One-Day Adventures by Car

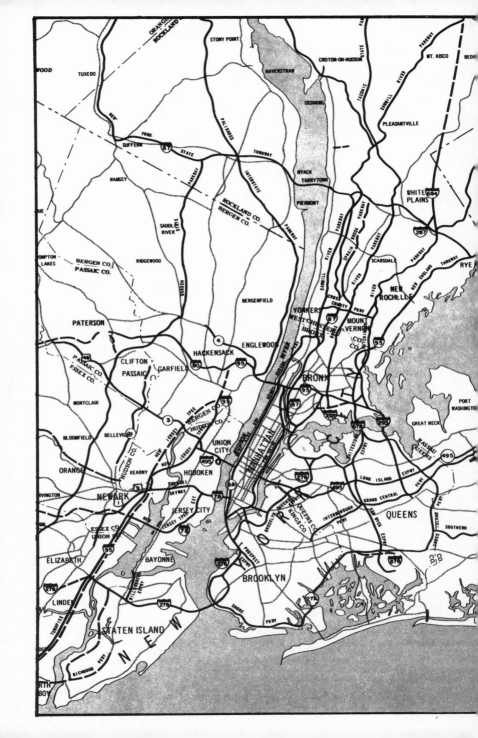

One-Day Adventures by Car

With Full Road Directions for Drives Out of New York City

by
Lida Newberry

HASTINGS HOUSE · PUBLISHERS
New York

Published simultaneously in Canada by
Saunders, of Toronto, Ltd., Don Mills, Ontario

Library of Congress Cataloging in Publication Data

Newberry, Lida.
    One-day adventures by car.

    Includes index.
    1. New Jersey—Description and travel—1951—Tours. 2. New York
(State)—Description and travel—1951—Tours. 3. Connecticut—Description and
travel—1951—Tours. 4. Automobiles—Road guides—New Jersey. 5. Auto-
mobiles—Road guides—New York (State) 6. Automobiles—Road guides—
Connecticut. I. Title.
F132.3.N48 1980   917.4   79-27901
ISBN 0-8038-5393-9

Printed in the United States of America

Contents

List of Maps

KEY TO MAPS

LIMITED ACCESS

EXISTING   UNDER CONSTRUCTION
as of November, 1969

MAJOR ARTERIALS

ROUTE SYMBOLS

INTERSTATE   U.S.   STATE

0   5   10   20 MILES

SCALE : ONE INCH EQUALS APPROXIMATELY 7 MILES

Maps by courtesy of Tri-State Transportation Commission

Invitation to Adventure

In all directions from New York City superb highways lead to a wonderland of scenic beauty and historical lore, to noble houses and spacious gardens, to villages cultivating the arts and crafts, and to an ever-changing shoreline. All these can be reached in motor-car drives usually within a 100-mile radius, inside of one day.

One day there and back—no overnight stay—and an exhilarating adventure of exploration and discovery, right on our doorstep.

REGULAR TRIPS include attractions within a radius of 60 or 70 miles of New York City. EXTENSION TRIPS are farther out, but can be completed in one day.

The territory covered is divided into eight adjoining AREAS. These begin to the south along the New Jersey coast and form an arc that includes New Jersey, southeastern New York, western Connecticut, Long Island and Staten Island. Longer drives take us across the borders of Pennsylvania and Massachusetts.

EXIT POINTS. These lead out of New York City to the principal highways, and include the George Washington Bridge, the Verrazano-Narrows Bridge, the Hutchinson River Parkway, Major Deegan Expressway and the Throgs Neck Bridge. Two others to the north, the Tappan Zee Bridge and Hawthorne Circle, are easily reached via all parkways. Tunnels out of Manhattan are not recommended because of heavy trucking and traffic jams.

EASY DRIVING. The best time on the most-used highways is between 10 a.m. and 3 p.m. Avoid the hours between 7 and 9 a.m. and 4:30-7 p.m. Week-day driving is better than week-end. Try to avoid roads near beach areas in season.

TOLLS. These are collected one way only at most crossings. We pay double coming in, none on leaving. However, in our listings we give *half the round trip rate* which is then doubled for the complete tour. SOME BRIDGE TOLLS RAISED.

FOOD. Restaurants, inns, some diners are mentioned when we pass them. We do not endorse any.

CHECK FIRST before making a special trip. Sometimes attractions close temporarily.

NATURE AREAS call for use of insect repellent, on the advice of authorities.

GROUPS should arrange in advance before visits, for reduced rates. N.J. SR. CITIZENS (only): No charge to N.J. State Parks, sites.

HANDICAPPED persons will find helpful information in our directions.

PLAN-IT-YOURSELF. Many trips start where the previous one ended. Those with more time may proceed to the next, or else blend features from several.

Have a good day.

LIDA NEWBERRY

New Jersey Shoreline and Colonial Trails

● *Our first trips unlock the treasure chest that lies close to New York City in New Jersey. Nature has been lavish with this shoreline, providing over 120 miles of white ocean sand, rolling breakers, and fresh, unpolluted air. Long Branch, Asbury Park, Atlantic City are on our route. Seaside amusement parks, marine museums, wildlife refuges with tours guided by a naturalist invite us. Turning inland, we follow historic trails that lead us to the white mansions preserved from Colonial days.*

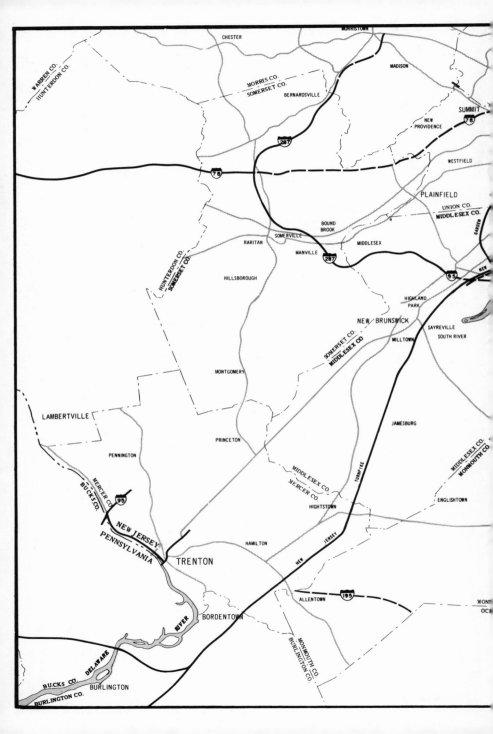

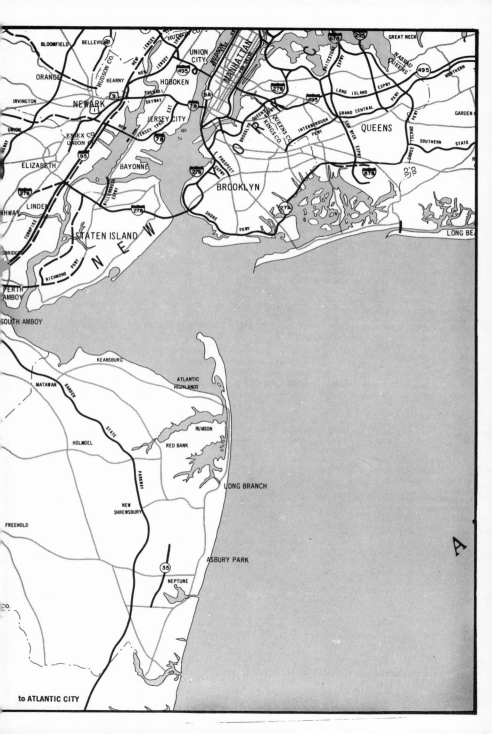

To reach Area A from New York City use Exit Points George Washington Bridge or Verrazano Bridge. Main roads: Garden State Parkway, New Jersey Turnpike and Route US 22.

From G.W. Bridge: To Garden State Parkway: Follow signs to Rte. 80 and drive 10 *m.* to Parkway south. To N.J. Turnpike: Follow signs at bridge. To US 22: Take Garden State Parkway south to Exit 140A at Rte. 22 west.

From Verrazano Bridge: To Garden State Parkway south: Cross Staten Island to NY 440 and follow signs across Outerbridge into New Jersey. Pick up signs here to Garden State Parkway south. To N.J. Turnpike: Cross Staten Island then Goethals Bridge into New Jersey. Immediately are signs to N.J. Tpke. south. To US 22: Cross Staten Island then Goethals Bridge. Take Bayway Ave., (NJ 439) and proceed 3 *m.* to jct. with NJ 82. Turn left on Rte. 82; shortly are signs to US 22 west toward Somerville.

Sandy Beach and Highlands
at New York's Doorstep

TRIP A-1. *We'll Visit:*
MOUNT MITCHELL
TWINLIGHT MUSEUM, Highlands, N.J. (Summer)
SANDY HOOK PARK

DISTANCE AND TOLLS: Via G.W. Bridge, about 65 *m.*, $1.50. Via Verrazano
Bridge, about 45 *m.*, $1.25. Plus return trip. Fast or average speeds.
FOOD: On Mt. Mitchell, Bachert's Hofbrauhaus, closed Tues. In Highlands, Bahr's
Seafoods, closed Mon.

Mount Mitchell: One of the highest points on the mainland along the
Atlantic Ocean between New York and Florida (250 ft.) VISTAS of
distant New York, Sandy Hook and the Atlantic Highlands Municipal
Harbor. Binoculars for rent; better to bring yours.

Twinlight Museum, Highlands, N.J. 07732. *Grounds open daily 8 a.m.
to dusk. Museum, Memorial Day thru Labor Day, 1-4, closed
Mon. Fees: Donations. Rest rooms. Picnics. Handicapped: Steps up into
Museum.* A small, shipshape marine display includes authentic exhibits,
many from the local area so rich in nautical history and legends. Climb
the Tower for spectacular VISTAS. Fine views off-season from grounds.

Sandy Hook Unit, Gateway National Recreation Area, P.O. Box 437,
Highlands, N.J. 07732. *Presently open year around, sunrise to 8 p.m.
Fishermen permitted at any time. Entrance fee may be charged, in
which case an annual Golden Eagle Passport will allow unlimited access
to this and all other Federal Fee Areas. Golden Age Passport, free to
those 62 years of age or older, allows same privile. :s. Available at the
site. Protected ocean bathing in season. Check new schedule on surfing
and scuba diving, as well as Nature Walks and other activities. Picnics in
limited areas; no tables, no fires. Pets leashed.* INFO. CTR. 8-5.
In 1972 an Act of Congress established Sandy Hook as part of the new
Gateway National Recreation Area, first of its kind in a crowded urban
location. Eventually there will be 26,000 acres of much-needed park-
land in the New York Harbor area. Watch for expanding programs and
recreational facilities as the project is developed.

This oceanside natural park features seascapes that include ocean,
river, a bay, and a cove lined by a wildlife sanctuary, as well as the
Hook itself. A nearby lighthouse, built 1762, rising 103 ft., is in the
background. The area has 8 distinct habitats for plant and animal life, a

rarity in such a small space. The famed HOLLY FOREST is largest along the coast below Massachusetts. Of particular interest to bird watchers—this is part of the great Atlantic Flyway.

FOR THE DRIVER: Take Garden State Parkway south to Exit 117 to Keyport. Take NJ 36 south through Keansburg. Shortly below, exit at sign to Atlantic Highlands Business District. Proceed across town. Before Municipal Harbor, turn right at sign to Mt. Mitchell via Scenic Drive. Here are several VISTA points, also a Brauhaus restaurant and in season, snacks.

Continue briefly to jct. with NJ 36, turn left (south). Proceed through Highlands; just before bridge is a sign to Historic Twin Lights. Exit here for the Museum; go one block then right again on Highland Ave. to a point on left where 2 branching roads start up hill. Take right hand road to top and Twinlight Museum.

Back to the bridge area. For Bahr's restaurant follow signs to Business District and Bay Ave. Then back to bridge. Cross bridge, turn left to Sandy Hook Park.

Return Trip: Take NJ 36 back to Garden State Parkway north. Exit 127 for Outerbridge, Exit 159 for G.W. Bridge.

Where Eight Presidents Sought the Sea Breezes

TRIP A-2. *We'll Visit:*
LONG BRANCH
ASBURY PARK

DISTANCE AND TOLLS: Via G.W. Bridge, 75 *m.*, $1.75. Via Verrazano Bridge, 55 *m.*, $1.50. Plus return. Mostly fast speeds.
FOOD: Numerous restaurants in both resorts.

Long Branch. *Open most of year for outdoor activities, spectator sports, pageants, etc. Fees: Small beach fees, also for boardwalk games. Swimming: May-Sept. Surfing, May-Oct. on reserved beach. Fishing from pier, surf, boat. Boating on river and ocean. Waterskiing on river. Summer boat races; winter ice boating, ice fishing.*

In the second half of the 19th century Long Branch became the resort of rich New Yorkers and the summer capital of Presidents. Grant, Garfield, Arthur and Wilson attended services at the little Church of The Presidents (Episcopal) on Ocean Ave. *Open weekends from Memorial Day to Sept., 2-6 p.m.; weekdays by appointment.* This today houses the Long Branch Historical Museum. Excellent beaches for the more sports-minded.

Asbury Park. *Open year around. Beach and boardwalk activities from Memorial Day to mid-Sept. Some places open from Easter through October. Fees for swimming incl. locker & shower. Parking, metered on* *city streets. Handicapped: Ramps to boardwalk but not beaches; benches on boardwalk, chairs on porch of Convention Hall. Rest rooms not designed for wheelchairs. No picnics. No scuba diving or surfing. Two amusement parks are open daily in summer, weekends, spring and fall.*

James A. Brady, a New York businessman, in 1870 bought 500 acres and laid out Asbury Park as a summer resort for Temperance advocates and people who attended Methodist camp meetings at Ocean Grove. Today the keynote is recreation. Historically, on Sept. 8, 1934, the *S.S. Morro Castle* burned at sea off the northern side of Convention Hall, with a loss of 125 lives.

FOR THE DRIVER: Take Garden State Parkway south to Exit 105 and follow signs to Long Branch. If skipping Long Branch, continue on Parkway to Exit 102 to NJ 66 and follow signs to Asbury Park. .

From Long Branch, continue south along the shore to Asbury Park.

Return Trip: Take NJ 66 west from Asbury Park, following signs to Garden State Parkway north.

To a Religious Beach Resort, a Country Store, an Antique Train

TRIP A-3. *We'll Visit:*

THE DESERTED VILLAGE OF ALLAIRE, Farmingdale, N.J.

PINE CREEK RAILROAD, Allaire State Park (Weekends and holidays, May-Oct. Daily, mid-June-Labor Day.)

OCEAN GROVE

DISTANCE AND TOLLS: G.W. Bridge to Allaire, 65 *m.*; to Ocean Grove, about 90 *m.* $1.75. Via Verrazano Bridge, about 20 *m.* less. $1.50. Plus return. Mainly fast speeds.

FOOD: Restaurants in Ocean Grove, and on Parkway.

Deserted Village of Allaire, Allaire State Park, Box 218, Farmingdale, N.J. 07727. *Park open all year, 8-dusk. Bldgs. open daily Apr.–Oct. 10-5; weekends in March. Closed Nov.–Feb. Parking Mem. Day–Labor Day $2. Weekends & Hol. $3. Daily in May & Sept. $2. Plus 50¢ all over 12. Bus $10. for N.J. groups; $25. out of state. Acoustiguides for walking tours, fee. Free brochures for self-guiding walking tours of village, also of natural area, with or without guide. Food: Snacks, picnics, cooking. Fishing in Mannasquan River, subject to N.J. regulations. Adjacent riding academy. Write for list of special shows and fairs. Handicapped: Can watch demonstrations and railroad activities; some paths hilly, and there is climbing in the buildings.* Braille Trail. (201) 938-2371.

An engrossing display of Americana is shown to good advantage in this peaceful village, once a noisy industrial town. In the 19th century, James Allaire, a New York ironmonger, took over Monmouth Furnace here and built a foundry, brick kilns, and houses for 500 employees. Later the works were moved to Pennsylvania and the village became deserted. Today we watch the blacksmith and carpenter at work, perhaps attend church services in summer. Costumed hostesses escort and explain. There are nature trails to hike.

The Pine Creek Railroad, Allaire Park. *Runs May thru Oct., weekends and holidays; daily, mid-June to Labor Day. 75¢ per ride.*

This is for everybody, old and new. It's one of the 3-foot gauge railroad types used to open the West. There are rolling stock, a tool shed and machine shop to inspect, and a train whistle we can record both on tape and on film.

Ocean Grove. *Season is from Memorial Day to weekend after Labor Day. Beach fees. Food: Restaurants; beach picnics. Handicapped: Ramps to boardwalks. Benches throughout town. Sports: Swimming (ex. Sunday) in ocean or pool, fishing, horseback riding, boardwalk activities.*

An attractive small town is background for religious and cultural programs, Bible meetings, evangelical talks, organ recitals. Founded for Methodist camp meetings in 1869, Ocean Grove has large facilities for revivals. Leading to the Auditorium is the Pilgrim's Pathway, built without use of nails. A clay model of the City of Jerusalem stands nearby. Repentance of sinners is preached from the big stage. Beach meetings are held at the Boardwalk Sundays at 6 p.m. Motor cars are not permitted on the streets on Sunday.

FOR THE DRIVER: Take Garden State Parkway south to Exit 96 and follow signs to Allaire State Park and the Deserted Village of Allaire. Pine Creek Railroad is in the park.

Back to Garden State Parkway north. Proceed on it to Exit 100 to NJ 33. Take this east through Asbury Park to Ocean Grove.

Return Trip: Follow signs in town to Garden State Parkway north and return.

A Jungle Flourishes in the Pine Barrens

TRIP A-3(A): *We'll Visit:*

GREAT ADVENTURE

DISTANCE AND TOLLS: From G. W. Bridge, 75*m*, Turnpike toll $1.55. Via Verrazano Bridge about 55 *m*, 75¢. Plus bridges. Plus return. Fast speeds.

Great Adventure, P. O. Box 120, Jackson, N. J. 08527. Phone (201) 928-2000. *Open: (Check papers for latest dates.) Entertainment Park, May-Sept. daily, 10-10; weekends in Oct. Safari Park, May-Sept. daily, 9-6; weekends in April and Oct. Adm. fee; combination ticket to both parks at reduction. Ticket good for unlimited rides, shows. Free parking. No pets; kennels, free, for first 80 pets - owner provides food. Moderate charge for bus (optional) through Safari. Park open rain or shine. Food: No picnics in park, but picnic area adjoins parking lot. Many restaurants and snack bars in Entertainment Area serve a variety of menus at reasonable prices. Limited number strollers and wheelchairs available, no charge. Handicapped: Ramps to buildings and to all shows except Great Arena. Rest rooms adapted for wheelchairs. Plenty of benches and shade. Walks level.*

Great Adventure, opened in 1974 on 1,500 acres of Pine Barrens, is two parks, a jungle safari and a theme park. Since every year brings new attractions and improvements, it is becoming an annual affair for many visitors. The Safari Park is a maze of winding auto roads through living quarters of animals such as Bengal tigers, lions, rhinos, bears, llamas, giraffes, baboons and ostriches. Three lanes provide stopping on either side, or through driving. Note: Animals take noontime siestas so are best viewed early or late in the day. *Caution:* Motors tend to overheat on the safari trail; best preventative is to turn them off at every stop.

The Entertainment Park is alive with jousters, chariot racers, rodeo performers and dancing dolphins, for spectators. Those preferring to participate have a large choice including roller coasters, runaway trains, flying waves, and not one but two great flume rides. A newer Kiddie Kingdom gets the smallest fry into the act. There's an elaborate 19th-century Carousel, and a 15-story high Ferris wheel is in constant motion. Elsewhere, a miniature village built to 1/25th scale at a cost of $1½ million, contains 76 historic castles, churches, Dutch marts, three of the Kremlin's cathedrals, and vessels at sail in an 18th-century harbor. It's a photographer's dream.

We can shop at international bazaars and eat in an oversized Conestoga Wagon, an emporium shaped like an ice cream sundae, perhaps in a filigreed gazebo, or else outdoors at an umbrella-shaded table.

FOR THE DRIVER: Take the N. J. Turnpike south to Exit 7-A, then I-195 East to Exit 6 at Rte. 537. South on this 3 miles to the park.

Sea Breezes and Sunshiny Beaches

TRIP A-4. *We'll Visit:*
POINT PLEASANT BEACH
SEASIDE HEIGHTS and SEASIDE PARK
ISLAND BEACH STATE PARK

DISTANCE AND TOLLS: To Point Pleasant Beach, from G.W. Bridge about 80 *m*. To Seaside Heights, add 10 *m*. $1.75. Via Verrazano Bridge, about 20 *m*. less. $1.50. Plus return. Add 25¢ on return if via NJ 37 to Pkwy. Mainly fast speeds.
FOOD: Point Pleasant Beach, Lobster Shanty. On return, at Tom's River, Howard Johnson's.

Point Pleasant Beach. *Open year around for swimming, ocean or pool; especially favorable for surfing, which is extended to swimming beaches before 8 a.m. and after 6 p.m. Shops sell or rent equipment. Fishing in ocean or river. Food: Lobster Shanty, snacks. No pets on beach.*

There are three main attractions here—boating, fishing and art. It's home port to a fleet of commercial fishing vessels. Moonlight sails are popular and provide good views of the Thursday night fireworks in summer. What may be the oldest native folk festival in the state draws large crowds annually.

Seaside Heights and Seaside Park. *Season from mid-June to mid-Sept. Handicapped may find it hard to reach beaches. Pets: not on beaches.*

Plenty for whole family here including a large amusement park. In May, Father Neptune opens the beaches for the season and throughout the summer are all kinds of exciting events. Mardi Gras in September.

Island Beach State Park, Seaside Park, N.J. 08752. *Open year around for fishing or nature walks, 8-8. Swimming, mid-June to Labor Day, 10-6 in protected beaches only. Surfing in special area when lifeguards are on duty; must first pass proficiency test given free at park. Scuba diving in special areas. Parking: Weekdays, Mem. Day-Labor Day, $4. Weekends, Hol, $5. Rest of year $2. (50¢ over 12 years of age). Annual fishing permit $40., 2nd Gate fee, Mem. Day - Labor Day, 50¢/car. Food: Snacks in season. Picnics; no tables, no fireplaces. Pets leashed, not allowed in bathing areas. Handicapped can drive part way into sanctuary; walking may be rugged. Guided nature tours at 10 a.m. and 2 p.m. free.*

One of the few barrier beaches remaining in this part of the country, Island Beach is a valuable spot for naturalists. The 2,300-acre ten-mile strip of land contains high and low dunes, holly clumps, briar thickets and bird refuges.

FOR THE DRIVER: Take Garden State Parkway south to Exit 96 and follow NJ 34 east. Take NJ 35 at jct.—this goes to Point Pleasant Beach. Lobster Shanty is off NJ 35.

For Seaside Heights and Seaside Park, continue south on NJ 35. Below these, on same road, is Island Beach State Park.

Return Trip: Back to Seaside Heights; take NJ 37 west toward Tom's River, thence to Garden State Parkway north. Howard Johnson's at Tom's River.

We're approaching an area beyond an average day's drive from New York City but which may be reached on a round trip by getting an early start. The following EXTENSION TRIPS are given at this point because they are next in line from the section just visited.

A Day-Long Marine Drive, from Barnegat Light to Beach Haven

TRIP A-5 EXTENSION. A Day-Long Marine Drive, from Barnegat Light to Beach Haven. As this trip is primarily for the enjoyment of the drive rather than for any one major attraction, it will be written out as such, FOR THE DRIVER.

We'll Visit:

LOVELADIES ART COLONY, Long Beach Island (Summer)

BARNEGAT LIGHTHOUSE STATE PARK

BARNEGAT LIGHT MUSEUM (Summer)

BEACH HAVEN: BAY VILLAGE (Summer)

HOLGATE WILDLIFE REFUGE

DISTANCE AND TOLLS: To center of Long Beach Island, from G.W. Bridge, about 120 *m.*, $2.25. Via Verrazano Bridge, about 100 *m.*, $2. Plus return. Round trip on island to either end about 20 *m.* Mainly fast speeds.

FOOD: Adjacent to Barnegat State Park, restaurants and snacks.

FOR THE DRIVER: Take Garden State Parkway south to Exit 63, then NJ 72 east to Long Beach Island. Cross the Causeway to Ship Bottom in the center of the island; go ahead a block or two and turn left, north. The road goes straight up the island. Pass Loveladies Art Colony, *open July to Labor Day.* This has exhibits, antiques, and a location comparable with Cape Cod. The Foundation of Arts and Sciences may be visited. For details about their art classes, films, concerts, lectures, write them at Box 87, Harvey Cedars, N.J. 08040.

Continue to the end of the Island where road forks. Go straight ahead to pass the Barnegat Light Museum, *open July to Labor Day daily 2-5, weekends in June. Contributions.* This marine display includes the prism from France that was used in the original light crown, a lens that had 1,024 individual prisms forming 24 bulls-eye lens belts 15 feet high.

Just ahead, turn left to road to Barnegat Lighthouse State Park (right). *Open daily Memorial Day thru Labor Day; weekends in May and thru Oct. Parking: Mem. Day-Labor Day, $3., daily & weekends. Walk-in fee, 50¢. Lighthouse fee, 25¢. (Plus 50¢ over 12 years of age). N.J. bus groups $10.; out of state, $25. The Park is open off-season, no fees. Lighthouse open 10-4:45. Under 12, free with adult. Food: Picnic area. Snacks and restaurant nearby.*

Main attraction here—Old Barney, the famous lighthouse. It has a 172-foot base and we may climb 217 steps for an unforgettable VISTA. A sizeable beach provides both ocean and more protected swimming. There's good fishing on all sides.

We now return to Ship Bottom then follow signs to Beach Haven. Before we reach the red water tower comes a sign, right, to Bay Village, a small shopping complex, and a dory, all that remains of the schooner *Lucy Evelyn.* Nearby is an amusement area. In town is the Surflight Theatre for summer shows.

Continue as far as road goes, to parking lot for Holgate Wildlife Refuge. *Open daily, daylight hours. Fee. Fires on beach only; no camping. Pets leashed. Fishing permitted. Beach buggies must have permit.* This somewhat remote park is popular with naturalists as a typical shore area. Birdwatchers will discover nesting and migrant shorebirds.

Return Trip: Back to Causeway and NJ 72 to Garden State Parkway north.

Protected Forest, Bird Refuge, Rebuilt Towne

TRIP A-6 EXTENSION. *We'll Visit:*

BASS RIVER STATE FOREST

BATSTO

TOWNE OF SMITHVILLE and OLD VILLAGE

BRIGANTINE WILDLIFE REFUGE

DISTANCE AND TOLLS: To Smithville via G.W. Bridge, about 125 *m.*, $2.50. Via Verrazano Bridge, about 105 *m.*, $2.25. Plus return. Mainly fast speeds. If going to Batsto, add 25 *m.*
FOOD: In Smithville Towne, restaurants, snacks. Also on Parkway.

Bass River State Forest and **Lake Absegami.** *Open year around. Swimming, Memorial Day to Labor Day. Parking: Mem. Day-Labor Day, $3. Weekends, Hol. $4. Weekends May & Sept., $2. Walk-In, 50¢, plus 50¢ 12 years and over. N.J. bus groups, $10.; out of state, $25. Boat launching $1. Fees collected daily in swimming season, also on weekends May-Nov. Food: Picnics. Pets, leashed, not allowed near beach.* This large and beautiful woodland has facilities for boating, camping, fishing, picnicking, hiking, horseback riding. There's a playground for children, a nature area for all. Impressive plantings of trees are labeled.

Batsto, R.D. Hammonton, N.J. 08215. *Open daily year around. Tour of buildings Memorial Day to Labor Day, 10-6. Weekends and holidays, 11-6. Rest of year, 11-5. Parking: Weekends & hol. only, $2., Mem. Day - Labor Day. Tour $1. Nature Tour 50¢. Stage Coach Ride 50¢. Under 12, 50¢. Nature tours with naturalist, same fees, last 1½ hours.* (609) 561-3262.

The Dutch and Scandinavians called their steam baths "baatstoo," a word the Indians adopted, and which eventually turned into "batsto," a bathing place. There is a feeling of mystery here; the great mansion rising out of nowhere should be in a thriving town, not among tall forest trees in the Pine Barrens. On our tour we learn that nearly 1,000 people once lived here and worked at the iron furnace which produced arms needed at Valley Forge. We can visit the Mansion, carriage house, blacksmith shop and some of the original workers' homes. BATSTO NATURE AREA, located just beyond the village, is always open. It contains over 130 species of plants and many small animals.

Towne of Smithville, Smithville, N.J. 08201. *Open year around, daily. Shops open at 10:30 and after dinner. Free. Ample parking. Food: Three inns and an informal Posset Shop, which includes light snacks. No picnics. Handicapped: Limited facilities as buildings are old-style, but only a few steps into one of the inns and the Shop. Walks of brick, mainly, with curb. Benches on Village Mall and at Pond.* (609) 652-7777.

The original Smithville Inn was established in 1787, and that era provides the flavor of the Towne reconstructed around it. Over 30 restored buildings are open for business: The Pewterer, Ship Chandler, Buttery, Gryst Mill, Clam House, and many more. THE OLD VILLAGE, *open spring & fall Tues.-Fri. 11:30-5. Weekends 10-3. Closed Mon. In summer, open daily & Mon. 12-5.* (609) 652-7777. This is an authentic restored crossroads town of over a century ago where more than 100 people live today, performing tasks of yesterday. Special programs scheduled for weekends.

Brigantine Wildlife Refuge, P. O. Box 72, Oceanville, N.J. 08231. *Open daily, daylight hours. Free. Food: picnics. Rest rooms. Handicapped can see well from car and visit all Tour stops.*

We travel by car over 8 miles of dikes and through holly groves, with 15 stops for viewing. Photographers with proper equipment may obtain permits to use the blinds. Over 250 species of birds have been listed here and at neighboring Holgate Refuge. The spring and fall migrations are spectacular. The birds nest in Canada, winter in Florida, and regularly pass through here via the Atlantic Flyway. Besides these transients, over 150,000 waterfowl winter here. And all this with the long, gray skyline of swinging Atlantic City a distant backdrop across the bay.

FOR THE DRIVER: Take Garden State Parkway south to Exit 52 to New Gretna. Follow signs to Bass River State Forest; drive to recreation area, then to Lake Absegami.

To continue to Batsto, follow signs from park; however, it may be easier to return the way you came, passing the Parkway, continuing to Rte. 9. Turn right on 9; shortly is sign, right, to Batsto.

Go back about 13 *m.* to jct. with US 9. Turn right (south); you soon join the Garden State Parkway. When Rte. 9 leaves Parkway, stay on 9 to Smithville. The Brigantine Refuge is on your left, but the only car entrance is below Smithville. US 9 goes through Smithville Towne.

Take US 9 south. Watch for small sign at a road, left, just before Leeds Luncheonette. This directs you to the Brigantine Wildlife Refuge. You drive over dikes on unpaved but good roads.

Return Trip: Take US 9 north. When it merges with Garden State Parkway, remain on the Parkway.

To Atlantic City and Environs

TRIP A-7 EXTENSION. *We'll Visit:*

ATLANTIC CITY

ABSECON LIGHTHOUSE (Summer)

DISTANCE AND TOLLS: Via G.W. Bridge about 140 *m.* $2.50. Via Verrazano Bridge, about 120 *m.*, $2.25. Plus return. Fast speeds. Best route is via Atlantic City Expressway from Garden State Parkway.

Atlantic City: For information write Visitors Bureau, Convention Hall, Atlantic City, N.J. 08401. Added to the famed seaside activities, boardwalk and amusement piers is casino gambling, starting in 1978. Check progress at Gardner's Basin, a maritime village opened in 1976, with a clipper ship to board and below decks, a sight and sound show; a sailing ship for ocean cruises in summer; shops, restaurants, museums. Still comparatively small, this will be worth watching as more ships and historic buildings are added.

Absecon Lighthouse, open Memorial Day thru Labor Day, daily except Wed., 10-5. Fee 50¢.

To Monmouth Old and New and Historic Environs

TRIP A-8. As this is primarily for the enjoyment of the drive, it will be written out FOR THE DRIVER.

We'll Visit:

MARLPIT HALL, Middletown (Open part of week)

FORT MONMOUTH SIGNAL CORPS MUSEUM

MONMOUTH COUNTY HISTORICAL SOCIETY MUSEUM, Freehold (Closed Monday)

NATL. BROADCASTERS HALL OF FAME, Freehold. (Closed Mon.)

GARDEN STATE ARTS CENTER, Holmdel

CHEESEQUAKE STATE PARK

DISTANCE AND TOLLS: From G.W. Bridge, about 80 *m.*, $1.50. Via Verrazano Bridge, about 60 *m.*, $1.25. Plus return. Add 15¢ toll on return. Average speeds after Parkway.

FOOD: Near Marlpit Hall, Howard Johnson's. Off Rte. 35 below Red Bank, Rod's Shadowbrook. Opposite Fort Monmouth, Crystal Brook Inn. In Freehold, American Hotel.

FOR THE DRIVER: Take Garden State Parkway south to Exit 117. Take NJ 35, right (south) for 5 *m.*, till sign King's Highway. Turn right; immediately on left comes:

Marlpit Hall, Middletown, N.J. 07748. *Open Tues., Thurs., Sat. 11-5, Sun. 2-5. Closed Jan. Donations. $1. Guided tours. First floor easy for handicapped.* A Dutch Colonial house with period furnishings, this appeals to lovers of the antique. (201) 671-3237.

Back on NJ 35, turn right (south) toward Shrewsbury. Pass Rod's Shadowbrook at Broad St. At Sycamore Ave is:

Old Christ Church, with a rare copy of the *Vinegar Bible,* so called because vineyard, in the parable, was misspelled.

Continue to County Rte. 537, Tinton Ave. Turn left to Fort Monmouth. Pass gate to Myer Hall and:

Fort Monmouth Signal Corps Museum, Ft. Monmouth, N.J. 07703. *Open year around. 8-4 daily except holidays. Free. Rest rooms. Handicapped can manage first floor.* Here we learn what a big part communication plays in military campaigns. We'll view quantities of apparatus from the signal flags of the Civil War to the syncom satellites of today, a segment of military operations rarely seen by the civilian.

Across from the Fort on Rte. 35 is Crystal Brook Inn. After the Museum follow Rte. 537 back, but this time remain on it to Freehold. Here NJ 79 merges with yours in town, then goes left. Do not turn; instead, continue ahead, passing on right the Hall of Records. On next corner, Court St., turn right to Monmouth Battle Monument Park. Across from park is:

Monmouth County Historical Museum and Library, 70 Court St., Freehold, N.J. 07728. *Open daily 11-5, Sun. 2-5. Closed Mon. and last half of July, and in Dec. Library open Fri. & Sat. only, 11-5. Donations, $1. Sr. Cit. 75¢ 6-18, 50¢.* (201) 462-1466.

A beautiful three-storied Colonial building (1931) is the setting for one of the best museums in the area. Fine examples of period furnishings and Americana are well displayed. One whole floor is devoted to a popular Junior Museum. The Library is primarily for research and includes a genealogical and historical reference section.

In Freehold is the American Hotel and restaurant on E. Main St. Other dining places in town. From the Museum go to next corner, Haley St., then left to the end at Throckmorton. Turn left, soon passing, left:

St. Peter's Episcopal Church. This was used as a hospital by the British, later as barracks by the Continentals.

Just beyond the church is Main St., where railroad tracks cross.

National Broadcasters Hall of Fame, 19 W. Main St., Freehold, N.J. 07728. (201) 431-4656. *Open daily exc. Mon. 12-5. Adm. $2. Sr. Cit. $1.50. 6-13 $1.*

Here's a museum, comparatively new, crammed with all things pertaining to radio broadcasting from its early years into the projected future. There are tangible mementoes of the industry and actual programs can be heard in the small theater.

FOR THE DRIVER: From here, back on W. Main St. to jct. with NJ 79. Follow Rte. 79 north, branching left. Proceed 13 *m.* to jct. with road to Holmdel and Garden State Parkway, right. Take this to Parkway North. A few miles ahead, off the Parkway, is:

Garden State Arts Center, with picnic areas, nature trails. This is the center for performing and creative arts built by the New Jersey Highway Authority. It was designed by Edward Durrell Stone and seats 5,000 with room for 3,000 more on the lawn. No charge, except for performances, which may be orchestral, folk songs, ballet and opera. Special events for Senior Citizens, handicapped, school children, ethnic groups, free. Heritage Festivals. On Sundays, free concerts. Phone (201) 264-9200.

Continue on Parkway to Exit 120 and follow signs to CHEESE-QUAKE STATE PARK. *Open year around. Parking: weekdays Mem. Day-Labor Day, $2. Weekends & hol. $3. Weekends, May & Sept. $2. (50¢ each 12 and over.) N. J. bus groups, $10.; out of state, $25., collected Memorial Day to Labor Day, also weekends May thru Oct. Small fee for picnic groups.*

This attractive park includes a small lake and a camping area. Its nature trails are popular with botanists; tours in season. There are swimming, fishing, hiking.

Return Trip: In the park is a jct. with sign to Garden State Parkway *south.* It directs those going north to take southbound ramp to Exit 120 then cross over to northbound lane.

To the Biggest Flea Market of Them All on Molly Pitcher's Battleground

TRIP A-8(A): *We'll Visit:*

ENGLISHTOWN AUCTION SALES

DISTANCE AND TOLLS: From G. W. Bridge, about 64 *m.*, $1. plus bridge. Via Verrazano Bridge about 23 *m,* bridge tolls only.

Englishtown Auction Sales. *Open every Saturday from about 3 a.m. to 3 p.m. Free parking and entry.*

The mileage for this may look incongruous for a trip to a kind of glorified rummage sale, but not so to the avid auction buff, the antique enthusiast, the bargain sale fanatic. To some 40,000 of these, coming from places like upper New England, the mid-west, far south, and most major cities hereabouts, these 20 or more acres of flea market, located on the site of the Battle of Monmouth, are one of the highlights of the week. Sales begin during the night; from about midnight, truckloads of merchandise arrive and the owners set up shop until showtime, in this case, 3 a.m. for the antique market. By daylight, things are in full swing and 1,500 or more outdoor stands and many more indoors are exchanging for cash livestock (to be taken alive), evening dresses, Army boots, cut-rate games, kitchen tables, ice cream molds, an elephant (so the story goes) and other treasures in untold categories. Frozen foods are dispensed indoors, while outside New Jersey farm produce is piled high; home-made delicacies are popular with those who don't do-it-themselves.

By about 9 a.m. parking has become a problem, but the area is large and those with good walking shoes manage.

For a different route home and possibly an ocean dip after the dust of the battlefield, take NJ 33 east to Asbury Park *(see Trip A-2).*

FOR THE DRIVER: Speediest: N.J. Turnpike to Exit 9 at New Brunswick; Route 18 south to Old Bridge and jct. with County Rte. 527 which goes to Englishtown. OR: From G.W. Bridge, I-80 to Garden State Pkwy. South, taking *local* lane after Raritan toll, to exit no. 123 to Rte 9 south. Rte 9 south to jct. with Co. 522 to Englishtown. Via Verranzo Bridge, Outerbridge Crossing then NJ 440 to jct. with US 9. South on Rte 9 to Co. 522 to Englishtown.

How to Jump From A Parachute in Easy Lessons

TRIP A-9. *We'll Visit:*

OCEAN COUNTY PARK, Lakewood, N.J.

LAKEWOOD PARACHUTING CENTER, Lakewood, N.J.
(Daily, May to Nov., then weekends)

NAVAL AIR ENGINEERING CENTER, Lakehurst, N.J. (Sunday)

DISTANCE AND TOLLS: From G.W. Bridge, about 80 *m.*, $1.75. Via Verrazano Bridge, 60 *m.*, $1.50. Plus return trip. Mainly fast speeds.

Ocean County Park: *Open year around, daylight to dark. Fee in Summer. Picnics; no liquor. Buses allowed in winter, not in summer.*

Four miles of roadways run through an arboretum of fine trees, brought in originally by John D. Rockefeller, Sr. In season there are carriage rides along winding roads.

Lakewood Sport Parachuting, Box 258, Lakewood, N.J. 08701. (201) 363-4900. *Open daily May thru Oct., rest of year, weekends. First jump course, Mon., Thurs., Fri. 11 a.m. Weekends 10 a.m. & 1 p.m. Cl. Tues. & Wed. Fees for instruction & first jump, incl. rental of equipment. Candidates 16-18 yrs. must produce parental consent — forms on request in advance. Guided Target Tours 50¢ adults, 25¢ under 12 yrs. Picnics, snacks.*

This is a professional place, with the latest in safety controls. Equipment may be rented or bought outright. Free Fall Parachuting is also performed here, after a certain number of static line jumps. Spectators may observe by taking a tour, in order to learn the techniques from the ground while watching actual jumps.

Naval Air Engineering Center, Lakehurst, N.J. 08733. *Tours Wed. by appointment only, for groups of between 10 & 35 people.* (201) 323-2620.

Back in 1923 the first American blimp, the *Shenandoah,* was launched here. In 1937 the Hindenburg landed in flames at Lakehurst. Since then the dirigible has faded from the scene. Meanwhile the station has become a helicopter base, and also conducts experiments in aircraft development.

FOR THE DRIVER: Take Garden State Parkway south to Exit 91. Follow signs to NJ 88 and Lakewood. This passes Ocean County Park, right.

From the park turn left (east) back toward the parkway. Just ahead at N. Hampshire Ave. turn right (south) to County 528, Cedarbridge Rd. Turn left (east) to Ocean County Aviation Airport where the Parachuting Center is located.

Continue on Rte. 528 for U.S. Naval Air Station. Drive to jct. with NJ 70, turn right and proceed about 9 *m.* to Lakehurst.

Return Trip: From Lakehurst, back on NJ 70 east; follow signs to Garden State Parkway north.

From Parachuting Center, go back on Rte. 528 to left, and turn right on N. Hampshire Ave. to NJ 88. Turn right on Rte. 88 to Garden State Parkway north.

Milking Time on an Ideal Farm and Boy Scouts

TRIP A-10. *We'll Visit:*

RUTGERS HORTICULTURAL GARDENS, New Brunswick, N.J.

RUTGERS COLLEGE OF AGRICULTURE FARM

NATIONAL BOY SCOUT HEADQUARTERS, JOHNSTON HIS-
TORICAL MUSEUM, New Brunswick

EAST JERSEY OLDE TOWNE

DISTANCE AND TOLLS: From G.W. Bridge, about 50 *m.*, $1.25. Via Verrazano Bridge, about 30 *m.*, $1.40. Plus return. Average speeds after highways.
FOOD: At jct. US 1 & NJ 18, Howard Johnson's; The Edgebrook, closed Sun.

Rutgers Horticultural Gardens. *Open dawn to dusk, daily, exc. Sat. during hunting season. Free.*

Here are seen the finest in plantings, including a section with American holly tree varieties and another with rhododendron and azaleas. Also in this area is Helyar's Wood and nearby, the Log Cabin. We may take self-guided tours of the woods (booklet free at office). Also, guided tours for a fee.

Rutgers College of Agriculture Farm. *Open year around daily. Barns close at milking time, 3 p.m. Free.*

We can wander about on our own here, enjoying the fine animal specimens in their typical quarters. Students of agriculture will find it of special interest. So will photographers. And kids.

National Boy Scout Headquarters, Johnston Historical Museum, New Brunswick, N.J. 08903. *Open year around. Tues.-Sat. 9-4:30. Sun. from 1. Closed 5 major holidays, and Good Friday. Free. Picnic area. Handicapped: 1 low step into Museum.* (201) 249-6000.

Here we follow the Trail beginning with the Tenderfoot and progressing in rank as he does. We'll see exhibits of equipment used by explorers who once were Eagle Scouts; a replica of the study where Lord Robert Baden-Powell, founder of scouting, did much of his work. There are a weather observatory and an operational shortwave station.

A space capsule is appropriate, for out of the first 30 astronauts, 27 were either scouts or scout leaders. The half-mile Nature Trail outside will be enjoyed by visitors of all ages.

EAST JERSEY OLDE TOWNE, INC., P. O. Box 431, New Brunswick, N.J. 08972. *(New project, hours uncertain.)* Eventually this will be a reconstructed village of buildings now in neighboring towns, brought to this site and filled with furnishings of the period. Several buildings are on the grounds, others undergoing renovation. We may visit a farm house, tavern and barn. Historians and architects will follow the progress with interest. Opening ceremonies were July 4, 1976.

FOR THE DRIVER: Via G.W. Bridge, take Garden State Parkway south about 30 *m.* to Exit 130 to US 1 south. Drive south 8 *m.* to New Brunswick. Via Verrazano Bridge: Take New Jersey Turnpike south to Exit 9 at New Brunswick. Here take NJ 18, right, to jct. with US 1 southbound. At this jct. is a Howard Johnson's, also the Edgebrook.

All: Southbound on Rte. 1: just below jct. with NJ 18, pass a Sears shopping center. Beyond this is Ryder's Lane. Take second exit to this, to Milltown. Turn right, from ramp. The gardens are just across the highway; turn left after the median, into small road with sign Rutgers Garden, Horticultural Farm No. 1. Drive through, or walk.

Back to Ryder's Lane, turn right and take US 1 south toward Trenton. Immediately is College Farm Road, right. Enter this to College Farm.

Return to US 1 and continue south to rotary at jct. with US 130. Take Rte. 130 south. Immediately watch on right for Boy Scouts and Johnston Historical Museum.

Go back to Rte. 130. Start to the right, but cross to other lane where indicated. Return to rotary. Back at US 1 turn right to jct. with NJ 18. Take this through New Brunswick, crossing river then passing Johnson Park, where are picnic areas, playfields, a race track, special events. Shortly above, on left, is the hq. of the County Park Dept. Turn in here for East Jersey Olde Towne.

Return Trip: Back on Rte 18 thru town. For Goethals Bridge continue to N.J. Turnpike and go to Exit 13. For G. W. Bridge, at jct. with US 1 turn north to Garden State Pkwy. north.

On Washington's Trail and Princeton University

TRIP A-11. *We'll Visit:*

ROCKINGHAM, WASHINGTON'S HEADQUARTERS, Rocky Hill, N.J. (Closed Monday)

PRINCETON UNIVERSITY

DISTANCE AND TOLLS: From G.W. Bridge about 70 *m.*, $1.25. Via Verrazano Bridge, about 50 *m.*, $1.40. Plus return. Average speeds.
FOOD: Restaurants along the way. In Princeton, principal ones are Nassau Inn, Princeton Inn, King's Court.

Rockingham (Berrien House) Rocky Hill, N.J. 08553. *Open year around daily exc. Mon., 10-12, 1-5. Sun. 2-5. Closed 3 major holidays. Fees: 50¢, ages 12 and over.* (609) 921-8835.

While waiting for the signing of the peace treaty with England, the Continental Congress convened at Princeton University. General Washington was invited to attend and made his headquarters at nearby Rockingham, using the Blue Room for his study. Here in 1783 he wrote his *Farewell Address to the Army* and stood on the balcony outside his room to read it. We will visit his study then step out as he did on the balcony. But we won't look out on the same terrain he saw for the building has been moved from its original site. It has since been restored to an 18th century period. In a small separate building is a typical kitchen of that era.

Princeton University: *Guided Tours the year around last an hour. They start from office in Stanhope Hall. Daily. Inquire for hours. Phone (609) 452-3603. No. Sat. aft. tours during football season.*

Tours include Nassau Hall, which was the nation's capitol in 1783, the Firestone Memorial Library, with more than 2 million volumes and some priceless documents, and the largest University Chapel in the country. We may also take self-guiding Tours, first stopping at the Information Office for maps and directions. No charge; no tipping allowed.

For interested parties, on advance notice, Tours may be taken through the Art Museum, the Forrestal Scientific Research Center, and the Museum of Natural History. Write to Orange Key Guide Service and Campus Information Office, Stanhope Hall, Princeton University, Princeton, N.J. 08540.

FOR THE DRIVER: Follow directions in Trip A-10 as far as jct. in New Brunswick with Rtes. 18 and US 1 southbound. Continue south on US 1 until sign, right, to Franklin Park. Turn here, go to the end of the road, at NJ 27. Turn left on Rte. 27 and proceed to a fork, where 27 goes left and County 518 goes ahead toward Rocky Hill. Take Rte. 518; just beyond this jct. is Rockingham, right.

Continue on Rte. 518 for several miles to jct. with US 206. Take this left (south) into Princeton. In town at jct. with County 583, to your right is the Battle Monument and beyond it, Morven, home of the Governor of New Jersey. To your left is Princeton University. Campus Tours start at Stanhope Hall.

For parking, stay as far as possible from the heart of town. You may want to extend your campus tour by walking to Palmer Square for shopping. You'll find the King's Court restaurant on Witherspoon St., Nassau Inn at Palmer Square, and the Princeton Inn on Alexander St.

Return Trip: From Princeton campus take any route going east as far as Rte. 1. Turn left (north) on this. For Goethals Bridge, take NJ 18 at New Brunswick and drive to N.J. Turnpike, to right. For G.W. Bridge, stay on US 1 to Garden State Pkwy., north.

A Day at the State Fair

TRIP A-12. *We'll Visit:*

The New Jersey State Fair, Hamilton Township. *Open for 9 days in Sept., usually starting about the middle of the month. Nominal fees for admission and parking. Activities day and night.*

Everyone who enjoys the excitement of a fair should try not to miss the biggest ones of all, the State Fairs. This one features all the favorites: Grange displays, contests and judging; exhibits—culinary, commercial and industrial. Large amusement areas and assorted parades add to the atmosphere. Plenty of good food is available.

FOR THE DRIVER: Take N.J. Turnpike, I-95, south to Exit 8, then proceed on NJ 33 which goes directly to the Fair.

Where Glass of Fine Quality Comes From

TRIP A-13. *We'll Visit:*

FLEMINGTON CUT GLASS CO.

FLEMINGTON FUR CO.

STANGL POTTERY

TURNTABLE JUNCTION

LIBERTY VILLAGE

RAILROAD: BLACK RIVER & WESTERN R.R. (Mid-Apr. thru Nov. weekends and holidays; July, Aug. afts., exc. Mon.)

FLEMINGTON FAIR

DISTANCE AND TOLLS: Via G.W. Bridge, about 70 *m.*, $1.25. Via Verrazano Bridge, 55 *m.*, $1. Plus return. Fast or average speeds.
FOOD: Howard Johnson's on Parkway, also on Rte. 22. In Somerville, the Stockholm; other restaurants on Rte. 22, in Flemington and Turntable Junction.

Flemington Cut Glass Co., 156 Main St., Flemington, N.J. 08822. *Open 9-6 weekdays, 11-6 Sun. and holidays. Closed 4 major holidays. Rest rooms. Ample free parking. Handicapped: ramps.*

A series of stores and houses contains a wide assortment of gifts and home decorations and fixtures. There is an enormous selection of glassware as well as lamps. Towels sold by the pound.

Liberty Village. *Open daily, except major holidays. Adm. fee.* Opened 1972. Fascinating demonstrations of Early American crafts in recreated village, already a major tourist attraction.

Flemington Fur Company, 8 Spring St., Flemington, N.J. 08822. *Open daily and Sunday, 10-6. Tours by appointment only: March 1 - June 15, Tues., Wed., & Thurs. between 10:30 and 3:30, last about ½ hour. Handicapped, ramp with hand rail. Rest rooms. Free parking.*

The Tour includes the storage vaults, where the temperature is 36° and the humidity, 40%; the workshop where fur garments are made, repaired and restyled; the Fur Salon, Fun Fur Department and the Town and Country Fashion Center. There is no obligation to buy.

Turntable Junction: *Open year around, daily & Sun., 10:30-5:30. Food: Snacks, restaurant. Rest rooms. Limited parking. Best days, Mon. & Tues. Very crowded weekends and holidays. Handicapped: Low curbs, brick walks. Stores small, difficult for chairs.*

Built around an old railroad turntable is a picturesque collection of specialty shops housed in reproductions of historic buildings, many seen in Williamsburg, Virginia, Sturbridge, Mass., and nearby Rockingham. We'll visit places like the Button Boutique, Nut Kettle, Candy Caboose and Granny's Folly, and warm (or cool) ourselves at the Spread Eagle Inn. Rounding things out are an art gallery, a gazebo for concerts, and many railroad embellishments.

Black River & Western Railroad. *Open mid-April thru Nov., weekends and holidays. Moderate fees. Group rates. Weekday trains July & Aug. afternoons except Mon. First train leaves Flemington for Ringoes at 11:30 a.m. Trains leave every 1½ hours until 5:30. Food: Picnics at Ringoes. Write for information on group plans, company outings, birthday parties, to Black River & Western R.R., P.O. Box 83, Ringoes, N.J. 08551. (201) 782-6622.*

We ride in coaches, some built in 1875, with oil-burning lamps, pot-belly stoves, plush seats, all in perfect condition. This is a standard-gauge steam railroad, not a miniature, and its colorful rolling stock attracts all buffs. But we don't have to be buffs to get a thrill out of our ride through the historical countryside.

Stangl Pottery, Mine St. *Open daily & Sun. 10-5:30. Closed 3 major holidays. Demonstrations from mid-June to Labor Day, when there is usually a potter hand-throwing pieces of pottery for the public to watch. Ample free parking. Rest rooms. Handicapped: No steps, but crowds in summer and on weekends.*

Here the famed Stangl dinnerware and artware is hand-crafted and hand-painted while we watch. There are fine displays of Stangl pottery, some made early in the century, and of the way it was manufactured. Some of these exhibits are inside a large walk-in kiln (pronounced *kill*). Merchandise, both perfects and seconds, is available.

Flemington Agricultural Fair. *Open Tues. before Labor Day thru Labor Day. Nominal admission. Free parking.*

This well-advertised event is a treat for all, and an especially good opportunity to show the youngsters what a typical small country fair is like.

FOR THE DRIVER: Take US 22 west through Somerville. Pass numerous restaurants, diners. At jct. with US 202 and 206 (merged) take them south (left) toward Flemington.

Right on Rte 12 to Main St. just ahead. Turn right on Main; just beyond railroad tracks is the Flemington Cut Glass Co. Parking on both sides of street. Turn right and go thru parking lot to Broad St.

Turn left and proceed to first street where you can turn left (Maple St.) Drive 1 block on Maple, turn right on Spring St. Just ahead, right, is the Flemington Fur Co. Park across street.

Continue past the Fur Co., turn right and go back to Broad St. Turn right to Church St. Turn right, cross Main St. Just ahead are Turntable Junction shopping center, and Liberty Village.

Beyond are the railroad tracks off Central Ave. Turn right to the station for the Black River and Western Railroad.

Continue on Central Ave. to next corner, Mine St., and cross tracks to Stangl Pottery.

For Flemington Fair Grounds: Go back past Turntable Junction to Church St. Take this back across town to NJ 31. Go north (left), shortly are the Fair Grounds.

Return Trip: From town, go back to Turntable Junction and Church St. Take this across town to US 202, turn left (north) to jct. with Rte. 22 in Somerville. Take Rte. 22 east, back to either Garden State Parkway north, or to NJ 82 to Elizabeth and Goethals Bridge.

From Fair Grounds: Go back down NJ 31 to Church St., then left to US 202. Turn left (north) on Rte. 202, and return as directed above.

Milestones in Locomotion; Canal Barge to Steam Locomotive

TRIP A-14. *We'll Visit:*

PARRY BARN MUSEUM, New Hope, Pa.

CORYELL'S FERRY (Summer)

MULE BARGE RIDES (Summer, exc. Mon.)

NEW HOPE IVYLAND RAILROAD (Weekends & Hol. spring and fall)

PEDDLER'S VILLAGE, Lahaska
THE YARD, Lahaska
FONTHILL MUSEUM, Doylestown
MORAVIAN POTTERY AND TILE WORKS, Doylestown
MERCER MUSEUM, Doylestown

DISTANCE AND TOLLS: From G.W. Bridge to New Hope, about 80 *m.*, $1.25.
From Verrazano Bridge, about 65 *m.*, $1. To Doylestown, about 10 *m.* more each
way. Plus return. Average speeds.
FOOD: Restaurants and snacks on US 22. In Lambertville, Lambertville House;
River's Edge, closed Mon. On US 202 near The Yard, Boswell's closed Mon.
Restaurants in New Hope, The Yard, Peddler's Village.

This is a large and important area, deserving more than a one-day trip.
Those with more time should ask at any place listed below for free
brochure *Highways of History*, with several good car tours. If planning
your trip in advance, write for copy to *Bucks County Historical-Tourist
Commission, Fallsington, Pa. 19054.*

Parry Barn Museum. *Open daily 1-5 incl. Sun. Closed Mon.* This is
operated by the County Historical Society and has changing exhibits.

Coryell's Ferry. *Runs mid-June to Labor Day, daily 1-5; weekends from
Memorial Day and after Labor Day. Summer weekends, 1-9 p.m.
Round trip lasts half hour. Moderate fees; group rates. Parking is better
on New Jersey side.*
 River sightseeing in a small boat, especially suitable for
photographing.

Mule Barge Rides. *May-Sept., daily incl. holidays, exc. Mon. In April and
thru Oct., Wed., Sat., Sun. only. Trips at 1, 3, 4:30, 6: last 1 hour. Fees:
$3. 2-11 yr. $1.50. Food: Picnic tables at start. Rest rooms. Free parking.*
 Here's a chance for a quiet, relaxing ride along a historic canal that
takes us through New Hope, then into the countryside. In season there
are flowering shrubs, gardens and arching trees along the way. Bring
your camera; forget your problems. (717) 862-2842.

New Hope & Ivyland R.R. Between New Hope and Buckingham Valley,
*weekends & hol. May-Oct. at 1, 2:45, 4:30. Apr., Nov. weekends, 1 & 3
p.m. Fees: $3. 2-11 yrs. $1.* (215) 862-5206.
 This round trip takes in 14 miles of Bucks County with its scenic,
historic countryside. We cross the trestle that includes the curve from
which Pearl White was rescued in the silent film, *Perils of Pauline*. The
locomotive, a ten-wheeler, is one of the few remaining coal-burners in
use. Avoid congestion by driving to Buckingham terminal (free parking)

and riding the train back to New Hope. Picnics, snacks at Buckingham; Dining Car at the New Hope Station.

The Yard, Lahaska, Pa. 18931. *Stores open Mon. thru Sat. and holidays, 10-5. Sundays, largely closed.*

Here is a collection of 14 picturesque shops surrounded by enclosed walks and offering some unusual merchandise. Located at the crossroads where we turn off for the larger Peddler's Village, The Yard has a gay, bazaar-like atmosphere.

Peddler's Village, Lahaska, Pa. 18931. *Open daily all year inc. most holidays. Many stores close Sundays. Hours: Mon. thru Sat. 10-5. Fri. until 9. Food: Restaurant; snacks. Rest rooms. Handicapped: Some climbing, and some hilly areas; stores are small, but those on crutches might manage.*

Originally a series of barns and chicken coops reconstructed into shops, this is today a large, impressive village with stores and arcades grouped around a handsome Common. Almost every kind of ware is found here and the emphasis is on crafts, antiques and unusual items. The Cock 'n Bull Restaurant has a cocktail lounge and a Peddler's Pub, while Punch & Judy caters to the ice cream and soft drink crowd. For fidgety youngsters, pony rides just across the way.

Fonthill Museum, E. Court St., Doylestown, Pa. 18901. (215) 348-9461. *Open same hours as Mercer Museum. Guided tours every 15 min; last tour 3:45. Fees: $2. Sr. Cit. & children, $1.*

This was the home of the late Dr. Henry C. Mercer, manufacturer of pottery and tile and curator of archaeology at the University of Pennsylvania. He built the Mercer Museum and Moravian Pottery and Tile Works. His home is maintained as a museum. It is constructed of reinforced concrete in the style of a castle, and is filled with fine examples of his tiles.

The Moravian Pottery and Title Works, E. Court St., Doylestown, Pa. 18901. *Open Wed. thru Sun. 10-5. Last tour at 4. Fees: $1.75. Sr. Cit. & students $1. Family, $3.50.*

Designed after the style of the Spanish Mission churches of Southern California, this concrete structure was opened in 1912 for the production of pottery and the now famous Moravian tiles. Dr. Mercer had earlier become interested in the pottery created by the Pennsylvania Germans who had learned their trade in the Black Forest. Distressed to find these skills dying out, he became an apprentice potter. The available clay was too soft for utensils but excellent for tiles. Eventually he built the tile works which we'll visit today.

Mercer Museum, Pine & Ashland Sts., Doylestown, Pa. 18901. *Open daily exc. Mon., March-Dec., Tues. thru Sun. 10-5. Closed Jan.-Feb. Fees: adults $2., Students $1., Sr. Cit. 75¢ Under 6, free. Family, $4.50. Rest rooms. Gift shop. Library of Bucks County Historical Society open Tues., 1-9 p.m., Wed.-Fri. 10-5. Comb. tickets to 3 bldgs.* (215) 348-4373.

Every youngster who relished fairy tales should have a chance to explore this castle. They'll find 33 rooms and 36 alcoves, all on different levels, located in cubby holes, towers, even on the roof. They'll see, among other things, tools used by butter and cheese makers, glass blowers, confectioners, tanners, wheelwrights. There is a fine collection of toys and dolls. If these are too juvenile for their taste, happily there's also a prisoner's dock and a gallows.

FOR THE DRIVER: Same as for Trip A-13 as far as Flemington. Continue south on US 202 then left on Rte 179 through Lambertville. Cross the Delaware River into Pennsylvania. At first light, turn left on PA 32. On left are the Parry Barn Museum, the Golden Door Gallery, and others. In same area is the Bucks County Playhouse. Drive from the Playhouse parking lot to West Ferry St., which goes to Coryell's Ferry.

Go back to Pa 32, South Main St. Turn left, cross bridge to West Mechanic St. Turn right 1 block to New St., then left to parking lot for Mule Drawn Barges.

Back on any street to Bridge St. Turn left; on right is the New Hope & Ivyland R.R. Proceed about 5 m. to Lahaska joining US 202 above town. At The Yard shopping center turn right to Peddler's Village.

Back to Rte. 202, turn right and proceed to jct. with Pa 413 to Buckingham-Valley. At jct. is Boswell's restaurant. To reach the trains, turn left on Rte. 413.

Back to US 202 follow signs south to Doylestown. For Fonthill and the Moravior Tile Works turn right on Pa. 313 about a mile to Court St. then back to US 202.

For the Museum, on Rte. 202 just after sign Borough of Doylestown, a road (E. Ashland St.) branches left. Follow signs to Mercer Museum.

Return Trip: Back to Rte. 202 which bypasses New Hope. Continue to jct. with US 22 at Somerville. East on Rte 22 to jct. with Garden State Parkway north, or to NJ 82 to Elizabeth and Goethals Bridge.

We Cross the Delaware with General Washington

TRIP A-15. *We'll Visit:*

　WASHINGTON CROSSING STATE PARK, PENNSYLVANIA
　　THOMPSON-NEELY HOUSE OF DECISION
　　BOWMAN'S HILL TOWER
　　BOWMAN'S HILL STATE WILDFLOWER PRESERVE
　　MEMORIAL AUDITORIUM
　　POINT OF EMBARKATION
　　OLD FERRY INN

WASHINGTON CROSSING STATE PARK, NEW JERSEY
NATURE CENTER (Tues., Thurs., weekends)
McCONKEY'S FERRY HOUSE MUSEUM (Closed Monday)
FLAG MUSEUM

DISTANCE AND TOLLS: From G.W. Bridge, about 90 *m.*, $1.25. Via Verrazano Bridge, about 70 *m.*, $1. Plus return. Average speeds.

FOOD: Restaurants on Parkway, Rte. 22, in Lambertville, New Hope. Near Old Ferry Inn, Pa., Washington Crossing Inn; '76 House.

Washington Crossing State Park, Pennsylvania. *Open year around daily until 9 p.m. No fees. Picnics and light cooking permitted. Pets leashed.*

We are lucky indeed to be able to view, after a few hours' drive, the tangible records of a great spectacular episode in American history, Washington's Crossing of the Delaware on that stormy Christmas night in 1776. Here is the river, once filled with blocks of ice; here are the banks where the frost-bitten Continentals embarked and landed; here are the houses they used for shelter, and here is that heroic painting that has stirred our imaginations since school days.

Our tour begins where the Continentals massed before their raid on Trenton—on the Pennsylvania side in Concentration Valley. Here the 2,400-odd patriots, pushed back by the disheartening campaigns of 1776, assembled. Special celebration Washn. Birthday.

A 16-mm color film, a documentary of the Crossing, narrated by Chet Huntley, may be rented at the park office, the Old Ferry Inn or the Memorial Auditorium.

Thompson-Neely House. *Open year around, weekdays 10-5, Sun. 1-5.*

Known as the House of Decision, this is a stone structure of early Pennsylvania farm architecture. It was used by General Lord Stirling (Alexander) and other officers and is believed to have been the place where Washington's strategy was decided. It now contains period furnishings.

Bowman's Hill Tower. *Open 8 a.m. to sundown. Rest rooms in adjacent building.*

The 110-ft. Tower, built in 1930, may be climbed to the open top. Here we'll get a VISTA that includes the winding Delaware, rolling hills and distant towns. When Washington encamped nearby the troops built a wooden platform for observation. At the tower's base, foot trails start down the hill. Easter Sunrise Service is held here.

Bowman's Hill State Wildflower Preserve. *Open 8 a.m. to sundown.*

Something is usually in bloom from March thru Nov. Peak bloom is in April thru June. During winter, seasonal exhibits are in the Preserve Building. Guided Tours available. Write for details to Park Botanist,

Washington Crossing, Pa. 18977. Free pamphlets describing Tours and trails, available at Preserve Building. Rest rooms. Parking areas.

About 100 acres in the Preserve have been planted with flowers, trees and shrubs native to Pennsylvania. There are marked trails, each named after a flower.

Memorial Auditorium. *Open year around daily, 9-5. Sun. 10-6.* Library of American Revolution *open 11-5, Sun. 12-5. Free. Rest rooms. Gift and souvenir shop. Handicapped can enter through special door, wide enough for wheelchairs.*

This native fieldstone building is primarily a large auditorium. Here we can sit comfortably while we listen to the narration of the Crossing, played every half hour, and look at a copy of the Emanuel Leutze painting. This might be a good place to start the tour of the two parks, as it sets the stage for the story of the dramatic events.

Point of Embarkation. Footpaths lead to the spot at the river bank where the Crossing began on Christmas night, 1776, and monuments commemorate the raid. Here the Crossing is reenacted annually on Christmas Day, beginning at 2 p.m. The Durham boat on display near the Auditorium is used and volunteers in uniform embark with "General Washington" and paddle across, hopefully under conditions less hazardous than those of 1776.

Durham Boat Replica. A full-scale reproduction of the Durham boats used by the army for the Crossing is exhibited near the Memorial Auditorium and used in the annual reenactment. Durham boats were flat-bottomed barges about 60 ft. long used for hauling iron ore on the river. They were propelled by oars or sails.

Old Ferry Inn. *Open year around, Mon. thru Sat. 9-5, Sun. 1-5. Food: Light snacks and drinks in season.*

Built 1757, this is the Inn where the General may have eaten his Christmas meal before starting across the river. There are furnishings from the wartime period, donated by local historic groups.

Washington Crossing State Park, New Jersey. *Open year around. Parking Fees: weekends only, May thru Sept., $2. For use of picnic table, 50¢. Food: Picnics, cooking. Handicapped: Easy access to first floor, Ferry House. 2 steps up at Nature Center, short step to rest rooms. Braille Nature Trail. Pets must be leashed.*

We are now on the east bank of the Delaware River, where the Continental army landed and began its march to surprise the Hessian camp at Trenton. Here is preserved Continental Lane, the road the soldiers used. This park of 293 acres has been turned into attractive groves of evergreens, three named for Generals Washington, Sullivan and Greene. It is also a wildlife sanctuary. Besides the historical memorials it has a Memorial Arboretum, a Nature Center, and an Open Air Theatre. Flagpole, markers, and garden plots have been provided by patriotic societies.

Nature Center. *Open year around, Tues., Thurs., weekends 10-4.*

A small museum with good exhibits, of special interest to naturalists studying the botanical specimens of the area, and to birdwatchers. For sports there is hiking through fire trails and along deer trails into more rugged terrain. For Guided Nature Walks, inquire at the Center.

Open Air Theatre. This natural amphitheatre hosts a summer festival of performing arts. For details, write in May to: Theatre Committee, Washington Crossing Association of New Jersey, Box 1776, Titusville, N.J. 08560.

McConkey Ferry House Museum. *Open year around daily ex. Mon., 10-12, 1-5. Sun. 2-5. Fees: Ages 12 and over, 50¢. Handicapped can see first floor.*

Originally a tavern, this house belonged to the son of the owner of the McConkey Ferry, across the river in Pennsylvania. Here General Washington waited after crossing with his troops before starting the march toward Trenton. It has been restored as a Colonial Inn and we can visit the kitchen, taproom and a bedroom.

Flag Museum. Comparatively new, this is located in the McConkey barn near the Museum.

FOR THE DRIVER: From both G.W. and Verrazano Bridges, same as for Trip A-13 as far as Flemington.

Continue south through Lambertville and cross into New Hope, Pennsylvania. Just over the bridge take Pa 32 left (south). Proceed about 3 *m.* to entrance, left, to Washington Crossing State Park, Pennsylvania.

Note: If bridge traffic is too heavy, turn south on NJ 29 before crossing river. This goes to both Washington Crossing Parks.

Turn off to your left for the Thompson-Neely House of Decision. Then continue along the same road to picnic areas and Soldiers' Graves.

Back on PA 32, turn left (south) and proceed to a road, right, to Bowman's Hill Tower. Continue from here to Wildflower Preserve and parking area.

Continue to jct. with Pa 32, passing picnic areas, and turn right. Proceed about 4 *m.* to the Memorial Auditorium. Near it is the Point of Embarkation and the replica of the Durham Boat.

Drive to next corner to Old Ferry Inn. Nearby are the Washington Crossing Inn and the '76 House, for food. Drive past the Inn and cross the river into New Jersey. On the other side watch for sign, on left, to Washington Crossing State Park and Open Air Theatre. Go up the hill, passing picnic areas, playgrounds, and the Nature Center. Eventually you reach the McConkey Ferry Museum and Flag Museum.

Return Trip: At this point you are just off NJ 29, going up along the river. Take this to your right (north) and proceed above Lambertville to jct. with 202. Turn right on 202 and return to jct. with US 22 in Somerville. Take Rte 22 east to jct. with Garden State Pkwy. north for G.W. Bridge. For Verrazano Bridge, at jct. take NJ 82 toward Elizabeth and Goethals Bridge.

New Jersey, from Edison Land to the Poconos

● *Here are attractions closer to New York City. Unlike those in Area A, which follow one another in a fairly straight line, these come in clusters and are spread out across some of New Jersey's more populated regions. The larger industrial cities are not included because of their heavy traffic. Eventually there are some enjoyable trips 100 miles from Manhattan, to the Poconos, where the extraordinary scenic beauty and the hospitality of the resorts give these adventures a special value.*

See map pp. 2-3

To reach Area B from New York City, use Exit Points: George Washington Bridge, or Verrazano Bridge. Main roads: Garden State Parkway, NJ 24, US 22. From G.W. Bridge: To Garden State Parkway: Follow signs to Rte. 80, drive 10 *m.* to Parkway southbound. To NJ 24: Take Garden State Parkway south to Exit 140 to NJ 82 west toward Morristown. (1 extra toll this way, but it saves driving through heavy city traffic.) Remain on Rte. 82 to jct. with NJ 24 and continue on Rte. 24 toward Chatham. To US 22: Take Garden State Parkway south to Exit 140A to US 22 west.

From Verrazano Bridge: To Garden State Parkway northbound: Cross Staten Island and take Goethals Bridge into New Jersey. Continue on NJ 439 (Bayway Ave.) following signs to Roselle and Garden State Parkway. Just beyond railroad overpass, at light, turn left on NJ 28 to Pkwy. north. To NJ 24: Cross Staten Island and Goethals Bridge. Proceed on NJ 439 (Bayway Ave.) for 3 *m.* to jct. with NJ 82. Turn left on Rte. 82. When it joins NJ 24 continue on latter toward Chatham. To US 22: Same as to Rte. 24 as far as NJ 82. Turn left on Rte. 82 and proceed to jct. with US 22 westbound.

A Mid-April Journey to Cherry Blossom Land

TRIP B-1. *We'll Visit:*

BRANCH BROOK PARK CHERRY BLOSSOM FESTIVAL, Newark, N.J.

DISTANCE AND TOLLS: From G.W. Bridge and Verrazano Bridge, under 25 *m*. G.W. Bridge $1. Via Verrazano Bridge, $1.35. Plus return.

Branch Brook Park Cherry Blossom Festival. Every spring in late April the cherry blossoms appear throughout the New Jersey Park System. Some of these displays are lavish. We will devote a separate trip to the most spectacular of these where over 2,000 trees bloom for about 3 weeks. At the parking area we may picnic or play games. A small lake with picturesque reflections lies at the southern end of the park. Caution: This is very popular and is crowded on weekends, especially Sundays. The Park is open the year around.

FOR THE DRIVER: Via G.W. Bridge, take Garden State Parkway south to Exit 149 at Belleville Ave. After ramp, turn right to light at Belleville, then turn right and proceed through town to Washington Ave., at a light. Turn right and proceed several blocks to light at Mill St. Signs on right direct into the Festival area. Follow Park drive, bearing left to remain in Park. By continuing to the other end you reach the lake.

Via Verrazano Bridge: Take Garden State Parkway north to Exit 148 at Bloomfield Ave. (County 506 Spur). After ramp go to light, then turn right on Bloomfield Ave. Your road goes through Branch Brook Park. The lake is to your right; main blossom display is to your left.

Return Trip: For G.W. Bridge, back to Belleville Ave., turn left to Pkwy. north. For Verrazano Bridge, back to Bloomfield Ave. (506 Spur) the way you came, following signs to Pkwy. south. Take Pkwy. to Exit 137 to NJ 28 to Goethals Bridge.

We Visit the Statue of Liberty, Ellis Island, New York Harbor, All from A Park in New Jersey

TRIP B-1(A): *We'll Visit:*

LIBERTY STATE PARK, Jersey City

DISTANCE AND TOLLS: From G. W. Bridge, 22 *m*., Tpke. 90¢, plus bridge. Via Verrazano Bridge & Goethals Bridge, 10 *m*., Tpke. 60¢, plus bridges.

Liberty State Park, Jersey City, N.J. 07304. *Open daily year around. Free. Picnic tables; refreshment stand in season, limited menu. Pets leashed. No alcoholic beverages. No fires in picnic area, but contained fires are permitted between the fence and water. Boat trips to either Ellis Island or N.Y. Harbor, three times daily: Lv. 10:30, 12:30, 2:30. Ret. 12:15, 2:15, 4:15. As of Sept., 1977, additional trips to Statue of Liberty. Fares: Adults $2.50, Senior Citizens $2.00; 11 and under, $1.25. Groups by reservation, 15 or more, adults only, $2. each. Handicapped: Special parking area. Paths level, paved. Some benches but little shade. Wheelchairs fit boat gangplank (about 34" wide), but many steps at Ellis Island; at Statue of Liberty, access into American Museum of Immigration; Harbor Tour best, no walking. Boats seasonal.* Contact Circle Lines (201) 435-9499.

Here is a glorious panoramic view we'll never forget. After our drive down an avenue lined with flags we see just 1,500 feet ahead the Statue of Liberty. To our left lies Ellis Island and beyond, the confluence of the mighty Hudson and the East Rivers. Between the two is all of lower Manhattan with its incomparable skyline. Brooklyn Bridge is prominent, backed by the others across the East River. From Brooklyn, the Verrazano-Narrows Bridge reaches to Staten Island, bearing to our right. Finally, over the rooftops of Bayonne, is Bayonne Bridge, completing a giant arc linking three boroughs with New Jersey. Staten Island Ferries and the popular sightseeing cruisers come and go; tugs, cargo vessels and, as an occasional bonus, one of the great ocean liners, make a never-ending pageant on the waters.

Only a few years ago this area of New Jersey was one of rotting docks, derelict boats and marshlands. The State is developing it into a State Park. The section we are in is Phase One; adjacent to it will be a wild-life refuge and lagoon. A promenade is in the future, to lead toward Ellis Island. Afternoon concerts on Sundays (2 p.m.) are drawing many to the park. These have included jazz groups, the New Jersey Symphony Orchestra, the Army Band, the Coast Guard and a Persian Drill Team.

FOR THE DRIVER: Take the N.J. Turnpike to Exit 14 where there is an extension to Jersey City and Bayonne and exits 14A, B & C. Go to Exit 14B. From ramp, turn left toward Burma Road, to Liberty State Park. Return same way.

To the Workroom of a Genius Who Changed Our Lives

TRIP B-2. *We'll Visit:*

THE LABORATORY OF THOMAS A. EDISON, West Orange

GLENMONT, Edison's home (Closed Sundays and holidays)
EAGLE ROCK RESERVATION

DISTANCE AND TOLLS: From G.W. and Verrazano Bridges, about 25 *m*. Via
G.W. Bridge, $1., via Verrazano Bridge, $1.35. Plus return. Average speeds to
slow, after parkway.
FOOD: Near Eagle Rock at Prospect Ave., Pal's Cabin; The Manor.

Edison Laboratory, Main St. & Lakeside Ave., West Orange, N.J. 07052.
*Open year around daily 9:30-3:30 (last tour starts), closed 3 major
holidays. Fees: Age 16 and over, 50¢. (Sr. Cit. free.) School groups free
by appointment. Tours: Guided only, last 90 min., start continuously.
Handicapped: Ramps into buildings; one with stairs reached without
steps from a second door. Crutches no problem.* (201) 736-5050.

This pilgrimage to West Orange, New Jersey, should be a duty for
every American who realizes how Thomas Alva Edison changed the
economy and pleasures of our world. Here is the birthplace of the
motion picture, of the talking machine, of the dictation recorder, of
many other inventions now in daily use, all produced by a man who
knew how to use his imagination.

Thomas Edison came to West Orange in 1887, after he had invented
the electric light in Menlo Park. We have an opportunity to come close
to the man himself, and a touching picture of him emerges as we pass
through his old laboratory, see his coat hanging in its accustomed place,
his tools at his work bench. In the theater we watch *The Great Train
Robbery*, and films about the life and friends of Edison.

Glenmont. *Open year around, Mon. thru Sat. 10-4, closed Sundays and
holidays. Fees: Same as for The Laboratory. Guided Tours start every
hour on the hour, last about ¾ hr. Make arrangements at the
Laboratory unit. Only 15 on a Tour. Mornings, and early in week are
least crowded times to visit. Handicapped: Steps and no railings into
house. Inside, can see a good deal without climbing to 2nd floor.*

Thomas Edison bought this house furnished, but added so many
personal touches that the elegant house became a much lived-in home.
Outside the well-kept grounds are lovely. Walk over to see the graves
nearby of Edison and his wife.

Eagle Rock Reservation. *Open year around, daily. Free.*

Here is a popular VISTA point where we can look out and down
upon towns, parks, rivers, and the distant New York skyscrapers. There
are picnicking, hiking and general park activities here.

FOR THE DRIVER: Via G. W. Bridge, take Garden State Parkway south to Exit
145 to I-280. Take this west, toward the Oranges.

Via Verrazano Bridge, take Garden State Parkway north to Exit 145 to
I-280. Take this west, toward the Oranges.

All: Shortly is the exit from I-280 marked to 508, Oranges and Montclair. Exit here. Immediately is 508, Northfield Ave. Turn right on this; just ahead is a traffic light. A sign has pointed this out as the direction to Edison's Site; however, it does not say what to do next.

At the light is Main St., tho it may be hard to find the name. Turn left. The street bears left, passing the municipal buildings. Follow Main St. for several blocks to the Edison Laboratory on Lakeside Ave., on right. Parking is at next corner, on left.

All: At the Laboratory, if continuing to Glenmont, make appointment here and get directions. Leaving Glenmont, turn left on Main St., again passing the Laboratory. From Laboratory, continue on Main. A short way ahead, left, is Eagle Rock Ave. Take this to top of hill and sign to Eagle Rock Reservation. Turn in here. Just ahead, off Eagle Rock Ave. on Prospect Ave. are Pal's Cabin and The Manor.

Return Trip: Go south (left) from top of park, on Prospect Ave. to junction with I-280. Take this toward Newark (east), to Garden State Parkway exit.

Art and a President's Birthplace

TRIP B-3. *We'll Visit:*

MONTCLAIR ART MUSEUM (Afternoons. Closed Monday, also July & Aug.)

ISRAEL CRANE HOUSE (Sun. afts., except Summer)

GROVER CLEVELAND BIRTHPLACE, Caldwell (Closed Monday)

DISTANCE AND TOLLS: From both Exits, under 35 *m.* Average speeds, slower in towns. Via G.W. Bridge, $1. Via Verrazano Bridge, $1.35. Plus return.
FOOD: On Pkwy. from G.W. Bridge. Restaurants also in towns.

Montclair Art Museum, South Mountain and Bloomfield Aves., Montclair, N.J. 07042. *Open weekdays 10-5, Sun. 2-5: closed Mon., and July & Aug. Concerts Sun. at 4 p.m. in Jan., Feb. and early March, Free. Handicapped: Exhibits, rest rooms, on main floor.* (201) 746-5555.

Considered one of our finer small museums, this one features a permanent collection that includes the works of many famous artists who lived in Montclair. One of the first was Charles Parsons (watercolors and marine lithographs); his friend, Harry Fenn, one of the founders of the American Water Color Society, also lived in town and soon George Inness moved here. Other painters and sculptors followed. Today we will see not only their works but also those of contemporary artists of the region.

Israel Crane House, 110 Orange Road, Montclair, N.J. 07042. Phone (201) 783-4322. *Open Sundays 2-5, or by appointment. Closed July, Aug.*

Headquarters of the Montclair Historical Society, this 1796 Federal style house has noteworthy furnishings of the past 2 centuries, with one room devoted to Americana, and an appropriately furnished schoolroom of yesteryear. The Montclair Junior League has done much to promote interest in this historic building and to provide special events here for schools and for the general public.

Grover Cleveland Birthplace, 207 Bloomfield Ave., Caldwell, N.J. 07006. *Open year around Tues. thru Sat. 10-12, 1-5. Sun. 2-5. Fees: 25¢ age 12 & over. Guided Tours. Parking in street before 4 p.m.; limited space behind house.* (201) 226-1810.

The Old Manse of the Caldwell First Presbyterian Church was just five years old when Grover Cleveland was born there. It's a homey place, furnished in the 19th-century style of the time when Cleveland, the only President of the United States to be born in New Jersey, was alive. Although he lived in it just three years, it has been kept as a memorial to him. Visitors may see the rooms on the first floor, including the one in which he was born. Personal mementoes, pictures and letters from the famous are displayed in wall cases.

FOR THE DRIVER: Same as to Edison's Laboratory, Trip B-2, as far as the Laboratory.

All: Continue on Main St., bearing left. A short way ahead is Eagle Rock Ave., left. Take this up the hill, turning into Eagle Rock Reservation at the sign at top, right. Drive to pavilion and VISTA point, then take the road from there going down a winding hill; at the foot, go straight ahead to South Mountain Ave. Turn left, briefly, to Bloomfield Ave. Just before you cross it is the Montclair Art Museum.

To continue to nearby Crane House, turn right on Bloomfield Ave. Just ahead is a traffic light at Orange Road. Turn right. Crane House is on right, at No. 110 (look for flag). From here, continue to next street going to right. Take this to South Mountain Ave., turn right, passing Museum.

Turn left on Bloomfield Ave. and drive about 3 *m.* into Caldwell. Shortly after the sign Caldwell, and just before the large church grounds, right, is the Grover Cleveland Birthplace.

Return Trip: Go back on Bloomfield Ave. to Garden State Pkwy. Take it north to Exit 159 for G.W. Bridge, or south to Exit 137 and NJ 28 for Verrazano and Goethals Bridges. Try to avoid Bloomfield Ave. during rush hours.

Youngsters' Delight: Farm Animals and Zoo

TRIP B-4. *We'll Visit:*

TURTLE BACK ZOO, West Orange, N.J.

DISTANCE AND TOLLS: To Zoo from both Exits, about 30 *m.* From G.W. Bridge, $1., via Verrazano Bridge, $1.35. Plus return. Average speeds after Pkwy. **FOOD:** Restaurants on Pkwy., from G. W. Bridge. Snacks at Zoo.

Turtle Back Zoo, Northfield Ave., West Orange, N. J. 07052. *Open all year, weather permitting. Daily, 10-5, Sun. & Hol. 11-6. Winters until 4:30. Closed Thanksgiving, Christmas Eve and Christmas, New Year's Eve and New Year's. Fee: Adults, $1.75; children over 12, 50¢ (also Senior Citizens); under 12, free with an adult. Small fee for train ride. Food: picnics, no fires; snacks. Handicapped: It's hilly, but most walks level, all well-paved. Benches, shade. Beginning in 1977, a Handicapped Day may become annual event. Inquire.* (201) 731-5800.

A picture-card zoo with an overall toytown atmosphere, this has exhibits easily viewed by the smallest in the party. There's the Mayflower, the barnyard, the Animal Contact Area, and in the grove by the Orange Reservoir, mile-long rides on a scale model of an 1865 Iron Horse. A word to adults: This is not a big, sprawling affair so you won't need sprinting shoes to keep up with the kids. However, this 15-acre zoo happens to be located right up the side of South Mountain, which may convey a message. Especially crowded weekends in season.

FOR THE DRIVER: Same as for Trip B-2 as far as exit from I-280 to 508 and Oranges. All: Exit here; first major road is Northfield Ave., 508. Turn left on this and proceed about 2 *m. Caution:* A sign at traffic light for turn-off is marked: Turtle Back Zoo Picnic Area. This is *not* Zoo entrance. Continue to bottom of hill, to another sign to Zoo, and to Arena; turn left.

Return Trip: Back on Northfield Ave. to jct. with I-280.

A Deer Paddock, A Fine Arboretum, and Potters at Work

TRIP B-5. *We'll Visit:*

SOUTH MOUNTAIN RESERVATION

DEER PADDOCK (March thru Oct.)

WASHINGTON ROCK LOOKOUT

CORA HARTSHORN ARBORETUM AND NATURE CENTER, Short Hills. (Arboretum year around. Museum Oct. to mid-June on Tues. and Thurs. afts., Sat. a.m.)

CHATHAM POTTERY SHOP, Chatham (Closed Sunday)

MUSEUM OF EARLY TRADES AND CRAFTS

DISTANCE AND TOLLS: From both Exits, about 30 *m*. From G.W. Bridge, 75¢. Add 25¢ on return. From Verrazano, $1.35. Plus return tolls. Average speeds. **FOOD:** On Pkwy. from G. W. Bridge. Restaurants on NJ 24 West, The Arch., Short Hills Mall; Altman's Charleston Garden, Stouffer's. In Chatham, the Wm. Pitt, closed Monday.

South Mountain Reservation. *Open year around, parts in season. Hiking trails; fishing at Diamond Mill Pond, picnic areas, vistas. In winter skiing and sledding.*

Washington Rock (554 alt.) Here Washington and his staff had a panoramic view of Continental troops trying to impede the British approach to Morristown in 1780. The Deer Paddock enables us to watch a large herd of deer roaming in their native setting and willing to be fed.

Cora Hartshorn Arboretum, 324 Forest Drive South, Short Hills, N.J. 07078. *Open year around. Museum open Oct. to mid-June. Tues. and Thurs. 3:30-5, Sat., 10-12. Fees: Donations. Handicapped: Some areas accessible to wheelchairs. Rest rooms in Museum. No picnics.* (201) 376-3587. The Arboretum has two miles of wooded paths within 17 acres. Many fine specimens of flowering shrubs make this a must during the seasons for azaleas, mountain laurel and rhododendron. The Museum exhibits change with the seasons. There's also a natural science reference library.

The Pottery Shop, 32 Watchung Ave., Chatham, N.J. 07928. *Open Mon. thru Fri. 9-5. Sat., 9-6. Free. Handicapped: 2 steps into workroom; narrow aisles.*

A small but interesting workshop produces fine quality handcrafted Early American Stoneware, a durable pottery in soft colors with embossed designs in different motifs—Federal, Pennsylvania Dutch and nautical. After watching the potters we visit the shop where both seconds and odd lots may be purchased.

Museum of Early Trades and Crafts, Main St. and Green Village Road, Madison, N.J. 07940. Phone (201) 377-2982. *Open Mon. - Sat. 10-5; Sun. 2-5. In winter, until 4. Closed major holidays. Contributions.*

An eye-catching pink limestone building, almost a small castle, for the early New Jersey villagers. Conducted tours provide much detail. Be sure to note the building itself, a turn-of-the-century gem.

FOR THE DRIVER: Via G.W. Bridge, take Garden State Pkwy. south to Exit 144 to South Orange Ave. After ramp turn right and take local road along Pkwy. back to first light, at South Orange Ave. Turn left on this (County 510), proceed through town and up mountain. Just before blinking light, turn left following signs to Crest Drive to Washington Rock Lookout.

Via Verrazano Bridge: Take Garden State Pkwy. north to Exit 144 to South Orange Ave. After ramp go ahead to next major street, South Orange Ave. Turn left on this (County 510), proceed through town and up mountain. Just before blinking light, turn left following signs to Crest Drive to Washington Rock Lookout.

All: Drive to end of road for Lookout. On the way, pass Deer Paddock, right.

Back to South Orange Ave. and turn right, down the hill. Just ahead at first traffic light after top of hill is Wyoming Ave. Turn sharp right on Wyoming and proceed about 3 m. to Millburn Ave. (County 527), just after crossing railroad tracks. Turn right on Millburn; detour as directed at Essex St. then return to Millburn. Continue past Saks Fifth Avenue. Across from this on right is building housing New Eyes for the Needy. At this corner, Baltusrol Way, turn right and go to railroad station at Chatham Road. Turn left on Chatham to Forest Drive, then left again to the Cora Hartshorn Arboretum and Bird Sanctuary.

Back to Millburn Ave. and turn right to NJ 24, Morris Ave. Go right on this (west) for several miles. On Rte. 24 pass The Arch restaurant; soon is the Short Hills Mall, with Stouffer's Restaurant and in Altman's, the Charleston Garden. Continue past Mall for several blocks to light at Hillside Ave. Turn left for two lights to Watchung Ave. Left on this to # 32, Chatham Pottery.

Go back to Rte 24; turn left a short way to junction with Green Village Rd. On left is the Museum of Early Trades and Crafts, in the pink building.

Return Trip: Back on NJ 24, passing the William Pitt in Chatham.

For G. W. Bridge: Less traffic, 1 extra toll by going ahead East on Rte. 82 after Rte. 24 branches off. Follow signs to Garden State Pkwy. north and take this. Otherwise, take Rte. 24 to Pkwy.

For Verrazano Bridge: Take Rte. 24; when it branches, continue in left lane, east on Rte. 82 to jct. with NJ 439. Turn right on Rte. 439 to Goethals Bridge.

Easy Access into the Heart of the Great Swamp

TRIP B-6. *We'll Visit:*

THE GREAT SWAMP, NATIONAL WILDLIFE REFUGE

DISTANCE AND TOLLS: From G. W. Bridge, about 40 *m.*, $1.25. Via Verrazano Bridge, about 25 *m.*, $1. Plus return. Average speeds.

FOOD: Restaurants on Parkway. For others on NJ 24 see Trip B-5.

The Great Swamp, National Wildlife Refuge, R D 1, Box 148, Basking Ridge, N.J. 07920. *Open year around, daily, dawn to dusk. Free. For self-guiding tours get map and information at Park Office. Pets, leashed. No picnics or smoking. Rest rooms.*

holds an interesting museum of tools and the products they produced

A natural area, the only one of its kind in the North Atlantic States, this is a haven for naturalists. Even the novice, however, can learn much by taking the self-guiding tour. We come first upon a remarkable boardwalk that extends out of sight into the swamp beyond, and from which we are able to see terrain usually unknown to the layman. Our tour booklet describes what we are passing, the small animals, about 180 species of birds and over 500 of plants. A Nature Center provides educational programs weekdays.

FOR THE DRIVER: Take Rte. 24 west. Proceed past Short Hills Mall for several blocks. Turn left on Fairmount Ave. at sign to Meyersville and go to jct. with Southern Boulevard. Turn right and proceed a mile to sign, left, Outdoor Educational Center. Turn in for The Great Swamp.

Return trip: Back to Fairmount Ave., turn left toward Chatham and proceed to NJ 24. Turn right and continue on Rte. 24. When this branches off, go straight ahead, now on NJ 82 east. For G.W. Bridge, follow signs Garden State Pkwy. north and take this. (Rte. 24 also goes to the Pkwy., but there is a longer stretch through traffic en route.) For Verrazano, continue on Rte. 82 to Rte. 439 and follow signs to Goethals Bridge.

The Continental Trail After Trenton, Before Yorktown

TRIP B-7. *We'll Visit:*

MORRISTOWN NATIONAL HISTORIC PARK, including
  FORD MANSION and HISTORICAL MUSEUM
SCHUYLER-HAMILTON HOUSE (Open Tues. & Sun. afts.)
FORT NONSENSE
JOCKEY HOLLOW
WICK HOUSE (Closed winter.)
SUGAR LOAF HILL

DISTANCE AND TOLLS: From G.W. Bridge, about 50 *m.*, $1.25. Via Verrazano Bridge, about 35 *m.*, $1. Plus return. Average speeds, slow in towns.
FOOD: On Parkway, restaurants. In Madison, Bottle Hill; Paul's Steak House. In Convent Station, New Hampshire House, closed Mon.; Rod's 1890 Ranch House. In Morristown, Governor Morris Inn. Diners on Rte. 24. See Trip B-5 for others.

Ford Mansion, 230 Morris Ave., Morristown, N.J. 07960. *Open year around daily 10-5, closed 2 major holidays. Fees: 50¢. Self-guiding tours. Handicapped: many steps. No charge for holders of Golden Eagle or Golden Age passports.* (201) 539-2016.

Morristown and environs are indelibly associated with the hardships of Washington's army. Here at different times in 1779, 1780 and 1781 the patriots rested between campaigns; drilled, endured cold and shortage of food. Here occurred the mutiny of the 2,000 Pennsylvanians who were fed up with promises and mean conditions. This handsome American Colonial mansion, built in 1772 by Col. Jacob Ford, Jr., was later placed at the disposal of General Washington, wife and staff. We will view many furnishings and personal objects that they used and others of the same period.

Historical Museum, located behind the Ford Mansion, was opened by the National Park Service February 22, 1938. It is open same hours as the mansion and one fee covers both. Here are military pieces, china, pewter, and a link of the Hudson River chain, weighing 104 lbs. Dioramas depict the mutiny and Washington's meeting with Lafayette on the steps of the Ford Mansion. There is a Gilbert Stuart painting of Washington. Here we pick up a map of the historical tour by car.

Schuyler-Hamilton House, 5 Olyphant Place, Morristown. *Not part of Park Tour. Open Tues., Sun. & Washn. Birthday, 2-5. Donations.*

This 18th-century Colonial house was the setting for the courtship of Betsy Schuyler by Alexander Hamilton in 1779. It has been furnished in period style by the local chapter of the D.A.R.

Fort Nonsense. Did he or didn't he, order his troops to build a fort, just to keep them occupied during a slack season? Anyway, a marker on top of a scenic hill shows where Washington's men executed his command and built the fort. It was named years later in derision. Today we'll get fine VISTAS from the site.

Jockey Hollow. *Open daily 9 to sunset, closed major holidays. Free. Picnic areas.* (See also Trip B-8.)

Here units of the Continental Army camped in 1779-1780. Replicas of their huts have been rebuilt on identical sites. The markers start at the Bettin Oak, beside the grave of Capt. Adam Bettin, who was killed when the Pennsylvania line troops mutinied here on January 1, 1781. The troops had suffered many grievances and intended to confront the Continental Congress at Philadelphia with demands for their bounties, back pay and reforms. General Anthony Wayne was threatened with death when he tried to stop them. He helped negotiate a settlement at Princeton, by which many of the men were released from service.

Wick House, Jockey Hollow Road. *Open daily. Same hours as Ford Museum. Closed major holidays. Handicapped: Several steps in yard; can approach from path near road. 2 steps into house.*

This house is very different from the Ford Mansion in its homey air and evidence of how some families lived comfortably without all the conveniences. It was owned by Henry Wick, captain in the cavalry, and is celebrated for the action of his daughter Tempe (pronounced *Tempy*—Temperance). When the Colonial troopers came to requisition her horse she led it into the house and hid it in a closet.

Sugar Loaf Hill is part of our Park Tour. Here are reconstructed huts used by officers, as well as a reproduction of an army hospital. As we proceed markers designate the location of nature trails, parade grounds and picnic areas.

FOR THE DRIVER: From G. W. Bridge, I-80 west to junction with I-287. South on I-287 to exit marked to National Historical Park in Morristown. Exit here, following signs to the park.

Via Verrazano Bridge, same as for Edison's Laboratory, Trip B-2, until on Main St. going toward the Lab. At a traffic light, get into left lane for a left turn onto Mt. Pleasant Ave., toward Whippany. This becomes NJ 10. Take it to junction with I-287, then south on I-287 to Morristown. At exit marked Historical Park, leave, and follow signs to park.

All: Because of one-way streets, check at Museum for best way to next destination. Can walk back a short way toward town to Olyphant Place and Schuyler Hamilton House, No. 5, on right. Then, choice: Drive right from Ford Mansion, to any street going right, into town, proceed to South St. (Rte 24), and turn right. OR: Take I- 287 south to next exit at South St. Take this west toward center of town.

All: On NJ 24, route goes (one-way) around Morristown Green. Stay to right and follow Rte 24 briefly when it turns right. If you miss it, go straight ahead from green to Ann St., then turn right to Tour sign.

On Rte. 24, just beyond the square, turn left on Western Ave., following signs for Park Tour. First, turn left on Ann St.. then right, up the hill. Bear left and follow winding road to site of Fort Nonsense.

Then back to Western Ave., turn left and follow signs to Jockey Hollow. Pass Bettin Oak and Wick House then on through Jockey Hollow.

Return Trip: From Jockey Hollow take Tempe Wick Road, by Wick House, east to junction with US 202 and I-287. North on I-287. For G. W. Bridge, continue to junction with I-80, take this east to the bridge. For Verrazano, off at Rte 10, east to West Orange. Road ends at Main St. Turn right on Main, passing municipal buildings, right; road bears right. At next traffic light turn right on Northfield (Rte 508); immediately is the junction with I-280. Take this east, toward Newark, to Garden State Pkwy. South.

More To See in Morristown and Southward

TRIP B-7(A).*We'll Visit:*

SPEEDWELL VILLAGE (Apr. thru Oct., Thurs.-Sun.)
FRELINGHUYSEN ARBORETUM (Daily March - Nov. then weekends)

ACORN HALL (Thurs. & Sun., Cl. Jan., Feb., Hol.)
BASKING RIDGE OAK
U. S. EQUESTRIAN TEAM HEADQUARTERS, Gladstone
U. S. GOLF ASSOCIATION HEADQUARTERS, Far Hills

DISTANCE AND TOLLS: From G. W. Bridge about 55 *m.*, each way. Bridge toll only. Via Verrazano Bridge, about 48 *m.*, Pkwy. tolls 35¢ plus bridge.

FOOD: In Morristown, restaurants; Old Mill Inn on Rte 202; a few snacks.

This trip is not to some blockbuster attraction for a day's outing. Rather, it's a historical ramble for those whose interests include fine antiques, villages of quaint homes, buildings connected with the development of the telegraph by Samuel Morse and Alfred Vail, training grounds for the Equestrian teams we send to the Olympics, and a newly arrived museum all about the game of golf.

Since one trip already has introduced us to the side of Morristown General Washington and his army knew, this next will give us a chance to continue from that or to come back some other day.

Speedwell Village, 333 Speedwell Ave. (Rte 202) Morristown, N.J. 07960. Phone (201) 540-0211. *Open Apr. thru Oct., Thurs. - Sat. 10-4; Sun. 2-5. Rest of year by appointment. Adm. fee; special rates for Senior Citizens and those under 18.*

The old Speedwell Iron Works once supplied General Washington's army with munitions. Fallen to ruin, its site is today preserved and a number of historic buildings have been gathered here. These include the Telegraph Building, the Vail factory where Morse and Vail in 1837 conducted their famous experiments with the Morse code and telegraph. Others are the homestead of Stephen Vail, owner of the iron works, and a carriage house and wheel house. Exhibits of models and documents and other memorabilia pertaining to the iron works and to the electro-magnetic telegraph are on hand. A detailed pamphlet permits self-guided tours and reminds that grounds are much as they were in the past, with no paved walks between houses. This is a developing project, organized in 1966, and will have additions in the future. It has been listed in the National Registry of Historic Sites.

Frelinghuysen Arboretum, E. Hanover Rd. *Open daily, 9-5, mid-March-Nov. Rest of year, weekends. Closed major holidays. Free.*

A country estate of the Victorian era is now headquarters of the Morris County Park Commission. Elaborate gardens, flowering shrubs, displays of roses and spring bulbs make this worth a visit in almost any season. Blind guests will welcome a Braille Trail. Horticulture library, also programs related to gardening available. (Fee for lectures.)

Acorn Hall, 68 Morris Ave., Morristown, N.J. 07960. *Open Thurs. 11-3; Sun., 1-4. Adm.: Adults, $1., students, 50¢. Closed Jan., Feb. & Hol.* This excellently preserved Victorian house is headquarters of the Morris County Historical Society. The scrollwork embellishments on the exterior indicate what to expect inside. Some of the rooms have been praised by the highest authorities as possessing unusual charm. Most of the house is exactly as it was when built in 1853; furnishings include many priceless objects from around the world. New Jersey designated the house a Historic Site; it is in the National Register of Historic Places and Buildings.

Basking Ridge is a small historic town, proud of its past and heedful of the present, making certain its appearance remains unchanged - and attractive. Markers along the main street tell of the earliest settlement here (1720), point out the site of the Widow White's tavern where Gen. Charles Lee was captured ignominiously by the British, and relate that the Presbyterian Church supplanted a log church that had been erected underneath an old oak tree. In the adjoining cemetery the ancient tree, now known as the Basking Ridge Oak, still stands. It is said to be second in size only to the Salem Oak.

U. S. Equestrian Team Headquarters, Gladstone, N.J. 07934. Phone (201) 234-1251. *Open year around, Mon. - Sat. 10-1. May be adm. fee. To make sure team is not on tour call first. Handicapped can enter stables, watch some of the activities.*

This is an extraordinary treat, for here the riding teams are trained for the Pan American and Olympic Games. Rehearsals for the contests include dressage (testing obedience), steeplechase and cross-country jumping. The organization has a long record of important awards. It has no Federal subsidy.

U. S. Golf Association Headquarters, Far Hills, N.J. 07931. Phone (201) 234-2300. *Open year around daily; Mon. - Friday 9-5; weekends 10-4. Closed hol. Free*

In 1972 the United States Golf Association moved from New York into the red brick Georgian Colonial estate once owned by the W. J. Sloane family in Far Hills. Part of the building is a Museum, filled with the sort of exhibits most appealing to golfers. The history of golf is followed from its origin to the present day; rules of the game likewise are traced. There is a fascinating display depicting the evolution of golfing equipment and another of clothing worn on the links, past and present. We also see trophies, photographs, pictures of many golf courses, and clubs and balls used by today's champions. A golf library is valuable for reference.

FOR THE DRIVER: From G. W. Bridge take I-80 west to jct. with I-287. South on Rte 287 briefly to exit to Rte 10 "to Whippany". Note: Do *not* turn toward Whippany - take road west a short way to jct. with US 202. Turn left (south).

Via Verranzo Bridge, same as for Edison's Laboratory, Trip B-2, until on Main St. going toward the Lab. At traffic light, get in left lane to turn left on Mt. Pleasant Ave. Take this - it soon becomes NJ 10 to Whippany. Proceed past jct. with I-287 to next major road, US 202 and turn left.

All: Shortly, cross Hanover Ave. at light. Just beyond on left is Speedwell Village. Watch for sign.

Return to Hanover Ave. and turn right on E. Hanover. Proceed past the Mennan Arena to the Frelinghuysen Arboretum, on right. Then back on E. Hanover to I-287. Take this south, toward Morristown. Just ahead is the exit to National Historical Park. Follow signs to Park, passing the Ford House *(see Tour B-7)*; park in street, and walk a short way to 68 Morris Ave. and Acorn Hall.

To continue southward, the most enjoyable route will be US 202, but best to take it after leaving Morristown. Take I-287 south again, skipping exit to South St. in town. Any exit below will connect, to the right (west) with US 202. Take Rte 202 left, south, through an area of small towns and antique shops. Photographers may be interested in the Old Mill Inn, on left (open as restaurant) and across from it, right, the historic mill built in 1842 by Ferdinand Van Dorn.

A road goes from here into Basking Ridge, but another below goes directly into the heart of town. Take either. Ahead, at N. Finley Ave. at a light, turn left about 1 mile into town. At N. Maple St. at a light is a church. Adjacent to this is the cemetery where the Basking Ridge Oak stands. Good views of the center of town are obtained by driving, or walking, up the hill in front of the church. Then return to US 202; turn left.

At junction with County 512, turn right toward Pottersville. Just beyond a field, left, is the road to the U. S. Equestrian Team Headquarters. (Road unpaved but useable.) For the golf museum, turn left from Rte 202 on County 512 and drive about 2 miles to the entrance.

Return Trip: For G. W. Bridge follow signs back on 512 to I-287 north. Take this to I-80 to G. W. Bridge. For Verrazano Bridge, take I-287 south toward Somerville and remain to the end where are connections with NJ 440 to Staten Island. This goes to I-278, to Verrazano Bridge.

Sound Waves, Indian Relics and a Log Hospital

TRIP B-8. *We'll Visit:*

MORRIS MUSEUM OF ARTS AND SCIENCES, Morristown. (Closed Sun. & Mon. in summer)

JOCKEY HOLLOW

DISTANCE AND TOLLS: To Morristown from G.W. Bridge, 50 *m.*, $1.25 going, $1. returning. From Verrazano Bridge, about 35 *m.*, $1., add 35¢ on return. Mainly average speeds after Pkwy.
FOOD: See Trips B-5 and B-7 for restaurants on Rte. 24.

Morris Museum of Arts and Sciences. P.O. Box 125, Convent, N.J. 07961. *Open Mon.-Sat. 10-5. Sun. 2-5. From July 1 to Labor Day, open Tues.-Sat. 10-4. Closed major holidays. Adm. fee. $1. adults, 50¢ students & Sr. Cit., under 12, 25¢. Small fee for guides for groups. Handicapped: Ramp into building, special elevator for wheelchairs.* (201) 538-0454.

An excellent museum in an imposing red brick mansion, this holds just about everything from live animals to sound wave demonstrations to old-time toys. Downstairs a model of a railroad is being constructed by members of a local railroad association. A shop sells inexpensive souvenirs and educational matter.

Jockey Hollow. *Open daily, 9-sunset. Closed Christmas & New Year's Day. Free. Picnic area.*

This is part of the Historic Tour (Trip B-7) but for youngsters not yet ready for too much history it's a good place to relax after the Museum. They can watch an orientation movie at Visitor Center then play on the old Parade Grounds, climb to the reconstructed Officers' Huts and marvel at the primitive log hospital. Daily in summer and weekends in winter a costumed soldier demonstrates musket loading and firing. People who prefer a good walk may follow a nature trail through a wildlife preserve. The Wick House is a short distance away, by foot, and worth a visit.

FOR THE DRIVER: Follow directions in Trip B-7(A) into Morristown and the National Historical Park. From here, on Morris Ave., proceed to junction with Columbia Road, County 510, near the Gov. Morris Inn. Turn right on Columbia. Shortly ahead, at Normandy Parkway, on left, nearly hidden by large shrubbery, is the Morris Museum of Arts and Sciences.

Go back, following signs to I-287 South. Go to Exit 26B, Bernardsville, ahead to traffic light on Rte. 202. Right on 202 to next light then left on Tempe Wick Road to the Park.

Return Trip: Follow directions in Trip B-7.

From A Stage Coach Stop to the High Hills

TRIP B-9: *We'll Visit:*
STAGE HOUSE INN AND VILLAGE, Scotch Plains
TERRY LOU ZOO
WATCHUNG RESERVATION, Mountainside, N.J.

DISTANCE AND TOLLS: From G. W. Bridge about 50 *m.*, plus 35 on return; 75¢ Pkwy. tolls plus bridge, plus return. Via Verrazano Bridge, about 26 *m.*, plus 10 on return to Goethals Bridge. Just bridge tolls.

FOOD: Numerous places along Rte 22 and in towns. Refreshments in Watchung Reservation. Picnic areas. In Scotch Plains, Stage House Inn (lunch & dinner).

Stage House Inn and Village, Front St. & Park Ave., Scotch Plains, N.J. 07076, Phone (201) 322-4224. *Open during business hours or by appointment.*

This is a collection of 18th-century buildings that have been preserved and today hold a number of small shops surrounding a courtyard. The Stage House Inn on the corner, built in 1737, once served weary travelers taking the 2-day trip between New York and Philadelphia on the Swift Sure Stage Line along the Old York Road. Other houses now contain shops featuring early crafts, leatherwork, antiques, silverware, marble furniture and more. Across the street is the Cannon Ball Museum, hit by one of the cannons during the Battle of Short Hills. House contains a museum, open Sundays 2-4 or by appointment.

Terry Lou Zoo, Raritan & Terrill Rds., Scotch Plains, N.J. 07076. Phone (201) 322-7180. *Open daily, 10 to dusk. Adm. fee, adults $2., children $1. (subject to change).*

A privately owned zoo, this has an outstanding collection of game. About 275 birds and animals live here, including some endangered species. Some of the animals and waterfowl are free to roam, allowing children to pet them. Pony rides available, small fee.

Watchung Reservation. *Open 8 a.m.-11 p.m. daily year around. Trailside Museum, Sept. thru June weekdays exc. Fri., 3-5. July & Aug., 1-5. Weekends and holidays all year, 1-5. Free. Planetarium shows weekend afts & Wed. eve. over 8 yrs. only. 50¢. Fees for horseback riding, boating. Food: Picnics, snacks. Tours: Guided, by appointment only. Write Trailside Nature and Science Center, Coles Ave. & New Providence Road, Mountainside, N.J. 07092. Pets leashed only. (201) 232-5930.*

There's much to do in this scenic, 2,000-acre park. In season there is a wonderful display of rhododendron; peak bloom occurs usually a little past mid-May. An Observation Tower 575 feet above sea level provides not only good VISTAS but an excellent spot from which birdwatchers can observe migratory flights. Look, too, for the Deserted Village and the mile-long Lake Surprise, where there's boating and fishing; also, in winter, ice skating. Small fees. The Stables are popular because of 12 miles of bridle paths. Riding instructions are available. Much of the Reservation has been left in its natural state, meaning that many Indian trails have been preserved. Indians also left us the term "Wach Unks," High Hills. Sometimes, in the quiet woods of the Watchung Mountains, you get the feeling they're not so far away from their old camping grounds.

FOR THE DRIVER: Take Rte 22 west toward Somerville. After passing New Providence Road (to Watchung Reservation - we return later), watch for sign from Rte 22 to take Mountain Ave. to Scotch Plains. Branch left on this and proceed into town, and Park Ave. Turn left on Park Ave. to Front St. At this jct. is the Stage House Inn and Village.

Right on Front St. several blocks to jct. with Terrill Road. Left on this to the end, at jct. with Raritan Road. At this junction, on right, is the Terry Lou Zoo.

Back on Terrill Rd., continue to its jct. with US 22. Take Rte 22 east. At New Providence Road, follow signs off of Rte 22 and continue up the mountain to the Watchung Reservation.

Return Trip: Back to Rte 22, turn left (east). For G. W. Bridge, proceed to jct. with Garden State Pkwy. North, take this to I-80 to bridge. For Verrazano Bridge, take Rte 22 east, then NJ 82 toward Elizabeth and Goethals Bridge. This goes to NJ 439, to right, to the bridge.

Shops and Houses Out of America's Past

TRIP B-10. *We'll Visit:*

WALLACE HOUSE, Somerville, N.J. (Closed Monday)

OLD DUTCH PARSONAGE, Somerville (Closed Monday)

CLINTON HISTORICAL MUSEUM, Clinton (Apr. thru Oct.)

HUNTERDON COUNTY ART CENTER, Clinton (Afts. Closed Monday)

VOORHEES STATE PARK

NEW HAMPTON GENERAL STORE

DISTANCE AND TOLLS: To Clinton from G.W. Bridge, about 70 *m.*, $1.25. From Verrazano, about 55 *m.*, $1. Plus return trip. Adding Voorhees Park and General Store, 20-25 *m.* more. Mainly fast speeds, average in towns.

FOOD: On Rte. 22 at Whitehouse near Clinton, Ryeland. Restaurants and snack places along Rte 22 and in towns.

Wallace House, Washington Place, Somerville, N.J. 08876. *Open year around, daily exc. Mon., 10-12, 1-5, Sun. 2-5. Fees: 50¢ ages 12 and up. Guided tours.* (201) 735-1015.

This restored Colonial house probably was one of the best of its kind when General Washington made it his headquarters. The typically furnished kitchen has special interest, and the slave quarters remain unchanged. We are made acquainted with the military and social life of the house during the Revolution. The furnishings are authentic 18th-century.

Old Dutch Parsonage, Across the street from Wallace House. *Same hours and fees. Caretaker next door, 38 Washington Place.*

Rutgers University was born here, established by the Rev. Freling-huysen as a Dutch Reformed theological seminary, which became Queens College and later, Rutgers. The building was constructed of bricks from Holland in 1751. An interesting novelty is the smokehouse, usually built outdoors but, because of the constant wartime foraging, installed here on the third floor. General and Madame Washington often dropped in here while staying at the Wallace House.

Clinton Historical Museum, Old Red Mill, Clinton, N.J. 08809. *Open April thru Oct. Mon. thru Fr. 1-5. Sat. & Sun., 12-6. Fees: Adults $1.75, Senior Citizens, $1., children 50¢. Guided tours. (201) 735-4101.*

You don't have to be an antiquarian to enjoy this reconstructed old mill, which since 1763 has processed flaxseed oil, grain and lime, and today is crammed with reminders of the past economy. Lifelike figures in costumes illustrate the uses of the period rooms. The Mill today is part of a growing village of that era. Excellent special events held here—phone for schedule.

Hunterdon County Art Center, Old Stone Mill, Clinton, N.J. 08809. *Open weekdays exc. Mon., 1-4. Sun. 1-5. Closed Holidays. Donation.* (201) 735-8415.

In a large, cool, barnlike gallery beside a waterfall we'll find a variety of arts and crafts on display. This is more than a gallery, it is a cultural center with numerous activities throughout the year that include evening meetings and chamber music sessions.

Voorhees State Park. *Open daily, year around; free, but 50¢ for use of picnic table in season.*

Fine hiking, nature area and children's playground here, plus a superior VISTA.

New Hampton General Store, R.F.D., Hampton, N.J. 08827. *Open* *weekdays 10-5, weekends 12-5 inc. Sun., closed major holidays.*

A museum piece itself, this 100-year-old bazaar and emporium recreates a turn of the century general store. It's packed with eye-catching antiques and vintage household items, clothing, old-fashioned candy. This is no souvenir shop operation; it is both store and mail order house, with attractive merchandise.

FOR THE DRIVER: Take US 22 Take US 22 westbound. Proceed to jct. with US 202 and 206, merged. Take these south, toward Princeton. When they branch, continue on US 206 past railroad overpass. Just beyond it, at light, is Somerset St. Turn left for 1 block, then right on Middagh to the end. Turn left to Wallace House and Old Dutch Parsonage. (Caretaker at 38 Washington Place, next door.)

Back to US 206, turn right to rotary, then take NJ 28 west. Continue to jct. with US 22 and turn left (west). Soon it merges with I-78. There are 2 exits in Clinton. Take second one, marked Clinton-Pittstown. Turn right from ramp—this is W. Main St. Continue to street just before small bridge. On left is Clinton House. Just beyond is Clinton Historical Museum.

Cross the river to Hunterdon County Art Center, opposite museum, on Lower Center St. On leaving, continue, bearing right on Center St., and stay on this to jct. where you turn left to Rte. 31 north. Take Rte. 31 a mile or so to County Road 513, right, and drive to Voorhees State Park.

Back on Rte. 513 to NJ 31; turn right, continue past Spruce Run. Do not take the road to Hampton but wait for one, right, marked New Hampton. Turn here to the New Hampton General Store. Park in street or in lot opposite. Antique shops are nearby.

Return Trip: Back to Rte. 31, turn left and return to Rte. 22 east. Take this back to Garden State Pkwy. north for G.W.Bridge, or to Rte. 82 east for Verrazano and Goethals Bridges.

For a scenic alternate route back, take Rte 31 to right, to junction with NJ 57. Turn right on 57 to NJ 24 and take this to Morristown. This goes over the scenic Schooleys Mountain, passing several good dining places in Chester, more in Morristown area. At junction with I-287 follow directions from Trip B-7.

A Tour of the Famous Duke Gardens

TRIP B-11. *We'll Visit:*

THE DUKE GARDENS FOUNDATION, INC., Somerville, N.J.
(By appointment only.)

DISTANCE AND TOLLS: From G.W. Bridge, 55 *m.*, $1.25. Via Verrazano Bridge, 40 *m.*, $1. Plus return.

Duke Gardens Foundation, Inc., Rte. 206 South, Somerville, N.J. 08876. *Phone (201) 722-3700. Tours by reservation only, 7 days a week, 12-4; Wed. & Thurs. also from 8:30-10:30 p.m. Last about 45 min. Closed from June 1 to Oct. 1., also Thanksgiving, Christmas & New Year's Day. Fee: $2.50. School sponsored groups complimentary Mon. & Fri. Handicapped: some paths are narrow and there are a few stairs. No cameras permitted. And no spike heels.*

An acre of gardens flourishing under glass in controlled temperatures comprises a major attraction of this part of the country. Despite requiring an appointment to visit them, they are listed at this point because they are close to the destinations in our preceding trip and could be combined.

Visitors discover an unforgettable collection of twelve individual and atmospheric gardens from around the world. Each has its own flavor; experts in the style of each country have made them as authentic as possible, and we'll find ourselves in Victorian England, in China, France, Japan, India, Hawaii. There are also lovely seasonal displays in spring and summer.

FOR THE DRIVER: See directions for Trip B-10 to Somerville and the jct. where US 206 turns south. Pass the turn-off for Wallace House on Rte. 206. A short distance farther at traffic light are signs to the Duke Gardens.

Return Trip: Go back the way you came.

Boating, Canoeing, and Model Railroading

TRIP B-12. *We'll Visit:*

CRANFORD BOAT & CANOE CO., Cranford, N.J. (Spring thru fall, afts. & eves.)

BOWCRAFT'S SPORT SHOP AND PLAYLAND, Scotch Plains.

MODEL RAILROAD CLUB, INC., Union, N.J. (Eventually open evenings & weekend afts.)

DISTANCE AND TOLLS: To Bowcraft's from G.W. Bridge, about 40 *m.*, $1.25. From Verrazano Bridge, under 30 *m.*, $1. Plus return trip. Fast and average speeds.

FOOD: Restaurants and snack bars along Rte. 22.

Cranford Boat & Canoe Co., Springfield & Orange Aves., Cranford, N.J. 07016. *Open for rentals, spring, summer and fall, daily 11 a.m. to 11 p.m. Fees by the hour, week, month or by season; moderate rates. Special party rates.*

We'll paddle up the Rahway River, a winding waterway through a variety of scenery. We can bring our own canoe or rent one here. There are other rivers nearby to explore, as well as dams to conquer. We will learn the correct way to handle a canoe, if we didn't know before; there are safety regulations to be obeyed. Plenty of boats are available, but a large group should arrange in advance.

Bowcraft Sport Shop and Playland, Route 22, Scotch Plains, N.J. 07076. *Open all year, 10-10. Two weather-controlled tents permit arcade games and other sports "indoors".* *Fees vary with activity. Food: Snacks. Fireplaces reserved, free. Rest rooms. Handicapped may play some of the games.* (201) 233-0675.

This lively area, a clean, well-groomed playland, provides activities to suit most ages and interests. The sports line-up includes miniature golf, archery, pony rides, water cycling, table tennis, whiffle golf, and more. A small lake and an attractive garden are good for relaxation between games. Ticket books available for the games, reduced prices, transferable.

Model Railroad Club, Inc., Box 1146, Union, N.J. 07083. Phone (201) 964-9724. *Meetings eventually every weekday evening, and weekend aft. Phone first because Club is adapting to new schedule and new quarters. All visitors welcome. Beginners and experts urged to join and to follow their special interests. Full membership for anyone over 18; limited openings for those 15-17.*

How would you like to view the start of what may be the world's largest model railroad, with over 10,000 feet of track? This dream will come true with a visit to the Model Railroad Club, formerly located in Murray Hill but now in fine new quarters in Union. Visitors have their own balcony for observing both the railroad and the permanent displays. They may even operate the trains by push-button control when the Club is not in session. Exhibits show how to start the hobby and where supplies may be purchased. The project, a quarter of a century old in Jan., 1974, includes completion of a point to point railroad that eventually will reach from Hoboken to Pittsburgh. Interest groups meet on different nights; the N, HO, and O layouts are kept separate physically in order for the groups to retain an informal atmosphere. Once a year visitors are invited to a full public show and allowed to walk through the operating aisles. Watch for the date.

FOR THE DRIVER: Via G.W. Bridge, take Garden State Pkwy. south to Exit 137 at NJ 28, turn right from ramp and drive several blocks and cross a small river.

Via Verrazano Bridge: Take NJ 28 as far as Garden State Pkwy. north, but continue past the Pkwy. and across small river.

All: After crossing Rahway River turn right at sign to Kenilworth and Springfield, on Springfield Ave. Drive several blocks to Orange Ave., at light. On right is Cranford Boat and Canoe Co.

Continue on Springfield Ave. past Nomahegan Park to end of street; turn left, still on Springfield Ave., until jct. with US 22. Take second entrance, west. After passing turn-off to Mountainside, Bowcraft's is at your right, on Rte. 22. Turn back on US 22 to jct. Jefferson Ave. Turn right to Model Railroad Club.

Return trip: Back to US 22, right to jct. Garden State Pkwy. For G.W. Bridge, take Pkwy. north. For Verrazano, at this jct. take NJ 82 east toward Elizabeth and follow signs to Goethals Bridge.

Biblical Gardens and an Edison Museum

TRIP B-13. *We'll Visit:*

BIBLE GARDENS OF ISRAEL, Woodbridge (Closed Sat.)

EDISON MEMORIAL TOWER AND MUSEUM, Menlo Park (Closed Mon.)

CEDAR BROOK PARK, Plainfield

DRAKE HOUSE, Plainfield (Mon., Wed., Sat. afts.)

WASHINGTON ROCK STATE PARK

DISTANCE AND TOLLS: From G.W. Bridge about 55 *m.*, $1.25. From Verrazano, about 40 *m.*, $1. Plus return trip. Average speeds.
FOOD: Near Metuchen, en route Plainfield, Oak Hills Manor, closed Mon. & last 3 weeks in July. Others on Rte 1 and in towns.

Bible Gardens of Israel. Beth Israel Memorial Park, Route 1, Woodbridge, N.J. 07095. *Open daily 9-4:30, closed Sat. Flowers usually blooming by June. Rest rooms. Handicapped: Good walks.*

Here are miniature gardens with authentic plants that were mentioned in the Bible. There are four main displays: The Garden of the Promised Land, the Garden of Moses, the Garden of Jerusalem, and the Garden of the Kings. Architecture features marble from Mt. Carmel and stones from the Holy Land. This is a comparatively small park, yet people of all faiths come to enjoy the plantings.

Edison Tower & Museum, Menlo Park, N.J. 08817. *Open year around, Tues.-Sat. 10-12, 1-5; Sun. 12-5. Fees: 25¢, over 12 years. Rest rooms. Free parking. Exhibits on one level.* (201) 549-3299.

This small museum is essentially a memorial to Thomas Edison on the site of the laboratory in which he began work on the incandescent lamp. Several scale models may be seen, including one of the original laboratory. There is also a model of Edison's first tinfoil phonograph and the first successful light bulb. Pictures of the inventor and his friends line the walls. We cannot climb the tower, but inside at its base we'll see the ever-burning light that Edison himself lighted in 1929. On top of the tower, 131 ft. above us, is a 13 ft. replica of his original lamp.

Cedar Brook Park, Park Ave., Plainfield. *Open daily, year around. Iris Display: Early May to mid-June. Dogwood: Early to mid-May. Other flowers in season. Picnic areas.*

An attractive small park, this features a Shakespeare garden containing plants mentioned in his works, as well as the iris and dogwood (cornus) collections. We can drive past some of these, but others should be inspected on foot. At the height of the season this will be crowded on weekends.

Drake House, 602 W. Front St., Plainfield. *Open year around Mon., Wed., Sat. 2-5 p.m. Fees: Donations.* (201) 755-5831.

During the Battle of Short Hills in 1777 this striking appearing house became Washington's Headquarters. Built in 1746, it now is filled with period furnishings as well as an interesting diorama depicting one of the nearby battles. Today as headquarters of the local Historical Society it provides us with a good chance to look back over a portion of America's past.

Washington Rock State Park. *Open year around. Fees: For use of picnic table only, 50¢. Rest Rooms.*

This small, 36-acre park is worth the trip for its fine VISTA. During the Revolution General Washington used it to view enemy troop movements below him. A monument commemorates this, erected in 1912 by the Continental Chapter D.A.R. and people of Plainfield and North Plainfield.

FOR THE DRIVER: Via G.W. Bridge, take Garden State Pkwy. south to Exit 130 to US 1 south. Exit to Rte. 1, but at first jug-handle, cross over and come back the other side, north. Just beyond the parkway overpass a sign, right, directs to Beth Israel Memorial Park—Bible Gardens.

Via Verrazano Bridge: Cross Staten Island to NY 440 and take this south across Outerbridge into New Jersey. Continue on 440 to US 9. Go north on Rte. 9 toward Newark. Shortly comes a rotary at jct. with US 1. Turn left onto Rte. 1 Southbound. Watch for sign, left, to Bible Gardens of Beth Israel, off Rte. 1. Take jug-handle turn to cross highway and proceed to gardens.

All: Take US 1 north, to right, back to rotary; turn left following sign to Iselin, on Greene Ave. Just beyond Mt. Lebanon Cemetery is a railroad overpass then a light. Turn left here, onto NJ 27 toward Metuchen. Proceed past the Parkway to a road, right, to Edison Tower, just ahead.

Back on NJ 27, turn right toward Metuchen. At traffic light at Main St. is a sign, to Plainfield, right. Take this road, County 531. You pass Oak Hills Manor restaurant.

At Oak Tree Ave. light, turn left briefly, then right again onto Park Ave., still on 531. Continue on Park Ave. and watch for sign, left, to Cedar Brook Park. Turn in here; a road, right, leads to the Iris Gardens. Look up the Shakespeare Garden and the Dogwood display.

Continue through park, bearing right, to return to Park Ave. Turn left on Park and proceed toward town to Fifth St., NJ 28. Turn left on this and follow it through town, turning twice with it. The second time will be at West Front St. Here, where Rte. 28 turns left, is the Drake House.

Leaving Drake House, turn right and continue on Rte. 28 for a couple of miles. Eventually, pass Rock Ave. The following one is Washington Ave. Turn right (north) at light here on County 529. Shortly, cross US 22. Continue beyond this, following signs to Washington Rock Park.

Return Trip: Go back to US 22 and take it east (left). Soon you'll pass Bowcraft's (Trip B-12) and the road to the Watchung Reservation (B-9). Diners, Restaurants on Rte. 22. Continue to jct. with Garden State Pkwy. For G. W. Bridge take this north. For Verrazano Bridge at this jct. take NJ 82 toward Elizabeth and Goethals Bridge.

A Castle in New Jersey

TRIP B-14. *We'll Visit:*

VON STEUBEN (ZABRISKIE) HOUSE, State Historic Site. North Hackensack (Closed Mon.)

VAN SAUN COUNTY PARK, Paramus

PATERSON MUSEUM (Closed Sun., Major Hol.)

LAMBERT CASTLE (Wed. thru Sun.)

GARRET MOUNTAIN RESERVATION

DISTANCE AND TOLLS: To Garret Mountain; via G. W. Bridge, *15 m*, plus bridge toll. Plus return. Average and slow speeds.

FOOD: Numerous restaurants on all state roads and in Malls *(see Trip B-14 (B).*

Von Steuben (Zabriskie) House, New Bridge Road, North Hackensack, N.J. 07661. *Open year around, daily 10-12, 1-5, ex. Mon. Sun. 2-5. Fees: 25¢ aged 12 & over. Guided Tours.* (201) 487-1739.

The State of New Jersey gave this attractive dwelling to Baron von Steuben in gratitude for his help in drilling and training the American army during the Revolution. He later chose not to live in the house and eventually it reverted to the State, which now owns it; it is today headquarters for the Bergen County Historical Society. Visitors will find a good variety of authentic period furnishings including handcrafts, Colonial furniture, antiques, even Indian artifacts.

Van Saun County Park, Paramus. *Open year around, daily, daylight hours. Free. Picnic and game areas.*

Primarily a County Park, this is likely to be crowded at the height of the season but at other times, especially when the early gardens bloom, it's worth a visit. Particularly noteworthy is the Washington Spring Garden—the General is said to have drunk from the waters of the spring. Children will like the farmyard and the train and pony rides.

Paterson Museum, 268 Summer St., Paterson. *Mon. to Fri. 1-5. Sat. 10-12, 1-5. Closed major holidays. Free.* (201) 742-4820.

An exceptional collection of minerals makes this small museum outstanding. Besides the fluorescent rock exhibit is a room filled with gems from around the world. For those who are not rock hounds there are Indian displays, natural history items and artifacts dug up in the immediate neighborhood. There's also a 14-foot submarine, noteworthy because it happens to be the one John Holland invented.

Lambert Castle, 5 Valley Road, Paterson, N.J. *Open year around, Wed., Thurs., Fri. 1-4:45, weekends, 11-4:45. Donations. Guided Tours.* (201) 523-9883.

Modeled after Warwick Castle in England, these great halls contain old firearms, machinery of past days, period furnishings, paintings, and items made by a neighbor named Thomas Edison.

Garret Mountain Reservation. *Open year around, daily. Free.*

A woodland park on top of a mountain (alt. 502 ft.) provides good hiking and excellent VISTAS. There are picnic areas and in season, various activities.

FOR THE DRIVER: Exit Point for all: G.W. Bridge. Follow signs to Rte. 4 west. Take this 5 *m.* to exit at Hackensack Ave. near Bloomingdale's, right. From ramp, follow signs to the Von Steuben House, bearing right.

Back to Rte. 4 west, continue briefly to exit to Forest Ave. At traffic light, keep right on County Route 13 (still Forest Ave.) and drive about 1 *m.* Signs, right, direct you to Van Saun County Park. Do not turn here but continue to second entrance to park near stables and farm. Drive thru Park.

Back on Forest Ave., turn left back to jct. with Route 4. Caution: Turn left at small sign to Rte. 4 west, at light. Continue on Rte. 4 west.

Continue into Paterson, on Broadway. Several blocks beyond railroad tracks watch, left, for sign on Summer St. to Paterson Museum, a small building this side of the Library. Parking for both Museum and Library in same lot.

Go back to Broadway, turn right, the way you came. Just after crossing the tracks again, turn right, at light, on Madison Ave. and continue to its end, at Main St. Turn right on Main, following signs to City Hall, and Hawthorne. Just ahead, go under railroad overpass, then across the tracks. Hospital is on right; opposite the entrance at the far end is Barclay St., left. Take this up the hill; cross bridge, just beyond light, toward Montclair on Valley Road. Almost at once, turn right, up mountain, to Lambert Castle.

For Garret Mountain Reservation, return to Valley Road, turn right to where first road goes right up the hill at Fenner St. This is Mountain Park Road. Take it to top of mountain. Here a road goes right, and small sign: Garret Mountain Reservation. Drive through park, bearing right. On return, bear left, to stay in park, to the place you entered.

Go back to Valley Road, turn right and proceed to jct. with US 46 east. Take this to G.W. Bridge. For Verrazano Bridge, branch right on Rte. 3 to Parkway South.

Note: After Garret Mountain, turn right on Valley Road to jct. with US 46 but take it west and follow directions in Trip B-15 to Dey Mansion.

Submarines and Waterfalls

TRIP B-14(A): *We'll Visit:*

SUBMARINE LING, Hackensack
GREAT FALLS / S.U. M. HISTORIC DISTRICT, Paterson
WESTSIDE PARK, Paterson

DISTANCE AND TOLLS: Via G. W. Bridge, 19 *m.*, bridge toll only. Fast speeds, slower in cities.

FOOD: Restaurants and snack places in Hackensack. Picnic areas at the Great Falls, also in the park.

Submarine USS Ling, Borg Park, Court & River Sts., Hackensack, N.J. 07601. Phone (201) 488-9770. *Open daily year around 10-6, weather permitting. Closed major holidays. Last tour begins at 5:15. Contribution: Adults $1.50; under 12 and Senior Citizens, 75¢. Group rates (15 or more), arrange in advance. Night visits by arrangement. Gift shop. Free parking. Birthday parties for youngsters may be held on board. Inquire.*

The Ling is a real submarine, used in WW II, later as part of a Reserve Fleet, then as a valuable training vessel that could simulate all operations such as diving and surfacing for trainees. Since 1973 she has been berthed on the Hackensack River, donated as a memorial to all submariners who lost their lives in service. Visitors have an unforgettable tour for the ship is in perfect working condition. We travel through the entire 312-foot long vessel which includes the crew's living quarters, the engine rooms, torpedo rooms, conning tower, maneuvering room and more. Improvements in later models are discussed along with some of the problems that brought about the need for them.

The ship is heated, but in winter it's wise to dress warmly for the tour. As for agility needed for entering each compartment, it helps to have some, but Senior Citizens have made it easily and enjoyed every minute.

Great Falls / S.U.M. National Historic Landmark, Paterson.

Great Falls Tours, 80 McBride Ave., Paterson, N.J. 07501. Phone (201) 345-1407. *Guided tours Mon.-Fri., 9-5; weekends and holidays by appointment. Booklet available for self-guiding tours. Tour of entire Historic District lasts about 2 hours; shorter one, 1 hour. Picnic tables, rest rooms down steps at Haines Memorial Park below the Falls.*

Nearly half the height of Niagara Falls and 100 feet wide, the Great Falls of the Passaic River can be counted on for a spectacular display almost every season and especially after heavy rains and in winter. They are only one part of the Great Falls / S.U.M. Historic District which became a National Landmark in 1976, but they are the most indispensable feature. Historically, Alexander Hamilton was one of the originators of a plan to harness the tremendous power of the falls for use in industry; this eventually brought about the Society for Establishing Useful Manufactures (S.U.M.), and Paterson became the first city in America to be planned just for industry. At one time it produced half the silk used in the nation with 120 silk mills operating. Samuel Colt turned out Colt revolvers here; Rogers locomotives were built close by. Raceways for the various mills (some still visible on the tour) were constructed in 1792 by Pierre L'Enfant who also planned Washington, D.C.

After many of the mills closed down the falls were part of a general dumping ground until 1971 when a park was constructed around them. During the Labor Day weekend there is an annual Great Falls Festival which includes a high-wire act and fireworks.

There's more to see from above the park. Walk up the street to the road this side of the river which goes across a footbridge over the falls. This leads to the other section of the park and views of the Valley of the Rocks. Much of the walk is paved; wheelchairs can manage part of it including the footbridge.

Westside Park, Totowa and Preakness Avenues. *Playing fields, picnicking.*

An almost idyllic spot just outside the busy industrial section of Paterson, this park along the Passaic River above the falls has a special attraction on view, the *Fenian Ram,* one of the first practical submarines built by John Holland in 1878 and dedicated originally to the sinking of the British Navy to gain freedom for Ireland. An earlier model, dug up from the Passaic River half a century after it sank there, is now in the Paterson Museum *(see Trip B-14).*

FOR THE DRIVER: Exit point for all, G. W. Bridge. Follow signs "To Rte 80" but take the *local* lane of Rte 80, to the right. Exit at Hudson St., just across the Hackensack River. At STOP sign, stay on E. Kennedy St., crossing Hudson St., then one more block to River St. Turn left. The submarine is a few blocks ahead. (Note: That castle-like structure is the County jail.)

Back onto I-80 westbound. Continue through Paterson to exit at Squirrelwood Road. After ramp turn right to Glover St. just ahead, then left following sign to William Paterson College. At light at McBride Ave., before bridge, turn right. McBride ends at a bridge. Turn right part way down hill, then left to entrance to Haines Memorial Park at foot of falls. Parking area here.

To drive to another section of the falls, go back up hill, right, from park, but continue ahead. Just before bridge is another entrance to footbridge over falls. Then continue across bridge and turn right to the other end of park by a stadium. If no game, can park here for falls. Otherwise, public parking lot (free) is one block above. Streets are one-way, go around any block and enter Walnut St. with parking lot.

Continue on any street going away from falls, up the hill. A block or two ahead is Totowa Ave. Turn left on this a short way to Westside Park. Then continue briefly on Totowa Avenue, following signs to I-80 to G. W. Bridge.

For A Change of Pace—A Shopping Spree at the Jersey Malls

TRIP B-14 (B): *We'll Visit:*

> RIVERSIDE SQUARE, Hackensack
> BERGEN MALL, Paramus
> GARDEN STATE PLAZA, Paramus
> PARAMUS PARK, Paramus
> THE FASHION CENTER, Paramus
> WILLOWBROOK MALL & WEST BELT MALL, Wayne

DISTANCE AND TOLLS: Via G. W. Bridge, about 10-11 *m.*, covers first five malls. Willowbrook about 20 *m.* via I-80. No tolls after bridge.

FOOD: Besides numerous restaurants on Rtes 4 & 17, every Mall has good eating facilities for snacks or meals.

This is an area of shopping malls. Its proximity to New York City as well as its location in or near four counties and nearly 3 million people, make this form of merchandising practical and, for the customer, convenient, comfortable and attractive.

A suggestion: Each mall resembles a small city and cannot adequately be covered quickly. Best to plan not to take in more than one, two at the most, in one day. Each has its own individuality; some are geared for that elegant feeling, others for kids and strollers and gaiety. All are enticingly seasonal. During the year there are almost constant exhibits of various kinds, attractions like the Mickey Mouse Club (and train), petting zoos, motor boats, trailer homes, craftwork, school exhibits, choruses from Broadway musicals, fashion and art shows, perhaps a display of hang-gliding equipment or a farmers' mart. In general, lush foliage (living) is used in profusion; plenty of benches provide rest zones for shoppers; natural light comes through cleverly structured skylights; and all but one (Garden State Plaza) are enclosed and temperature controlled.

Riverside Square, Rte 4 & Hackensack Ave., Hackensack, N.J. *Open weekdays 10-9:30; Saturday, 10-6. Closed Sun. Parking for 3,000 cars, 3 levels. Elevators.*

Opened March, 1977, this is newest and probably the most elegantly luxurious of the malls. The selection of anchor stores sets the theme; here are Bloomingdale's, Saks Fifth Avenue and Martins, with about 90 smaller shops and boutiques lining walkways of 2 floors. Softly shaded nature tints are used in the decor. Food is both plain and gourmet; a special section is set apart to permit diners to eat on benches amid the sun - or moon - lit landscaping.

Bergen Mall, Rte 4 at Forest Ave., Paramus. *Open Mon.-Sat. 10-9:30. Closed Sun. Parking for over 4,800 cars on 2 levels. Mall on 1 level, elevators available in Stern's. Separate group of shops, the Village Square, on a lower level (access only by escalators or stairs from mall), open Tues., Wed., Sat. 11-5:30; Thurs., Fri. 11-9:30. Closed Sun., Mon.*

There is almost a World's Fair atmosphere here with rows of flags and a large shimmering ball that is a gushing fountain. Anchor stores are Stern's, Ohrbach's and Newberry's with about 70 other shops handling a big variety of merchandise. Stern's floral department fronts on the center promenade and within it is a restaurant, one of several in the mall where both snacks and larger meals are available. Here, too, is the well-known Playhouse on the Mall featuring Broadway shows and musicals. *Phone for information: (201) 845-3040.*

Downstairs is a quaint little slice of time out of the past called Village Square with a number of narrow "streets" and cubby-hole shoppes selling craft materials, metals, leatherwork, objects d'art, and antiques including doll houses and toys. Also downstairs are the auditorium, post office, headquarters for several youth organizations and a bank.

Garden State Plaza, Jct. Rtes 4 & 17, Paramus. *Open Mon.-Sat. 10-9:30. Closed Sun. Parking for over 8,000 cars.*

This large mall is out of doors with attractive shopping lanes named for flowering trees embellishing each one in spring — magnolias, cherries, dogwood. Anchor stores are Bamberger's, Gimbels and J. C. Penney; 75 stores and services attract huge crowds who find the outdoors pleasant and relaxing. Snacks or meals are available. At Christmas a jumbo Santa Claus waves from his chimney to the passing world.

Paramus Park Mall, Rte 17 nr. Midland Ave., Paramus. *Open Mon.-Sat. 10-9:30. Closed Sun. Parking for over 4,000 cars.*

Between Abraham & Straus and Sears, nearly 100 stores line an enormous S-shaped walkway with a variety of merchandise appealing to those of many ages and tastes. Youngsters are beguiled by special shows put on for them, and by a carousel. In the 2-story high center section escalators and a "bubble" elevator rise amidst banks of plantings and waterfalls to a second level with a Pic-nic area. Here are 20 more shops; two of them restaurants, one featuring all kinds of crepes, the other a Farrell's Ice Cream Parlour. The others sell an unbelievable assortment of good food at good prices, to be eaten at one of the many tables on the surrounding gallery. Menus include Greek, Alpine, Pennsylvania Dutch, Contemporary Chinese, Mid-East, Italian, Mexican, fish 'n' chips, Nathan's hot dogs and deli concoctions. A health food center sells its products to those who prefer something different. (Crowded at high noon.)

The Fashion Center, Rte 17 near Ridgewood Ave., Paramus. *Open Mon.-Sat. 10-9:30. Closed Sun. Parking for over 1,800 cars on 2 levels.*

The tone of this mall is set by its anchor stores, B. Altman and Lord and Taylor. There is a less hurried atmosphere here, a feeling of relaxed shopping in a very pleasant setting of fountains and soft lights. Among the more than 20 additional stores are those of Georg Jensen, W & J Sloane, F A O Schwarz and Rogers Peet. Food is available and includes Altman's Charleston Garden.

Willowbrook Mall, Jct. I-80, Rtes 23 & 46, Wayne. *Open Mon.-Sat. 10-9:30. Closed Sun. Parking for 9,000 cars.*

This is one of the biggest, and a single visit won't cover nearly all of it. Four anchor stores here — Bamberger's, Ohrbach's, Stern's and Sears — are just part of a line-up of 153 more shops on two levels. Escalators and elevators are available. One section is a fashion gallery with hanging gardens and fountains and places to relax away from the throngs. All kinds of eating places on hand.

West Belt Mall, adjacent to Willowbrook but a separate unit, has a Korvette, J. C. Penney and an Arcadian Garden outlet.

FOR THE DRIVER: Exit Point for all: G. W. Bridge. For all but Willowbrook and West Belt Malls, follow signs to Rte 4 and proceed to the exit to Hackensack Ave., at Bloomingdale's. Turn in here for Riverside Square. *(Same exit used for Von Steuben House, Trip B-14.)* Parking, side or back.

Follow signs to Rte 4 west, take briefly to exit to Forest Ave. where signs direct to Bergen Mall, on left side of road.

To continue to Garden State Plaza, follow signs back to Rte 4 west and continue to jct. Rte 17 south. Take this across the road and exit at Mall.

For next 2 malls take Rte 17 North about 3 *m.*, to entrance on right to Paramus Park on either the Sears, Roebuck Drive, or above, the Abraham & Straus Drive.

From here, take the A. & S. Drive north of mall to a light, and follow signs here to Fashion Center. OR take Rte 17 north, briefly.

For Willowbrook and West Belt Malls, from G. W. Bridge take I-80 about 20 miles to jct. with NJ 23. Entrances are only from local roads. Best to follow signs to Rte 23 south. Just beyond cloverleaf is entrance to West Belt Mall, and also to Willowbrook.

For a different approach to the first 5 malls: Those living nearer the Tappan Zee Bridge and N.Y. Thruway can take Thruway to jct. with Garden State Pkwy. South on this (1 toll) to Exit 165 to Ridgewood & Oradell. Follow sign to Oradell at first, then stay ahead on "From Road", beside Pkwy. Continue on side road; just beyond motels is Abraham & Straus Drive, right, to Paramus Park Mall. Signs from here to Fashion Center. Then take Rte 17 south to jct. with Rte 4, and take Rte 4 east to the other malls. For Willowbrook, stay on parkway to exit to I-80 west to Paterson and exit at Rte 23 south.

Return Trip: Via G. W. Bridge, Rte 17 south to Rte 4; east to bridge. For N.Y. Thruway, follow signs to Garden State Pkwy. north. From Willowbrook, back the way you came.

Old Interior Furnishings in Perfect Condition

TRIP B-15. *We'll Visit:*

DEY MANSION, Wayne, N.J. (Tues., Wed., Fri. and weekends)

VAN RIPER-HOPPER HOUSE, Wayne, N.J. (Tues., Fri., and weekends)

DISTANCE AND TOLLS: From G.W. Bridge about 25 *m.*, bridge toll. Via Verrazano Bridge, 40 *m.*, 2 bridge tolls, Pkwy. 50¢. Plus return. Average speeds.

Dey Mansion, Preakness Valley Park, Wayne N.J. 07470. *Open year around, Tues., Wed. & Fri. 1-4, weekends 10-4. Fees. 60¢, age 16 and over. Guided Tour, about 40 minutes. Last tour 4 p.m.* (201) 696-1766.

A costumed guide escorts visitors through this attractive red brick and brownstone house. Washington was here during most of July, 1780, as it was strategically situated for his military maneuvers. The house has great appeal for anyone interested in furnishings, for the articles are original or exact duplicates, and in perfect condition.Thus Dey Mansion (pronounced *Die*) becomes a treasure house of information on restoration. Outbuildings also have been restored and we see an ancient barn, wagon shed, smoke house, forge and spring house.

Van Riper-Hopper House (Wayne Museum), Berdan Ave., Wayne, N.J. 07470. *Open year around. Fri.-Tues., 1-5. Closed 2 holidays. Other times by appointment. Donations.* (201) 694-7192.

This Dutch style house stands on land once belonging to the Lenni Lenape Indians. It was built in the 1780's, an excellent example of careful planning. It faces south, in order to take advantage of the sun's light and heat, and has no windows on the north side. Six fireplaces provided warmth and the kitchen fireplace was big enough to keep a fire burning continuously. Furnishings are from around 1860.

FOR THE DRIVER: Via G.W. Bridge, take Express road to I-80 west thru Paterson to exit to Rte NJ 62.

Via Verrazano Bridge, take Garden State Pkwy. north to Exit 159; follow signs to I-80 West (toward Paterson); go to exit to NJ 62.

All: Take second exit at NJ 62, marked "62 south to Little Falls." Almost at once follow small sign to fork right—"West on 46 to Dover." Take US 46; shortly is exit, right, to Riverview Drive to Wayne. Small sign here to Dey Mansion. After ramp follow signs to Wayne on Riverview Drive for about a mile. At intersection just before golf course, right, is Totowa Road. Turn right on this to the Dey Mansion, on left.

Back to Riverview Drive, turn right and follow signs, right, to Valley Road. Drive several miles to end at Hamburg Turnpike. Turn left and proceed for two traffic lights to Berdan Ave., right. Take this a little over a mile to far end of reservoir and the Van Riper-Hopper House.

Return Trip: Go back to Hamburg Turnpike, turn left for two lights to Valley Road, right to Riverview Drive, then follow signs, left, to G.W. Bridge. For G.W. Bridge, take US 46 east to jct. with NJ 62. Take this north toward Paterson, and connect with I-80 east to the bridge. For Verrazano Bridge, US 46 east, then follow signs to Garden State Pkwy. south, branching right on Rte. 3. Take Pkwy. to Exit 137 to NJ 28.

Wild West in New Jersey

TRIP B-16. *We'll Visit:*

LAKE HOPATCONG

HOPATCONG STATE PARK

BERTRAND ISLAND AMUSEMENT PARK (Memorial Day thru Labor Day)

WILD WEST CITY, Netcong (Late June to Labor Day; weekends from May and thru Oct.)

DISTANCE AND TOLLS: To Wild West City, via G.W. Bridge, about 50 *m.*; 85¢. Via Verrazano, about 65 *m.*; $1.50. Plus return tolls. Mainly fast speeds. Add miles driven around lake, optional.
FOOD: Restaurants, diners en route US 46.

Lake Hopatcong. Nature has provided a wonderful freshwater lake in northwest New Jersey, where it has a shoreline of more than 40 miles 900 ft. above sea level. For many years it has drawn thousands of campers and vacationists. It is available for swimming, fishing, boating, water skiing and winter ice-fishing. At the southern end of the lake is:

Hopatcong State Park. *Open year around. Beach open Memorial Day to Labor Day. Walk-in: 50¢. Parking: weekdays, Mem. Day - Labor Day, $3. Weekends, Hol., $4. Weekends, May & Sept., $2.Plus 50¢ each person 12 yrs. & older. Small locker fee. N. J. bus groups, $10., out of state, $25. Collected weekends in May and Oct., daily in season. Rest of year no charge. Picnics; snacks in season.*

This relatively small area provides a certain amount of supervision and some facilities in an exceptionally scenic spot.

Bertrand Island Amusement Park. *Open Memorial Day thru Labor Day, Noon-11. Sat. to midnight. Sun. to 11. Free entry, small parking fee, charge for rides. Group rates. Picnics, snacks.* (201) 398-0136.

There are rides and games for all ages and tastes in this park on Lake Hopatcong's shores. Besides boardwalk activities there is boating and of course, swimming. Rides for both adults and kiddies. Not to mention a lively midway.

Wild West City. Route 206, Netcong, N.J. 07857. *Open daily from late June thru Labor Day, 11-6. Adults $3. 2-12 yrs. $2.50, combination tickets, group rates. Food: Snacks, picnic area.* (201) 347-8900.

They say you can spend the day here in this three-dimensional reproduction of your favorite television westerns. There are rides—horseback, pony and hay; old-time railroad forays into Indian territory; gunslingers on the stagecoach. Finally, square dancing rounds out the day.

FOR THE DRIVER: From both G.W. and Verrazano Bridges follow directions for Trip B-15 onto I-80 west.

There are 3 exits from Rte. I-80 to Lake Hopatcong. Take Exit D to ·Lake Hopatcong and Ledgewood. Just after ramp, the road forks; take left road to West Shore, bearing left. Road ends at Lake Hopatcong, at Landing. Follow small sign left to West Shore, then signs to State Park, on right.

Turn left from Park to jct. at Landing. Continue on road bearing left, now toward East Shore. Just ahead, left, is entrance to Bertrand Island Park. You may drive around the lake, bearing left to follow shoreline.

Return to jct. at Landing, where small sign directs you back to Rte. 46. If going on to Wild West City, take US 46 west to rotary and jct. with US 206. Go north on 206 toward Newton, passing turn-off to Waterloo (Trip B-17). Just beyond, on right, is the road to Wild West City.

If skipping Wild West City, from Lake Hopatcong return to I-80 and take it east.

Return Trip: Back on US 206 to I-80 east, to G.W. Bridge. For Verrazano Bridge, take Garden State Pkwy. south to NJ 28. If desired, you can go back on US 206 to Rte. 46 but take this west and proceed to Hackettstown and the Fish Hatchery (Trip B-18).

New Jersey, too, Has a Waterloo, in a Rustic Setting

TRIP B-17. *We'll Visit:*
WATERLOO VILLAGE, Stanhope, N.J. (April–Dec. weekends.
July & Aug., Tues.-Sun.)
STEPHENS-SAXTON FALLS STATE PARK, Hackettstown.

DISTANCE AND TOLLS: From G.W. Bridge, about 55 *m.*, 85¢. Via Verrazano
Bridge, about 70 *m.*, $1.50. Plus return. Mainly fast speeds.
FOOD: Eating places all along US 46.

Waterloo Village Restoration, Stanhope, N.J. 07874. Phone (201)
347-0900. *Open mid-Apr. thru Dec., daily exc. Mon., 10-6. May close
holidays, also part of Dec. Adm. $3.50. Sr. Cit. $2.50. Children $1.50.
group rates. Luncheons in Wellington House for 25 or more, by
reservation. Snacks at outdoor grill; picnic area. House tours led by
costumed guides. Handicapped: one step up to rest rooms, some
climbing in houses.*

They named the village after an iron foundry which, in turn, was
named for Napoleon's battle of 1815. It is now a showplace of
authentic 18th-century houses along the old Morris Canal. These are
original buildings, not reproductions, and they are located today
exactly where they were constructed back in the 1700's and 1800's.
Their appeal is greatest to those who prefer the genuine to the more
flamboyant.

We can visit a dozen houses, an inn resembling Mount Vernon, a
canal house, church, stagecoach inn, general store and blacksmith shop.
Touring the homes we see about 80 rooms with antique furnishings.
Throughout the summer there are music festivals on Saturday evenings.

Stephens-Saxton Falls State Park, Hackettstown, N.J. *Open year
around, daily. Fee for use of picnic tables in the Stephens section. No
parking fees.*

This attractive park has two areas—Saxton Falls, which utilizes part
of the Morris Canal, and the Stephens section about a mile below.

At Saxton Falls, besides a spectacular waterfall in the Musconetcong
River, there is not only great fishing, but also swimming where a guard
lock of the old canal has been filled, and is under lifeguard protection.
Snacks in season.

Stephens State Park is used mainly for camping, picnicking and fishing. We'll notice an air of relaxed contentment here as the fishermen spread out along nearly a mile of the Musconetcong.

FOR THE DRIVER: From both G.W. Bridge and Verrazano Bridge, follow directions in Trip B-15 to where all are westbound on Rte. I-80. Proceed to jct. with US 206, and drive north on 206. Watch for small sign to left to Waterloo Village.

From village, turn left and continue, shortly passing Saxton Falls State Park. About a mile farther is Stephens State Park, both sections of the same park.

Return Trip: Continue in the same direction to jct. with US 46 in Hacketts-town. Turn left (east) to I-80. Take this east to G.W. Bridge, or to Garden State Pkwy. south to Exit 137 to NJ 28, for Verrazano Bridge.

About Fish, Pheasants, and Jenny Jump

TRIP B-18. *We'll Visit:*

STATE FISH HATCHERY, Hackettstown, N.J.

STATE PHEASANT FARM, Rockport

LAND OF MAKE BELIEVE, Hope, N.J. (June to Christmas, Sun. aft. July, Aug. daily.)

JENNY JUMP STATE FOREST

DISTANCE AND TOLLS: From G.W. Bridge, about 75 *m.*, 85¢; via Verrazano Bridge, about 90 *m.*, $1.50. Plus return. Mainly fast speeds; slower in town.
FOOD: In Hackettstown, Clarendon Hotel restaurant. En route, restaurants and diners on US 46.

State Fish Hatchery, Hackettstown, N.J. 07840. *Open year around, daily: 8-4:30. Free. Tour guides available. Rest rooms.*

This could just be the hit of today's trip. Every fisherman in the family will want to pay a visit here, but even the amateur will be impressed. Sportsmen (and cooks) stand drooling at the sight of thousands of bass, trout, blue gill, and perch that soon will stock the New Jersey waters. Indoors, the first steps in hatching may be observed. This might be a perfect place to start a father-and-son trip, for just up the road in Stephens and Saxton Falls State Park are two splendid fishing areas.

State Pheasant Farm, Rockport, N.J. *Open year around daily; week-days, 8-4:30, weekends and holidays, 8-6. Free.*

The drive alone is worth this trip through the Jersey hills. Not a very large spread, the Farm contains pheasants, turkeys, geese, even deer. Sportsmen are always interested. So are the kids.

Land of Make Believe, Hope, N.J. 07844. *Open June to Christmas, Sun. from noon to 5. July & Aug., daily, 10:30 to 6:00. Mod. charges for adm. and rides. Food: Picnics, snacks. Handicapped may be able to visit some of the exhibits.* (201) 459-4220.

Aimed at children up to about 9, this is a delightful mixture of old and new. It's located on the slope of Jenny Jump Mountain and contains a restored house where the legendary Jenny may have lived. Those who prefer Santa can climb up to see him. An alfalfa ride through the meadows, and a fire engine ride are always a thrill. Good VISTA from picnic area. Snacks for sale, also souvenirs, toys and Christmas decorations.

Jenny Jump State Forest. *Open year around, daily. Fees: 50¢ for use of picnic table. Get written permission from park officer. Food: Picnics; cooking with wood or charcoal only. Campsites and shelters for rent, April thru October. Handicapped can drive to VISTA points.*

The settler looked up in horror to where his daughter was picking berries above the clearing, saw the raised tomahawks of Indians coming up behind her and cried out, "Jump! Jenny, jump!" Legend has it that Jenny did.

A small but exceedingly scenic park commemorates this tale, and we're invited to come and explore, either by car or on foot. Here lived the Minsi (Wolf) Tribe of the Lenape Indians. Campsites now rest on ground where many artifacts have been found. The main attraction is the superb view. Scenic drives are marked. For the Land of Make Believe crowd, if finishing the day here, there's a playground at the entrance. For the city tap water crowd, a fresh water spring emerges at the roadside.

FOR THE DRIVER: From both G.W. Bridge and Verrazano Bridge, follow directions in Trip B-15 to where all are westbound on I-80. Take I-80 west to exit to US 46 to Hackettstown. In town, watch for sign on Grand Ave., at light, to turn left to Rockport. At this jct., left, is the Clarendon Hotel and restaurant. Follow signs to State Fish Hatchery.

Return to Grand Ave., but turn left. About 3 *m.* ahead is the State Pheasant Farm in Rockport.

Go back to Hackettstown and US 46. Turn left (west) and proceed several miles to the road, right, marked Mountain Lake and Hope. Follow signs to Land of Make Believe.

Continue as far as road goes, then turn right following signs to Jenny Jump State Forest. Road branches, going up mountain; last portion is unpaved, but not difficult to drive.

Return Trip: Take I-80 from Hope, east to G.W. Bridge or to Garden State Pkwy. south to Exit 137 to NJ 28, for Verrazano Bridge.

Much to Learn about Minerals on This Tour

TRIP B-19. *We'll Visit:*

MORRIS COUNTY CENTRAL RAILROAD
(Daily in Summer, weekends in Spring)

FAIRY TALE FOREST, Oak Ridge, N.J. (Daily in summer; weekends, spring and fall)

FRANKLIN MINERAL MUSEUM, Franklin, N.J. (Early April to mid-Dec., closed Mon.)

FRANKLIN MINERAL DUMP

GINGERBREAD CASTLE, Hamburg, N.J. (Daily, April thru Oct. Rest of year, weekends.)

VERNON VALLEY SKI AREA (all year)

DISTANCE AND TOLLS: From G.W. Bridge, 50 *m.*, 85¢. From Verrazano, 65 *m.*, $1.50. Plus return. Mainly average speeds.

FOOD: O On Rte. 23, many dining places: Jorgensen's Inn, closed Mon. and Tues. In Hamburg, Gov. Haines, closed Mon. and last week in March, 1st in April. Near Fairy Tale Forest, restaurant. At Gingerbread Castle, restaurant. Plus diners along Rtes. 46 and 23.

Morris County Central Railroad, Rte 23 & Green Pond Rd., Newfoundland, N.J. 07435. P. O. Box 179. *Train runs: Weekends from early April, at 1, 2:30 & 4 p.m. July & Aug., daily 1, & 2:30. Fares (subject to change) Adults, $2.50, under 12, $1.25. Senior Citizens 10% discount. Babes in arms, free. Group rates. Special trips: Fall foliage trip in Oct. (check date); Santa Claus trips, last 2 weekends in Nov. In Feb., mid-winter excursion. Other trips for schools, reservations needed. Phone (201) 267-8608 or 697-8446, day or evening. Picnic facilities on grounds, also a souvenir shop for buffs.*

Formerly at Whippany, this authentic steam locomotive and its coaches provide a magnificient outing for all and an eye-opener for the TV-oriented kids. At the station are additional cars and cabooses to explore and photograph. The ride is along the scenic banks of Pequannock River. This is a good chance to tape record the once familiar sounds, the chugging and whistling, the clicking over trestles, the hissing stops.

Fairy Tale Forest, Oak Ridge, N.J. 07438. *Open daily mid-June-Labor Day. Weekends only from Easter Sun., and to end of Oct. Adm. Adults $2.50. Under 12, $1.25. Food: Snacks, picnics. Restaurant nearby.*

Children can hardly wait to enter this enchanted land filled with scenes from their favorite stories. They go from castle to Swiss Village, from a street model of Jerusalem to the home of Red Riding Hood's grandmother, renewing acquaintances along the way with Cinderella, Snow White and the dwarfs. A train ride is popular.

Franklin Mineral Museum, 6 B Evans St., Franklin, N.J. 07416. *Open April to Dec., daily exc. Mon. 9-4:30; Sun., 12:30-4:30. Adm. fee. Same fee for Buckwheat Dump. Tours last 1 hr. Last one starts an hour before closing time. Food: Bring picnics. Handicapped will find ramp to show rooms. Rest rooms. Groups should arrange in advance.* (201) 827-3481.

Franklin is noted for its minerals; this museum contains over 3,000 specimens. We will descend into a replica of the original Franklin Mine which was 1,250 feet deep (18 levels) when it was closed. Some tracks and part of a typical train are shown. Next we climb upstairs (good railings) to the top of the mine to learn how mines are drilled and what equipment is needed. Then to the fluorescent room to see a brilliant display of superb specimens. Beginners: This trip is specially geared for you. You find out how to start this hobby, and buy prospecting equipment here (hammers, chisels) moderately priced. The Gift Shop carries two good lines of hobby materials, Ultraviolet Science and Hobby Kits and fluorescent lamps.

Buckwheat Dump, near the Museum. Amateurs can climb piles of rocks that have been dumped here, then look under a lamp for colors in the specimens they found. Ask at museum about prospecting, curator will inform the Dump. Among others, we may discover Calcite; under the fluorescent lamp this glows pink, and Willemite, in green, yellow and other shades. Also open 1st & 3rd Sat. eve. each month, 8:30-10:30 p.m. Adm. fee.

Trotter Dump. Across the street from the Museum, this one is privately owned. Better minerals may be found here, but it's primarily for experts who know what they're looking for.

Gingerbread Castle, Hamburg, N.J. 07419. *Open year around. From Apr. thru Oct. daily from 10 a.m. Rest of year, weekends only. Open thru June until 4:30; in the summer, until 5:30; in Sept. and Oct. until 4. Fees: $1. adults, 3-11 yrs. 75¢. Also fees for train rides. Food: Picnics, snacks, restaurant. Handicapped: There's a good deal of climbing through the castle, including a spiral staircase 45 steps high. Special rates for schools and organizations. Tours last about 20 minutes, conducted by Hansel or Gretel, trained school children in period costumes.* (201) 827-9540.

While the kiddies are relishing the Witch's Trophy Room, the black cauldron in the evil kitchen, the wise old owl and the spitting cat, their elders will be casting second glances at a beautifully designed background for the familiar folk tales. For this is no mere roadside park; it was designed by Joseph Urban, and it cost $250,000. It began as a boyhood dream of F.H. Bennett, who eventually was able financially to make it come true. Since opened in 1930 it has become a tourist objective. Our youthful guide points out every exhibit. While we don't usually mention specific foods, warm, home-made gingerbread with whipped cream can be a big part of a pleasant memory.

VERNON VALLEY SKI AREA, Rte 94. (201) 827-2000. *Year 'round activities from snow skiing to frisbee golf to water slides to grass skiing. Fees for each.*

FOR THE DRIVER: From both G.W. and Verrazano Bridges follow directions in Trip B-15 onto I-80 West.

Continue to where NJ 23 branches right (north) toward Butler, and take this. You pass several rotaries: focus on signs 23 North toward Sussex.

At junction with Rte 513 at Green Pond Rd., exit and cross over to south side. Morris County Central R.R. is about 100 yards in.

Then back to Rte 23 west; take to exit to Oak Ridge and Fairy Tale Forest.

Back to NJ 23 toward Sussex (must cross road at light, turn left). Pass Jorgensen's Inn. Shortly is a small shopping center, right, and sign to turn left to Franklin. Follow sign, then pick up signs, right, to Franklin Mineral Museum. Across the street from this is the Trotter Dump, with entrance on Main St. at rear of bank. Buckwheat Dump, connected with the museum, is reached from the road below.

Return to NJ 23, turn left, continue into Hamburg. Just beyond railroad overpass turn sharp left and follow signs to Gingerbread Castle. At this jct. is the Governor Haines Restaurant. Continue on Rte 23 briefly to jct. with NJ 94. Turn to right, to Ski Area.

Return trip: Back to Rte 23 then left to jct. with I-80, and return.

A Long Drive to the Mountains to Watch Fine Craftsmen At Work

TRIP B-19 (A): *We'll Visit:*

PETERS VALLEY CRAFT VILLAGE

DISTANCE AND TOLLS: About 70 m., from G. W. Bridge. Only bridge tolls. Fast speeds.

Peters Valley Craft Village, Layton, N.J. 07851. Phone (201) 948-5200. *Open: Studios, Apr. thru Dec. Tues. thru Sun. 10-4. Craftsmen discuss their work and the school, 1-4 p.m. Store and gallery open same dates. Closed major holidays. Crafts Fair in late July, 1 weekend: craft and food sales, demonstrations, performing musicians.*

This is a trip primarily for people interested in observing or possibly joining craftsmen in many media. They are professionals who have been selected by a jury to live in a craft village in exchange for instructing students and having their studios open to the public.

Visitors may tour the village and observe such activities as spinning, weaving, dyeing, woodworking, blacksmithing, and the creation of ceramics and jewelry by different methods. Products are sold by consignment in the shop.

Programs are available allowing those especially interested to work with a professional in his line for a 10-13 week period. Also provided are weekend workshops which accept both professionals and the general public. A summer session lasting 1 to 3 weeks aids beginners with basic information on the crafts. Some educational institutions offer college credits to students. Write or visit the Village for details.

FOR THE DRIVER: Exit point for all: G. W. Bridge & I-80. Take I-80 west about 38 *m.* to jct. with NJ 15. North (right) on this to jct. with US 206, and continue on 206 passing Stokes State Forest. Just ahead is County 521 to Layton. *(Caution:* Rte 521 comes in below from left and merges with US 206. Wait for second jct. when it goes to Layton.) On County 521 go about a mile, *not* reaching Layton, and turn left on County 615 for about 2 *m.* to Peters Valley.

Note: The village is located in a good focal point from which to branch out on other trips. Stokes State Forest was on Rte. 206. *(Trip B-20.)* Or by continuing into Layton on County 521, it's a short distance to the Delaware River and the bridge to Dingmans Ferry, leading into Pennsylvania's Poconos. Take US 209 south from this passing several of the renowned waterfalls *(see Trip B-23 Extension).*

A Family's Private Zoo and Other Attractions

TRIP B-20. *We'll Visit:*
    SPACE ZOOLOGICAL FARM, Beemerville, N.J. (May thru Oct.)
    STOKES STATE FOREST and TILLMAN RAVINE
    HIGH POINT STATE PARK

DISTANCE AND TOLLS: To High Point, via Stokes Forest: From G.W. Bridge, about 100 *m.,* plus return trip of about 65 *m.* From Verrazano, about 15 *m.* more each way. Mainly average speeds. Via G.W. Bridge, total 85¢, via Verrazano, $1.50. Plus return.

FOOD: See Trip B-19 for restaurants en route. Also, dining at Inn at High Point Park, and snacks at Space Zoo.

Space Zoological Farm, Beemerville, N.J. P.O. Sussex, N.J. 07461. *Open May thru Oct., daylight hours. Adults $3. 3-12 yrs. $1. No charge to Indian Museum, mink ranch and dairy farm. Food: Snacks, picnic* *area. Handicapped: Somewhat hilly, paths unpaved, but many can get around fairly well. Dairy Farm: Milking time 5 a.m., again at 3:30 p.m. daily.* (201) 875-5800.

These are not Zoo animals from Outer Space, but a collection of native live North American wild animals gathered by the Space family. They have been studying these creatures for over 40 years and today have about 500, of 100 different species, including birds and reptiles. Some of them have been seen in movies and on television. An added attraction is an operating fur farm with a large mink herd. Visitors may look in on the pens. Furs from the farm are sold in a fur shop on the premises. Nearby is a dairy farm where registered Holstein cattle may be seen. A gift shop and an Indian Museum are in the main building with the snack bar.

Stokes State Forest: *Free, except for Stony Lake Section. Parking: weekdays, Mem. Day - Labor Day, $2. Weekends, $3. No charge May & Sept. In some sections, small charge for picnic table, collected in season. Food: Picnics; cooking by permit; no picnics in Tillman Ravine. Handicapped can drive to many scenic areas.*

There are more than 75 miles of hiking trails in this forest, including a number with excellent VISTAS. Don't miss Tillman Ravine where you climb through a scenic gorge. Nearby is a small bathing area (at your own risk) and places for camping. Trout fishing in Flatbrook, subject to state laws. Get a map of the forest from the office on Rte. 15 as you enter.

On the way to High Point State Park, follow signs to Sunrise Mountain, a well-known Lookout, over 1,600 feet high.

High Point State Park. *Open daily, year around. Parking: $3, weekdays Memorial Day - Labor Day. Weekends & Holidays, $4. Weekends in May & Sept. $2. Monument, 25¢. Plus 50¢ each person 12 and over. Collected daily, from Memorial Day thru Labor Day; weekends in May and thru Oct. Small fees for picnic tables, bathing, and to enter monument. Food: Picnics, cooking with permit, snacks. Dining room service at the Inn, in season. Handicapped: Some walking, some climbing, but roads are paved. Fine vistas from parking area.*

The highest point in New Jersey (alt. 1,803 feet), this of course boasts wonderful views. From the top of the Monument, a memorial to the State's heroes of all wars, we can see the Delaware Water Gap and the Poconos to the south, the juncture of three states—New York, New Jersey and Pennsylvania—to the west, and northward, the Catskills. Beautiful in laurel time, it's equally magnificent in the fall. Naturalists come to observe the unusual variety in plant life; hikers enjoy good trails, some of them part of the Appalachian Trail. Spring-fed Lake

Marcia provides a refreshing dip. In winter when weather conditions are right the park is open for winter sports, including hiking on skiis or snowshoes.

FOR THE DRIVER: From both G.W. and Verrazano Bridges, follow directions in Trip B-19 to where all are northbound on NJ 23. Proceed through Hamburg. There are two routes to the left to the Space Farms. The first, a cut-off, is via County 565. Follow signs to the Farms, shortly making a right angle turn and then continuing straight ahead after the route becomes 565 Spur. This goes to County 519 where you turn left to the Farms, as directed (about 5 *m.* from Rte. 23.)

A slightly longer way is to stay on Rte. 23 to County 519, then turn left and go directly to the Space Zoological Farms.

Continue on Rte. 519 the direction you were going for several miles to jct. with US 206. Turn right and proceed on 206 to Stokes State Forest. Take road marked to Park Office, right, and get map; follow highway signs to various sections including Tillman Ravine and Lake Ocquittunk. Just before you reached Park Office road, signs directed, right, to Sunrise Mountain and the north shore of Culver Lake. Start on this road to our next objective, High Point Park. Almost at once the main road bears right while a smaller park road forks left. In season there's a sign here to Sunrise Mountain Road. When sign is not up, look for Caution sign: Road hazardous, travel at own risk. By taking this road you drive along the crest of the mountain, with VISTA points en route. At a fork in the road you can drive, right, up to Sunrise Mountain VISTA point. Then return to fork. Soon watch at side of road for signs to High Point Park, Monument and Rte. 23. Follow signs for several miles. At Rte. 23 turn right, to entrance, left, to High Point State Park.

When weather is unfavorable for mountain road, start out for Sunrise Mountain and north shore of Culver Lake, but bear right on main road. This goes to jct. with County 519. Turn left toward Beemerville, passing the zoo, to Rte. 23. Turn left on 23 to High Point State Park, right.

Trip B-19(A) to Peters Valley Craft Village passes Stokes State Forest before turning off toward Layton.

Return Trip: From park, turn left on NJ 23 through Hamburg; continue to jct. with I-80 east. For G.W. Bridge, stay on I-80. For Verrazano Bridge, take Rte. 46, to Rte. 3 following signs to Garden State Parkway south, and take this to Exit 137 to NJ 28.

First Long Trip to the Poconos

TRIP B-21 EXTENSION. We are going to take four different routes through this famous region. They will permit us to see a good variety of attractions, for each has a good assortment of scenic drives, VISTA points, shops, craft demonstrations and places for sports. As they are primarily for the enjoyment of the drive rather than for any single attraction, they'll be written out FOR THE DRIVER.

We'll Visit:

POINT OF GAP, Delaware Water Gap
POCONO WILD ANIMAL FARM, Stroudsburg (May into Oct.)
QUIET VALLEY LIVING FARM MUSEUM, Stroudsburg (late
    June thru Labor Day)
SCIOTA CRAFT SHOP
HOUSE OF BASKETS, Gilbert
HICKORY RUN STATE PARK AND BOULDER FIELD
BIG POCONO STATE PARK

DISTANCE AND TOLLS: To the Gap from G.W. Bridge, 85 *m.*, $1.10. Via Verrazano Bridge, 100 *m.*, $1.75. Add about 100 *m.* if taking entire trip, plus return trip from Gap. Mostly fast, some average speeds.
FOR THE DRIVER: Exit Points: G.W. Bridge, Verrazano Bridge, Easton, Pa. From both G.W. and Verrazano Bridges, follow directions in Trip B-15 on to I-80 westbound. Take this to next exit after Hope, at jct. with US 46, then take bridge across the Delaware River to Portland, Pa. Go north on US 611.
    From lower areas of New Jersey: Take US 22 or I-78 west to Easton, Pa. (toll bridge.) Immediately after bridge turn right, and take US 611 north.
    All: Drive north on US 611, stopping for VISTAS at Lookout Points, including POINT OF GAP. This has diagrams showing how the Gap was created.
    Continue north on Rte. 611 a few miles and follow signs to:

Pocono Wild Animal Farm. *Open May into Oct., 9-5:30. Adults $2.50. Sr. Cit. $2.25. 2-12 $1.25. Picnics, snacks.* (717) 421-7871.

An attractive, woodsy background for a natural history tour with infinite photographic possibilities.

    Continue on US 611 into Stroudsburg and follow signs to Business Rte. 209. (Not the regular Rte. 209.) Where 209 and Bus. 209 branch, follow Bus. 209 south. A few miles beyond follow sign, left, to:

Quiet Valley Living Farm Museum. *Open late June thru Labor Day, 9:30-5:30. Sun. 1-5:30. Adm. fee. Tour lasts about an hour.*

Costumed guides show us a Pennsylvania Dutch Farm out of the past, demonstrating how they cared for their needs using materials on hand. We watch them at farming, spinning, weaving, baking, tending the animals.

    Back on Bus. 209 south (left).
    About a mile or two on down Bus. 209 is the SCIOTA CRAFT SHOP, right, with 2 floors of handcrafted items, enamel, copper, also many imports.
    A few miles below we find the HOUSE OF BASKETS in Gilbert, open all year, where we have a purchaser's choice of over 1,000 styles and sizes.
    A short distance farther, watch for jct. with Pa. 534 west (right), to Jonas and Hickory Run Park. Take this about 18 *m.* to:

Hickory Run State Park. A Trout Nursery is near entrance. Drive to Main Park Entrance and turn in, right. Day Use area on right, for parking and swimming. Follow signs to left to:

Boulder Field. Here we find a lake, 2,000 ft. by 500 ft., with shores scenically contoured and trees coming down to the shoreline—but no water. Instead, boulders: pinkish, rounded and piled like a heap of giant jelly beans. One of the more startling views is of energetic young people climbing the lake, almost out of sight as they near the opposite "shore". Plan to take home some pictures so people will believe your story.

Return to the Day Use area, then back to highway. At exit turn right, on Pa 534 west, and proceed to jct. with Pa 940. Drive east on this following signs to I-80 east toward Stroudsburg. Take this to Exit 45 at Tannersville; at foot of ramp turn right briefly, then left, following signs to Camelback Ski and Big Pocono State Park.

This is part of the old Sullivan Trail, where in 1778, Gen. John Sullivan made his famous march from Easton to quell an uprising of hostile Iroquois Indians. The Trail continues to Pocono Pines, but we leave it shortly to go to the most spectacular viewpoint in the region. Follow signs, left, to:

Big Pocono State Park. *Picnics, snacks, rest rooms, gift shop.* Turn off at sign to Scenic Drive which goes past picnic areas and around the entire mountain. Back at the main road, turn left and drive on up to the top, to the gift shop and more VISTA points. This is accessible all year because of roads cleared for skiers.

Return Trip: Go back to Tannersville and take I-80 east toward New York. For New York: Instead of returning on Rte. 611 on the Pa. side, cross bridge with I-80 and follow that back.

For Easton, take Exit 53 from I-80, and go south on US 611.

NOTE: For those with more time: At Tannersville, instead of taking Rte. I-80, turn left briefly to jct. with US 611; take it to left to Scotrun, and the start of Trip B-22 Extension.

Second Long Trip to the Poconos

TRIP B-22 EXTENSION. *We'll Visit:*
  POCONO KNOB
  MEMORYTOWN, U.S.A., Mt. Pocono
  PENNSYLVANIA DUTCH FARM (Apr. thru Nov. daily, then weekend
  SCHNEIDER'S GEM CRAFTS

DREISBACH'S ART GALLERY, Mountainhome (July-mid-Oct.)

BUCK HILL FALLS (Waterfall: Early April to mid-Nov.)

HOLLEY ROSS POTTERY SHOP, La Anna (May to about Dec. Dec. 1)

LAKE WALLENPAUPACK: WHITE BEAUTY VIEW RESORT & MARINA

SCENIC CRUISER (Memorial Day thru Labor Day)

PADDLE WHEEL BOAT RIDES (Summer)

PENNSYLVANIA POWER & LIGHT COMPANY TOUR, Lake Wallenpaupack (Daily in season)

DISTANCE AND TOLLS: To the Gap from G.W. Bridge, 85 *m.* $1.10. From Verrazano, 100 *m.*, $1.75. Plus return. To drive to all places listed, add about 100 *m.* Trip back via Milford bridge: To G.W. Bridge, add 75 *m.*, to Verrazano, 90 *m.* Mostly fast or average speeds.

FOOD: Near Tannersville, Rhineland Inn, Old Heidelberg. Near Memorytown, Norway House. In Memorytown, restaurant; snack patio in season. White Beauty View Resort, restaurant. In Milford, Fauchere's Inn, closed Jan. to April. Tom Quick Inn, closed Sun.

FOR THE DRIVER: Exit Points: G.W. Bridge, Verrazano Bridge, Easton, Pa. All: Start the same way you did for Trip B-21 Extension as far as the bridge at Portland just below the Gap.

Via New York area: Stay on I-80 without crossing the bridge to Portland. You pass more VISTA points, and receive Pocono information. Continue on I-80, crossing bridge to Pennsylvania (toll).

Via Easton, continue north on US 611 as before, to the Gap. Branch right at sign to I-80 and take this west toward Stroudsburg.

All: Proceed west on I-80 to the exit beyond Tannersville, following signs to Scotrun. Take US 611 north, from ramp, passing several eating places including Rhineland Inn and Old Heidelberg. Shortly come signs to Memorytown. However, before visiting it we're adding a brief side trip for a VISTA. Continue just beyond the railroad overpass to small road, right, Knob Road. Signs here to Mt. Pocono Motel. Take this road to the end, at Pocono Knob. Snacks available here. The road encircles the Knob then returns to US 611. Turn left on Rte. 611 and this time take road, left, to:

Memorytown, U.S.A. *Open year around, 10-5.*

A series of shops originally a horse barn, cow barn, corn crib, carriage shed, are today the Mountain Greenery, Hex Shop, Phoebe's Little Wax Works, Country Store, St. Nick's Nook. There's a restaurant by the lake, a Backyard Snack Patio under an old apple tree, even a motel. Paddle boats on the lake, in season, and a covered Kissing Bridge for all seasons.

Pennsylvania Dutch Farm, adjoins Memorytown. *Open 10-5. Daily, June-Oct. Cl. Mon. in April. May & Oct. Closed Dec.-March. Adm. $1.75. 2-12 yrs. $1.* (717) 839-7680.

We'll learn of the Amish and their customs from people who know. Sitting on benches similar to those used by this sect we watch excellent slides taken in the Lancaster area. The Tour includes rooms set up authentically, the barns with their buggies, sleighs and machinery, and perhaps in closing, a wagon ride around the Farm.

Continue in the direction you had been going; almost at once you reach Pa. 940. At this jct. is Norway House restaurant. Turn right on 940. Watch for signs to Cresco and Mountainhome and turn left to jct. shortly with Pa. 191. Left again on 191 to jct. where it goes left and Pa. 390 goes ahead toward Skytop. We're going to turn left on 191 to La Anna, but first you may want to stop at a small shop specializing in antiques, semi-precious stones and mineral specimens, where jewelry is made on the premises. For this, continue on Pa. 390 north briefly to small shop on your left, SCHNEIDER'S GEM CRAFTS. Just beyond is Broadway in the Poconos — the POCONO PLAYHOUSE.

Return to jct. with 191 and turn right, following signs to La Anna. Almost at once, left, is DREISBACH'S ART GALLERY. *Open July–mid.-Oct., daily & Sun.* Here are paintings of the Poconos and the Pennsylvania Dutch regions; art classes also scheduled.

Continue on Rte. 191 to a road to the right to Buck Hill Falls. Take this briefly to entrance to the Inn, and follow signs, left, marked Falls. Soon they direct you to the right; at this point, the road branches. Take the one passing the tennis courts, left, and continue to entrance to BUCK HILL FALLS (Waterfall). *Open early April until about mid-Nov., depending on weather, daily, till 5 p.m.* Moderate Fees.One of the famed Pocono Waterfalls, this would be a place to spend a good part of the day if time permitted. Scenic trails wind through woods and ravines to the 200-foot waterfalls surrounded by banks of laurel and rhododendron as well as birch groves and hemlock stands.

Back to Rte. 191 north (turn right); continue a few miles to the village of La Anna, and watch for signs, right, for:

Holley Ross Pottery Shop. *Open May till about Dec. 1, daily. Demonstrations usually weekdays at 11 a.m. and 3:30 p.m. Factory store hours 9:30-5:30. Picnics in adjoining park.*

Even if you miss the demonstrations you'll probably want to browse through the room filled with pottery and china made on the premises—unusual gift ideas, over-proof ware, plus seconds. This is a popular attraction, not only for the pottery but the surrounding park as well. Highlight is the Swinging Bridge across a small river. Picnic tables here, a lake nearby, and good trails for hiking.

Continue on Pa. 191 to your right.

Continuing, we're soon passing the NEWFOUNDLAND ARTS CENTER, a cultural year-round center featuring theatre-in-the-round, Broadway shows, concerts, fashion displays, dance festivals. Shortly take Rt. 507. Bear right.

A few miles beyond we begin to see glimpses of LAKE WALLENPAUPACK; soon we pass the WHITE BEAUTY VIEW RESORT and MARINA, where the public may rent boats, scuba diving gear, canoes, rowboats. The SCENIC

CRUISER is on hand daily in season, providing a trip lasting nearly an hour. Also available, SPEEDBOAT RIDES. Moderate fees. There are a restaurant and gift shop, a small public beach and places for snacks and picnics overlooking the lake.

Continue along the lake to the end, where US 6 comes up from Milford. Follow signs, left, to Hawley. Almost at once is the Wallenpaupack Motor Lodge from which we can take a PADDLEWHEEL BOAT CRUISE. *Leaves every hour, 12-5. Moderate Fees.*

Near this, off US 6, are signs, left, to the PENNSYLVANIA POWER & LIGHT CO. Go to Supt.'s office for an interesting tour. Daily in season 9:30 a.m. - 4:30 p.m. Free. On this Guided Tour we get background information about Lake Wallenpaupack straight from the company that created it several decades ago. We'll visit the hydroelectric facilities, the dam and power plant, after which we proceed in our own cars to the generating station.

Return Trip: Go back on US 6 and continue toward Milford,   At jct. of Rtes. 6 and 209, we go ahead on US 206 and 209 toward toll bridge. First, for Fauchere's Inn and Tom Quick Inn, turn left on US 6 briefly, then back to jct.

Follow US 206 across toll bridge into New Jersey. Pass Stokes State Forest (B-20). Continue to jct. with NJ 15; take this, branching left toward Sparta and proceed to jct. with I-80 east; this connects with G.W. Bridge. For Verrazano Bridge, take Garden State Pkwy. south to Exit 137 (NJ 28) to Verrazano and Goethals Bridges.

For Easton: Start down US 6 toward Milford but a mile or two ahead take Pa. 402, right, toward Blooming Grove. Continue to jct. with US 209 just above the Gap. Go right on Rte. 209 to jct. with I-80. Near this jct. is a Holiday Inn. Take I-80 east to Exit 53 to US 611, and take this south.

Four Famous Waterfalls on One Tour

TRIP B-23 EXTENSION. *We'll Visit:*

MOON VALLEY PARK, Milford, Pa. (Weekends in May thru Oct. Daily, mid-June thru Labor Day.)

RAYMONDSKILL FALLS, Milford (Mid-May thru Oct.)

DINGMANS FALLS & SILVER THREAD FALLS, Dingmans Ferry, Pa. (mid-April thru Oct.)

BRISCO MT. WOODCRAFTERS, INC., Dingmans Ferry

BUSHKILL FALLS, Bushkill, Pa. (April to Nov.)

WINONA FIVE FALLS, Bushkill (April thru Nov.)

POCONO'S MAGIC VALLEY

DISTANCE AND TOLLS: To Delaware Water Gap at end of trip: From G.W. Bridge, 125 *m.*, $1.10. From Verrazano, 140 *m.*, $1.75. Plus return tolls. Returning from Gap: To G.W. Bridge, add 85 *m.*, to Verrazano, 100 *m.* Mostly fast or average speeds.

FOOD: In Milford, Pa., Fauchere's Inn, closed Jan. to April. Tom Quick Inn, closed Sun. In Apple Valley Village, Pancake House. In Bushkill, Fernwood Resort. Near jct. I-80 and US 209, Holiday Inn.

FOR THE DRIVER: Exit Points: G.W. Bridge, Verrazano Bridge, Easton, Pa., Quickway (Rtes. 6 & 17) from Northern New York State.

Via G.W. Bridge and Verrazano Bridge: Same as for Trip B-15 on to I-80 westbound. Proceed to jct. with NJ 23 and take this north toward Sussex. This passes High Point State Park. In Port Jervis join US 6. Take Rte. 6 across bridge (no toll) and proceed south to Milford, Pa. Follow signs in town to Moon Valley Park.

Via Easton, Pa.: US 611 north to Delaware Water Gap. Branch right at sign to I-80 and take this west to next exit, 52, to US 209. Drive north on Rte. 209 to Milford and follow signs in town to Moon Valley Park.

Via Quickway (Rtes. 6 & 17): Leave at Exit 121 where I-84 goes to Port Jervis and follow that. In Port Jervis take US 6 west and cross bridge (no toll) then proceed on Rte. 6 to Milford, Pa. Follow signs in town to Moon Valley Park.

Moon Valley Park, Milford, Pa. 18337. *Open weekends in May thru Oct. Daily, mid-June to Labor Day. Adm. $2.75. Children $1.75. Sr. Cit. discounts. Group rates. Picnics; snacks.* (717) 296-6211.

A picturesque park with an Old West flavor, this is located appropriately in rustic woodlands. We find Conestoga wagons, brightly painted buildings of a Pioneer Town, babbling brooks, roaming animals and walks through flowering shrubbery to Rainbow Falls.

Back to US 6, turn right passing Tom Quick Inn and Fauchere's Inn. Shortly Rte. 6 turns right, toward Hawley. We go to the left here on US 209.

Take US 209 south along the Delaware River. A couple of miles below comes turn-off to:

Raymondskill Falls. *Open mid-May thru Oct. Moderate fees. Snacks in season. Picnic groves. Gift shop. Rest rooms.*

Here the Battle of Raymondskill was fought in 1780. Today we find peaceful, all-hemlock woodlands surrounding the 175-ft. waterfall. We can walk to the top of the falls, or climb down to the bottom for an even more scenic view. Along the way we pass compounds with animals native to the area.

Back on US 209 south; proceed to Dingmans Ferry, where signs direct us to:

Dingmans Falls and Silver Thread Falls. *Open mid-April thru Oct. 9-5:30. May have fees. Picnics, snacks in season. Gift shop. Rest rooms.*

The Pocono's highest waterfalls are surrounded by deep woods and many hiking trails. Two distinctive falls are seen, a long, silver, threadlike flow near the entrance, and farther in, another livelier cascade that rushes down past banks of rhododendron. We need not climb to get excellent views of both, but the trails are all about us if we care to try them.

Back to US 209 south. Continue a short distance watching for a small sign to:

Brisco Mt. Woodcrafters, Inc., Dingmans Ferry, Pa. 18328. *Open year around daily and Sunday, 9-5, depending on weather. Guided tour of factory optional.*

We follow the signs leading up the mountain to the factory and showrooms. This is the home of the combination pepper mill-salt shaker, known as Pepsal Mill®. We may observe expert craftsmen at their meticulous work, then select gifts made of fine wood sold at the shop upstairs. Over it all, the aromatic fragrance of wood shavings.

Continue south on US 209 a few miles to Bushkill and follow signs to:

Bushkill Falls. *Open April – November, daylight hours. Moderate fees. Picnics, cookouts, snacks, gift shop, playground, boating.*

We reach the main falls without too much climbing, but there are tempting paths to take through the banks of laurel and rhododendron to Thunder Gorge, Bridal Veil Falls, Upper Canyon, Twin Lakes. The Niagara of Pennsylvania is largest of its kind in the state and it's a beauty.

Continuing South on 209 we shortly pass the resort FERNWOOD, *food service and gift shop.* Just beyond, follow signs to:

Winona Five Falls. *Open Apr. thru Nov., daylight hours. Picnics, snacks, gift shop, playgrounds. Displays of Indian relics. Moderate fees.*

Here we find a series of five cascades totaling 175 feet. Hiking trails through pine, laurel and rhododendron take us to the falls, which have been kept just as they were at the time of the legend. Hundreds of years ago, Indian Princess Winona is said to have leaped into the rushing waters in an effort to stop her father's tribe from warring with that of her lover.

Pocono's Magic Valley, Amusement Park near Winona Five Falls. *The Falls are now included in adm. Adm. includes unlimited rides. Restaurants, snacks. Open daily in summer, 10-10. Weekends, spring & fall, 10-8. Adm. $5.50; Sr. Cit. $5. 4-11 yrs. $4.50.* (717) 588-9411.

Opened June, 1977, this is the only amusement park in the Poconos. It's located at the foot of Winona Five Falls and includes turn-of-the-century themes, plus games, rides, performing arts, and petting zoo.

Return Trip: For G.W. and Verrazano Bridges, continue south on US 209 to jct. with I-80. Holiday Inn near jct. Take I-80 east to G.W. Bridge, with exit to Garden State Pkwy. for Verrazano connection to exit 137 to NJ 28 to Verrazano and Goethals Bridges.

For Easton, Pa. Go south on US 209 to jct. with I-80. Holiday Inn near jct. Take I-80 east 1 exit to Exit 53 to US 611 south, and return.

For Quickway to northern N.Y. State: Go back up US 209 north. At Milford, take Rte. 6 to Port Jervis and follow it to I-84 east toward Middletown, which connects with the Quickway.

Remarkable Engineering Exhibits in the Delaware Valley

TRIP B-24 EXTENSION. *We'll Visit:*

ELDRED PRESERVE FOR TROUT FISHING

FORT DELAWARE MUSEUM OF COLONIAL HISTORY, Narrowsburg, N.Y. (End of June thru Labor Day, daily; weekends, June.)

MINISINK MONUMENT AND PARK, Minisink Ford, N.Y.

BOB LANDER'S CANOE RENTALS, Minisink Ford (Summer, daily; weekends, spring & fall)

ROEBLING SUSPENSION BRIDGE

ZANE GREY INN, Lackawaxen, Pa.

GRAVITY COACH, Hawley, Pa.

STOURBRIDGE LION, Honesdale, Pa.

LAKE WALLENPAUPACK, Pa.

DISTANCE AND TOLLS: Round trip, except for branch trip: From G.W. Bridge, total 240 *m*. From Verrazano Bridge, total 270 *m*. Adding branch trip, about 14 *m*. more. Via G.W. Bridge, total $1.10; via Verrazano, $1.75. Plus return tolls.

FOOD: In Barryville above Port Jervis on NY 97, Reber's, closed Jan. to mid-March exc. weekends. Restaurant at Eldred Preserve. On return trip in Milford; Fauchere's Inn, closed Jan. to April; Tom Quick Inn, closed Sun. Also in towns en route, and on US 46.

FOR THE DRIVER: Exit Points: G.W. Bridge, Verrazano Bridge, Easton, Pa., Quickway (Rtes. 6 & 17) from northern New York State.

From both G.W. and Verrazano Bridges, same as for Trip B-15 onto I-80 westbound. Turn off on NJ 23 north to Sussex and continue to jct. with US 6 in Port Jervis. This goes to jct. in town with NY 97 north.

Via Easton, Pa.: North on US 611 to Delaware Water Gap, then branch right following sign to I-80. Take I-80 west to next exit, 52, to US 209 north. Drive north on this through Milford, then take US 6 on up to Port Jervis. Pick up the trip in town at jct. with NY 97 north.

Via Quickway: Take this to Exit 121 and I-84 to Port Jervis. Here, take US 6 west to jct. in town with NY 97 north.

All: Northbound on NY 97: Proceed up the river for 17 miles to Barryville and jct. with NY 55. Reber's restaurant at this jct. Turn right on Rte. 55 and drive 7 *m* to Eldred, and to the:

Eldred Preserve for Trout Fishing. *Open year around. Admission to Pond $2.50, children $1.50. Free to motel guests. Plus $2.80 per pound for fish caught. No license needed; all equipment for sale or rent. Picnic* *facilities, snacks. Motel and restaurant at the Preserve. Fish prepared for mailing anywhere.*

This might be a good spot to spend some time. You have a choice of rainbow, brook, brown trout or tigers. A smaller pool for children and novices holds an ample supply of somewhat smaller fish. You can fish by the day for a flat rate, also fish and release.

To come directly here, follow directions above via Quickway, but exit from Rte I-84 at Exit 104 to Rte. 55. West on 55 to Eldred.

Continue on NY 55 for 3 or 4 *m.* and watch on left for road marked Narrowsburg and Ten Mile River Boy Scout Camps. Follow signs to Narrowsburg, about 10 *m.*, and jct. with NY 97. Go straight ahead on 97 (north) and proceed about 1 *m.* Do not turn into town but remain on 97 and watch on left for the stockade of:

Fort Delaware Museum of Colonial History, Narrowsburg, N.Y. 12764. *Open end of June thru Labor Day, daily 10-5:30; Sun. 12-6. Weekends in June. Moderate fees, family tickets available. Snacks. Gift shop. Gift shop.*

This unusual exhibit shows the living conditions within a frontier fortification of 200 years ago. It is not a playground; there are no cowboy shoot-outs. Rather, here is an authentic reproduction, which the State Dept. of Education has chartered as a museum to show the life in a buckskin type of fort. Besides the stockade and blockhouses, through which visitors may climb, there are a store house, armory and the Meeting House Shop where pictures depicting life during the era of the fort are shown. Craft work and daily chores as well as games are demonstrated. Especially popular is a lesson in the firing of cannon and muskets.

Go south on NY 97 to Minisink Falls. Watch for sign, left, to MINISINK BATTLEGROUND MEMORIAL PARK. We can drive almost to the monument. Picnic facilities. Markers describe the 1779 battle.

Back to NY 97. Across the highway is the bridge to Lackawaxen which we take next. However, canoeists may want to stop at Bob Lander's nearby. For this, go south (left) on Rte. 97 about 1 mile. Motel is on left; just beyond, right, is:

Bob . Lander's Canoe Rentals, Minisink Ford, N.Y. Phone (914) 252-7101. *Open weekends from April, daily in summer. After Labor Day, weekends until Oct. or Nov. depending on the river.. Write Main Lodge, Narrowsburg, N.Y. 12764, for brochure and rates. Future plans call for clambakes, smorgasbords, etc., with advance notice. Snacks. Plenty of canoes available in summer; in fall, crowded on weekends—check first.*

They'll transport the canoes ("unsinkable") upriver for you to one of several likely points such as Hancock, Callicoon or Skinners Falls. You then paddle them back along the exceptionally scenic, winding river that includes a number of white water stretches. Only swimmers may rent canoes. Special weekend package trips are available for clubs. Inquire.

Go back up Rte. 97 to jct. with road to Minisink Park. On left is the:

Roebling Suspension Bridge (toll). Bridge is always open; drive over to the barrier and cross into Pennsylvania.

This, the oldest suspension bridge in the world, was built in 1848 and is a model for the Brooklyn Bridge. Now a National Landmark, it is a fine picture subject.

Turn right at stop sign, following winding road back to the river. Soon comes a cemetery, left, with the grave of the Unknown Soldier of the Revolutionary War, who died in the Battle of Minisink. Just beyond is:

Zane Grey Inn. Lackawaxen, Pa. 18435. *Museum open mid-April – Oct. daily exc. Mon., 10-4. Adm. fee.* (717) 685-7522.

Here, Zane Grey said, he first experienced really wild country. And here he wrote many of his books about the West, becoming the most popular writer of western adventure. He filled his workroom with mementoes of his career, including pictures used to illustrate his books. He died in 1939 and both he and his wife are buried in the adjoining graveyard.

Just beyond the author's house, the Lackawaxen River flows into the Delaware. Continue to the highway that crosses the Zane Grey Bridge, right, and take Pa. 590 north toward Hawley, to left. Soon Rte. 590 turns right toward Hawley. For an exceptional scenic drive, don't turn, but continue along the river. Eventually this road bears right and rejoins Rte. 590. Pick it up here to Hawley and jct. with US 6. Turn left (east) on Rte. 6; just beyond the bridge, on your left is a red railroad car, the famous

Gravity Coach. This pioneer coach, operating between Hawley and Pittstown, was completed in 1850 and in service until 1880. Instead of using locomotives to haul the cars, the operators used stationary engines for power up the hills, then depended on gravity to get the cars down the other side.

Branch trip: To reach the Locomotive Exhibit and replica of the Stourbridge Lion, turn back on Rte. 6 from the Gravity Coach. Go west to Honesdale. Pass the Wayne County Historical Society Museum, 810 Main, behind which is one model of the locomotive. Continue on US 6 across a bridge. Just ahead, left, is a white building in which is the replica of the STOURBRIDGE LION. The original was brought from England in 1829. Here also is the Eclipse, passenger coach and pay car, used on the B. & H. Gravity R.R.

Resume Regular Trip. On Rte. 6 return east thru Hawley to Lake Wallenpaupack.

Return Trip: Same as for B-22 Extension, except if using Quickway. For Quickway (Rtes. 6 & 17). Take US 6 from the lake to Milford and follow it, left, passing Fauchere's Inn and Tom Quick Inn, through Port Jervis. Continue to I-84 east to Middletown, which connects with the Quickway.

Up the Hudson River Valley

● *To many New Yorkers the Hudson is the Enchanted Valley, a wizard's mixture of history and legend, evoking memories of Dutch mariners, British grenadiers, Continental veterans, Bear Mountain, West Point, and the wooded Highlands. Houses of stone that have lasted 300 years; miles of apple orchards; parks and waters for outdoor fun, embellished by the imagination of Washington Irving and Fenimore Cooper. From Manhattan to Rip van Winkle's hideout, every mile is an exhilarating experience.*

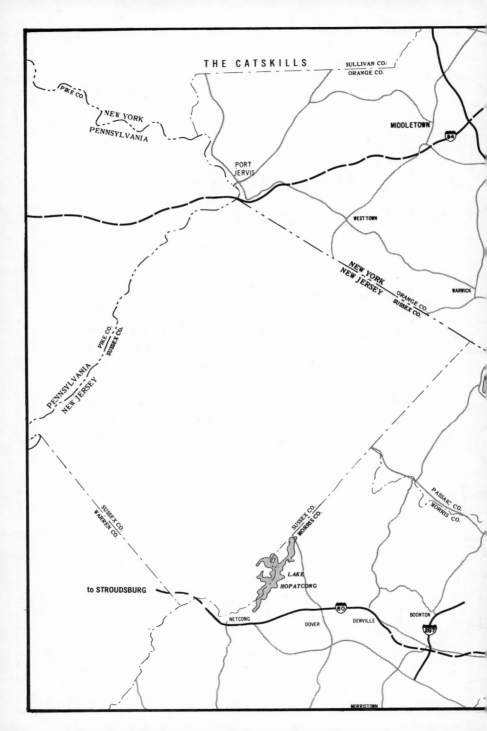

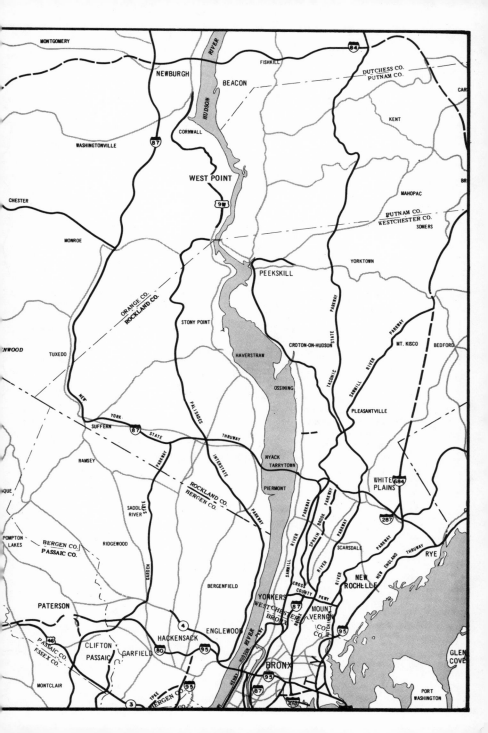

To reach Area C from New York City, use Exit Points: George Washington Bridge, Tappan Zee Bridge, and Garden State Parkway, from the northern end.

Main roads: Palisades Interstate Parkway, New York State Thruway (extension of Major Deegan Expressway).

From G.W. Bridge: To Palisades Interstate Parkway: It starts at the bridge on the New Jersey side; follow signs. To N.Y. State Thruway: Take Palisades Interstate Parkway north to Exit 9 marked Thruway to Albany.

From Tappan Zee Bridge: To Palisades Interstate Parkway, continue on Thruway after crossing bridge, to Exit 13, for Parkway northbound.

For N.Y. State Thruway: You are on it, on bridge. Proceed as directed.

From Garden State Parkway: To Palisades Interstate Parkway, go to northern end of Garden State Pkwy. and take N.Y. Thruway toward N.Y. City and Palisades Parkway. Proceed to Exit 13 on Thruway to Palisades Pkwy. northbound.

To N.Y. State Thruway: Go to northern end of Garden State Pkwy. and follow signs, either toward N.Y. City or Albany, as directed.

For A Clear Day,
the Most Remarkable Panorama

TRIP C-1. *We'll Visit:*
ROCKEFELLER AND ALPINE LOOKOUTS
STATE LINE LOOKOUT
LAMONT NATURE SANCTUARY

DISTANCE AND TOLLS: From G.W. Bridge, 11 *m.* 50¢. Plus return.

Palisades Interstate Park (not Amusement Park) Minutes from Manhattan we'll stand on cliffs 300 to over 500 feet high as we survey a panorama that includes the mighty Hudson River, the New York skyscrapers, Long Island, Westchester and far beyond. Looking straight down we'll have awesome views of tops of trees that literally grew up the sides of the precipice. The 12-mile long park extends north across the New York State line. Along its shores are picnic grounds and boat basins, most easily reached by car, all open to the public for a small parking fee. Caution: Obey signs; climb only where permitted.

Rockefeller Lookout. *Open daily year around. Handicapped: One curb; can walk to VISTA points.*

We're across the river from the Riverdale section just above Manhattan Island. To our right is the George Washington Bridge and behind it, the New York skyscrapers. Beyond them is Long Island Sound and finally, Long Island.

The hills north of the bridge rise to become Washington Heights, highest point on Manhattan Island. During the Revolution it was the site of Fort Washington, one of the city's ill-fated defenses. Fort Tryon Park stretches along the top; at the upper end stands the Cloisters, a medieval museum maintained by the Metropolitan Museum of Art.

Underneath the New York end of the bridge at Jeffries Hook we can just make out the Little Red Lighthouse, slated to be demolished when the bridge went up, but spared through protests and publicity.

Look straight down the side of the cliffs, for staggeringly effective views of treetops mingling with gigantic columns of rock.

Alpine Lookout. *Open year around, daily. A few steps; walk to the promontory is mostly unpaved.*

Here the Blue Hiking Trail along the top of the Palisades comes through. This is part of the Long Path that some day may take us on a

400-mile hike to Lake Placid. Presently we'll follow it a short distance to our right to a vantage point from which we can get startling views from the very edge of the cliffs. We're safely fenced in but naturally we'll stay on the marked trails and keep the kids with us. Here we are among the great, craggy pillars that poured out of the earth then solidified so many eons ago. That's Yonkers across the river.

State Line Lookout. *Open year around, weather permitting, Parking fees for picnic area only. No charge for parking for viewing. Food: Picnics; snacks in season.*

We're now across from Hastings-on-Hudson and we're 532 feet tall. Our best view is to the north where the Tappan Zee Bridge carries the New York Thruway across 3 miles of river between Tarrytown and Nyack. The Long Path (Blue Trail) still clings to the top of the cliffs and we may join it for a hike up the road to the Lamont Nature Sanctuary not far above.

Lamont Nature Sanctuary. *Open year around, weather permitting.*

This is an extension of the Palisades Park area, 23 acres of unspoiled woodlands that reach to the cliffs. The Sanctuary contains winding trails and VISTAS, stone stairways and waterfalls unexpected so close to the city. To make the round trip, with stop-offs to enjoy the superb views could take one or two hours so don't hurry.

If approaching from State Line Lookout, a walk of about 20 minutes takes you to the gate. You enter the Sanctuary at the top of a hill with a choice of paths leading downward. By making your way toward the Hudson River you'll find Moss Rock, the first VISTA and above it the best one of all, High Gutter Point. You will also see Totem Pole, one of the needle-like crags, and you may climb the Stairway to the Sun.

FOR THE DRIVER: Exit Point for all: G.W. Bridge. Follow signs to Palisades Pkwy. Drive north about 3 *m.* to Rockefeller Lookout, off road to right. Continue on parkway another 3 *m.* to Alpine Lookout. 3 *m.* farther turn off to State Line Lookout.

For Lamont Nature Sanctuary, choice: Park at State Line Lookout and walk to the Sanctuary—about 20 minutes along the road, all down hill. Or drive back to Palisades Pkwy. north to Exit 4 at US 9W. Turn left from ramp; almost at once is entrance, right, to Columbia Observatory. The Sanctuary entrance is past the chain between two boulders. Park here and walk in a short way.

Return Trip: Back to Palisades Interstate Pkwy. south, from Lamont Sanctuary parking area. From State Line Lookout, start north on Pkwy.; almost at once is a turn-off, left, to southbound lane. All: Follow signs to G.W. Bridge.

Exploring the Palisades From Below

TRIP C-2. *We'll Visit:*

ROSS DOCK PICNIC AREA (Summer)
ENGLEWOOD BOAT BASIN & PICNIC AREA
UNDERCLIFF BEACH (Summer)
ALPINE BOAT BASIN & PICNIC AREA

DISTANCE AND TOLLS: Farthest point about 6 *m.* from G.W. Bridge. 50¢. Plus return.

Ross Dock Picnic Area. *Open from mid-Apr. and after Labor Day thru Oct., weekends and holidays. After school closes, daily. Daylight hours. Parking fee. Picnics, snacks. No swimming.*

This is the first picnic area we reach. The view is especially interesting because we're almost beneath the George Washington Bridge.

Englewood Boat Basin and Picnic Area. *Open year around, weather permitting, from sunrise to midnight. Parking fee, from mid-Apr. to mid-Nov., plus weekends from late March. Free at other times. Food: Picnic areas with cooking; snacks in season. No swimming.*

Here is a good sized area with fine views, and a road to the top, if you care for a steep climb. The Dyckman Street Ferry used to dock here.

Undercliff Beach. *Open May to Labor Day, weekends and holidays only; daylight hours. Parking fee. Food: Picnics; no cooking. Snacks. No swimming.*

Located on the cliff side of the road, it provides walks across to the river. Follow trails only.

Alpine Boat Basin. *Open year around daily, sunrise to midnight. Parking fee collected from close of schools to Labor Day, also weekends and holidays from mid-April to mid-Nov. Other times free. Food: Picnics, cooking; snacks. No swimming. May be reached from Palisades Interstate Pkwy. (see Trip C-1) when lower road is closed.*

Above us hang the great cliffs with trees growing at all angles from the rock crevices. Man-made embellishments include picturesque pavilions and a historic house that once was Cornwallis' headquarters (we have to look through the windows). Finally, trails lead not only along the river banks but also right up the side of the Palisades. If these seem pretty steep for us, we might note that during the Revolution the

British soldiers climbed them, carrying all their equipment, on their way to capture Fort Lee.

FOR THE DRIVER: Exit Point for all: G.W. Bridge. From upper deck: Take exit marked Hudson Terrace and turn sharp right, going down hill. Turn right again under bridge. Shortly branch left on County Rte. 505 toward Edgewater. Just beyond, left, is entrance to Palisades Interstate Park.

From lower deck: Take the first exit to Fort Lee & 9W. First light after ramp is on 9W. Turn left, crossing bridge approaches, and continue straight ahead several blocks to Main St. (County Rte. 56). Turn left on Main to the end, at jct. with Hudson Terrace, then bear right down the hill. Shortly, left, is entrance to Palisades Interstate Park.

All: Take this road along the river and back under the bridge for picnic areas. When road is closed take Palisades Interstate Pkwy. as for Lookouts (Trip C-1) and exit at Englewood or at Alpine then follow signs to either boat basin.

Return Trip: Go back via the lower road, then turn right and follow signs to G.W. Bridge. Or, just before Alpine Basin take road to top and Palisades Interstate Pkwy. Take this south and follow signs to G.W. Bridge. For State Line Lookout (Trip C-1) take Pkwy. north to next exit.

History and Vistas from A Revolutionary War Site

TRIP C-2 (A): *We'll Visit:*

FORT LEE HISTORIC PARK

DISTANCE AND TOLLS: Located at N.J. end of G. W. Bridge. Bridge tolls only.

Fort Lee Historic Park, Hudson Terrace, Fort Lee, N.J. 07024. Phone (201) 461-3956. *Open daily year around: Park, 9-dusk. Museum, 9:30 - 5. Fees: Memorial Day to Labor Day, and all weekends, parking $1.50 for 3 hours; 50¢ per hour thereafter. At other times, free. Buses, $5. Groups reserve in advance; civic groups may arrange for after-hour tours. Bicycles not permitted, but those cycling in may park them in a special rack. Picnic tables; vending machines in season sell soft drinks, coffee. No picnicking or sunbathing in historic section. Handicapped: Special parking area; ramps to walks and into buildings; rest rooms adapted for wheelchairs. Walks level and paved. Benches and shade.*

Since 1976 we have had a rare opportunity to visit the reconstructed site of a memorable segment of the Revolutionary War and at the same time obtain spectacular views of the Palisades, Manhattan, the Hudson River and George Washington Bridge and including both 20th-century landmarks and 18th-century battlefields.

This is a historic park, planned for study rather than recreation. A modern Visitor's Center holds a museum, one of the few historical ones in this part of the State, with an orientation movie and automated maps and dioramas depicting the Revolutionary War battles in and around New York. Two observation towers may be scaled for even more sweeping VISTAS. Historic trails cover the southern portion of the 33-acre park. We pass 3 reconstructed gun batteries (with cannon). Signs explain fully their necessity, their actual use, and the results.

Historians, of course, are eager to corroborate their knowledge of this phase of the Revolution. However, the park has a special significance for many people who never fully understood the importance of the strategic battles and enemy activity taking place within our viewing range, and of the dramatic impact they had on American history.

The park is comparatively new. Fascinating projects are in the planning stage which should keep visitors returning. Organizations are encouraged to get details for using the park for historic or cultural activities.

FOR THE DRIVER: Exit point for all: G. W. Bridge. Follow directions for Trip C-2 to Hudson Terrace. Park entrance is just above the one to the road at the foot of the Palisades (which has a different entrance and is closed winters). If approaching via Main St. in Fort Lee, at jct. with Hudson Terrace turn left to the park.

Return Trip: Follow signs back to G. W. Bridge to N.Y. OR: To extend the trip, take either the upper road (Palisades Interstate Parkway) or the lower (Trips C-1 and C-2).

The End of the Road for Major John André

TRIP C-3. *We'll Visit:*

GEORGE WASHINGTON MASONIC SHRINE (DE WINT HOUSE),
Tappan, N.Y.

THE '76 HOUSE

ANDRÉ HILL

TALLMAN MOUNTAIN STATE PARK, Sparkill

DISTANCE AND TOLLS: From G.W. Bridge, under 15 *m.* 50¢. Plus return.

George Washington Masonic Shrine (De Wint House), Tappan, N.Y. 10983. *Open year around, 10-4 daily exc. Christmas. Donations. Handicapped: Paths well graded; a step or two into house.*

General Washington made this house his headquarters five times, and he was here the last week in September, 1780, when Major John

André, convicted as a spy in the Benedict Arnold conspiracy to betray West Point, was brought to Tappan. A military court appointed by Washington held an inquiry on Sept. 27, 1780 and declared André should be considered a spy and suffer death. Washington is said to have signed the order for his execution at a table now in this house. The house, dating from 1700, was subsequently bought by the Masonic order and is preserved as a memorial to Washington, a member. On the grounds is a Carriage House, built 1800, which contains historic objects.

The '76 House. *Open daily, as a restaurant.*

This house, built in 1755, was a tavern when Major André was detained in a small room later torn out during remodelling. It was from this tavern that André walked with a military escort to the place of execution.

ANDRÉ HILL. Efforts of British Headquarters in New York to get André's release by an exchange of prisoners failed. He had written Washington asking for a soldier's death by shooting, but received no reply. In full uniform as Adjutant General, he was marched up the hill to the drumbeat of the *Dead March*, on October 2, 1780, and hanged. André was buried where he died; in 1821 his remains were removed to Westminster Abbey in London.

Tallman Mountain State Park, Sparkill, N.Y. *Open daily year around. Fees: $1.50 per car ($1 after 4 p.m.). Collected late June – Labor Day. Swimming – lockers & showers, adults 50¢ children 25¢, late June thru Labor Day. No buses, no dogs. Food: Picnics, snacks.*

A scenic park contains handball and tennis courts, a cinder track and a large stadium, as well as several VISTA points. Swimming is in a pool at the foot of the mountain near the Hudson River.

FOR THE DRIVER: Exit point for all: G.W. Bridge. Take Palisades Interstate Parkway north, passing 3 Lookouts (Trip C-1) to Exit 4 for US 9W. Turn left on this and follow sign to Nyack north. Shortly at Oak Tree Road (traffic light) turn left and drive until crossing NY 303. A block beyond, left, is the De Wint House. Parking left.

Drive back to Oak Tree Road, turn left until road merges with Main St. in Tappan. Turn right to '76 House, just across street. Then go back to the corner you turned on, but continue straight ahead on Main. If you skipped the '76 House, at jct. with Main St. turn left and proceed.

All: Continue up hill, bearing right, to André Hill. Turn right and ascend this then turn right again to Monument. On return go back to Oak Tree Road, turn right, passing De Wint House, and return to jct. with 9W. Turn left, north, to Tallman Mountain State Park, on right.

Return Trip: Go left, south, on US 9W to jct. with Palisades Interstate Parkway south and follow directions to G.W. Bridge.

Up the Scenic Hudson to High Tor

TRIP C-4. *We'll Visit:*

NYACK BEACH STATE PARK, Nyack, N.Y.

ROCKLAND LAKE STATE PARK, North & South, Nyack, N.Y.

HIGH TOR STATE PARK, Haverstraw (Late June to Labor Day.)

LITTLE TOR, Haverstraw.

DISTANCE AND TOLLS: To Haverstraw from New York City exits, 35 *m.*, mainly fast speeds. Via G.W. Bridge, 50¢; via Major Deegan & Thruway, 75¢; via Hutchinson River Pkwy. 75¢. Plus return.

Nyack Beach State Park. *Open year around. Fees: $1.50 per car ($1 after 4 p.m.). Collected Mem. Day – mid-Oct. weekends and Holidays, daily in summer. Food: Picnics, cooking. Snacks in season. Fishing year around. No swimming.*

This small 61-acre park is hard to beat for scenery. Main attraction is the river itself; children love to play on its banks; adults think first of the fishing. Paths start here for the two-mile hike to Haverstraw; they also connect with others from Rockland Lake State Park above.

Rockland Lake State Park, North & South Areas. *Open year around for fishing and hiking. Fees: $1.50 ($1 after 4 p.m.), collected daily late June – early Sept., and weekends and hol. May – mid-Oct. Bathhouse open daily late June to early Sept. Fees for lockers and activities. Food: Picnics, cooking; snacks in season. Handicapped: Not much climbing, but not much shade in main areas. A dock will accommodate wheelchairs to permit fishing. Pets not allowed.*

Built around an attractive small lake, this park provides swimming and boating. A network of paths spreads out in several directions for hiking. Fairly new is the Nature Center with trails that include a boardwalk into a swamp area where plants of the region are marked for identification. Wild fowl also gather here and during winters are a constant attraction. Also available, golf and tennis.

High Tor State Park, Haverstraw. *Open daily from late June to early Sept. Fees: $1.50 ($1 after 4 p.m.) per car. Lockers and showers, pool swimming, Adults 50¢ under 14, 25¢ Food: Picnics, cooking. Vending machine for snacks. Handicapped: Hilly. Pets not allowed.*

This is a newer park, located up the side of the famous High Tor Mountain, popular mainly for hiking and swimming. It's part of the Long Path, on its eventual 400-mile journey to Lake Placid. Hiking here is for the more experienced. You can climb to High Tor, to your right, or by going left, the Little Tor area. Trails are marked and connect with those from Nyack and Rockland Lake Parks as well as others from the Hook Mountain region.

Little Tor. *Open year around for hiking and VISTA. Free.*

This is an entry point for those who prefer to start their hike from the crest of the mountain rather than its foot. It also is a wildlife sanctuary as well as a fine Lookout. Little Tor is not a formal park—we pull off the road to a parking area then hike in. Trails lead eastward to High Tor and west to Mt. Ivy.

FOR THE DRIVER: Via G.W. Bridge: Take Palisades Interstate Parkway north to Exit 4 for US 9W then left (north) to Nyack. In town, turn right on High St. (next after NY 59) and drive to Broadway, then left to Nyack Beach State Park.

Via Tappan Zee Bridge: Take Exit 11 to Nyack. You're on High St. after ramp; proceed straight ahead to Broadway, then left to Nyack Beach State Park.

All: From park, turn back on Broadway about a mile, then right on Old Mountain Road (small sign) and go to top. Follow signs, right, to US 9W. Take 9W north, right, to Rockland Lake State Park.

Continue north on 9W to jct. with NY 304 to New City. Turn left on this to first small road, (Ridge Rd.), then turn right, to the end at South Mountain Road. Go left to High Tor State Park on the mountainside.

Back on South Mountain Road, turn right from park to blinking light at Central Highway. Turn right to top for parking area and VISTA. Just beyond is parking for hikers at Little Tor Wildlife Sanctuary.

Return Trip: Continue over the mountain to jct. with US 202. Turn left to jct. with Palisades Interstate Pkwy. and take it south.

To A Peaceful Religious Shrine and A Battlefield

TRIP C-5. *We'll Visit:*

MARIAN SHRINE, West Haverstraw, N.Y. (May-Oct.)

STONY POINT BATTLEFIELD RESERVATION (May thru Oct.)

DISTANCE AND TOLLS: From New York City exits about 40 *m.*, mainly fast speeds, some average. Via G.W. Bridge, 50¢; via Major Deegan & Thruway, 75¢; via Hutchinson River Pkwy. 75¢. Plus return.

FOOD: Diners and Restaurants along 9W.

Marian Shrine, West Haverstraw, N.Y. 10993. *Open May-Oct. daily 9-6, weekdays, Mass at noon, services at 3:30. Weekends, arrival and blessing of pilgrims, a.m., Masses at 11 and noon: afternoon tours, procession* *through Rosary Way, benediction. Food: picnics, snacks. Handicapped: Good pavement; shade. Rest rooms.*

Here a beautiful woodland path winds past fifteen white Carrara marble statues that comprise the Rosary. While not as spectacular as Graymoor, across the river, it has an intimacy all its own. Visitors may attend Mass at an outdoor altar under a marble dome. The guardians are the Salesians of St. John Bosco. There's quite a little walking, for the statues are spaced some distance apart. Photographers try to capture the expressions on the finely sculptured faces. There are fine VISTAS of the Hudson and the distant mountains.

Stony Point Battlefield Reservation, Stony Point, N.Y. 10980. *Open mid-April thru Oct. daily 9-5, free. Museum, 9-5. Free. Food: Basket picnics only. Handicapped may be driven to top of park near Museum, then car returned to Parking Area at foot of hill. Groups by advanced reservation.* (914) 786-2521.

The park commemorates the Revolutionary War battle when "Mad" Anthony Wayne on the night of July 15, 1779, captured the fortress held by the British. Although the post was considered too difficult to hold afterward, the victory was great for American morale and discouraged the enemy from further offensives. Markers allow us to walk out the battle: we learn where the outer and inner line of the British abatis was located, where the final hand-to-hand combat was fought. Artists and photographers will be delighted to come upon a picturesque Lighthouse at the tip of the Point.

In the Museum we'll find documents on the history of Stony Point with maps of the battlegrounds. There's also material on the Arnold-André treachery. Look for a self-portrait by André. There are many artifacts from the war, firearms, musket balls. On the north bank of the Point is the site of the famous King's Ferry, which carried thousands of Continental soldiers from Verplanck's across the river.

FOR THE DRIVER: Take Palisades Interstate Parkway north about 9 *m.* above jct. with NY Thruway. Leave at Exit 13 to Willow Grove Road. Turn right and proceed to Marian Shrine, off Filors Lane.

Return to Filors Lane, turn right and continue to US 9W. Turn left on this, (North). After crossing NY 210, watch on right for turn off to Stony Point Battlefield Reservation.

Return Trip: Back on US 9W to Stony Point. Here, take NY 210 west, right, for several miles to Palisades Interstate Pkwy. Take Pkwy. south, the way you started.

To Bear Mountain State Park and Environs

TRIP C-6. *We'll Visit:*
IONA ISLAND
BEAR MOUNTAIN STATE PARK
PERKINS MEMORIAL DRIVE (April into Nov. depending on Weather)

DISTANCE AND TOLLS: To Bear Mtn., from NYC exits, about 40 *m.*, mainly fast speeds.

FOOD: Restaurant, snacks at Bear Mtn. Inn.

Iona Island. This was formerly a vineyard, then an amusement park and summer resort, later a naval ammunition depot. Today the Palisades Park Commission owns the property and is preparing a new park with swimming pool, marina, and picnic and recreation facilities.

Bear Mountain State Park. *Open year around. Swimming in pool, Memorial Day to Labor Day. Rowing, roller skating, hiking. Winter sports: Skiing, with Ski Jumps on weekends; ice skating. Trailside Museum, open year around, 9-5, free. Fees: Parking $1.50 ($1 after 4 p.m.) exc. weekdays off-season. Museum free. Charges for activities vary. Food: Restaurant at the Inn; Cub Room for luncheons; cafeteria, snack bars, many picnic areas. Handicapped: ground level for most activities; Nature Trails and Trailside Museum in hilly area. Pets must be leashed and are not allowed in Nature Trail area.*

We're at the biggest playground of them all. Bear Mountain Park, lying within the larger Harriman Park region, is a remarkable tourist attraction. It is in the Highlands that caused the Hudson to become known as the Rhine of America. It features beautiful mountain lakes, hiking trails for beginners and advanced, playfields, sports for summer and winter. This means great throngs in season. The popular Trailside Museum and Zoo has attraction for botanists, zoologists, geologists and historians. NEW: Santa, pageants, fun at Xmas Festival, 3 wks. in Dec. Crafts Exhibition and Fair in mid-Oct. Ski-jumping tournaments weekends in winter.

Perkins Memorial Drive. *Open April to mid-Nov., depending on weather. Maybe small fee in Season. Food: Picnic areas; no fires allowed. Handicapped: Good views from parking area, also on Scenic Drive. Rest* *rooms have stairs and approaches are hilly. Pets must be leashed in park, not allowed in Tower. Tower is open 9:30-6.*

Here's one of the best mountain drives available near the city. We ascend a scenic, winding road with continual VISTAS, many of them identified by markers telling of historic battles that took place directly below.

On the mountain top are many parking places, with views. Numerous trails find their way here, including one starting near Bear Mountain Inn, which comes directly to the Tower. On a clear day we can see the High Point Memorial Tower in New Jersey, the skyscrapers in New York and closer, Anthony's Nose and Sugar Loaf. Binoculars may be rented.

Drive down to picnic areas on unpaved roads. Just below the Tower a road runs to the Scenic Drive which goes to that well-photographed overlook above Bear Mountain Inn.

FOR THE DRIVER: Take Palisades Interstate Parkway north to the end at Bear Mountain circle. Turn right to Bear Mountain Inn and parking lot.

Leave parking lot at far (southern) end, turn right and follow the Seven Lakes Pkwy. to where the road branches right at toll booth for Perkins Memorial Drive.

Return Trip: Go back to Seven Lakes Pkwy., turn right. Just ahead is entrance to Palisades Interstate Pkwy. Cross to southbound lane, bear left for New York City, and return the way you started.

Picnics, Swimming, Sports, in Bear Mountain Area

TRIP C-7. *We'll Visit:*

ANTHONY WAYNE DEVELOPMENT (Late June thru Labor Day)

SILVER MINE

TIORATI BEACH

SEBAGO BEACH (Late June thru Labor Day)

WELCH BEACH (Late June thru Labor Day)

DISTANCE AND TOLLS: To Beaches from NYC exits about 50 *m.*, fast speeds. Via G.W. Bridge, 50¢; via Major Deegan & Thruway, 75¢; via Hutchinson River Pkwy. 75¢. Plus return.

Anthony Wayne Development. *Open late June thru Labor Day. Fees: $1.50 per car ($1 after 4 p.m.), locker & shower, adults 50¢, under 14, 25¢. Pool swimming. Picnics, charcoal available. No pets. Buses reserve in advance, $6.*

This park is built around a large swimming pool, with scenic picnic areas and playgrounds. For those who don't require things to be too rustic.

Silver Mine. *Open year around. Fees: $1.50 per car ($1 after 4 p.m.), collected daily from late-June to Labor Day; weekends and holidays, mid-May – mid-Oct., daily in summer. Rest of season free. Free parking for skiing, but charge for skiing. No swimming. Food: Picnics with cooking, snacks in season. Handicapped: Paths to picnic areas close to parking lot. Rest rooms a little farther away. Pets must be leashed. Rowboats: Small fee by hour or day. Buses reserve in advance, $6.*

A beautiful woodland park by a picturesque mountain lake, this has paths all around the lake for fine hiking, and picnic areas at every scenic turn. Fall foliage is outstanding here. Rowing and fishing on lake but no swimming. In winter, free parking for skiing, but not for watching.

Tiorati Beach. *Picnic area open year around. Beach, daily, late June thru Labor Day, 9-7. Fees: $1.50 ($1 after 4 p.m.) per car, including picnic area and parking for beach, collected weekends and holidays mid-May thru mid-Oct. Daily in summer. Swimming fees: 25¢. Small fee for lockers, towels (optional). Suits rented. Food: Picnics with cooking; snacks in season. Handicapped: Hard walking in most of picnic grove, but can park close to some tables. Bathing, down a ramp; gate opened so you can avoid stairs. Pets on leash in picnic area only.*

A large, clear lake, Tiorati is a truly scenic spot with little tufts of islands providing intriguing destinations for boatsmen. There's good rowing, and mountain hiking. The lake water is refreshing for swimming, and just across the road the aroma of food cooking over charcoal is the best kind of stimulant to the appetite.

Lake Askoti and Lake Skannatati. *Open for fishing only. No charge for parking; rowboats $2. a day, no deposit.* We pass these after leaving Tiorati.

Sebago Beach. *Open late June thru Labor Day. Fees: $2 per car ($1 after 4 p.m.) Buses reserve in advance, $8. Small fee for lockers (optional). Suits rented. Rowboats, $1.50 an hour. Food: cooking; snacks. Handicapped: paved walks mainly, including to snack bar, rest rooms and lockers. A fairly high step or two onto beach. Pets not allowed.*

One of the larger beaches in the area, this is an excellent place to spend the whole day. The setting is superb and the walks take us to some fine spots for viewing the lake and hills. Rowing is good too, and there's more general activity here than at some of the other beaches. There is another section for cabin camping. No trailers.

Welch Beach. *Open late June thru Labor Day. Fees: $2. per car ($1 after 4 p.m.) Buses by reservation, $8. Lockers 25¢. Suits and towels rented. Rowboats, pedal boats. Food: Picnics with cooking; snacks. No buses. No pets.*

Another large beach area, this one is able to handle the biggest crowds in Harriman Park. Excellent swimming and boating here and plenty of picnic areas. Adjacent is a tent and trailer camping area.

FOR THE DRIVER: Take Palisades Interstate Parkway north into Harriman Park, to the Anthony Wayne Development.

From here, turn right then follow signs to left, to the Seven Lakes Pkwy. Take the Pkwy. past Silver Mine.

Continue on Seven Lakes Pkwy. to Tiorati Beach.

Proceed past the lake and two others used for fishing only. Continue past traffic circle at jct. with NY 210, and shortly comes Sebago Beach.

Continue to where you can cross back into the other lane, and return to jct. with NY 210 at the circle. Take Rte. 210 right, to Lake Welch.

Return Trip: Continue on NY 210 to Palisades Interstate Pkwy. south. At the fork, take speedier road to your right.

Ringwood State Park and Ringwood Manor

TRIP C-8. *We'll Visit:*

RINGWOOD MANOR, Ringwood, N.J. (Park all year, Manor, May thru Oct.)

SHEPHERD LAKE, RINGWOOD STATE PARK, N.J.

SKYLANDS MANOR SECTION
RINGWOOD STATE PARK

DISTANCE AND TOLLS: To Ringwood Park from NYC exits, about 35 *m.*, mostly fast speeds. Via G.W. Bridge, 70¢; via Major Deegan & Thruway, 95¢; via Hutchinson River Pkwy., 95¢; via Garden State Pkwy., 20¢. Plus return.
FOOD: At Suffern exit from Thruway, Restaurant on the Mountain; at Shepherd Lake, Lodge dining room. Snacks, picnics at Ringwood Manor.

Ringwood Manor State Park. *Park is open daily year around. Manor House, May thru Sept. daily, 10-4; weekends till 5. Parking: $2. daily, Mem. Day – Labor Day. Weekends & Hol. May & Sept., $2. Plus each person 12 yrs. and over, 50¢, collected in season: Memorial Day thru Labor Day, daily; weekends from May 1 and thru Sept. Manor House,*

50¢. Comb. fee $3. – Ringwood and Skylands. Small picnic fees for groups. Food: Picnics, cooking. Snacks in season. Handicapped: can see grounds and gardens; a few steps into house.

A picturesque park with a mill pond, wildlife sanctuary, and formal gardens surrounds a Manor House of historical significance. In it we'll tour rooms furnished in 19th century style and filled with valuable pieces which two well-known families collected over the years. Peter Cooper, founder of Cooper Union, lived at Ringwood and later, Abram Hewitt, the ironmaster, resided here. General Washington made it his headquarters occasionally. Outside a water wheel stands on the site of an iron forge.

Three art galleries are open in season, Wed., weekends and holidays, 1-5. A summer workshop is held for various performing arts. Inquire.

Shepherd Lake, Ringwood State Park, N.J. 07456. *Open year around for various activities. Parking, weekdays Mem. Day – Labor Day, $3. Weekends, Hol., $4. Weekends, May & Sept. $2., plus 50¢ each person 12 yrs. and over. Small fees for bathhouse and locker (optional). Rowboats $1. per hr., boat launching $1. See attendant for shooting rates. Parking fees collected daily from Memorial Day to Labor Day, also weekends from May 1 and thru Sept. Swimming from Memorial Day thru Labor Day. Food: Lodge dining room open all year. Snacks, picnics, cooking in fireplaces only. Charcoal for sale. Handicapped might manage, but it's hilly. Beach is near parking area. (201) 962-6377.*

Here 541 acres of the Ramapo Mountains are ours to enjoy. There is swimming in the spring-fed lake, and the fishing is excellent, if you like trout (rainbow, brown or tiger), pickerel and northern pike. Subject to New Jersey fishing laws. Hiking is along trails leading to good viewpoints at the elevation of 500 to 1,040 feet above sea level.

Skylands Section, Ringwood State Park. *Grounds open all year. Parking fees Memorial Day-Labor Day, daily $2., also weekends in May & Sept. Comb. fee for Ringwood & Skylands, $3., daily Memor. Day-Labor Day, & weekends, May & Sept. Tour of house, daily exc. Mon., same dates as parking fees, 10-4., Sun. from 12, 50¢. Rest rooms. No picnics. Handicapped can manage house tours – all on one floor. Most paths level and paved. Garden tour 50¢.*

Skylands Manor House is a beautiful rustic estate, built in 1924, patterned after English baronial mansions. The rooms are not furnished, but the walls, ceilings, fireplaces, stained glass windows and paneling, imported from ancient European castles, are noteworthy. Inquire about using Manor for special functions. Formal gardens, elegantly landscaped, provide continual bloom. Miles of hiking trails afford splendid VISTAS.

FOR THE DRIVER: Take NY Thruway toward Albany to Exit 15 at Suffern. Take NY 17 north. Watch lanes carefully — you loop back; be sure to stay on Rte. 17N. Just beyond this jct. is entrance to Restaurant on the Mountain. Continue on Rte. 17 to the road marked To Ringwood. Take this, passing left, entrance to Shepherd Lake. Continue to Ringwood Manor State Park, on right.

From Ringwood Manor Park, go straight ahead; shortly is Morris Road where a small sign on *right* directs a *left* turn up hill to Skylands.

Return Trip: Back the way you came, to Rte 17 South, then Thruway to N.Y.

A Day in the Clear Air of the Ramapo Mountains

TRIP C-9: *We'll Visit:*

CAMPGAW MOUNTAIN COUNTY RESERVATION, Mahwah
DARLINGTON COUNTY PARK (Apr.-Nov.)
RAMAPO RESERVATION

DISTANCE AND TOLLS: From Tappan Zee Bridge & N.Y. Thruway, under 25 m. to 3 parks, plus return; 25¢ Thruway, plus bridge toll. Fast, average speeds.

FOOD: Picnic grounds; snacks in summer in Darlington County Park.

Campgaw Mountain County Reservation, Campgaw Rd., Mahwah, N.J. *Open all year, free. Permit needed for horseback riding and instruction, also for camping: Bergen County Park Commission, 575 Main St., Hackensack, N.J. 07601. Fees in winter for skiing.*

The two Reservations on today's tour provide decided contrasts in hiking opportunities. At Campgaw Mountain paths are not unusually strenuous, as they follow old Indian trails through hemlock groves or skirt the swamplands. The park contains a wildlife refuge. Picnic tables and shelters are scattered throughout; children have play equipment. The woods are laced with bridle paths. Winter sports include a 1650-ft. main ski slope and a toboggan chute.

Darlington County Park, Darlington Ave., Mahwah, N.J. *Open Apr.-Nov.; in summer, fees of $1. to $3. Children under 12 must be with an adult. Snacks.*

Three lakes, many playfields, a golf course, boating, fishing and swimming provide a change of pace from hiking. The setting is beautiful without being rugged.

Ramapo Reservation. Rte 202, Ramapo Valley Rd. *Open all year, free. Picnic areas. No cars beyond entrance. No swimming, but if we bring our own canoe we may use it on the Ramapo River. Camping; fishing; hiking.*

Be careful not to miss the somewhat unobtrusive entrance to this surprisingly rugged park. At roadside are a phone booth, a parking lot, and a sign: Ramapo Reservation of the Bergen County Park Commission.

Here are trails for the more adventuresome, under really tall timber. There's more climbing than walking and the boulders are piled high. Among several hikes is one up the mountain side to a clear lake about a mile or so away, not far from Skylands in the Ringwood section.*(Trip C-8.)*

FOR THE DRIVER: Take N.Y. Thruway toward Albany to Exit 15 at Suffern, then Rte 17 south into New Jersey. (If coming via the Garden State Pkwy., take it to upper end and follow signs toward Albany.) US 202 crosses Rte 17 shortly below Thruway. Take Rte 202 south (to right) toward Oakland, to a junction with County Rtes. 2 & 3 on Darlington Rd. Turn left, to where road forks. For Campgaw Mtn. Reservation, take right hand road up the hill. For Darlington County Park, take left fork to the park.

Return to Rte 202, turn left and continue briefly to entrance on right to Ramapo Reservation.

Return Trip: Back on Rte 202, to Rte 17, then north to Thruway to N.Y.

Picturesque Lake and Period Houses

TRIP C-10. Since this is primarily for the enjoyment of the drive, it will be written out FOR THE DRIVER.

We'll Visit:
   GREENWOOD LAKE
   SHINGLE HOUSE, Warwick (July & August, Tuesday & Saturday
      afternoons)
   1810 HOUSE, Warwick (Same)

DISTANCE AND TOLLS: To Warwick from NYC exits, about 60 *m.* Fast and average speeds. Via G.W. Bridge, 70¢; via Major Deegan & Thruway, 95¢; via Hutchinson River Pkwy., 95¢; via Garden State Pkwy., 20¢. Plus return.

FOOD: Near Suffern exit, Restaurant on the Mountain. On NY 17, Duck Cedar Inn, closed Mon. At Greenwood Lake, Linden House; New Continental Hotel, closed Wed. In Warwick, Warwick Inn, closed Mon. & Feb.

FOR THE DRIVER: The start is the same as for Trip C-8 as far as NY 17 north from Suffern exit from Thruway. Shortly pass entrance to Restaurant on the Mountain. Above, on NY 17, is Duck Cedar Inn, also other dining places. Turn left on Rte 210 at light, passing several VISTA points. About 8*m.*, above Rte 17 is:

Greenwood Lake. *Boats for rent, horseback riding, hiking, swimming, fishing, including ice fishing, also iceboating, skiing and sledding.*

If you recall the story of Molly Pitcher, the cannon she used at Monmouth was cast here. We'll drive all around the lake. In the vicinity are Linden House restaurant, on Rte. 17A, New Continental Hotel, and other dining places.

Continuing around the lake, at the far end, to the south (in New Jersey) turn left on first road in that direction, following signs to G.W. Bridge. Shortly, on left, is a road to Awosting and East Shore. Make sharp left turn and proceed to jct. with another major road. Turn left on this to the lake. Continue to the other end of the lake where you started, and NY 17A.

Turn left on 17A,, again passing end of lake; this time follow Rte. 17A to your right. You're now climbing Mount Peter, which has more panoramic VISTAS, also a ski area. Continue to sign, Village of Warwick. Just beyond sign is Forester Ave., right. Take this several blocks, crossing the railroad tracks. Just beyond Church St., on right is:

Shingle House, Historical Society of Town of Warwick. *Open July to Aug., Tues. & Sat. 2-4:30. Free.*

This is the oldest house in the village. The shingles for its roof and siding are said to have been cut from one tree. The house has been restored to its earlier period, 1764.

Check here whether best to walk the short distance to next objective, or to find parking space on Main St. Go to next corner, Colonial Ave., turn left to next intersection, at stop sign, then turn left again onto Main St. To right, this is Maple Ave. Go past Church St.; in next block on left is Village Green, and the:

1810 House, formerly Warwick Valley Museum. *Open July and August, Tues. & Sat. 2-4:30. Free.*

This quaint house has been restored to between 1805 and 1810. It contains good examples of Duncan Phyfe work, also displays of Americana including an exhibit of antique dolls.

Return Trip: Continue down Main St. the direction you were going; this is NY 94 and 17A. Just before they separate, pass Warwick Inn, right. At this jct. there are two possible routes home. The quickest: Take NY 17A left the way you came, to Rte. 17 south. This goes to Thruway to Westchester and New York.

A little longer trip, for additional scenery: Continue south on NY 94 after Rte. 17A turns off. Watch for sign, shortly, to turn left to Upper Greenwood Lake. Take this road, eventually passing the small lake. Continue, following signs to G.W. Bridge. This time go straight ahead on County 511 to Wanaque Reservoir.

Its capacity of 28 billion gallons of water are a scenic highlight—and wait until you see it in the fall! This area also is noted for a number of sightings of flying saucers. Something for everybody here.

Watch on left for a road branching away from the reservoir and sign Skylands of New Jersey Regional State Park System, to Ringwood Manor and Shepherd Lake. (Trip C-8). This road passes both; continue on it to jct. with NY 17 south, and take this back to the Thruway toward Westchester and New York.

United States Military Academy at West Point

TRIP C-11. *We'll Visit:*

THE UNITED STATES MILITARY ACADEMY, its Museum, Chapels and Parade Ground.

DISTANCE AND TOLLS: About 45 *m.* from New York City exits, mainly fast speeds. Via G.W. Bridge, 50¢; via Major Deegan & Thruway, 75¢; via Hutchinson River Pkwy., 75¢. Plus return.

United States Military Academy, West Point, N.Y. 10996. *Open daily year around. Visitors' Information Center open 8:30-4:30 Apr.-Nov. Daily. Then Wed.-Sun. Closed major Hol.* (914) 938-2638. *Get map and brochure for self-guiding tour here. Food: Restaurant and cafe at Hotel Thayer on the grounds. Closed 2 major holidays. Limited cafeteria facilities by reservation in Post Exchange Snack bars; vending machines in Information Center. No picnic grounds, but visitors may eat box lunches in the car. Parking free at specified locations, inquire at gate. Photographing everywhere except during Chapel services. Rest rooms at Center, Museum, elsewhere. Handicapped: Steps into Cadet Chapel; Museum will accommodate you if called in advance.*

Launch to Constitution Island. For tours of historic WARNER HOUSE, June to October, Tuesday and Wednesday at 1 & 2 p.m. Adm. $1.50. By apt. only. Phone (914) 446-8676.

Cadet Chapel. This is an impressive structure in "military Gothic" with an exceptionally large organ and magnificent stained glass windows. It is open daily and has services on Sunday at 10:30 a.m. Sept. thru May. In summer services are held at Trophy Point.

Catholic Chapel is another fine building, open from 6 a.m. to 9 p.m. daily.

Old Cadet Chapel is open Wed. through Sun., with Jewish services at 8:30 a.m. Sundays. In the Cemetery adjoining the oldest headstone is dated 1782; a more recent one is that of Major Edward White, the astronaut who lost his life in a space test in 1967.

West Point Museum. *Open 10:30-4:15 daily and Sun. exc. Christmas and New Years Day. Free.*

"Weapons change," said General George S. Patton, Jr., "but man who uses them changes not at all." This quotation is called to mind as we visit one of the finer displays emphasizing the importance of weapons of land warfare. We'll see uniforms of the Corps from 1822 to the present; dioramas of past wars; some of the Selden Chapin military miniatures such as his Grande Armée of Napoleon. There are memorabilia from the War with Spain, the Boxer Rebellion, the Civil War, Vietnam, and even Viet Cong weapons.

We'll learn how the Renaissance changed warfare through two introductions—gunpowder and the printing press. We observe a frontier stockade and block house. The Gift Shop carries a good variety of items including kits with guns to assemble. There are also pins, wall plaques, printed matter.

West Point Grounds. The Hudson River bends sharply here before continuing toward Poughkeepsie, providing a fine scenic VISTA from Trophy Point. The region was originally favored by the military for its strategic location. Here the great iron chain of 300-pound links was laid across the river to Constitution Island to keep British ships from using the waters to split the colonies during the Revolution. Benedict Arnold planned to turn West Point over to the British in 1780, for which his contact, Major John André was hanged.

FOR THE DRIVER: Take Palisades Interstate Pkwy. north to Bear Mtn. traffic circle, just before the bridge. Follow signs 9W North to West Point. A few miles above, take turn-off to Highland Falls and West Point on NY 218, right. When the road forks follow sign, right, to West Point entrance at South, Thayer, Gate. Turn left to Visitor's Information Center for maps, tours. When Center is closed ask directions at gate. Tour starts from Mills Road, just beyond Cavalry Flats near the Center. Turn left, then follow sign for Thru Traffic, bearing right past Smith Rink, Lusk Reservoir and Michie (*my-kee*) Stadium. Beyond on right is sign to Cadet Chapel. Drive in here. Then continue down hill to Washington Road for Catholic Chapel.

Turn right on Washington Rd. past Trophy Point, Battle Monument and Washington Monument. Public parking area to the right. Parade Grounds and Athletic Fields are also at this location. Park here for the West Point Museum.

Go back on Washington Road passing Trophy Point. Continue past the Cemetery and Old Cadet Chapel. Drive through grounds then continue, right, following sign to Rte. 9W, to Washington Gate. Go ahead to US 9W, take it south to jct. with Palisades Interstate Pkwy. and return.

To add the scenic Storm King Drive: At Washington Gate, turn right toward Cornwall. Pass the Museum of Hudson Highlands (C-12). Continue on Rte. 218 to jct. with US 9W. Either go south passing more VISTA points, to jct. with Palisades Pkwy., or go north to Newburgh and Washington's Headquarters (Trip C-12).

Washington and the Army's Winter of Discontent

TRIP C-12. *We'll Visit:*

WASHINGTON'S HEADQUARTERS, Newburgh, N.Y. (Wed.-Sun.)

KNOX HEADQUARTERS, Vails Gate (Same)

NEW WINDSOR CANTONMENT, Vails Gate (Mid-Apr. thru
Oct. Wed. thru Sun.)

MUSEUM OF THE HUDSON HIGHLANDS, Cornwall-on-Hudson
(Closed Fri.)

DISTANCE AND TOLLS: To Newburgh from N.Y.C. exits: about 60 *m*. Fast speeds. Via G.W. Bridge, 50¢; via Major Deegan & Thruway, 75¢; via Hutchinson River Pkwy. 75¢. Plus return.
FOOD; In Cornwall, Cornwall Inn. Diners on Rte. 9W and in Newburgh.

Washington's Headquarters, Liberty and Washington Sts., Newburgh, N.Y. 12550. *Open Wed. thru Sun. all year 9-5; closed major holidays. Free. Handicapped: A few steps. Rest rooms in museum basement.* (914) 562-1195.

The Hasbrouck House, which General Washington occupied for sixteen months in 1782-83, is the jewel in the collection of Revolutionary relics that make Newburgh important to all lovers of historical places. Its distinctive quality is that it remains practically as it was when Washington—and Madame Washington—lived here. Part of the house was built in 1725, but by 1770 the last addition had been made. In 1850 the State of New York took it over from the Hasbrouck family. A remarkable feature is its large room, which has seven doors, one window, and a fireplace practically inside the room, with a huge smoke vent in the ceiling above it. The house stands in seven acres called Headquarters Park. On the grounds is the Tower of Victory, 53 ft. tall, which formerly sheltered a life-sized statue of Washington based on Houdon. It now stands near the Museum. The Tower was erected in 1887 to commemorate the 100th anniversary of the disbanding of the Continental Army. Recently renovated it is now a modern interpretive center.

The Museum has a short orientation film on the importance of the site during the Revolution.

A short walk from the house is the foundation of the Ellison gristmill, visited by George Washington, and a stone bridge which leads to the Native Plant Sanctuary.

Knox Headquarters, Vail Gate, N.Y. 12584. *Open Wed.-Sun. all year 9-5; closed major holidays. Free. Rest rooms.* (914) 561-5498.

This attractive house of stone and frame construction was begun in 1734 as a hunting lodge and received additions as late as 1782. It was the headquarters of Major General Henry Knox, Washington's commander of artillery, during the New Windsor Cantonment. At times it also sheltered Major Generals Horatio Gates and Nathanael Greene, and social affairs brought the presence of Madame Washington from Newburgh. A memorial garden is cared for by local garden groups.

New Windsor Cantonment and Temple Hill, Box 525, Vails Gate, N.Y. 12584. *Open Mid-April - Oct. 9-5, Wed. thru Sun. Free. Picnic area. Rest rooms. Visitors advised to attend explanatory movie. Handicapped: easy access to demonstrations but paths are hilly, unpaved.* (914) 561-1765.

This is a reconstruction by the State of New York of the camp of the American Army, often called the Last Cantonment, which assembled here in November, 1782, and lasted until disbandment 8 months later. The troops were chiefly from New England and New York. The winter was especially severe; the men were in rags and their meager pay was long overdue. A group of officers presumably aroused by General Gates, presented two appeals to Congress citing their distress, demanding their pay, and threatening to leave their "ungrateful country." These were the Newburgh Addresses written by Col. John Armstrong, who later became Secretary of War. On March 15, 1783, Washington convened the officers in the New or Publick Building (later called the Temple) and pointed out the serious implications of their threats, by which they were "sowing the seeds of discord and separation between the civil and the military," and promised their accounts would be fairly liquidated. The officers gave Washington their unanimous support.

Guides in Continental uniforms will lead us through the Cantonment. The Temple, used by the army for Masonic meetings, has been reproduced; in one room is the original Purple Heart badge. In every respect, authenticity is the keynote here, from the smallest details in the clothing to the construction of the buildings themselves.

Museum of the Hudson Highlands on the Boulevard, Cornwall-on-Hudson, N.Y. 12520. *Open year around daily exc. Fri., 2-5. Donations. Handicapped: Some Steps. Rest rooms.*

On the side of a mountain, surrounded by nature trails, stands this prize-winning piece of architecture housing a unique small museum of living animals. Young people had much to do with its planning, and now maintain the animals; they also provided the murals. There is an assortment of small animals of the region, many collected by students.

FOR THE DRIVER: Take Palisades Interstate Pkwy. North and drive to Bear Mountain traffic circle. Turn left, take US 9W north for 16 *m.* to Newburgh. Almost at once, look for overhead sign to Washn. Hdq. This is Washington St. Turn right for several long blocks to the park on Liberty St., which has Washington's Headquarters and the Museum on the right. Parking on premises any day but Sunday.

Back to US 9W, turn left, south. When NY 94 branches right, take this to Vails Gate and Knox Headquarters.

Continue on NY 94 to jct. with NY 32, where 5 roads meet. Take Temple Hill Road, following signs, right, to New Windsor Cantonment.

Go back on Temple Hill Road to jct. and take NY 32 south. Continue past turn-off to Storm King Art Center (Trip C-13). Just beyond, NY 307 goes left. Take this and proceed into Cornwall-on-Hudson. Your road merges shortly with NY 218. Proceed on this, bearing right. In town on Rte. 218 is the Cornwall Inn. Continue to Mountain Road where signs direct you, right, to Museum of Hudson Highlands.

Return Trip: Go back on Rte. 307 to US 9W; take this south, passing West Point (Trip C-11), to jct. with Palisades Interstate Pkwy. and return.

Or go back to Rte. 307 but turn right and proceed along an especially scenic drive, Old Storm King Highway, to Washington Gate to West Point (C-11). Then continue to US 9W, take this south to jct. with Palisades Interstate Pkwy., and return.

From an Indian Museum to a Winery

TRIP C-13. *We'll Visit:*

PLUME INDIAN MUSEUM, Highland Mills (Closed Sun.)

STORM KING ART CENTER, Mountainville (May to Nov., afts. Closed Mon.)

BETHLEHEM ART GALLERY, (Closed Sun.)

BROTHERHOOD WINERY, Washingtonville (Daily in season, then Sat. & holidays.)

DISTANCE AND TOLLS: From NYC exits to Winery via the others, about 65 m., mainly fast speeds. Via G.W. Bridge, $1; via Major Deegan & Thruway, $1.25; via Hutchinson River Pkwy., $1.25; via Garden State Pkwy., 50¢. Plus return. **FOOD:** On Thruway above Exit 15, Hot Shoppe Rest Area.

Plume Indian Museum & Trading Post. *Open year around. Mon. thru Fri. 9–5, Sat. 10–12. Fees: $1. adults, 50¢ children. Handicapped: 3 low steps into building. Most exhibits on ground floor.*

This is a mail order house dealing in Indian sourenirs sold by many trading posts and souvenir shops. The building is small and houses the private collection of the owner. Anyone interested in Indian history would find this authentic display of value. It includes a collection of artifacts from the Little Big Horn battlefield in Montana where Custer died June 25, 1876. Many tribes, especially from the West, are represented.

Indian Trading Post carries a large assortment of souvenirs and authentic and rare items for collectors.

Storm King Art Center, Old Pleasant Hill Road, Mountainville, N.Y. 10953. *Open Mid-May-Oct. Wed.-Mon. Tues. if hol., 2-5:30. Closed Wed. following Tues. hol., and Nov.-April. Donation $2. Concerts are held the 2nd & 4th Sun. afts. in July & Aug. On these days the gallery is open 2-3, and 5-7. Handicapped: A few steps into Museum, but you can see much on first floor. In gardens, the paths are well graded — outdoor sculpture and fine VISTAS seen from them. Rest room on main floor. (Check concert dates.)*

A superb collection of fine art is displayed impressively in an elegant cut-stone mansion set in landscaped gardens overlooking the Catskill Mountains. Besides a large permanent collection of creative art by well-known artists there are special exhibits throughout the season in a wide variety of media and subjects, on loan from other galleries. From the gardens we get a magnificent VISTA of the rolling foothills, seen through five enormous, Ionic granite columns. The Center is for those seriously interested in art. No gift shop or picnic grounds.

Bethlehem Art Gallery, *R.D. 2, Box 140, Newburgh, N.Y. 12550. Open year around, Mon. thru Sat. 10-5; Tues. eve., 7-9. Free.*

There is quite a different atmosphere from that at the Art Center. This is a bustling place, which not only exhibits more locally produced art, but sells a large variety of pertinent items.

Brotherhood Winery, Washingtonville, N.Y. 10992. (914) 496-3661. *Tours: Weekends mid-Feb. thru Nov., 10-4. Daily Apr. 30 to June 22,*

12 noon - 3 p.m. From June 25 thru Aug., daily 10-4. After Labor Day, weekdays from 12 noon - 3 p.m. Sunday closings in July & Aug. extended to 5 p.m. Closed Thanksgiving, Christmas, New Year's, Good Friday, Easter Sunday. No adm. fee, but parking is $1.50. Special fees for buses, reserve in advance. Picnic area. Handicapped: Use caution on damp floors; some climbing; railings. Rest rooms. Tours every half hour, last nearly an hour including tasting products.

If you expect hills of vineyards and rows of brown-robed monks picturesquely plucking grapes—forget it. Only the name Brotherhood remains in this commercial enterprise, although the original cellars were built by French monks in the early 1700's. The tour will take us on a long subterranean ramble through dank caverns among the great white oak aging casks. We'll hear the story of wine and champagne making over the years, with tips on the proper way to serve and enjoy them. Eventually we're invited to step up to an almost endless bar and sample some of the merchandise. The only time of year when we may see grapes used is during the fall harvest, when they are brought in by truck. This is the busiest and most crowded time for a visit, but any season is good for the Tour. Bring a wrap. Even in summer the cellars are cool.

FOR THE DRIVER: Take N.Y. Thruway north toward Albany. Pass a Hot Shoppe service area above Exit 15. Proceed to Exit 16 to Rtes. 6 & 17 (Quickway). Immediately after toll, turn right (north) on NY 32 and drive to Highland Mills. Here is jct. with NY 208 which goes left. Take this briefly, watching, left, for dirt road to Plume Trading & Sales Co.

Back to Rte. 208. turn right and go back to Rte. 32 where you turned off. Turn left and continue on Rte. 32 just past jct. with NY 307. Almost at once you cross a small creek; on left is Orrs Mills Rd. Follow signs on this about a mile to Storm King Art Center.

Go back the way you came to NY 32 and turn left to jct. with NY 94. Make sharp left turn onto Rte. 94 west toward Washingtonville. Watch for sign at Jackson Ave. to Bethlehem Art Gallery. Turn right and drive about half a mile in.

Return to NY 94 and turn right, continuing to Washingtonville. Just before center of town is North St. Turn right and drive a couple of blocks to entrance, right, to Brotherhood Winery. Drive in to parking fields.

Return Trip: Go back to NY 94, turning right, into town. Just beyond, NY 208 comes in from the right and joins yours. Almost at once it turns left, crossing the tracks. Follow Rte. 208 south (left) and proceed to jct. with Quickway (Rtes. 6 & 17). Take this east to NY Thruway and return.

Growing Up From Homespun

TRIP C-14. *We'll Visit:*

MUSEUM VILLAGE OF SMITH'S CLOVE, Monroe, N.Y.
(May to Oct. Closed Monday)

DISTANCE AND TOLLS: From NYC Exits, about 55 *m.*, fast speeds. Via G.W. Bridge, $1., via Major Deegan & Thruway, also Hutchinson River Pkwy., $1.25; via Garden State Pkwy., 50¢. Plus return.

FOOD: In Monroe, the Goose Pond, closed Mon. On Thruway above Exit 15, Hot Shoppe. In Museum Village, snacks.

Museum Village of Smith's Clove, Route 17, Monroe, N.Y. 10950. *Open May – Oct. daily 10–5. Adm. $3. adults, 6-15, $1.75. under 6, free. Food: Snack bars, refreshment areas. Tours: Self-guiding, with maps, Notices of daily demonstrations at entrance. Handicapped: Some hilly parts, but walks well paved for wheelchairs; several buildings have ramps.* (914) 782-8247.

There were three stages that a 19th-century village had to go through in the changeover from a homespun to an industrial way of life. During the Age of Homespun everything was produced in the home, so that each family had to know how to create whatever it needed. Next came the Age of Craft Shops, when town specialists worked on raw materials provided by the villagers. Finally we arrive at the Age of Industry, with stores importing products made in distant areas to sell to local people. Here is a village of museums that shows this transition in a graphic and fascinating manner.

We'll visit a log cabin home as it was early in the last century, then in separate buildings we'll see how people did their own weaving, candle-making, cobbling, blacksmithing, broom-making, wood carving. In other displays we trace the gradual changeover to the Industrial Age.

Don't miss the Natural History Exhibit, where we're invited to "please touch" one of the bones of what may be the best preserved skeleton of a Mastodon in the United States. Railroad buffs will enjoy a collection of non-rail steam engines.

The Village is expanding, but is being kept non-commercial in order to preserve the proper atmosphere. However, we may buy products made by the craftsmen. A brochure is available on request, listing seasonal events such as County Art Shows, Flea Markets, Fall Festivals, and Antique Automobile Shows.

FOR THE DRIVER: Take NY Thruway north toward Albany. Pass a Hot Shoppe rest area. Proceed to Exit 16 to Rtes. 6 & 17 (Quickway). Take these west about 4 *m.* to special exit to Museum Village of Smith's Clove.

Return Trip: You do not return to the Quickway the way you came. From parking lot, turn left on NY 17M and follow signs to Rtes. 6 & 17. Take this east to NY Thruway, and return.

For Goose Pond Restaurant, in Monroe: Take road from parking lot, to left; continue through town to light at Lakes Rd. Restaurant is at this jct. Then follow signs to Rtes. 6 & 17 and take them east to Thruway.

Goshen, Original Home of the Hambletonian

TRIP C-15. *We'll Visit:*

HALL OF FAME OF THE TROTTER, Goshen, N.Y.

HISTORIC TRACK

HISTORICAL SOCIETY MUSEUM (Afts., closed Wed. & Sun.)

DISTANCE AND TOLLS: From NYC exits, about 60 *m.*, fast speeds. Via G.W. Bridge, $1; via Major Deegan & Thruway, $1.25; via Hutchinson River Pkwy., $1.25; via Garden State Pkwy. 50¢. Plus return.

FOOD: On Thruway, Hot Shoppe Rest Area. Plus restaurants in Goshen.

Hall of Fame of The Trotter, 240 Main St., Goshen, N.Y. 10924. *Open year around Mon. thru Sat. 10-5. Sun. & hol. 1:30-5. Closed major holidays. Free. For Handicapped, the aisles are wide; much of the display is on one level.* (914) 294-6330.

The former Good Time Stable has been converted into a Hall of Fame dedicated to the trotters that made the town and the state famous. The displays are shown in stalls and former hay chutes; the atmosphere has much of the stimulation and flavor of the races. There are dioramas showing the immortals of the sport. Dan Patch has a special place here, and we can see Hambletonian 10 with his owner. Also on exhibit, the colors of famous drivers. Upstairs are sulkies that show the changes of the years. Children will find this exciting, especially if they have a fondness for horses, and they'll be interested to learn that here is one of the few harness racing tracks where children are welcomed, with adults, since the races are held in the afternoon.

Consider adding to this trip a visit to the nearby Monticello Raceway.

Monticello Raceway. *Harness races: May - Sept. daily. Post time, 8:30 p.m. Sat., Sun. also 2:30 p.m. Adm. $2.50, subject to change.*

Monticello Raceway. *Harness races: Apr.-Sept. daily. Post time, 8:30 p.m. Mon.-Sat., Sun. 2:30 p.m. Adm. $2.50, subject to change.*

Once a year there is daytime racing here, but don't wait for that—this famous track captures much of the atmosphere visitors come to find. Be sure to look for the Messenger oak tree located at the head of the home-stretch, named in honor of the stallion that grazed there in 1801. Originally a third of a mile, the track now is half a mile long. The fact that it was selected as a National Historic Landmark is significant, for this honor is given only to those places that have in some unique way made a definite contribution to American history.

Goshen Historical Society Museum & Library. *Open year around, daily except Wed. & Sun., from 3-6, 7-9. Located across the street from the Hall of Fame of the Trotter. Museum is downstairs. Free.*

Here the devotees of the sport can find historic documents and mementoes, not only on racing but on the village of Goshen as well. They include the original deed to the land that the British owners received from the Indians who first possessed it. Much valuable reference material is available here.

Good Time Park. East of jct. of US 6 and NY 207. *Open year around, for viewing.*

This is the former site of the famous Hambletonian Stake, which in 1957 was removed to Illinois. It is now a one-mile training track.

FOR THE DRIVER: Take NY Thruway north to Exit 16, then Rtes. 6 & 17 (Quickway) west to Exit 124B to Goshen. Turn right, after ramp, onto NY 207 and proceed into town to Main St. Turn right on Main then bear left past the Minisink Memorial and Orange Blossoms Monument. Turn left, still on Main St.; about half a block beyond, right, is the Hall of Fame of the Trotter. Park in street.

Behind it is the Historic Track. Across the street is the Library with the Historical Society Museum.

For a Walking Tour of Goshen, a map is available showing all monuments, famous houses, and location of Good Time Park, which we can pass when we leave. Write to Executive Secretary, Chamber of Commerce, Goshen, N.Y. 10924.

Return Trip: Go back on NY 207 to Quickway (Rtes. 6 & 17). Take this east to NY Thruway and return.

To the Resort Hotel Country

• *We're again approaching a region beyond an average day's round trip from New York City, but still possible to cover on a long drive. Even if you don't expect to be a guest at one of the famous Catskill resort hotels, you'll probably be curious to see them. This is only one of several good scenic drives. For additional suggestions write Monticello Travel Service, 219 Broadway, Monticello, N.Y. 12701. Also write Sullivan County Publicity and Development Committee, Monticello, N.Y. 12701.*

As this is primarily for the enjoyment of the drive, rather than to any single attraction, it will be written FOR THE DRIVER.

TRIP C-16 EXTENSION. *We'll Visit:*

WURTSBORO AIRPORT, SAILPLANING (May be closed in winter depending on weather)

CATSKILL RESORTS

MONTICELLO RACEWAY (May – Sept.)

DISTANCE AND TOLLS: Round trip from NYC exits, about 200-225 *m.* Mainly fast speeds to resort area, then average. Via G.W. Bridge, $1., Major Deegan & Thruway, $1.25, Hutchinson River Pkwy., $1.25, Garden State Pkwy., 50¢. Plus return.

FOOD: On Thruway, Hot Shoppe Service Area. Near Grossinger's, Howard Johnson's. Others in towns along the way.

FOR THE DRIVER: Take NY Thruway north to Exit 16, then Rtes. 6 & 17 (Quickway) west. If adding trip to Wurtsboro for Sailplaning, take Exit 113 to Rte. 209. (Skip first exit marked Wurtsboro.) Turn right (north) on US 209 about 4 *m.* and watch for small sign on road at right, "Airport." Just off this side road is the

Wurtsboro Airport, Wurtsboro, N.Y. 12790. Phone (914) 888-2791.

Open year around daily, 9 a.m. to sunset; sailplaning curtailed in winter depending on weather. Moderate fee for 20-min. ride. Limited craft available, best to reserve in advance.

Whether you want to experience the peaceful, unbelievable quiet of soaring like a bird, or to watch this fascinating sport from the sidelines, you'll find this visit unique. Graceful, slim-lined sailplanes are towed into the air then released to glide, silhouetted against magnificent mountain scenery, finally coming to rest easily back at the starting point. This is becoming increasingly popular.

Return to Rte. 17 and drive west toward Monticello to Exit 105 to NY 42 to Kiamesha Lake. Take Rte. 42 toward the lake, passing the Concord Hotel, and proceed to NY 52.

Turn left at light, onto NY 52 west, toward Loch Sheldrake. Continue to jct. with NY 17 (Quickway). At this jct is Grossinger's. Also a Howard Johnson's.

Continue on NY 52 past the Quickway, to jct. with NY 55 to Swan Lake, to left. Proceed on NY 55 to jct. with NY 17B at White Lake. Turn left here toward Monticello.

Turn left at light, onto NY 52 west, toward Loch Sheldrake. Continue to jct. with NY 17 (Quickway). At this jct. is Grossinger's. Also a Howard Johnson's.

Continue on NY 52 past the Quickway, to jct. with NY 55 to Swan Lake, to left. Proceed on NY 55 to jct. with NY 17B at White Lake. Turn left here toward Monticello.

Monticello Raceway. *Harness racing May – Sept. daily. Post time 8:30 p.m.; on Sat. and Sun. also at 2:30. Adm. $2.50 (subject to change).* If you're lucky, you may see trotters on the track.

Just beyond is the Quickway (NY 17). Take this east to the NY Thruway to New York and return the way you came.

A Good Summer Objective—the Ice Caves

TRIP C-17 EXTENSION. *We'll Visit:*

SAM'S POINT AND ELLENVILLE ICE CAVES (Apr. to Nov.)

DISTANCE AND TOLLS: To Ice Caves from NYC exits, about 100 *m.* Mostly fast speeds. Via G.W. Bridge, $1; via Major Deegan & Thruway, $1.25; via Hutchinson River Pkwy., $1.25; via Garden State Pkwy., 50¢. Plus return.
FOOD: On Thruway, Hot Shoppe rest area. Restaurants and diners along Rte. 209 and in Ellenville.

Sam's Point and Ellenville Ice Caves & Fire Tower. *Open daily, 9 a.m. to dusk, April to Nov. Fees: $2.95 adults. 6-12 $1.25. group rates. Food: Picnic area on top of mountain. Rest rooms at base lodge. Handicapped: The drive and VISTAS are splendid, but don't try the ice caves. Fire Tower: Open weekends Apr. to Nov., plus some weekdays. To climb to top, an observer must be on duty; otherwise you can climb part way. No collecting of nature specimens.* (914) 647-7989.

This natural scenic attraction is located on a 2,255-foot high rocky plateau in the Shawangunk Mountains. However, be advised this is not a paved, neon-lit, urban playground; rather, we are in rough, often undeveloped country with its own rugged beauty. VISTAS take in five states. There are short, easy hikes for beginners; the experienced discover longer, more challenging ones to waterfalls and distant caves.

We climb the mountain by car or on foot, passing the turn-off to the Fire Tower—a long, unpaved stretch good for scrub scenery and some VISTAS. Proceeding past Lake Maratanza, a haven for migrating birds, we're soon at the parking area for the caves.

The ice caves are fascinating. While the quantity of ice therein varies with the weather, even without any ice at all they would be memorable. We must use normal caution, but almost anyone can follow this trail. There are good handrails and the steps are sound. Listen through a crack for the voice of Lost River which spelunkers have traced into the mountain. This tour can be accomplished in half an hour or so, but why hurry? We may never pass this way again. Incidentally, we don't have to reclimb those stairs; at the end, we're surprisingly close to the top.

On to Sam's Point, the ledge from which the original Sam jumped to escape approaching Indians (and lived to tell of it). Trails lead in several directions, one following the very rim of the plateau.

FOR THE DRIVER: Take NY Thruway north to Exit 16; then Rtes. 6 & 17 (Quickway) west for about 30 *m.* to Exit 113 at US 209. Drive north, passing Wurtsboro Airport (sailplaning) for about 13 *m.* to Ellenville. Turn right (east) on Rte. 52 thru town, stopping for VISTAS. About 5 *m.* out of town is road to Ice Cave Mountain, to left. Drive through the artist colony of Cragsmoor to the base lodge and gift shop. Purchase tickets here.

Return Trip: Go back to NY 52, turn left through Walker Valley. In about 45 minutes you're at the NY Thruway south (small additional toll from Newburgh).

Ten Thousand Acres of Mountain Playground

TRIP C-18 EXTENSION. *We'll Visit:*
MINNEWASKA PARK
LAKE MINNEWASKA MOUNTAIN HOUSES

DISTANCE AND TOLLS: From NYC Exits, about 90 *m.*, fast speeds, mainly. Via G.W. Bridge, $1.45; via Major Deegan & Thruway, also Hutchinson River Pkwy. $1.70; via Garden State Pkwy. 95¢. Plus return.
FOOD: Lake Minnewaska Mountain Houses, restaurants, snacks. 2 Hot Shoppes on Thruway.

Minnewaska Park. *Open year around, weather permitting. Small parking fee. Pay officer on duty, or at Ski-Minne. Picnic areas, no fires.*

Hiking trails through a natural forest area include a good stretch along the Peters Kill stream, with some picturesque waterfalls and cascades to augment the trip.

Lake Minnewaska Mountain Houses, Lake Minnewaska, N.Y. 12561. Direct NYC phone: WA 5-5638. *Open year around. Moderate fees for day use, which may be applied to a meal. Food: Restaurant, snacks. Handicapped can enjoy superb scenery, possibly swim or go boating.*

This fabulous resort covers more than 10,000 acres of scenic lakes, cliffs, and woodlands interlaced with miles of carriage roads and hiking trails laid out carefully to make the most of the magnificent views. The first of its houses was built in 1879 by Alfred Smiley; more were added as the need grew and today there is a large and impressive estate where both day and overnight guests are welcomed. Day visitors enjoy all facilities, such as hiking, swimming, boating, canoeing, golf, tennis. Hiking lists have suggestions for those with varying degrees of experience. It's said you can hike over 15 miles without leaving the premises or retracing your steps. All seasons are beautiful here, Laurel Time and Fall Foliage are spectacular.

FOR THE DRIVER: Take NY Thruway toward Albany. Pass 2 Hot Shoppe Service Areas. Continue to Exit 18 at New Paltz. Turn left from ramp onto NY 299 and drive through town. Continue to jct. with US 44 and NY 55, the Minnewaska Trail. Take these ahead (west) through scenery that includes hairpin curves and VISTA points.

Continue, passing on left Minnewaska Park. Just beyond is the entrance to Lake Minnewaska Mountain Houses.

Return Trip: Quickest, back the way you came, remembering to take NY 299, following signs to Thruway, via New Paltz.

Or if it's apple blossom time, early May, or apple-picking season—usually in September and early October—and you'd like to enjoy the spectacular views of the blossoms, or pick your apples at roadside orchards: Start back on US 44 and NY 55 the way you came. However, do not turn on NY 299 to New Paltz, but stay with Rtes. 44 & 55 to jct. with NY 208. Turn right, to Wright Fruit Market. Close by are Dolan's and others. Check on picking fruit.

Continue southbound on NY 208 to jct. with NY 17K. Here you can go left (east) to Newburgh and take Thruway back to NYC. Or continue on 208 through Washingtonville to NY 17 (Quickway) and take that east to Thruway, thence back to city.

By the Blue Waters of Lake Mohonk

TRIP C-19 EXTENSION. *We'll Visit:*

MOHONK MOUNTAIN HOUSE, Lake Mohonk, New Paltz, N.Y.

DISTANCE AND TOLLS: From NYC exits about 80 *m.*, mostly fast speeds. Via G.W. Bridge, $1.45, via Major Deegan & Thruway, $1.70, via Hutchinson River Pkwy., $1.70, via Garden State Pkwy., 95¢. Plus return.
FOOD: 2 Hot Shoppe Service areas on Thruway. Meals & snacks at Mohonk.

Mohonk Mountain House, Lake Mohonk, New Paltz, N.Y. 12561. Phone (914) 255-1000. Direct NYC line: 233-2244. *Open year around for day and overnight guests. Fees for use of picnic areas, gardens, walks. Does not entitle you to use other facilities reserved for regular guests.*

Day visitors not taking a meal park at gate (free), then either hike in (2½ miles) or, for a fee, take shuttle service to the main house. Day guests may stay for meal, but reserve in advance. Fee includes meal, adm. to grounds, parking, and use of parlors, porches and walks.

The evening meal fee includes the evening entertainment. There are no bars. Children admitted for the 2 meals. Handicapped: If coming to dine, may use the building, which has facilities for crutches and wheelchairs. Many walks fairly level.

We're in a 7500-acre wonderland that the Smiley family laid out more than a hundred years ago. Visitors are welcome to enjoy the gardens or hike to Lookout points and Sky Top Observation Tower. Mohonk is used by geology and conservation classes and nature groups. It's a haven for birdwatchers, gardeners, photographers. Rock climbing is available, some people coming from afar to try their skill on the Trapps, a series of rugged cliffs. Climbing can be dangerous and new climbers must pass a safety test. Check at the above address for permit.

FOR THE DRIVER: Take NY Thruway north to Exit 18 at New Paltz. Turn left from ramp and take NY 299 through town. Just beyond, cross small bridge over the Wallkill River; almost at once a road goes right, to Mohonk. Take this, bearing left at fork in road. Shortly is the Gatehouse to Mohonk Mountain House. Drive in to parking area then report to official.

Return Trip: Back through New Paltz the way you came. Take NY Thruway south.

Where the Huguenots Built Centuries Ago

TRIP C-20 EXTENSION. *We'll Visit:*

HUGUENOT STREET STONE HOUSE TOURS, New Paltz (Mid-May to late Oct. Wed. – Sun.)

JEAN HASBROUCK HOUSE

LOCUST LAWN, COL. JOSIAH HASBROUCK HOUSE (Mid-May thru Oct., closed Monday & Tues.)

DISTANCE AND TOLLS: To New Paltz from NYC exits: About 75 *m.* Fast speeds. Via G.W. Bridge, $1.45; via Major Deegan & Thruway, $1.70; via Hutchinson River Pkwy., $1.70; via Garden State Pkwy., 95¢. Plus return.
FOOD: On Thruway, 2 Hot Shoppe Service Areas. In New Paltz, Old Fort Restaurant, closed Monday. Reservations advised.

Stone House Tours. Given by Huguenot Historical Society, P.O. Box 339, New Paltz, N.Y. 12561. (914) 255-1889. *Houses open mid-May till late Oct. Wed.-Sat. 10-4, Sun. 1-4. In summer, also Sun. from 10. Closed 4th of July and rest of year. Each house 50¢, 6-14 yrs. 25¢. Tours of 7 houses and French church at 10 a.m. & 1:30 p.m. Adults $3. Children $2. Groups by appointment. Handicapped: Some steps, but guides will assist you to avoid some of them. Rest rooms in Deyo Hall.*

Twelve families of Huguenots, fleeing from religions persecution, first in northern France, then in the Rhineland, came to this country during the 17th century and settled in this area. They bought their land from the Indians before having the land grant confirmed by the English governor. By 1692 these patentees had begun to build more practical stone houses to replace their original log dwellings. Today we will see a number of their skillfully constructed homes, located on what has been called "the oldest street in the United States with its original houses."

Our tour starts in the Deyo Assembly Hall, formerly a glass factory and now a meeting place and museum in the making. Then we visit the

Abraham Hasbrouck House, begun in 1692 and completed in 3 parts as the family's needs grew; the Bevier-Elting House, from 1698, the Hugo Freer House, 1694-1720, the Le Fevre House, 1799, a reconstructed French Church of 1717, and the Jean Hasbrouck House which is also the Historical Museum.

All of the houses have furnishings of many generations, for all have been lived in continuously since their origin. We'll see heirlooms brought from Europe, early American ware, Victorian pieces of great value. The expert construction is evident throughout in the large, hand-hewn mitered beams, wide floor boards, fireplaces. A Gift Shop includes items with Huguenot crosses, also slides, books, stationery.

Another stone house, the Le Fevre House, (1799) will be open, possibly under a separate fee.

Locust Lawn, Colonel Josiah Hasbrouck House, Rte. 32, New Paltz, N.Y. 12561. *Open mid-May to late Oct. Wed.-Sun. 10:30-4. Adm. $1. 8-14 yrs. 50¢.* (914) 255-1660.

Here is a departure from the nearby stone houses, a handsome 12-room mansion with overtones of the architecture of Washington and Virginia. Built in 1814, it contains furnishings of several periods; fine china ware, pewter, laces, paintings and a good-sized library. Tools of the times are exhibited in the adjacent smoke house, slaughterhouse and carriage house. A bird sanctuary is on the premises.

FOR THE DRIVER: Take NY Thruway north to Exit 18 at New Paltz.

From ramp, turn left on NY 299 and proceed in town to foot of hill and second light, North Chestnut St. Turn right and drive a couple of blocks. There are signs, left, to Stone Houses; turn at second sign, at Brodhead Ave. Cross railroad tracks; just beyond is the Deyo Assembly Hall where the tours begin. Those coming when houses are closed may inspect them from outside; the Jean Hasbrouck House is open year around.

Then back the way you came, turning left on NY 299 to top of hill. Turn right (south) on NY 32 and proceed about 4 *m.* to Locust Lawn, the Col. Josiah Hasbrouck House, on NY 32.

Return Trip: Quickest, go back to New Paltz; turn right on NY 299 and proceed to Thruway south.

Or for a different route, using shunpike roads, especially good for apple blossoms in early May, and for picking our own apples in Sept. and early Oct. Continue on NY 32 to jct. with US 44 & NY 55 (Minnewaska Trail). Take these, right, to jct. with NY 208. Turn left. Just below this jct. are roadside stands and apple orchards; inquire about picking apples at Wright's. Then continue on NY 208 to NY 17K. Turn left on this to Newburgh, and follow signs to NY Thruway south.

Where a Great Naturalist Found Solitude

TRIP C-21 EXTENSION. *We'll Visit:*

SLABSIDES, West Park, N.Y.

DISTANCE AND TOLLS: Under 90 *m.* from NYC Exits, mainly fast speeds. Via G.W. Bridge, $1.45; via Major Deegan & Thruway, also Hutchinson River Pkwy., $1.70; via Garden State Pkwy., 95¢. Plus return.
FOOD: 2 Hot Shoppes on Thruway.

Slabsides, West Park, N.Y. 12493. *Open for viewing, year around, weather permitting, including Woodland Sanctuary and Nature Trails. Limited guided tours led by John Burroughs' granddaughter, Elizabeth Burroughs Kelley. Two Open House days when public invited – 3rd Sat. in May and 1st Sat. in Oct. Fees: None. No picnics. Rest room in cabin but open only for tours. No water at cabin. Gas station at cross-roads.*

This is something more than just a woodland spot where a great writer built a rustic cabin and found solitude. Rather, it is the remarkable result of hard, creative manual labor, for John Burroughs (1837-1921) had decided to convert a marshy woodland area near his home into a garden. When cleared, the results were so attractive that he knew he must build himself a shelter here so that he could camp out and meet with his friends. He and a local carpenter accomplished this, and he even made some of his own furniture.

The scenery is magnificent and there is a feeling of quiet and solitude. Tours are by far the best means of appreciating Slabsides. Led by his granddaughter, they include going through the cabin and getting questions answered by an expert. Postcards, slides, booklets and copies of her biography of Burroughs are available. The family asks that we disturb nothing and take nothing away. As in all forest areas, there can be no smoking, no fires, and no littering. Take only the road directly to the cabin since Lake Drive is private property.

There is a John Burroughs Association composed of friends who made possible the preservation of the cabin, and also a John Burroughs Natural History Society. These hold meetings twice a year and the public is invited to take part.

FOR THE DRIVER: Take NY Thruway north to Exit 18 to New Paltz. After ramp turn right (east) on NY 299 and continue a short way to jct. with US 9W. Take this north (left). A few miles above is West Park. Beyond main part of the small town is a sign, John Burroughs. Turn left here at Park Lane; this becomes Floyd Ackert Road. Stay on this, bearing left; sign, left, indicates Burroughs

Sanctuary. Park along road and walk in about half a mile on Burroughs Drive to the cabin.

Return Trip: Back on US 9W, south to NY 299, turn right to New Paltz and NY Thruway south.

Kingston in the Seventeenth Century

TRIP C-22 EXTENSION. *We'll Visit:*

 THE SENATE HOUSE, Kingston, N.Y.

  (Wed.–Sun.)

 KINGSTON MUSEUM (Same)

 OLD DUTCH CHURCH (Sat. 2–4 in summer)

 KINGSTON WALKING TOURS (May-Oct., 3rd Thurs. at 2)

DISTANCE AND TOLLS: From NYC Exits, about 90 *m.*, fast speeds. Via G.W. Bridge, $1.65; via Major Deegan & Thruway, also Hutchinson River Pkwy., $1.90; via Garden State Pkwy., $1.15. Plus return.

FOOD: In Kingston, Governor Clinton Hotel; Judie's; Dutch Rathskeller; Holiday Inn; Howard Johnson's; Leherb's. On Thruway, 2 Hot Shoppes.

Senate House, 312 Fair St., Kingston, N.Y. 12401. *Open 9-5 all year. Wed.-Sun. Groups reserve in advance.* (914) 338-2786. *Free guided tours. Free parking in adjacent lot; get ticket here or at Museum.*

 The Senate House has a prime place in the beginnings of New York State. Built by Wessel Ten Broeck in 1676 of rock-cut limestone, with one wall of Holland brick, it was already a century old when John Jay opened the first State Court here on Sept. 9, 1777, and the first legislature convened Sept. 10 to Oct. 7, 1777. In the same month the British troops set fire to Kingston but only the roof of this remarkable relic was damaged. Since 1887 it has been owned by the State. Only the porch is "new"–it dates from 1888. This and more you will learn on the tour. The local garden club has restored the gardens, and the collection of children's toys suggests that more intimate activities than legislative debates went on here. House is now a State Historic Site.

 The Museum, adjacent to the Senate House (free) was opened June, 1930. This Dutch Colonial house has many historical objects. Its numerous pictures include marine paintings of the Hudson Valley and portraits by John Vanderlyn, who was born in Kingston.

Old Dutch Church. *Open Sat. 2–4 in summer, or by appointment.*

 This attractive 19th-century church, located close to the Senate House, has several documents of historical value, including a letter George Washington wrote to the church. The first governor of New York State, George Clinton, is buried in the graveyard.

Walking Tour: *From May thru Oct., on third Thurs. afternoons at 2. Also 1st Sat. of June and July 2:00. Donation $1.50. Tours start from the Senate House. No reservation needed.*

These are tours of the Historic Stockade area of 1658, once known as Wiltwyck. They cover about one mile and last 2 hours. All important sites are included, as well as a number of stone houses that have been restored for contemporary living. A network of tunnels was found underneath many of these buildings and identified as part of the Underground Railway. Also included on the tour is Sleight House, the DAR Headquarters.

FOR THE DRIVER: Take NY Thruway toward Albany. Pass 2 Hot Shoppe rest areas. Proceed to Exit 19 at Kingston. Follow signs to Kingston and at rotary take right hand exit marked Washington Ave. passing Howard Johnson's and Holiday Inn. Proceed to the block following the first traffic light on Washington Ave., North Front St., and turn left. Pass several stone houses on way across town. Finally, must turn right at Fair St. At this jct. on left is the Museum and behind it, the Senate House. Metered parking, or inquire at either house.

Continue on Fair St. to Main St. Turn right to the Old Dutch Church.

For Walking Tours: These start at Governor Clinton Hotel nearby. Check at the Senate House or Museum. In the Governor Clinton Hotel is a restaurant; a little beyond, at 395 Albany Ave., is Judie's restaurant. About a block from Senate House on Clinton St. is Kirkland Hotel with a Dutch Rathskeller.

Return Trip: Most direct: From Dutch Church entrance, Main St., proceed several blocks to light at Washington Ave. Turn right and return to rotary. Follow sign to I-87, Thruway, and take this south.

For a different route home: From Dutch Church, continue on Main St. to Washington Ave. Turn left and proceed to Boulevard where signs direct to New York 92 *m.* to right. This is NY 32, and it goes through apple orchard country where trees bloom in early May. A mile or so below town is Leherb's restaurant. Rte. 32 follows the Thruway south most of the way back to the Bear Mountain region. You can stay on Rte. 32 or else pick up the Thruway at New Paltz, Newburgh, or from the Quickway (Rtes. 6 & 17).

In the Catskills

● *We're now up in the Catskill Mountains where most of the attractions are tied in with magnificent scenery. As in the Pocono region, there is such a variety of drives and VISTAS, ski resorts and tourist attractions that almost anywhere we go will be spectacular.*

Three major roads start near the Hudson River then branch out through the mountains. We will take two of these, with an optional trip along the third. The first, NY 28 from Kingston, is the Onteora Trail which passes the Ashokan Reservoir. The second, NY 23A, the Rip van Winkle Trail, runs roughly parallel to this, winding through Haines Falls and the Hunter Mountain region. The third, most northerly route is NY 23, the Mohican Trail from Catskill that takes in Windham Mountain.

Season: Remember these areas are in a different weather pattern from New York City. Spring comes late here; by the same token, two or three weeks before the leaves turn in the fall they'll be at their peak in the mountains.

The World Seen From A Chair Lift

TRIP C-23 EXTENSION. As this trip is primarily for the enjoyment of the drive, it will be written out FOR THE DRIVER.

We'll Visit:

ASHOKAN RESERVOIR

BELLEAYRE SKI CENTER, Highmount, N.Y. (Chairlift July thru Labor Day, Fri., Sat., Sun., weekends through fall foliage)

DISTANCE AND TOLLS: To Ashokan Reservoir from NYC exits, about 100 *m.* To Belleayre about 25 more, mostly fast, some average speeds. Via G.W. Bridge, $1.65; via Major Deegan and Thruway, $1.90; via Hutchinson River Pkwy., $1.90; via Garden State Pkwy., $1.15. Plus return.
FOOD: On Thruway, 2 Hot Shoppe rest areas. At Kingston Exit, Howard Johnson's and Holiday Inn. Near Belleayre, Maison Lafayette.
FOR THE DRIVER: Take NY Thruway north to Exit 19 at Kingston. At Kingston rotary are a Holiday Inn and Howard Johnson's. Follow signs to NY 28 west and proceed about 4 *m.* to where NY 28A branches left. Take this, it's a scenic shunpike road, for 10 *m.* to the Aeration Plant. Drive to the top then turn left along Reservoir.

Ashokan Reservoir is 12 miles long and provides New York City with a large proportion of its daily water supply, sending 1,600 sprays about 200 feet high at the Aeration Plant. Mountains unfold in all directions; cloud formations and reflections in the clear waters are superb. Often when the fall foliage has petered out along the Thruway and across the river, this section will be ablaze with color.

Continue along the Reservoir to where NY 28A again joins you from the left. Go ahead on this a few miles to jct. with NY 28; turn left and soon reach signs to:
Belleayre Ski Center, Highmount, N.Y. 12441. *Open: summer schedule for chairlift: July to Sept. Fri., Sat., Sun. 10-5:30. Weekends in Sept. and early Oct. Fees for chairlift: Adults $1.50, ages 6–12 $1.25, under 6, 25¢. Food: Cafeteria at Base Lodge; snacks in shelter at summit, also outdoor fireplaces. No picnics at base of mountain. Pets: In parking fields only; kept in vehicles or leashed.* (914) 254-5601.
We drive up the mountain to the Base Lodge. Our visit here is primarily for the VISTAS of the surrounding mountains. We can get these in comfort through great picture windows in the Lodge, or we can hike up or ride the lift to the 3,420-foot summit. At the top are picnic grounds and food shelter. Here, too, is the Belleayre Fire Tower, reached either by taking the lift and following signs at the top, by following a trail from the Lodge, or by hiking from the town of Fleischmanns below. This is the tallest tower in the Catskills, although the one at Hunter Mountain has the highest elevation.

On Rte. 28 at Fleischmanns in the Maison Lafayette.
Return Trip: Go back the way you came. For quickest trip, stay on NY 28 directly to Kingston, skipping the Reservoir. At Kingston rotary the Thruway is marked I-87 in several places. Take Thruway south.
Note: To continue to Hunter Mountain and another chairlift (C-24 EXT): Start back from Belleayre on NY 28 but shortly turn left (north) on NY 214. Proceed to jct. with NY 23A. Turn left—Hunter is just ahead.

Woodstock, A Famous Artist's Colony

TRIP C-24 EXTENSION. As this is primarily for the enjoyment of the drive, it will be written out FOR THE DRIVER.

We'll Visit:

WOODSTOCK, N.Y.

HUNTER MOUNTAIN CHAIR LIFT, Hunter, N. Y. (July thru Labor Day, weekends, spring & fall for summer lift.)

DISTANCE AND TOLLS: To Woodstock from NYC Exits, about 100 *m.*, mainly fast speeds. To Hunter Mtn. add about 35 *m.* Via G.W. Bridge, $1.65; via Major Deegan & Thruway, also Hutchinson River Pkwy., $1.90; via Garden State Pkwy., $1.15. On return, add 15¢ toll.

FOOD: On Thruway, 2 Hot Shoppes. At Kingston exit, Holiday Inn, Howard Johnson's. In Woodstock restaurants, snacks. Also at Hunter Mountain.

FOR THE DRIVER: Take NY Thruway north to Exit 19 at Kingston. At rotary are Howard Johnson's and Holiday Inn. Follow signs at rotary to NY 28 west. Proceed to jct. with NY 375 to Woodstock, right, and drive a short distance into town.

Woodstock. For information, write Woodstock Township Chamber of Commerce, P. O. Box 36, Woodstock, N.Y. 12498. *Some activities year around. Summer season, June thru Sept., includes plays, opera, chamber music, arts and crafts.*

This famous artist's colony began in 1902, when Ralph Whitehead, student of John Ruskin, left England in search of a place suitable for a community of artists and craftsmen. By 1906 a summer school was established, and ever since the art center has grown rapidly. Woodstock artists have works hanging in major galleries, including the Metropolitan Museum of Art.

The town is filled with galleries, antique shops, craft guilds, workshops.

The road through town is NY 212. Take this west to jct. with NY 28, turn right briefly to NY 214 to Tannersville. Drive right (north) to jct. with NY 23A, then left to:

Hunter Mountain, Hunter, N.Y. 12442. *Open for summer lift, July thru Labor Day, daily 10–4:30; weekends, from Memorial Day and into Oct., depending on foliage. Fees for chair lift, adults $2.50, 6–12 yrs. $1.25, under 6 yrs. 50¢. Food: Restaurant, snacks, picnic areas.* (518) 263-9223.

We take a 20-minute mile-long ride in a lift to Colonel's Chair, at the summit. It's the longest and highest lift in the Catskills, 3,200 feet above sea level, and the views at the top are striking. From here we can hike to the Fire Tower, or climb 1½ miles farther on a trail to the second tallest peak in the Catskills, 4,025 feet. Hiking is more rugged here than at some of the other sites. Midsummer, GERMAN ALPS FESTIVAL. (Adm. & parking charges.)

Return Trip: Go back on NY 23A through Haines Falls. This village has hotels and restaurants catering to tastes of many countries.

Continue to jct. with NY 32A—this branches right and connects with NY 32. If you miss it, Rte. 32 is just ahead. Turn right (south) on Rte. 32 to the NY Thruway southbound.

A Game Farm in the Catskills

TRIP C-25 EXTENSION. *We'll Visit:*

CATSKILL GAME FARM, Cairo, N.Y. (Mid-April to late Oct.)

CARSON CITY AND INDIAN VILLAGE, Cairo (Memorial Day to Labor Day)

DISTANCE AND TOLLS: To Game Farm from NYC exits, about 120 *m.*, mainly fast speeds. Via G.W. Bridge, $1.80; via Major Deegan & Thruway, $2.05; via Hutchinson River Pkwy., $2.05; via Garden State Pkwy., $1.30. Plus return.
FOOD; On Thruway, 2 Hot Shoppe rest areas. At Game Farm, restaurant. Above Carson City, Bon Fire, closed Tues., Xmas, Jan. & Feb.

Catskill Game Farm, Cairo, N.Y. 12413. *Open, mid-April to late Oct. daily, 9-6. Admission Adults $4.50, 4-12 yrs. $2.25. (518) 943-4475. Small charge for rides. Food: Picnic areas, snacks, restaurant. Handicapped may drive to top parking lot near entrance. A train goes uphill, takes collapsed wheelchairs. Lower level good for seeing animals. Plenty of benches, shade.*

This game farm was started in 1955 as a conservation project to propagate wild species in danger of becoming extinct. About 3,000 animals and birds may be seen, with emphasis on horned and hoofed specimens. What impresses most is the remarkable air of contentment on the part of the occupants. Many roam the mountainside and even those who must be fenced in have ample space. There are two levels, with rather steep walks between them, but a train may be used to the top. We may feed the herds on the lower level with their, not our, crackers. Beyond is the Nursery, where the new arrivals are bottle-fed and on a strict diet; identities and vital statistics are to be seen on a bulletin board. On the upper level are exotic birds, reptiles, a baby elephant, and bear cubs which may be given ice-cream cones. Many deer are roaming among the trees. Playgounds and rides for the youngsters here.

Carson City & Indian Village, Cairo, N.Y. 12413. *Open daily, late June to Labor Day, 9:30–6, weekends from Memorial Day. Adm. $2.99 adults. Under 12, $1.99.* (518) 678-5518. *Plus small charge for rides. Picnics, snacks.*

This is a fairly large place, somewhat reminiscent of vanished Freedomland. A Wild West City, it's also quite picturesque and filled with all the trimmings. These include dancing Indians, shoot-outs among the cowboys, and a circus performance. We ride the stagecoach and if we're lucky, or unlucky, depending on our point of view, we may be held up by the James Boys.

FOR THE DRIVER: Take NY Thruway toward Albany. Pass 2 Hot Shoppe rest areas. Proceed to Exit 20 at Saugerties, about 80 m. above Spring Valley toll booth. Take NY 32 north after ramp and proceed to where signs indicate turn-off for Catskill Game Farm.

Back to NY 32, then left, north, passing Toy City Motel (games, shops). Next to this is Carson City and Indian Village. Also on this route is Bon Fire restaurant.

Return Trip: Back on NY 32 to Thruway south.

Dutch in the Catskills

TRIP C-26 EXTENSION. *We'll Visit:*

BRONCK HOUSE MUSEUM, Coxsackie (Late June to early Sept. Closed Monday)

DISTANCE AND TOLLS: From NYC Exits about 125 m. If adding mountain side trip, under 20 m. farther. Fast and average speeds. Via G.W. Bridge $2; via Major Deegan & Thruway, $2.25; via Hutchinson River Parkway, $2.25; via Garden State Parkway, $1.50. Plus return.
FOOD: On Thruway, Hot Shoppes.

Bronck House Museum, Coxsackie, N.Y. 12051. *Open late-June to early Sept. weekdays except Mon., 10–5, Sun. 2–6. Hourly tours begin at 10 except during noon hour, Sundays at 2. Fees, $1.50. 12-15 50¢. Tours by appointment also in May & Sept.* (518) 731-8386. *Food: Arrange for table in picnic grove with staff at Trading Post. Rest rooms adjacent. Historical research library open by appointment.*

This outstanding museum consists of a group of buildings covering 300 years of living in the Hudson Valley. The first of the dwellings was built in 1663 by Pieter Bronck on land purchased from the Indians, and is called the oldest house in the county. In 1685 a second stone house was added to serve a growing family, and in 1738 a third, this one of brick. All are fine examples of Hudson Valley Dutch architecture. Nothing was created just for exhibition; all are farm buildings adapted for museum purposes. So much research has gone into the project by the Greene County Historical Society, which maintains it as head-quarters, that it attracts experts in many fields.

The houses contain some of the earliest Hudson Valley portraits, and a whole room is devoted to Thomas Cole, his paintings and his equipment. Besides these are a number of other distinctive buildings. They include a Dutch barn, filled with authentic farm tools; a Stepmother's House built in the 1820's for Judge Bronck's second wife when his daughters by his first wife refused to live with her; a Victorian horse barn with a collection of Americana, and the Freedom Barn with 13 sides, after the original 13 states, the only one of its kind. Eight generations after Pieter Bronck came here from Albany (Beverwyck) his heirs donated the buildings.

FOR THE DRIVER: Take NY Thruway north toward Albany. Pass 3 service areas with Hot Shoppes. Take Exit 21 in Catskill, then NY 23 east toward the Rip van Winkle Bridge to jct. with US 9W. Drive north on 9W about 10 m to a group of stone houses and red barns, the Bronck House Museum.

Return Trip: Most direct—return as you came, 9W south to NY 23 then west to NY Thruway southbound.

For an additional drive in the mountains: Back on Rte. 9W to NY 23, then west to Thruway. Continue on Rte. 23, the Mohican Trail, up through E. Windham. Take NY 296, left, to Hunter, and route NY 23A. Turn left on 23A, passing Hunter Mountain with chair lift (Trip C-24 Extension). Continue on Rte. 23A to jct. with NY 32; turn right and proceed to entrance to NY Thruway south, and return.

Along the East Banks of the Hudson

● *Here are lands of great natural beauty, hills and valleys endowed with folklore, Colonial settlements, Revolutionary Memorials, parks and reservations. We'll follow the Hudson River northward through historic Westchester County into Putnam, then Dutchess County. Proceeding inland across the southeastern strip of New York State we reach attractions on the border of Connecticut.*

To reach Area D from New York City and its environs use: George Washington Bridge, Major Deegan Expressway (which becomes the NY State Thruway), Hutchinson River Parkway, Tappan Zee Bridge, and Throgs Neck Bridge from Long Island.

One Exit Point not always found on local road maps is the Hawthorne Circle. To reach this take the Saw Mill River Parkway, the Sprain Brook Parkway (to be completed soon), the Bronx River Parkway or NY 9A north of White Plains.

Main roads: NY State Thruway, Saw Mill River Parkway, Hutchinson River Parkway.

see frontispiece map

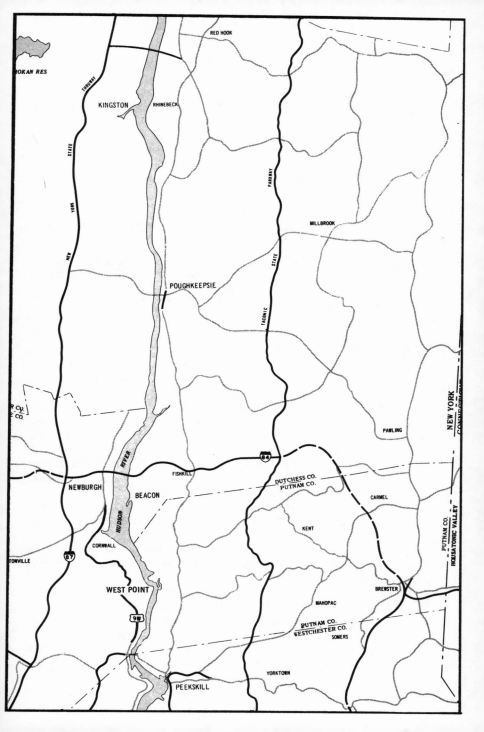

To the Seat of A Dutch-British Manorial Family

TRIP D-1. *We'll Visit:*

PHILIPSE MANOR HALL, Yonkers (Wed.–Sun.)

HUDSON RIVER MUSEUM, Yonkers (Closed Mon. and holidays)

GREEK GARDEN, UNTERMEYER PARK

SHERWOOD HOUSE, Tuckahoe (mid-May to Oct. Thursday, Sunday, holiday afts.)

DISTANCE AND TOLLS: Yonkers is directly north of the New York City line. Via G.W. Bridge, total 60¢; via Saw Mill River Pkwy. from suburbs, 25¢; via Hutchinson River Pkwy. from NYC, 50¢. Plus return.

FOOD: Near Sherwood House, Holiday Inn's Restaurant in the Sky. Restaurants and diners in towns.

Philipse Manor Hall, Warburton Ave. & Dock St., Yonkers, N.Y. 10701. *Open Wed.-Sun. 9-5; free. Groups arrange in advance: Call Mike Griffin, (914) 965-4027. Slide lectures also available, as are children's programs, concerts and demonstrations. Inquire for dates.*

This handsome Manor House was begun in 1682 by Frederick Philipse, a Dutch immigrant who became Peter Stuyvesant's carpenter-contractor and, under the British, first lord of the Manor of Philipsburg. By trading and shipping he became owner of houses, mills, and 90,000 acres on both sides of the Hudson up to Croton. During the Revolution the family remained loyalist and the manor was confiscated. At one time this house was the Town Hall of Yonkers and the northern household wing was stripped to provide a court room and a council chamber. The State of New York became custodian in 1908. It is today a State Historic Site.

Mary Philipse, sister of the lord of the Manor and said to have interested George Washington, was born in this Manor House and married in the east parlor to Captain (later Colonel) Roger Morris of the British Army on January 19, 1758. Two hundred years later the marriage service was reenacted on the spot. The house is largely an art gallery and contains portraits of the Philipses, as well as work by Copley, Gilbert Stuart, Charles Willson Peale, Rembrandt Peale, Benjamin West and other Americans. Also are exhibits of architecture and of the painstaking restoration of the Manor.

Hudson River Museum, 511 Warburton Ave., Yonkers, N.Y. 10701. *Open year around Tues. thru Sat. 10-5. Sun. 1-5, Wed. 7-10 p.m. Free.* Planetarium: *Tues. thru Fri. 3:30 & 7 p.m., Sat. 11:30, 1:30, 3, 4, 7 p.m. (Verify hours). Sun. 1:30, 3, 4, 7 p.m. Adm. fee. Handicapped: several low steps to Museum and Planetarium but wheelchair visitors can manage. Stairs to part of art display* (914) YO-3-4550.

A new $2 million addition to the Hudson River Museum houses a modern museum presenting exhibits in different media, and the Andrus Space Transit Planetarium, computer-driven. A Geophysical room includes space exhibits, a mural of the moon and a rotating globe showing the earth as astronauts see it, all shown under dramatic Black Light for greater effect. In the adjoining building, a large Victorian mansion built in 1879, are permanent exhibits connected with the city of Yonkers and the Hudson River Valley. Here are vast collections of objects from ancient toys to Indian relics; minerals, military displays, art and sculpture from the last century. Hours sometimes curtailed; check first.

Untermeyer Park and Greek Garden. *Open year around daily, dawn to dusk.*

A walled Greek garden, once part of the estate of New York Governor Samuel Tilden and later, of that of Samuel Untermeyer, this unique park contains beautiful walks and VISTAS, with its background of gardens, statues and fountains.

Boyce Thompson Institute for Plant Research, Inc., 1086 N. Broadway, Yonkers, N.Y. 10701. *Open year around Mon. thru Fri., closed holidays. Tours by appointment only.*

The grounds, not far from the Greek Gardens, contain the finest in plantings and may be visited at any time.

Sherwood House, 340 Tuckahoe Rd. at Sprain Brook Pkwy., Tuckahoe, N.Y. 10707. *Open mid-May thru Sept. Thurs.–Sun. 2–5 and by appointment. Fees: Adults $1., school children 50¢. Handicapped: Some climbing.*

One of the few pre-Revolutionary houses in the area, this Colonial farmhouse has been restored by the Yonkers Historical Society. Visitors will see the large fireplace and "beehive" bake oven, exhibits of period costumes, and many fine antiques. In September the holiday special Christmas in Sherwood begins.

FOR THE DRIVER: Via G. W. Bridge, follow signs to Henry Hudson Pkwy. North. Proceed past 2 tolls; after the second this becomes the Saw Mill River Pkwy. Immediately after junction with Cross County Parkway, just beyond, is an exit from Saw Mill Pkwy. to Yonkers Ave. Ramp leads to Ashburton Ave., at light. Turn right.

Via Major Deegan Expressway from N.Y.C. area, northbound: Go to exit to Cross County Pkwy. Take second exit to Pkwy. west to Saw Mill R. Pkwy. At jct. with Saw Mill Pkwy. turn right (north), then immediately exit at Yonkers Ave. Ramp leads to Ashburton Ave. at a light. Turn right.

Via Hutchinson River Pkwy., north to exit 13 to Cross County Pkwy. to Yonkers. Take this, joining parkway just ahead, and go to the end, at jct. with Saw Mill R. Pkwy. At this jct. turn right (north) then immediately exit at Yonkers Ave. Ramp leads to Ashburton Ave. at a light. Turn right.

All: Continue on Ashburton to top of hill. Here, Ashburton turns right, at light, then bears left down hill. Stay on this for about 2-3 m., to Warburton Ave. Left on Warburton. Manor is 3 blocks down. Turn at third light into Larkin parking plaza — metered, free on Sun. (Tour and school buses may park in front of south entrance on Dock St. Ring bell at far door on Warburton side.)

Back on Warburton to Trevor Park and Hudson River Museum, left. Use parking area.

Proceed on Warburton about 1 m. to small Odell Ave., right. Take this uphill to US 9. Turn right on this (south) passing hospital. Just beyond is Untermeyer Park and Greek Gardens.

Turn around on US 9, go north. After Odell Ave. goes right, the Boyce Thompson Arboretum is just ahead on Rte. 9.

Then go back to Odell, and turn left. Proceed across Bronx River Pkwy. to jct., just beyond, with NY 9A; turn right on latter to Tuckahoe Road at overpass. Turn left, following signs to NY Thruway. On left, pass Holiday Inn with the Restaurant in the Sky. Beyond Thruway entrance a sign, right, directs to Sprain Pkwy. southbound. Just before the ramp is a small road, right, and Sherwood House. Drive in to parking area.

Return Trip: For Major Deegan & NY Thruway, from Sherwood House go back to Thruway and take this south.

For Tappan Zee Bridge, back to NY Thruway and follow signs north; this crosses bridge.

For G.W. Bridge and Hutchinson River Pkwy.: Take Sprain Pkwy. south, at Sherwood House. Shortly is jct. with Cross County Pkwy.

For G.W. Bridge, take Cross County Pkwy. west to jct. with Saw Mill River Pkwy. and follow signs, left, to N. Y. This becomes the Henry Hudson Pkwy.

For Hutchinson River Pkwy., take Cross County Pkwy. east to jct. with Hutchinson River Pkwy. To return to city area follow signs to Whitestone Bridge (south). For upper regions, take Pkwy. north, returning the way you started.

To Washington Irving's House and Sleepy Hollow

TRIP D-2. Three major attractions with Tours are listed here because they are located close together. You may prefer to split your trip and visit one or two at a time.

We'll Visit:

SUNNYSIDE, WASHINGTON IRVING'S HOME, Tarrytown

LYNDHURST, Tarrytown

HISTORICAL SOCIETY OF THE TARRYTOWNS MUSEUM (Wed. aft., Sat. a.m.)
PHILIPSBURG MANOR, North Tarrytown
SLEEPY HOLLOW CEMETERY
OLD DUTCH CHURCH

DISTANCE AND TOLLS: From NYC exits about 20-25 *m*, mostly fast and average speeds. Via G.W. Bridge from N.J., 85¢. Via Hutchinson River Pkwy., 25¢. Via Major Deegan & Thruway, 25¢. Via Tappan Zee Bridge toward NYC, 50¢. Plus return.
FOOD: At jct. Thruway and US 9, Howard Johnson's; Hilton Inn. Nearby, Tappan Hill Restaurant. Diners en route.

Sunnyside, West Sunnyside Lane off Broadway, Tarrytown, N.Y. 10591. *Open daily year around 10–5. Closed 3 major holidays. Tours usually 1 hour long; summer weekend crowds may mean delays; midweek visits advised. Fees: Adults $2.25, 6–14 yrs. $1.50. Picnics on grounds. Handicapped: Long path to house, first floor easy but stairs narrow. Comb. ticket to 3 Sleepy Hollow Restorations, $5.75, adults; 6–14 yrs. $3.75.* (914) 591-7900.

Sunnyside was remodelled from a Dutch cottage by Washington Irving, who added the tower wing. He died in 1859. Later additions to the house were removed by Sleepy Hollow Restorations, Inc., originally supported by John D. Rockefeller, Jr. The house contains many original furnishings, including Irving's books. Special Christmas programs held annually. Theme tours of house. Inquire.

Washington Irving Memorial. As we turn into Sunnyside Lane from Broadway we find this wide brick, marble, and bronze memorial at its southwest corner. The work of Daniel Chester French, it portrays bronze reliefs of Rip Van Winkle and Boabdil, King of Granada, flanking a bust of Irving.

Lyndhurst, 635 So. Broadway, Tarrytown, N.Y. 10591. *Open daily year around, May-Oct. 10-5, Nov.-Apr. 10-4. Closed Christmas day. Thanksgiving and New Years. Fees: Adults $2.25, Students & Sr. Cit., $1.25; under 6, free. Handicapped: Some climbing, but you can see a lot on one level. Guided Tours. Most crowded on weekends.* (914) 631-0313.

This Gothic Revival castle, which was home to the financier, Jay Gould, is considered not so much a restoration as a reconciliation. Three different families lived in it, each one contributing its own style in furnishings, and apparently nothing was ever thrown away. Thus, anyone who likes variety in his surroundings will find this place a treasure house of late 19th-century elegance. There are Tiffany glass windows, Gothic furniture, rugs of silk and silver thread, paintings by well-known artists never seen outside this house. There are examples of *trompe l'oeil* (fool the eye) with wood painted to look like marble, ceilings painted to look like wood. The quarters once occupied by Anna Gould, Duchess of Talleyrand-Perigord, are shown.

Lyndhurst Festival, *Summer of Music is held on the grounds from late June to late August, Sat. evenings 8:30. Adm. $3, adults; $1.50, children.*

Museum of the Historical Society of the Tarrytowns, Inc. 1 Grove St., Tarrytown, N.Y. 10591. *Open year around on Wed. 3-5 & Sat. 10-12, only. Other times by appointment. Free.*

Located in the elegant home of the first president of the Village of Tarrytown, built in 1848, this museum deals with local and American history. In the Captor's Room paintings, lithos and documents record the capture of Major John André on September 23, 1780. There is an Indian collection and there are items from the Revolutionary War, the War of 1812, and the Civil War. Children may enjoy the room filled with dolls and doll furniture.

Philipsburg Manor, North Tarrytown, N.Y. 10591. *Open year around daily, 10–5. Fees: adults $2.25, 6–14 yrs. $1.50. Closed 3 major holidays. Tours last nearly an hour; add time for craft demonstrations. Handicapped: Stairs in all buildings, some steep; good handrails; no steps to barn for several demonstrations. Rest rooms in information center and on grounds. Comb. ticket to 3 Sleepy Hollow Restorations, $5.75, 6–14 $3.75. (914) 631-8200.*

This historic place, operated by Sleepy Hollow Restorations, Inc., was begun by Frederick Philipse, the Dutch immigrant who lived in the Manor House in Yonkers. Here he ground grain and shipped it on sloops on the Hudson. He built the south half of the present structure, a stone house of four rooms. His son Adolph, who inherited it in 1702, added the north half. The estate was confiscated after the Revolution because the third lord of the manor had remained a loyalist. All the Beekman accretions of the last century have been removed to restore the Philipse period. Today we see the house, a rebuilt grist mill in full operation, the dam on the Pocantico, and the barn where spinning and weaving are demonstrated.

Sleepy Hollow Cemetery. *Open year around.*

Here is the "sequestered glen" of which Washington Irving wrote, describing it as "one of the quietest places in the whole world." Today the author rests here, and so do William Rockefeller, Andrew Carnegie and many others, famous and little-known. A beautiful drive encircles it. Near the entrance are directions to Washington Irving's grave.

Old Dutch Church of Sleepy Hollow. *Open during summer, 12-4.*

This ancient landmark in Sleepy Hollow stands on a hill that was partly cut away to accommodate US 9, which crosses the Headless Horseman Bridge over the Pocantico River just below. The church was built by Frederick Philipse in 1697 or 1699 for his family and tenants of the Manor. The cupola contains the original bell, with the legend, in Latin: *If God be for us, who can be against us?* Philipse and his wife, Catherine van Cortlandt, are buried under the chancel. Around the church is Sleepy Hollow Cemetery.

FOR THE DRIVER: Take NY Thruway to Exit 9 to Route 9 southbound, just before Tappan Zee Bridge, on east side of the Hudson. US 9 is Broadway in Tarrytown. About 1 *m.* south a small road turns right, past the Washington Irving Memorial; follow this to Sunnyside.

Back to Broadway, US 9, turn left (north) and proceed to Lyndhurst just above.

Continue north on US 9. At jct. with NY Thruway are a Howard Johnson's and a Hilton Inn, with the Pennybridge restaurant. Nearby is Tappan Hill Restaurant. Follow signs.

Continue on US 9, a few blocks to center of town, at traffic light. The street, right, is Neperan Road. Take this for 2 blocks to corner of Grove St., where is the Historical Society Museum.

Back to US 9, turn right. Pass the statue marking the capture of Major André in a small park, left. Continue to North Tarrytown, where US 9 bears left; at the foot of the hill is the Philipsburg Manor Restoration.

Just beyond it, across the highway, is the entrance to the Sleepy Hollow Cemetery and the Old Dutch Church.

Return Trip: Go back down US 9 to Thruway and return the way you started.

In General Washington's Footsteps at White Plains

TRIP D-3. *We'll Visit:*

HAMMOND HOUSE MUSEUM, Valhalla, N.Y. (May thru Oct.,Fri. thru Sun.)

WASHINGTON'S HEADQUARTERS, ELIJAH MILLER HOUSE, North White Plains (Closed Mon. & Tues., also Dec. to Washington's Birthday.)

MILLER HILL RESTORATION

DISTANCE AND TOLLS: From NYC Exits, about 25 *m.* Fast or average speeds. Via G.W. Bridge, 85¢; via Major Deegan & Thruway, also Hutchinson River Pkwy., 25¢. Plus return.

Hammond House Museum, Grasslands Rd., Valhalla, N.Y. 10595. *Open May-Oct., Fri. thru Sun. 2-5. Other days by appointment. Adm. fee, $1. adults, 50¢ children. Handicapped: 1 low step into house. Guided tours.*

Standing at its original site, surrounded still by farmlands and fields, this 1719 house is a good example of a tenant farmhouse. It was built on the landed estate of Philipsburg Manor. Don't be misled by its small size—it is filled with an enormous variety of interesting items including authentic furnishings, especially tools needed for household and farm.

An incident at Hammond House during the Revolution is the subject of a pageant often enacted here. When General Washington called here in May, 1780, a Tory woman hurriedly informed the British. A British captain and squad rushed to capture him, but missing him, took Colonel James Hammond instead and imprisoned him in New York.

Washington's Headquarters, Elijah Miller House, National Historic Landmark, Virginia Road, White Plains, N.Y. *Open from Washington's Birthday to Dec., Wed.-Sunday, 10-4. Free. Guided tours. Handicapped: 1 low step; exhibits on 1 floor.* (914) 949-1236.

Washington slept here; he also made it his headquarters during three Revolutionary War campaigns. Today we may visit this 1738 white clapboard house and see it as it looked in the years when Elijah Miller and his family dwelled here. Everything on view is authentic or an exact duplicate; Washington used the table in the parlor during the Battle of White Plains; the Miller family baked in an oven similar to the model in the kitchen, and still in use for samplings of baked beans, cookies and breads. The house has been undergoing renovation by the Historic Workshop of the Natl. Trust for Historic Preservation in Tarrytown. Re-opened in March, 1979, it now shows the original look of the floorboards, walls, doors and trim. The White Plains Chapt. of D.A.R. owns the furniture and keeps it in perfect condition.

Check here on the Heritage Trail. This takes in the historic sites in the area and includes the Purdy House, 200 years old, and Chatterton Hill. The trail is marked; we can follow it by car or on foot.

In October a reenactment of the Battle of White Plains is held annually at nearby Silver Lake. Get details here. Shortly before Christmas, another celebration shows what the festive season was like back in 1776. George and Martha Washington are on hand to welcome us and we all join in singing carols.

Miller Hill Restoration. *Open year around for viewing. Free.*

Here the final shots of the Battle of White Plains were fired. Restored earthworks show where they were first dug; markers describe where the Redcoats fought in 1776, while a map gives the entire battle diagram.

FOR THE DRIVER: All except those using Hutchinson River Parkway take Saw Mill River Parkway north to exit marked Saw Mill River Road, Eastview. Exit here, turn right and proceed to jct. where NY 100C crosses bridge to left. Take this a short way to Hammond House.

Via Hutchinson River Parkway, go north to jct. with I-287 (Cross Westchester Expressway). Take this west to exit to Rte. 9A. Go north on 9A (right) to jct. with NY 100C. Take this, crossing bridge, and proceed a short way to Hammond House.

All: Continue in the same direction, passing Grasslands Hospital, and proceed down the hill. Near foot of hill, where are several gas stations and motor companies, turn left on Virginia Road. Take this across the Bronx River Parkway at a light, and continue across the railroad tracks then bear right. Just ahead, left, is Washington's Headquarters.

Continue on Virginia Road a short way to where signs direct, left, to the Miller Hill Restoration on top of the hill.

Return Trip: Continue the direction you were going; the road winds back down to Broadway. Turn right; just ahead follow signs, bearing right, to NY 22 south. At this point, signs direct to Hutchinson River Parkway to the left. Everyone else, take Rte. 22 south. A few blocks ahead is jct. with I-287. Take this west for Tappan Zee Bridge, or Thruway to New York. Return the way you started.

Program for a Fine Day and Refreshing Activity

TRIP D-4. *We'll Visit:*

AUDUBON CENTER OF GREENWICH, Greenwich, Conn. (Tues. thru Sat.)

WESTMORELAND SANCTUARY, Mt. Kisco, N.Y.

MIANUS RIVER GORGE WILDLIFE REFUGE, Bedford Village, N.Y. (April to Dec.)

DISTANCE AND TOLLS: To Mianus Gorge (farthest) via G.W. Bridge, 45 *m.*, 85¢; via Major Deegan & Thruway, 40 *m.*, 25¢; via Hutchinson River Pkwy. 30 *m.*, 25¢. Plus return. Add 20¢ toll on return. Fast and average speeds, slow to sanctuaries.

Audubon Center of Greenwich, 613 Riversville Road, Greenwich, Conn. 06930. *Open year around, Tues. thru Sat. 9-5. Closed holidays. Adults $1., children 50¢. Tours: Self-guiding, with maps, or guided by appointment. Handicapped can birdwatch from parking area. Rest rooms. Museum and Gift shop. No pets or picnics allowed in nature study areas.* (203) 869-5272.

This is the place to come for information on just about every phase of nature study. Established in 1942, the 477 acre Wildlife Sanctuary, because of a varied combination of natural habitat, is home to about 90 species of birds and many types of small animals. Trained naturalists conduct classes for hundreds of children yearly; in summers they also hold classes for adults interested in nature and conservation. Nature Trail booklets for walks are available.

Part of the Sanctuary is the nearby Wildflower Sanctuary, 127 acres of trails all marked, leading through different kinds of habitats of both flowers and small animals. Ask for road directions at the Center. Picnics permitted here.

Westmoreland Sanctuary, Box 335, R.D. 2, Mt. Kisco, N.Y. 10549. *Open year around, dawn to dusk. Free. Picnics and pets not permitted. Tours: Weekend guided walks for adults for a 6-week period each spring; ask for list.*

Five miles of trails give adults a chance seriously to study nature. The 115 acres include a number of different habitats. Although not along a regular bird migrating route, quite a few species seem to reach a peak during May, a good time to visit. April, with its warming days, is popular, as is brisk October; Indian summer is beautiful here.

Mianus River Gorge Wildlife Refuge, Mianus River Road, Bedford Village, N.Y. 10506. *Open April 1 thru Nov. daily, sunrise till 5:30. Guided Tours: Naturalists on duty mid-June to Mid-Sept. and on weekends and holidays rest of season. Fees: Donations. Food: No picnic areas, but eating in parking lot permitted. No smoking, or pets. Handicapped: Pretty rugged terrain but birdwatching possible near entrance. Rest rooms near parking lot. Groups on field trips must register 2 weeks in advance.*

A virgin forest of 260 acres has been made into a wildlife and botanical preserve and then left alone to flourish just as it did hundreds of years past. It runs for about a mile and a half along the Mianus River banks and gorge; naturalists have identified over 500 species of trees, shrubs, wildflowers, birds and animals within its borders. Five miles of paths are maintained and lists are available giving several suggested hikes. We may visit Little Tor with its scenic views, an abandoned mica and rose-quartz quarry, and a climax forest of hemlock, some of the trees possibly 300 years old.

FOR THE DRIVER: Take Hutchinson River Pkwy. north a few exits above jct. with I-287, to King St. After ramp follow signs, left, to Armonk. Proceed on King St., where shortly after passing blinking light a small road goes right–Sherwood Ave. Take this to jct. with Conn 128; turn left, proceed a couple of miles to John St. On this corner is entrance to the Audubon Center of Greenwich.

Back to Conn 128, turn right and continue to jct. with NY 22. Turn right (north), past Windmill Farms, then a country club. Soon afterward, small Chestnut Ridge Road goes left; take this about 1½ miles to Westmoreland Sanctuary.

Continue on this road to jct. with NY 172. Turn right and proceed to jct. with

NY 22. Take this, left, to Bedford Village. Here Rte. 22 turns left, but we take road to right, marked Pound Ridge. Proceed briefly to Long Ridge Road, Conn 104, and turn right, toward Stamford. Shortly is Millers Mill Road (unpaved) down hill to right. Cross a bridge to Mianus River Road; turn left about ½ mile to Mianus River Gorge Wildlife Refuge.

Return Trip: Go back to Rte. 104, Long Ridge Road, and turn right toward Stamford. This goes to the Merritt Pkwy. to New York, becoming the Hutchinson River Pkwy.

Historic American Villages

TRIP D-5. *We'll Visit:*

JOHN JAY (BEDFORD) HOUSE, Katonah, N.Y. (Wed. thru Sun.)

BEDFORD COURT HOUSE, Bedford Village, N.Y. (Wed. thru Sun.)

NEW CANAAN HISTORICAL SOCIETY MUSEUM., New Canaan, Conn. (afts. daily, exc. Mon., Sat., Hol.)

WILTON HERITAGE MUSEUM (Thurs., Sun. Closed Aug.)

DISTANCE AND TOLLS: Round trip from G.W. Bridge, 120 *m.*, $1.70; via Major Deegan & Thruway, 105 *m.*, 50¢; via Hutchinson River Pkwy., 90 *m.*, 50¢. On return trip, add 20¢ toll. Mainly average speeds after highways.

FOOD; In Pound Ridge, after Bedford Village, Emily Shaw's Inn, closed Mon. & hol. En route Lambert House from New Canaan, Silvermine Tavern, closed Tues. After Lambert House, at jct. Rte. 7 & Merritt Pkwy., Jolly Fisherman. Also dining places in towns and along Rte. 7.

John Jay (Bedford) House: See Trip D-10.

Bedford Court House Museum, Bedford Village, N.Y. 10506. *Open Wed. thru Sun. 2-5. Closed major Hol. Adm. charge, group rates. Handicapped: Steps into building, more to 2nd floor displays. Check first.* (914) 234-9328.

Our tour of this restored 1787 Court House begins in the court room where 150 years ago John Jay's son, William, was one of the presiding jurists. Typical accoutrements of a court of the stagecoach period surround the bench. Upstairs, besides two jail cells of the original building, is a museum containing memorabilia covering 300 years of town history. The Museum originally was located across the Green in the little stone school, now reopened as a typical one-room schoolhouse of the last century. A map outlining a Walking Tour of the Village is available at the Museum.

New Canaan Historical Society Museum, 13 Oenoke Ridge (Rte. 124), New Canaan, Conn. 06840. *Open daily exc. Mon & Sat., 2-4 p.m.*

Closed Hol. Donations: $1. Under 18, free. Handicapped: You could see some of the museums without climbing. Parking area. (203) 966-1776.

The Historic District of an attractive New England town contains a series of small, well-organized museums with eye-catching exhibits. The Hanford-Silliman House, built in 1761, where we start our Tour is a striking Connecticut Georgian house, now filled with antiques and a noteworthy collection of pewter. Nearby the small Tool Museum holds farm, carpenter and household tools. Another museum is the original studio of sculptor John Rogers and contains many of his Rogers Groups, once so popular in the American household.

A short distance away, down the hill is the Town House where we find a library containing exceptional collections of documents, genealogies, manuscripts and old newspapers on the history of Connecticut. Here, too, is the Costume Museum, showing clothing and accessories mainly of the 18th and 19th centuries, and the Drug Store Museum with late 19th century original merchandise.

Wilton Heritage Museum, 249 Danbury Rd. (Rte 7), Wilton, Conn. 06897. Phone (203) 762-7257. *Tours Thurs., Sun. 2-5. Closed August. Groups by appointment. Donations: Adults $1., children and Senior Citizens, 50¢. Library, office and gift shop open Tues. - Fri., 9-5.*

Built c 1757, this is headquarters of the Wilton Historical Society. Originally the Sloan-Raymond-Fitch House, the name was changed when the Society moved from Lambert House, which it still owns. There are interesting authentic furnishings of the period from 1750 to 1850; the gallery has changing exhibits. Lambert House (1724) is rented to the Hitchcock Chair Co. among others, part of a successful "adaptive use" project where parts of historic houses are leased, to help defray expenses. Many visit Lambert House just to view the historic rooms, now holding Hitchcock furniture.

FOR THE DRIVER: All except those coming via Hutchinson River Parkway: Take NY Thruway to Exit to I-287 toward White Plains. Proceed to the exit to I-684 to Brewster and take this.

Via Hutchinson River Parkway: North to jct. with I-684 to Brewster and take this.

All: Proceed to *second* exit to NY 22, near Katonah. Follow signs NY 22 south, Katonah and Cross River. After ramp, turn right following NY 22 south; at light, this goes to right toward Bedford. Proceed on Rte. 22 for *2m.* to John Jay House, left.

Back on Rte. 22, turn left and continue into Bedford Village, just past jct. with NY 121. In town, Rte. 22 turns right, passing the Village Green. Follow signs to Pound Ridge and Stamford. At this jct., on left, is the Bedford Court House. Park anywhere and walk in town.

Continue on the road to Pound Ridge several miles to jct. with Rte. 137 to Danbury and Stamford. Turn right, toward Stamford. However, for Emily Shaw's Inn, turn left briefly, then return to jct. Proceed on Rte. 137 about a mile then take road branching left to Scott's Corners, passing art and antique shops. Shortly you are on Rte. 124 in Connecticut. This makes a right angle turn onto Oenoke Ridge. A couple of miles ahead, just before the road jogs left, is the New Canaan Historical Society Museum at 13 Oenoke Ridge.

Proceed into town. Just ahead, at second light, follow sign Rte. 106 to left. Continue on Rte. 106 about 2 *m.* to where it makes a right angle turn to the left. We will turn left, but first, for Silvermine Artist's Guild (F-5) and for Silvermine Tavern, turn right at small sign: Silvermine Road. Then return and continue ahead on Rte. 106. Eventually we reach Conn 33 coming from Ridgefield. Turn right, following sign to Wilton on combined Rtes. 33 and 106. Almost at once reach US 7. Turn right, toward Norwalk. Shortly Rte 106 turns left, off Rte 7. Just before this, on right, is the Wilton Heritage Museum. Park in side street, where marked. Then continue down Rte 7. To visit Lambert House, go to corner where Rte 33 branches left. Just beyond is Lambert House, on left, and parking area for Hitchcock Chair Co.

Left again on Rte 7 about 2 *m*, to Merritt Parkway.

Take Merritt Pkwy. to New York—this becomes the Hutchinson River Pkwy. For Tappan Zee Bridge, follow signs at I-287.

To the Largest Public Park in Westchester

TRIP D-6. *We'll Visit:*

WARD POUND RIDGE RESERVATION, Cross River, N.Y.

DISTANCE AND TOLLS: From NYC Exits, about 40 *m*. Fast and average speeds. Via G.W. Bridge, total 85¢; via other NYC Exits, 25¢. Plus return.

Ward Pound Ridge Reservation, Cross River, N.Y. 10518. *Open year around. Museum: Wed. – Sun. 10–4. Parking fees: Westchester residents $1. Non-residents $2. Food: Picnics, cooking; snacks on weekends in season. Guided nature tours for groups. Pets must be leashed.* (914) 763-3493.

Over 4,000 acres of park are spread out across a scenic mountain to provide a great place for families or groups to spend the day. There are about 40 miles of trails, including one to a fire tower, for VISTAS; also, bridle trails, two rivers for fishing—for NY State licensed fishermen— and ball fields. Naturalists and gardeners will want to visit the Meyer Arboretum and Wildflower Garden to see native plants of this area throughout the year. A small but interesting Trailside Nature Museum contains natural history exhibits and has various programs appealing to children. In winter there are Snowmobile trails, a toboggan run, ski touring. Also during the year nature and hobby and sport activities, orienteering tours, Bonsai instruction.

FOR THE DRIVER: Same as for Trip D-5 as far as I-684 exit to NY 22 near Katonah. Follow exit signs to NY 22 south, Katonah and Cross River, and turn right from ramp. Take NY 35 east toward Cross River. At far end of the Cross River Reservoir is jct. with NY 121. Turn right; almost at once on left is entrance to Ward Pound Ridge Reservation.

Return Trip: Back on Rte. 121, right, to NY 35. Turn left, back to jct. with I-684. Can take Saw Mill River Pkwy. here to Hawthorne Circle, or return via I-684 toward White Plains, the way you came.

Superb Land and Water Trip; Cider and Donuts Too

TRIP D-7. As this is primarily for the enjoyment of the drive, it will be written out FOR THE DRIVER.

We'll Visit:

SCHULTZ' CIDER MILL, Armonk

WAMPUS POND, North Castle

MARSH MEMORIAL SANCTUARY, Mt. Kisco

TEATOWN LAKE RESERVATION, Ossining (closed Sunday, Monday)

DISTANCE AND TOLLS: To Teatown from NYC Exits, 40-50 *m.* Fast and average speeds. Via G.W. Bridge, 85¢; via Major Deegan & Thruway, 25¢; also Hutchinson Pkwy. Plus return.

FOOD: In Armonk, Rob Roy, Cider Mill Inn (closed Tues.). In Mt. Kisco, Kittle House, closed Mon.

FOR THE DRIVER: Same as for Trip D-5 as far as I-684 northbound toward Brewster. Drive about 4 *m.* to exit marked Westchester Airport and Rte. 120. After ramp turn left (north) on Rte. 120 and proceed to jct. with NY 22 at Kensico Reservoir. Continue on Rte. 22 following signs to Armonk, turning right at next light. Watch on left for small road and sign "Left lane must turn left." Take this road—Old Rte. 22. Just beyond a Garden Center is Rob Roy's restaurant. Continue on same road briefly to:

Schultz' Cider Mill. *Open year around. Roadside stand, snacks, coffee, cider. On weekends, only, home-made donuts. Adjacent to Cider Mill Inn (Closed Tues.).*

Continue to next corner and stop sign at NY 128. Turn left (north) and drive a couple of miles to:

Wampus Pond. *Open year around for various acitivities, daylight hours. Parking fees: Weekdays June thru Aug. 50¢; weekends and holidays, May thru Sept. $1. Fees for activities. Food: Picnics. Rest rooms. Pets must be leashed.*

A small, scenic park provides sports: rowing, fishing (State license required), and hiking. In winters, ice skating when red ball is displayed. No swimming.

Continue the direction you were going, for several more miles to jct. with NY 117 by Calico Corners (store). Turn right on 117 toward Mt. Kisco. For Kittle House restaurant, turn left on 117 briefly, then return. Just before main part of town, take NY 172 to your right. Just beyond the local park (for residents only) is the entrance to the next attraction. Park off the street, or on McLain St. to your left.

Marsh Memorial Sanctuary. Mailing address, Byram Lake Rd., Mt. Kisco, N.Y. 10549. *Open year around, daylight hours. Donations. Hdq. on Rte 172. Phone (914) 241-3363. Nature Museum & reference library open Tues.-Fri. or by appointment. Weekends, plays, concerts in amphitheatre. Handicapped: The Blind may touch flowers. Handicapped can birdwatch.*

On a rustic hillside surrounded by blossoming shrubs and wildflowers stands, of all unlikely things, a small natural Greek amphitheatre. Built in 1913, it is the setting for a number of activities both cultural and botanical. The sanctuary has two parts. Brookside, the more formal one, has 22 acres of gardens and trails. The other consists of 3 acres of marshland, reached by car by continuing past the sanctuary to Sarles St., turning right to Byram Lake Road, then right again: signs just ahead. The latter section is for more serious study of plant and bird specimens to be found in this largest fresh water marsh in Westchester.

Go back past Brookside on NY 172 the way you came. Take NY 117 to your right, into town. Watch for signs to NY 133, going left, toward Saw Mill River Pkwy. Take this, crossing a bridge. Immediately turn right, on Kisco Ave. Proceed on this to Pines Branch Road and bear left to jct. with NY 134 at Croton Lake.

Turn left on 134; shortly you pass the Kitchewan Field Station (open by appointment.) Continue for 3 miles; just after your road goes under the Taconic Pkwy., several smalls roads go to the right. One is Spring Valley Road. Take this briefly to the next stop.

Teatown Lake Reservation. Spring Valley Rd., Ossining, N.Y. 10562. *Open year around Tues.–Sat. 9–5. Sun. 1–5. Closed Mon. Free. Picnics in designated areas. Fires by permission only. Handicapped: A good deal of walking, not very level; could do birding near entrance. Fishing by permit, $1.25. Boats for rent.* (914) 762-2912.

This serene woodland area is operated, along with nearby Kitchewan Field Station, by the Brooklyn Botanic Gardens. Here the public is welcome at all times, but at the Field Station, we visit by appointment only. There are 8 miles of trails at Teatown, with six different walks laid out covering meadows and marshes as well as lakeside. We'll find something attractive in every season including winter. For those who have never taken a nature walk, this might be a good place to start.

Return Trip: Go back to jct. with NY 134 and turn left briefly to the entrance to the Taconic Pkwy. south to Hawthorne Circle. For Tappan Zee Bridge, NY Thruway and Henry Hudson Pkwy., take Saw Mill River Parkway south, following signs to your exit. For Hutchinson River Pkwy., at the circle, go ahead on Taconic southbound toward White Plains. Soon pick up signs to Hutchinson River Pkwy.

To the Manor House of the Van Cortlandts

TRIP D-8. *We'll Visit:*

VAN CORTLANDT MANOR, Croton

CROTON POINT PARK

CROTON GORGE

DISTANCE AND TOLLS: From NYC exits, about 30 *m.*, mainly fast speeds, average after Pkwys. Via G.W. Bridge 85¢; via Major Deegan & Thruway, 25¢; via Hutchinson River Pkwy. 25¢. Plus return.

Van Cortlandt Manor, Croton-on-Hudson, N.Y. 10520. *Open daily 10-5; closed 3 major holidays. Fees: Adults $2.25, 6-14 yrs., $1.50. Tours include both Manor House and nearby Ferry House, last about one hour. Food: picnic areas. Handicapped: Some on crutches might manage stairs into house; others can see parts on lower level. Long brick walk okay for wheelchairs; if slippery, a road runs parallel. Comb. ticket to 3 Sleepy Hollow Restorations, 6–14 $3.75, adults $5.75.* (914) 591-7900.

There is a flavor here that puts the visitor right back among the members of the bustling family that once lived in this Dutch Manor House. Part of the house was already standing when Stephanus Van Cortlandt acquired a patent to the Manor in 1697, when he already owned 200 square miles of land! In 1953 John D. Rockefeller, Jr., bought the house and land, now down to 20 acres, and it has been restored to 18th century decor. We'll watch demonstrations of crafts and cooking, and examine priceless antique furnishings, many from the original estate. Then we'll go down to the atmospheric Ferry House. The Van Cortlandts operated a ferry across the Croton River and were required to provide food and lodging for their passengers. Thus we find the picturesque structure with its Tap Room for the noisier, bawdier crowd, and a Common Room reserved for meals and for games for the quieter patrons. At Christmas time the house is decorated in 17th century style and a Candlelight Tour gives visitors a chance to see how things used to be. A Sleepy Hollow Restroation. Many special events year around.

Croton Point Park, Harmon-on-Hudson. *Park open year around, beach in season. Activities include swimming, mid-June thru Labor Day, 10-8; hiking, speedboating, ball games, use of driving range. Parking, May thru Sept. weekdays 50¢, weekends and holidays, $1. Beaches: Weekdays, adults 50¢, children 25¢; weekends and holidays, adults 75¢, children 50¢; without use of bathhouse 25¢ for all. Food: Picnics, cooking; snacks. Pets must be leashed.*

A large and popular recreation center of more than 500 acres, this park is quite scenic, even if the current approach to it is not. There are fine views up and down the river, and in winter we often can see ice-boating. It was off this point, in September, 1780, that the British man-of-war *Vulture* lay at anchor waiting to pick up Major John André after his secret interview with Benedict Arnold near Haverstraw. But Americans on Verplanck's Point opened fire with a small cannon and forced the ship to drop down. This made André take the land route, during which he was captured at Tarrytown.

Croton Gorge. *Open year around. Fees: Presently none, eventually, parking fees same as for Croton Point Park. Food: Picnics.*

This comparatively new, still undeveloped park has a remarkable attraction. With proper cooperation from nature, water pours down from Croton Lake above and roars past us toward the Hudson. We climb or drive to the top for an exciting view.

FOR THE DRIVER: Exit Point for all: Hawthorne Circle. Take NY 9A and drive north about 7 miles from circle to jct. with US 9, near Hudson River. Turn right (north) across the small bridge; immediately take the exit and follow signs to Historic Van Cortlandt Manor, bearing right from ramp, then right again, down dead-end street.

Return to jct. with NY 9A where you left the highway. Turn left, but go underneath Rte. 9 and continue straight ahead across railroad tracks. Proceed to Croton Point Park.

Back to NY 9A and the corner where you turned right for the Manor. This time turn left on 9A and proceed briefly to jct. with NY 129. Turn right (east) for 2 m. and watch on your right for a high, gray stone dam; just below is entrance to Croton Gorge Park.

For another view of this, continue on NY 129; almost at once a road branches right. This will take you across the top of the dam, for views. Then go back to NY 129 and turn left.

Return Trip: Back on NY 129 to jct. with US 9 south. Take this briefly, then branch left on NY 9A and return to Hawthorne Circle.

To a Nuclear Power Plant, Explained by Experts

TRIP D-9. *We'll Visit:*

GEORGE'S ISLAND, Crugers

INDIAN POINT ENERGY EDUCATION CENTER, Buchanan
(by appointment only)

BLUE MOUNTAIN RESERVATION, Peekskill

DISTANCE AND TOLLS: To Blue Mountain from NYC exits, about 35-40 *m*. Via G.W. Bridge, 85¢; via Major Deegan & Thruway, 25¢; via Hutchinson River Pkwy., 25¢. Plus return trip.
FOOD: Before entrance to George's Island, Springvale Inn.

Springvale-on-the-Hudson, Crugers, N.Y. 10521.

While not part of our trip, this residential apartment hotel for both senior citizens and younger transients is the scene of the Springvale Annual Rose Days. Inquire for dates. There is a restaurant here, open to the public.

George's Island, Crugers, N.Y. *Open year around. Fees: Parking weekends and holidays May thru Sept. $1; weekdays, June thru Aug. 50¢. Boat launching, small craft, maximum 21 ft. $1. Food: Picnics, cooking. Handicapped can watch launching activity. Parking lot is close to wildlife area (river marsh) for birdwatching or nature observation. Hiking paths pretty hilly and rugged. Picnic areas and rest rooms near parking lots.*

This particularly scenic small park has a lot going for it. There is the activity at the launching ramp and children's playgrounds; hiking trails extend along the crest of rocky shores that include intriguing little coves and patches of beach. Many species of small wildlife and birds can be found in the nature area. There are three different picnic grounds with circular picnic shelters for cookouts in all weather. Just remember this park is small and popular.

Con Edison Indian Point Energy Education Center, Buchanan, N.Y. 10511. Phone: from N.Y.C., 460-6910; other: (914) 737-8174. *Visits by appointment only, Tues.-Sat. 10-5, incl. most hol. Check summer schedule. Tours last 2-2½ hours. Come alone, with small group, or larger — 50 or more.*

Here is a splended opportunity to learn from experts the latest facts about our environment and the source and use of energy as related to electrical power. A handsome Education Center contains a movie theater where we watch films on nuclear power generation and conservation. We may look through windows of a simulator room and see operators being trained to run nuclear power plants, using computer-controlled situations to evoke rapid response. In an outdoor Plaza are exhibits graphically showing the production of energy and its use in the American home. Also here are tubes trained on various structures in the adjacent nuclear power plant. There are 3 plants on the premises, the first, called No. 1, in use since 1962 and the latest, No. 3, since 1976. The history and ecology of the Hudson River Valley is described in displays outside the center.

Blue Mountain Reservation, Peekskill, N.Y. *Open year around. Beaches, mid-June thru Labor Day, 10-8. Fees: Parking weekends, May thru Sept. $1; weekdays June thru Aug. 50¢; beaches, weekends and holidays 75¢ & 50¢; weekdays, 50¢ & 25¢. Without use of bathhouse, always 25¢. Fees for activities. All fees subject to change. Food: Picnics, cooking. Snacks in season. Handicapped: No pavement, but accessible if you can manage parks.*

Two of Westchester's highest peaks are within this forest preserve. We can hike to Blue Mountain and Mt. Spitzenberg; or if we prefer, there are bridle paths and we may ride up instead. Bathing is in Lounsbury Pond. Good hiking; playfields. In winter, ice skating when red ball is displayed.

FOR THE DRIVER: Exit point for all: Hawthorne Circle. Take NY 9A at the Circle and drive north about 7 m. to jct. with US 9 where roads merge. Turn right and continue on US 9 along the Hudson to the exit marked Montrose and Buchanan. Turn left and proceed on NY 9A north. Soon comes Springvale-on-the-Hudson.

Continue on Rte. 9A past the Veterans Hospital; just beyond is the road, left, to George's Island. Follow signs.

Go back to NY 9A; turn left and continue a short way to a group of traffic lights; at third light, on Bleakley Ave., turn left and follow signs for about a mile to the Con Edison Atomic Plant.

Return to NY 9A; turn left and drive to Welcher Ave. Turn right and proceed up the hill, crossing Washington St. Signs here direct you to the Blue Mountain Reservation.

Return Trip: Back to US 9 south and drive to turn-off where NY 9A branches left, then take this back to Hawthorne Circle.

Parks and Houses East of the Hudson

TRIP D-10. *We'll Visit:*
MOHANSIC STATE PARK, Yorktown
KATONAH GALLERY (Sun., Tues.-Thurs. afts. Fri., Sat. all day)
JOHN JAY HOUSE (BEDFORD HOUSE), Katonah (Wed.-Sun.)

DISTANCE AND TOLLS: From Hawthorne Circle about 35 *m.* to Jay Homestead. Mainly fast and average speeds. Via G.W. Bridge, 85¢; via Major Deegan & Thruway, also Hutchinson River Pkwy., 25¢. Plus return.
FOOD: On Rte. 202 above Mohansic Park, London Inn in Yorktown Motor Lodge. Diners en route.

Mohansic State Park, Yorktown, N.Y. *Open year around. Boating, Mem Day to late Oct. Swimming, late June to Labor Day. Fees: Parking in season, $2., swimming fees. Fee for boating. Food: Picnics, snacks in season. Pets leashed.*

A well-groomed park set on a hill overlooking a scenic lake, especially popular for group outings. Swimming is in a pool; the lake is used for boating and fishing. Baseball fields may be reserved, for a fee. Good picnic grounds.

Katonah Gallery, 28 Bedford Rd., Katonah, N.Y. 10536. *Open Sun., Tues.-Thurs. 2-5. Fri., Sat. 10-5. Free.*

Recently moved into a new modern building, this is an attractive setting for both interesting exhibits and well-researched background material. Exhibits are changed monthly and include painting, sculpture, and various types of museum pieces.

John Jay Homestead, State Historic Site (Bedford House) NY 22, Katonah, N.Y. 10536. *Open year around Wed.-Sun. 9-5, closed 4 major holidays. Free. Guided tours. Handicapped: Steps into house, but much on 1st level.* (914) 232-5651.

John Jay was our first Chief Justice. He negotiated the treaty with England in 1794, was Secretary of State and Governor of NY State. His descendents lived here continuously until 1958, when Westchester County bought the house and gave it to the state. The original farmhouse was built in 1788; the homestead seen today was rebuilt by Jay in 1800 and to it he retired. Furnishings are early 19th century. The wallpaper was reproduced from the original, discovered under five layers. The 18th century oil paintings include a number by John Trumbull and one by Gilbert Stuart. Mementoes and gifts Jay received during his career are displayed. Surrounding the house are fine plantings of trees and a garden.

FOR THE DRIVER: From Hawthorne Circle, take Taconic State Parkway north about 14 *m.* to Mohansic State Park. Exit is off parkway.

Take Taconic Pkwy. north to next exit, at US 202. At this jct. is the London Inn, at Yorktown Motor Lodge. Follow signs from ramp toward Yorktown, on 202.

When NY 118 comes in from right turn right (south) and proceed to Croton Lake. Turn left to traffic circle and jct. with NY 100. Take Rte. 100 north toward Somers 4 *m.* to jct. with NY 35. Turn right (east) to Katonah. Shortly, take NY 117 into Katonah, right. A few blocks ahead, in the center of town diagonal to you is the Katonah Village Library. The Katonah Gallery adjoins this. Park in street.

Go back to Rte. 35, turn right (east) and follow signs to NY 22 south to Bedford. About 2 *m.* ahead on Rte. 22 is the John Jay Homestead.

Return Trip: Go back the way you came on Rte. 22 to exit to Saw Mill River Parkway. For Hawthorne Circle, take Saw Mill River Pkwy. to the circle. For Hutchinson River Pkwy., start on the Saw Mill, but change to I-684 to White Plains. This goes to jct. with the Hutchinson Pkwy.

Note: At the Jay Homestead you are at the start of Trip D-5 to some historic houses and towns.

Two Enterprises That Have Influenced American Life

TRIP D-11. *We'll Visit:*

READER'S DIGEST, Pleasantville (Weekdays most of year)

CIRCUS MUSEUM, Somers (Fri. aft., Sat. a.m.)

HAMMOND MUSEUM AND ORIENTAL STROLL GARDENS, North Salem (Gardens, late May to late Oct., Wed. thru Sun. Museum, late May to late Dec.)

DISTANCE AND TOLLS: From NYC Exits about 50 *m.* Mainly fast or average speeds. Via G.W. Bridge, 85¢; via Major Deegan & Thruway, 25¢; via Hutchinson River Pkwy., 25¢. Plus return.

Reader's Digest, Pleasantville, N.Y. 10570. *Open year around weekdays 8:30-4, closed holidays. May close Fridays in May and one Fri. in midsummer—inquire first, phone (914) RO 9-7000, ext. 2200. Adult must accompany children under 12. Free. Guided tours by appointment, 10-3, exc. at 12 noon, last 1 hour each; reservation advised, especially for groups. Handicapped: a good deal of walking on tour; elevators, no ramps. Rest rooms.*

Persons driving along the Saw Mill River Parkway in Westchester long have been familiar with the outlines of the red brick buildings grouped around one with a handsome white cupola—headquarters of the world's most widely read magazine, the *Reader's Digest*. It is the objective of thousands of visitors each year and we may join some of them in a tour of the editorial and executive offices and the employees' lounges. Besides the luxurious furnishings, many of them antiques, we'll find a notable collection of French Impressionist and Modern paintings. We won't see the presses at work, for the printing is not done on these premises.

Circus Museum, Elephant Hotel, Somers Town Hall, Somers, N.Y. 10589. *Museum open Fridays 2-4 p.m., Sat. 10-noon. Free.*

Show Biz history was made in this small town. Once the center of a thriving cattle industry, it won national attention when a farmer named Hachaliah Bailey came into possession of an elephant, Old Bet, the second ever seen in the United States. His brother, a sea captain, had bought her in London and landed her at Ossining on the Hudson. The elephant caused such a sensation that Bailey exhibited her on tour for a fee. In Maine a farmer shot and killed Old Bet, which had ravaged potato fields. In a short time most of Bailey's neighbors started road shows. From his profits Bailey built the Elephant Hotel. This is today the Town Hall and in it is the Museum, with old circus posters and paraphernalia. In 1829 Bailey raised a monument to Old Bet opposite the Town Hall, an effigy made of wooden blocks standing high on a granite plinth.

Hammond Museum and Oriental Stroll Gardens, Deveau Road & Route 124, North Salem, N.Y. 10560. *Museum open late May to Dec. Wed. thru Sun. 11-5. Gardens, late May to late Oct. depending on weather, Wed. thru Sun. 11-5. Fees: Adults $1.50 to Museum, $1.50 to gardens; children under 12, $1. to each. Groups by reservation. Food: No picnics. Lunch, by reservation (for visitors to museum or garden, only) $7.50, incl. tips & tax. Served 12 noon-2 p.m., Sun. 1-3. Fri. & Sat. candelight dinners, 7-9:30.* (914) 669-5033. *Handicapped can use ramps into building; restrooms adapted for wheelchair visitors and their attendants. Garden paths of gravel but fairly level, with occassional benches.*

Here, apart from the rush of life, we can contemplate without pressure while we stroll through a miniature world carefully created to give the illusion of distance. We'll come upon a series of gardens, each with a different theme, including a Waterfall Garden—here the water runs from east to west into the lake, to conform with tradition—a Dry Landscape Garden with blue lava stones representing water, and miniature plants that give the effect of banks of a river. Across a small stone bridge is an island garden where sits Jizo, patron saint of children. The Zen Garden is of white gravel and lava rock grouped to symbolize heaven, man and earth, showing how each is separate yet all are part of the same universe.

The Museum of the Humanities, adjacent to the Gardens, is a showcase for art treasures from around the world collected by Natalie Hayes Hammond. Each year the exhibits have a different theme, the topic being selected for universal appeal and prepared with care. In its Guildhall are presented concerts, lectures, documentary films, ballets, period plays and masques.

FOR THE DRIVER: Exit Point for all: Hawthorne Circle.

Take Saw Mill River Pkwy. north toward Brewster to traffic light at Roaring Brook Road and Reader's Digest Road. Turn right and proceed to *Reader's Digest* headquarters.

Back to Saw Mill River Pkwy., turn right, continue to jct. with I-684. Continue north on I-684 to jct. with NY 116. Turn left on Rte. 116 into Somers and jct. with NY 100 and US 202. Turn left on these to where they branch; here is the Town Hall and monument to Old Bet.

Go back to Rte 116, turn right and proceed past I-684 and the Titicus Reservoir.

If skipping Somers, take NY 116 from I-684 right, toward Purdy's.

All: At far end of Reservoir a side road, right, gives opportunity for a visit to the Tool Shed Herb Nursery. Then continue on Rte. 116 toward North Salem. At top of hill is NY 124; turn left on this, passing June Farm Nursery. About a block beyond is Deveau Road, right, and sign to Hammond Museum.

Return Trip: Back to Rte. 124, then left briefly to Rte. 116. Turn right, passing the reservoir to I-684. Go south on this. Here you have a choice: For Hawthorne Circle, follow signs to Saw Mill River Pkwy. south. For Hutchinson River Pkwy., follow signs to I-684 south to White Plains, to jct. with Hutchinson River Pkwy.

From Maryknoll Seminary to Beautiful Boscobel

TRIP D-12. *We'll Visit:*

MARYKNOLL SEMINARY (tours by appointment, Wed., & most Sun. afts.)

GRAYMOOR

DICK'S (DIX) CASTLE, Garrison

BOSCOBEL (March thru Dec., closed Tues.)

FOUNDRY SCHOOL MUSEUM, Cold Spring (Wed. & Sun.)

CLARENCE FAHNESTOCK MEMORIAL STATE PARK

DISTANCE AND TOLLS: To Fahnestock Park (farthest point) from NYC exits, about 60 *m.*, fast or average speeds. Via G.W. Bridge: bridge 50¢, Pkwys. 35¢; via Major Deegan & Thruway, 25¢; via Hutchinson River Pkwy., 25¢. Plus return.

FOOD: In Peekskill above Maryknoll, Lamplighter (in motel). Near rotary above Peekskill, Oldstone Inn, closed Tues. Between Graymoor and Dick's Castle, Garrison Inn, closed Mon. & Tues. En route Fahnestock Park, Bird & Bottle, closed Tues. in summer, Mon. & Tues. in winter, and Jan.

Maryknoll Seminary, Maryknoll, N.Y. 10545. *Open daily, year around. Visiting days: Sundays, except the first in each month, and Wednesdays, 1-3. Groups make tour reservations 2 weeks in advance. Tour lasts an hour. Handicapped: some steps.*

Two groups are located here. On the east property is the Maryknoll Sisters' Mother House; for tours of this, write to Sister Marguerite Tighe. On the west property the Catholic Foreign Mission Society of America recruits young men for the priesthood and the Brotherhood, trains them for work in foreign missions and supports their work there. At administrative headquarters we can inspect the large collection of publications for mission education. The Tour includes the upper cloister where the Quadrangle below us and an infinity of splendid views may be seen. This is the scene of the annual Maryknoll Departure Ceremony when the Japanese temple bell is rung and the young priests leave for duty in missions in foreign lands.

Graymoor: Franciscan Friars of the Atonement, Graymoor, Garrison, N.Y. 10524. *Open year around daily. Pilgrimage schedule: First Sun. in June to last Sun. in Oct. Sunday Masses, 10:45, 11:45, 12:45; weekday Masses from June thru Oct. daily, 11 a.m. Outdoor service held at 3 p.m. Sundays. Group tours, guided, may be arranged at entrance; individuals may make their own pilgrimages. Anyone may visit without taking the tour. Food: Picnic area always open, cafeteria open Sundays only, June thru Oct. Handicapped: Some climbing in bldgs., but much to see outside. Outdoor services easily reached. Benches, paved walks, shade. Rest rooms. Gift shop.*

Situated on the top of a high hill and commanding a magnificent view is the Mount of Atonement, home of the Graymoor Friars. Pilgrims from around the world come here, many to attend services. The Tour includes the Pilgrim Shrine to St. Anthony, Our Lady of Atonement Chapel, the Hall of Memories, the Corpus Christi Cross, and the Crucifixion Group, where pilgrims may make the Stations of the Cross.

Dick's (Dix) Castle. Route 9D, Garrison, N.Y. 10524. *Open year around, weather permitting, 9 to 6. Art Gallery, Friday. Adm. $1, children 50¢. Handicapped: 2 steps into Castle; no need to climb to top. Picnic grounds.*

This one you have to see. "A photographer's paradise," they

advertise, and they're right. We'll climb through a unique structure that was a ruin before it was completed. Early in the century the Dick family began building a castle modeled after the Spanish Alhambra. After spending nearly $3,000,000 they were forced to give up the project due to business reverses. The castle remained on its hilltop while vandals destroyed great chunks of its ornamentation, tramps spent nights on its floors, and the building became a crumbling, photogenic ruin with Moorish characteristics.

Anton Chmela and his family own the castle and are living in it while transforming it into a museum of American industry. Members of the family will serve as guides. We climb narrow, winding staircases to different levels of the structure, look down into the lush courtyard gardens with their gay flowers and vines and pigeons. New: A popular Historical Miniature Museum includes 250 regiments of 2 1/8 in. soldiers garbed in authentic uniforms of the 1880-1914 prewar days. Museum gift shop sells foreign and domestic items related to many conflicts. Also are a modern art gallery and in summer, concerts and movies.

Boscobel, Rte 9D, Garrison-on-Hudson, N.Y. 10524. Phone (914) 265-3638. *Open March thru Dec. daily exc. Tues., Thanksgiving & Christmas. From April thru Oct., 9:30-5. Nov., Dec. & March, until 4. Fees: Adults, $3. under 21, $1.75. Tours last about 45 min. Gift Shop. Handicapped: Grounds and gardens accessible. However, the Mansion has steps outside and in. Slippers will be provided all visitors with spike heels, which damage floors.*

The picture-book house resembles a classical villa and is filled with rare and beautiful antiques, its rooms ornamented with flower-garland trimmings. This is the "beautiful wood", *bosco bello*, or, if you prefer, Boscobel.

Its builder, States Dyckman, wanted the finest of everything for his Dream House and despite his wife's pleas for economy, spared no expense. This, he told her, would be their "last sacrifice to Folly". Today we can be glad that he had his way.

Both the building and its furnishings were patterned after the style of Robert Adam. The Adam influence is delicate, flowery, pleasing to the eye. The mantels and moldings are exquisitely designed; outside across the portico are carvings resembling graceful draperies of wood.

Many furnishings are part of Dyckman's original collection, including a large library. Our tour ends in the kitchen where we can compare labor-saving devices of the time with ours of today. Following this we may walk about the picturesque grounds, orchards, and Orangerie.

Boscobel was reopened in 1977 after a number of changes. There is now a New York Federal style in some of the furnishings, and the authentic exhibits have been augmented. Performances of Sound and Light are discontinued, but the stately house and lush gardens in their scenic, historic setting, still make Boscobel one of our finer attractions.

Foundry School Museum, 63 Chestnut St., Cold Spring, N.Y. 10516. *Open year around, Wed. 9:30-4; Sun. 2-5. Free.*

This small museum, operated by the Putnam County Historical Society, is a treasure house filled with authentic and interesting exhibits that feature local history and economics. It's located in a refurbished school originally used by the children of the factory workers in the neighboring West Point Foundry. Permanent exhibits include artifacts connected with foundry products, both military and household. An annual Flea Market in May brings many visitors. There is good material for historic research in the Library, open Wed. or by appointment.

Clarence Fahnestock Memorial State Park. *Open year around; Activities from April to Nov. Fees from about Memorial Day to Labor Day. $2. for parking, small charge for activities. Food: Picnics, cooking. Pets, leashed and restricted to certain areas. Tent & Trailer camping; boat rentals and launching, bridle trails, fishing, hiking, skiing; no swimming. Winter sports.*

This park has 4,000 acres of woodland. The peak camping season is mid-July; in June you'll find it less crowded. This is a good place either to spend the day or to top off your trip.

FOR THE DRIVER: Exit Point for all: Hawthorne Circle. Take NY 9A north under 5 *m.* to exit at traffic light at NY 133. Turn right, toward Millwood, drive a few blocks to small Brookside lane where sign directs to Maryknoll, to left.

Leaving Maryknoll take first road, Ryder Ave., turn right, back to jct. with 9A north. Cross to entrance where you turn left to go north. Continue, merging with US 9 and remain on this. In Peekskill, pass Hillmann's Lamplighter, in motel. Shortly above Peekskill follow Rte. 9 across small bridge to rotary. For Oldstone Inn: take US 6 & 202 left at this point, then return to Rte. 9. Continue north on Rte. 9 toward Fishkill. About 4 *m.* ahead turn in to Graymoor. For Guided Tour make arrangements at Our Lady's Guest and Retreat House at foot of hill. For self-guiding Tour proceed to top where visitors may either drive through, or park and walk.

Back to US 9, turn right. Just ahead, NY 403 branches left to Garrison. Take this to jct. with NY 9D and turn right (north). For Garrison Inn, turn left on 9D briefly, then return. Proceed through Garrison. This town was made up to resemble Yonkers and used as the setting for the Barbra Streisand movie, *Hello, Dolly!*

A couple of miles farther just before small bridge is sign, right, Dix Castle. The road is unpaved, somewhat steep, but it's a short drive to Dick's Castle.

Back to Rte. 9D, turn right; shortly is entrance, left, to Boscobel.

Continue north on 9D. Almost at once, road bears left, then right again into town. Just after sign Village of Cold Spring, turn sharp left onto side road to Foundry School Museum, 63 Chestnut St. Then back to Rte. 9D northbound.

At this point, for a brief side trip to an unusual VISTA, continue on 9D to traffic light at jct. with NY 301. Turn left, go as far as you can then take the road, left, crossing railroad tracks. Follow it back to the one leading to the banks of the Hudson River, where there is an old-time band stand. Crow's Nest Mountain is across from you, Storm King Mountain to your right. Below is West Point. Then return to jct. with NY 301. This time cross 9D and proceed on Rte. 301.

From Museum, if skipping side trip, north on 9D, then turn right onto Rte. 301.

All: On NY 301 eastbound: a few miles ahead, cross US 9. For Bird and Bottle, turn left and follow signs a short distance. Then return to this jct. Continue on NY 301; shortly ahead is entrance, right, to Fahnestock State Park.

Return Trip: The park is at jct. with entrance to Taconic State Pkwy. Take this south to Hawthorne Circle where you started.

Maple Sirup from Tree to Table

TRIP D-13. *We'll Visit:*

APPALACHIAN TRAIL PURE MAPLE SYRUP CO.

(Carmel, N.Y.)

DISTANCE AND TOLLS: From NYC exits, about 50 *m*. Via G.W. Bridge, 85¢; via Major Deegan and Thruway, 25¢; via Hutchinson River Pkwy., 25¢. Plus return.

Appalachian Trail Pure Maple Syrup Co., RFD 3, Carmel N.Y. 10512. Phone (914) 245-2700 Ext. 339. *Call on school days between 9 and 3 p.m. Open in March on school days from 10-1. Tours given on the hour at 10, 11, 12. Visitors welcome to join school group tours. Also, weekend tours available, only in March, by advance reservation; call number above.*

The smoke curls from the chimney, the heady aroma of boiling sirup fills the crisp air, and at the plant we watch how it all takes place. They must work fast here; it takes about 50 gallons of sap to make one gallon of sirup and out of an 8 to 10 week season the heavy sap run may last only 10 to 20 days. We watch the sap bubbling along through the transparent pipeline; then the white liquid is heated, changing color in the process. Afterwards we can buy pure sirup and other maple products.

The weather, of course, makes a difference. It requires a spell of warm days with temperatures in the 40's and plenty of sun, followed by nights in the cool 20's to bring out the sap.

An Indian and a Colonial Maple sugar camp have been added, allowing for a fine overall picture of the process from earlier times.

John Madden donated the maple operation to the Putnam/Northern Westchester B O C E S in 1971. The mapling program is conducted by students from the Walden School who participate in the Walden-in-the-Woods Outdoor Education Program.

FOR THE DRIVER: Exit Point for all: Hawthorne Circle.
Take Taconic State Pkwy. north for about half an hour to NY 301 to Kent Cliffs and Carmel. Turn right on this and proceed about 3 miles. Here the main road turns right. However, you go straight ahead and at same jct. watch for small sign to Maple Sirup Plant. Immediately on your left is Miller Hill Road (unpaved). Turn left onto it and you'll begin to see the sirup bags and plastic lines. Drive about a mile up to the Maple Sirup Co. Plant.
Return Trip: Go back to the Taconic Pkwy. and return to Hawthorne Circle.

In Dutchess County With A Glimpse of Vassar

TRIP D-14. *We'll Visit:*

MADAM BRETT HOMESTEAD, Beacon (Mid-Apr. to mid-Nov. Wed.-Sat)

VASSAR COLLEGE, Poughkeepsie

GLEBE HOUSE, Poughkeepsie (Sun., Tues., Thurs. & Fri. afts.)

CLINTON HOUSE, Poughkeepsie (Wed.-Sun.)

JAMES BAIRD STATE PARK

DISTANCE AND TOLLS: To Baird Park via Beacon: From NYC Exits about 90 *m*. Fast or average speeds. Via G.W. Bridge, 85¢; via Major Deegan & Thruway, 25¢; via Hutchinson River Pkwy., 25¢; via Bear Mtn. Bridge, 25¢. Plus return.
FOOD: If coming via Bear Mtn. Bridge, Bear Mtn. Inn, also on 9D in Garrison, Garrison Inn, closed Mon. & Tues. On Rte. 9D below Beacon, Breakneck Lodge, closed Mon.; Dutchess Manor, closed Tues. In Poughkeepsie near Glebe House, Howard Johnson's. In James Baird Park, restaurant.

Madam Brett Homestead, 50 Van Nydeck Ave., Beacon, N.Y. 12508. *Open mid-Apr. to mid-Nov., Wed.-Sat. 1-4. Adm. Adults $1.50, 5-12, 50¢. Handicapped: A few steps in; can see much on first level. Parking in street. Rest rooms.*

The Homestead is one of the oldest buildings in Dutchess County. Since the original owners moved in on Christmas Day, 1709, seven generations of direct descendents of Catheryna and Roger Brett have lived here. At the time of the Revolution, a granddaughter and her husband were in residence and they were visited by many notables, including the Commander-in-Chief, Lafayette and Baron Von Steuben. During the war the house also served as storehouse for supplies for the American army. Antiquarians will be especially interested in the authentic furnishings of the Slocum memorial room.

Vassar College, Poughkeepsie. *Campus tours, self-guided; get map at main gate. Art Gallery open daily 9-5, Sun. 2-5, exc. during vacation periods. Summer hours usually 2-4. Gardens open any time.*
Taylor Hall Art Gallery includes sculpture, paintings and drawings. The Shakespeare Garden has on display plants mentioned in Shakespeare's plays and sonnets.

Clinton House, State Historic Site, 549 Main St., Poughkeepsie, N.Y. 12601. *Open year around, daily. Wed. thru Sun. 9-5. Closed 3 major holidays. Free. Handicapped: 4 wooden steps with railing to front porch. Rest room. Parking in street, metered.* (914) 471-1630.
The house was built in 1763 by the Everett family. It gets its name from Gov. George Clinton who used it as his office when Poughkeepsie was temporary capital of the state. We'll see excellent examples of authentic 18th-century furnishings in the style of a well-to-do mill owner. Displays are on ground floor only.

Glebe House, 635 Main St., Poughkeepsie, N.Y. 12601. *Open April – Sept., Sun., Tues., Thurs., Fri. 1-5. Rest of year, Sun., Tues., Fri. 1-4. Donations. Handicapped: You may enter at side of house and see the first floor, also the gardens. Rest rooms on second floor. Parking metered, or across the street – check at museum.*
A Glebe House is one for use by a minister. In this case, it was originally an Episcopal Church rectory, built in 1767 and first occupied by the Rev. John Beardsley. The next occupants were officers of the Continental Army when Poughkeepsie was the temporary state capital. Today the house is furnished in authentic Dutch style of the period. In December the home is trimmed in the fashion of the 18th century for an old-time Dutch Christmas celebration.

James Baird State Park, Freedom Plains, N.Y. *Open year around for picnics, hiking. Activities in season, mid-Apr. to November. Swimming pool, open late June thru Labor Day. Fees: $2. per car collected daily in summer, weekends spring and fall. Small fees for games, skating, swimming. Food: picnics, cooking. Restaurant open in season. Handicapped: Picnic areas are adjacent to parking lots. Rest rooms nearby. Pets: Leashed, in restricted areas.*
A large choice of activities may be engaged in against an unusually scenic background. There are golf, a driving range, swimming, roller skating, tennis, and much more. The restaurant is in the golf clubhouse and open to the public.

FOR THE DRIVER: Note: Those coming from the west side of the Hudson can add a scenic drive by taking the Palisades Interstate Pkwy. north to the Bear Mountain Bridge, passing close to Bear Mtn. Inn. Cross the bridge and turn left (north) on NY 9D, passing Garrison Inn. You also pass Dick's Castle and Boscobel

(D-12). Exit Point for everyone else, Hawthorne Circle. Take Taconic State Pkwy. north for about half an hour to jct. with NY 301. Drive west on this toward Cold Spring, crossing US 9, continuing to jct. with NY 9D in Cold Spring. Turn right (north) on 9D.

All: Northbound on NY 9D: A few miles ahead are Breakneck Lodge, then the Dutchess Manor Restaurant.

Continue into Beacon on NY 9D, which is Wolcott Ave. A few blocks ahead you cross a small bridge; shortly beyond is Teller Ave. Turn right on this and proceed to Madam Brett Homestead, a block before the traffic light.

Continue to the light and go straight ahead—you're now on Business Rte. 52. Proceed to jct. where Bus. 52 and NY 52 merge and continue on NY 52 east. At jct. where NY 82 branches left take this toward Hopewell Junction. Shortly, NY 376 merges with your road; just ahead, 376 turns left (north) to Poughkeepsie. Take this for several miles then watch for connector road from NY 376 marked To Routes 44 & 55. At this jct., Raymond Ave., on your right is Vassar College. Turn right from Rte. 376 to main gate at Raymond Ave.

Continue on Raymond Ave. following signs to 44 & 55 for several blocks to the jct. with these. Turn left (west) onto both (merged); shortly they bend left. Near this jct. are both Glebe House, 635 Main St., and Clinton House, 549 Main St. Metered parking.

Turn back on US 44 & NY 55 (east) and proceed to jct. where the two branch. Here is a Howard Johnson's. Take NY 55 right and proceed to Taconic State Pkwy. Drive north on this for about a mile; the entrance to Baird State Park is from the parkway.

Return Trip: Take the Taconic Pkwy. south to Hawthorne Circle and return the way you started.

Via Bear Mtn. Bridge: Take Taconic State Pkwy. south to exit to NY 301 and follow this west to Cold Spring. Turn left here on NY 9D and drive south to Bear Mtn. Bridge.

A Trip to Walter Beck's Innisfree

TRIP D-15. *We'll Visit:*

INNISFREE GARDEN, Millbrook (May thru Oct. exc. Mon & Tues. Open Labor Day)

DISTANCE AND TOLLS: From NYC Exits, under 80 *m*. Fast speeds. Via G.W. Bridge 85¢; via Maj. Deegan 25¢; via Hutchinson River Pkwy. 25¢. Plus return.

Innisfree Garden, Millbrook, N.Y. 12545 *Open May thru Oct., daily, exc. Mon. & Tues. Open Labor Day. Weekdays 10-4, weekends & holidays 11-5. Fees: $1.50 for age 16 & over on weekends only. No charge weekdays. Food: Picnic areas: also, on weekends, snacks at Teahouse. Handicapped: not advised. Pets: Must stay in car. Children should be supervised; no ball playing, etc., permitted.* (914) 677-8000.

It took 22 years for the late artist, Walter Beck, to design and build his "cup garden" as it is known in the East. He laid out trails and terraces, utilizing what nature provided in the form of streams, waterfalls, even the low surrounding mountains and the lake, to achieve the effect he wanted. The results are aesthetically gratifying and are of particular interest to horticulturists, especially experts on Oriental gardens. On weekends The Gallery, located in the former home of the owner, is open; here we can view his art collection, which includes many of his own tempera paintings.

FOR THE DRIVER: Exit Point for all: Hawthorne Circle. Take Taconic State Pkwy. north (toward Albany) for under 55 miles to exit to US 44. Take this east, toward Millbrook. Just beyond the jct. with NY 82, watch for road branching right—Tyrrell Rd. Follow signs here to Innisfree Garden.

Return Trip: Back to Taconic Pkwy. south, to Hawthorne Circle.

Note: If you have more time: Go back to Taconic Pkwy., but take it north a short way to exit to Salt Point Rd. Follow this west, to Franklin D. Roosevelt's Home and the Vanderbilt Mansion (Trip D-16 EXT.)

To the Roosevelt Home and Library in Hyde Park

TRIP D-16 EXTENSION. *We'll Visit:*

FRANKLIN D. ROOSEVELT NATL. HISTORIC SITE, Hyde Park.

(May close on Mon., Tues. in winter months.)

FRANKLIN D. ROOSEVELT LIBRARY

VANDERBILT MANSION (Same time as FDR Home)

DISTANCE AND TOLLS: To Hyde Park from NYC exits, about 95-100 *m.* Via G.W. Bridge, 85¢; via Major Deegan & Thruway, 25¢; via Hutchinson River Pkwy., 25¢. Plus return.

FOOD: No picnics. At entrance to Roosevelt's estate, Howard Johnson's. Another on Rte. 9 just below Poughkeepsie in Hudson Plaza; also Manero's Restaurant. Diners on Rte. 9.

Home of Franklin D. Roosevelt, Hyde Park, N.Y. 12538. *Open year around. Daily 9-5 during most of year, tentatively closed Mon. & Tues. during winter months, inquire first. Fees: Over 16, 50¢. Combination ticket, 50¢, includes Vanderbilt Mansion on same day. Rental of acoustiguide, 50¢ for single person, 75¢ for two. Handicapped: ramp to front door, 2 steps at end of first floor, railings part way to second. Seeing-eye dogs permitted. Rest rooms in separate building, 2 steps in. Cameras allowed but no flash bulbs. (Crowded in Season.) Free to holders of Golden Eagle and Golden Age passports (available here).* (914) 229-9115.

Franklin Delano Roosevelt was born in this house January 30, 1882, and kept it as his family home all of his life. With the voice of his wife, Eleanor Roosevelt, guiding us through the rooms by means of an acoustiguide, we sometimes have the uncanny feeling we're really visiting the living family, not just a house. We'll see some magnificent furnishings; the Dresden Room, heavy oak dining room pieces from the Netherlands, a Gilbert Stuart painting of one of F.D.R.'s illustrious ancestors. An Aubusson rug delights the connoisseur, but a small blanket on a comfortable chair brings a smile to everyone, for here in his master's bedroom lived the pet Scotty, Fala.

The Franklin D. Roosevelt Library. *Open year around, daily 9-5. Fees: 75¢, over 16. School groups free. Vanderbilt Mansion combination not valid here. Handicapped: Ramp to entrance, elevator to basement. Rest rooms in basement. Cameras allowed, but no flash bulbs.*

Those who experienced the Roosevelt period will be reminded of many things here—newsworthy gifts from rulers of many countries, oddities (remember him as The Sphinx?) and family heirlooms. Hobby collections include many naval paintings and ship models. Be sure to go downstairs to see the family cars, one of which is the Ford specially fitted to drive after he had contracted polio. The Research Room of the Library is open weekdays, free with prior notice.

The Graves of the President and His Wife.

The name Roosevelt comes from the Dutch, meaning field of roses. Thus it is appropriate that in a beautiful garden of roses, surrounded by century-old hemlocks and perennial flower borders, both Franklin D. Roosevelt and Eleanor Roosevelt now rest. The tombstone is of the same white marble used in the Thomas Jefferson Memorial in Washington, called Imperial Danby. A sun dial stands just beyond the graves; at its base is a small plaque flush with the ground and hard to see from the walk. Here, still close to his master, lies Fala.

Vanderbilt Mansion, Hyde Park, N.Y. 12538. *Open year around, daily 9-5. Grounds open all year, daytime. Fees: Over 16, 50¢. Combination ticket 50¢ includes the Roosevelt Home on same day. Tours. Handicapped: Many steps into house; no railings. Elevator. Cameras allowed but no flash bulbs.*

A turn-of-the-century palatial mansion, this relic of the Gilded Age is considered one of the best examples of Italian Renaissance architecture in the country. Its glittering opulence impresses, in different ways, everyone who visits it. This was the country home of a grandson of

Commodore Cornelius Vanderbilt and it expresses the influence of European art on American wealth in those days.

We take a self-guided tour through the mansion. Displays are all labeled; a booklet tells the source of the fine marble, the mahogany woodwork, the throne chairs, tapestries, beaded crystal chandeliers, heavily-napped rugs (one weighs 2,300 pounds), hand-embroidered silk.

Outside are magnificent trees and a stunning panorama of river and mountains.

FOR THE DRIVER: Exit Point for all: Hawthorne Circle.

Take Taconic State Pkwy. north and proceed about 55 m. to exit, above Poughkeepsie area, to Salt Point Tpke. Turn left (west) on this and follow signs to F.D.R. Home. Continue to jct. with US 9 (not 9G, which you cross first). At US 9 turn left and go 2 m. to the Roosevelt Home. F.D.R. Library on grounds. At entrance to estate is a Howard Johnson's. Another one, also Manero's Restaurant, 8 m. south on Rte. 9.

From F.D.R. Home, turn left, north, to traffic light where you came from Salt Point Tpke. Just beyond, left, is gateway entrance to Vanderbilt Mansion. Turn in here.

Following your visit, you have a choice: Return to south exit, this time driving past the Carriage House where you may stop to inspect the display. Then turn left from exit, back to Rte. 9, crossing it and continuing to the Taconic, the way you came. Or for more scenic trip, follow signs to North Exit and US 9, passing VISTA points. At exit onto Rte. 9, across the hwy. is lane leading to the Playhouse, with summer theatre attractions.

Turn right (south) on Rte. 9 to traffic light. Turn left and return to Taconic State Pkwy.; take it south to Hawthorne Circle where you started.

Antique Airplanes and Air Thrills

TRIP D-17 EXTENSION. *We'll Visit:*

MARGARET LEWIS NORRIE STATE PARK, Staatsburg

OGDEN AND RUTH LIVINGSTON MILLS MEMORIAL STATE PARK and MUSEUM, Staatsburg

MONTFORT REPTILE INSTITUTE, Rhinebeck

OLD RHINEBECK AERODROME (Mid-May thru Oct. Air shows Sun. afts.)

DISTANCE AND TOLLS: To Aerodrome from NYC exits, about 110 m., mainly fast speeds. Via G.W. Bridge, 85¢; via Major Deegan & Thruway, 25¢; via Hutchinson River Pkwy., 25¢. Plus return.

FOOD: Restaurant in Norrie State Park and in Mills Memorial State Park; in Rhinebeck, Beekman Arms Inn. Plus diners on US 9.

Margaret Lewis Norrie State Park, Staatsburg, N.Y. *Open year around. Food: Restaurant, picnics.*

This attractively located park includes tent camping facilities, cabin rentals, and for sports, fishing and hiking. There is boat basin for both launching and docking, but no boat rentals. Norrie Point Inn is within the grounds and features dining and dancing on a waterfront terrace.

Ogden and Ruth Livingston Mills State Park and Museum, Staatsburg, N.Y. 12580. *Park open year around. Museum, Mem. Day - Oct., Wed. - Sun. 9-4:30 Fees: Adults 50¢, children 25¢ for Museum. Free Parking. Museum tours, guided only, 10 persons at one time; last ½ hour. Last tour starts at 4. Food: No regular picnic areas but casual picnicking allowed. Public restaurant near golf course. Handicapped: 8 steps into building, no railings. Indoors, some could manage stairs to 2nd floor. Pets, leashed, in restricted areas.* (914) 889-4100.

There are over 300 acres to this ornamental park with great specimen trees, flower gardens and shrubbery planned to make the best use of the landscape.

The Museum: The Vanderbilt Mansion was a showplace. The Mills Estate illustrates how the very wealthy could turn an elegant mansion into a home without ostentation. Morgan Lewis, Governor of New York, once lived here, later, Ogden Mills, followed by his son, who was Secretary of the Treasury under President Hoover. On our tour we'll see priceless furnishings as well as historical maps and documents.

Montfort Reptile Institute, Schultz Hill Road, Rhinebeck, N.Y. 12572. *Open summer daily, 10-5. Rest of year, weekends or by appointment. Adults $3., children $1.50. Guided tours, only, last over 1 hr.* (914) 876-3769.

This is a scientific display with over 100 live reptiles and its purpose is to help remove some of our natural fear of snakes through a better understanding. Qualified herpetologists who have instructed the Armed Forces in reptile safety demonstrate the proper handling of poisonous snakes, with emphasis on the four most lethal species found in the United States. We'll watch the method of extracting venom; we'll learn the correct way to treat snake bites. This might be an especially advantageous trip for all sportsmen and hikers who will be in regions where snakes are found.

Old Rhinebeck Aerodrome, Rhinebeck, N.Y. 12572. (914) 758-8610. *Open mid-May thru Oct. 10-5. Air shows every Sat. & Sun. 2:30, last 1½ hr. Also on Sat. from July. Fees: Adults $3.50. 6-12 yrs. $2. For display only, adults $1.50, children $1. Pre-show activities start at 2 p.m.*

Food: Picnics, snacks. Free parking. Handicapped: Parking is across the road, but owner will see you are accommodated. Ground is fairly level; you can see a good deal near the entrance.

This one-of-a-kind exhibit, obviously a "must" for buffs and almost as intriguing to anyone who flies today, is located in a fair-sized field out in the farmlands. It is the private collection of Cole Palen, who sank everything he had into starting this collection. We'll see about 16 of the rare machines, antique aircraft right out of W W I.

The Air Show is possibly as exciting to the audience as to the pilots. Will they make it up? Will they make it back? The daring young men. garbed in aviators' costumes out of WW I, are aided in takeoffs and landings by a ground crew that apparently knows exactly how to handle planes without brakes or automatic starters, on runways of dirt that slope just enough to give the necessary boost. There's even a comedy routine, a light-hearted affair that would never be suitable for the clinically solemn modern jet.

Some of these planes have been used in movies, on television and in advertisements. They can also be rented for same.

FOR THE DRIVER: Exit Point for all: Hawthorne Circle. Take Taconic State Pkwy. north toward Albany and drive about 55 *m.* to exit at Salt Point Tpke. Drive west on this, following signs to F.D.R. Home, as for Trip D-16 Extension. Pass NY 9G and continue to jct. with US 9. Turn right (north), passing entrance to Vanderbilt Mansion, and continue several miles to entrance, left, to Norrie State Park.

Back on Rte. 9, turn left and continue about a mile to Ogden Mills State Park and Museum, entrance on left.

At exit to park, follow sign, left, to Rte. 9 north. Shortly you're in Rhinebeck. At jct. with NY 308 is one of the country's oldest hotels, the Beekman Arms Inn, built 1700. If going to the Reptile Institute, turn right on Rte. 308 for 2 *m.* to NY 9G. Turn right again; a short distance below is Schultz Hill Rd., on left, and sign to Montfort Reptile Institute.

Back on Rte. 9G, turn right and proceed to jct. with US 9. If skipping the reptiles, continue on US 9 to jct. with NY 9G.

All: At this jct., take US 9 a short distance to Stone Church Road, opposite a church. Follow signs here to the Old Rhinebeck Aerodrome.

Return Trip: Back to US 9. Turn right (north) and proceed to jct. with NY 199 in Red Hook. Turn right (east) on Rte. 199 and drive either to Taconic State Pkwy. (about 10 *m.*) where you take it south to Hawthorne Circle (quickest), or to jct. with NY 22 near Millerton, about 25 *m.* from Aerodrome; here, turn right (south) on NY 22 and drive about 55 *m.* either to jct. with Saw Mill River Pkwy., which goes back to Hawthorne Circle, or to jct. with I-684 which goes south to White Plains and to jct. with Hutchinson River Pkwy.

Chancellor Livingston's Home and the Upper Hudson

TRIP D-18 EXTENSION. *We'll Visit:*

CLERMONT STATE PARK and ROBERT LIVINGSTON'S HOME

OLANA CASTLE, Hudson, N.Y. (Mem. Day-Oct., Wed.-Sun.)

AMERICAN MUSEUM OF FIRE FIGHTING, Hudson (Apr.–Dec.)

HOUSE OF HISTORY, Kinderhook (End of May to late Sept., closed Mon.)

VAN ALEN HOUSE, Kinderhook (same)

DISTANCE AND TOLLS: To Kinderhook from NYC exits, about 145 *m*. Mainly fast speeds except in towns. If skipping Kinderhook, about 17 *m*. less. Via G.W. Bridge, 85¢; via Major Deegan & Thruway, 25¢; via Hutchinson River Pkwy., 25¢. Plus return.

FOOD: Occasional eating places in towns; restaurants in Kinderhook.

Clermont State Historic Park, R.D. 1, Germantown, N.Y. 12526. (518) 537-4240. *Grounds open for picnicking, hiking, riding, year around, 6 a.m. to 10 p.m. daily. Mansion open Wed. thru Sun. 9-5, Memorial Day thru Oct., also major holidays. May be adm. charge.*

Chancellor Robert R. Livingston, whose house we'll visit, helped make history, both political and scientific. He was one of 5 men chosen to draft a Declaration of Independence. Because of his strong views on Colonial rights and the American cause, the British set fire to his house and property after burning Kingston in 1777. His family escaped and rebuilt. As minister to France, Livingston met Robert Fulton and gave him financial aid and encouragement in his work perfecting the steamship, which was renamed Clermont in his honor.

Olana Castle, State Historic Site, Hudson, N.Y. 12534. *Open Mem. Day - Oct. Wed.-Sun., 9-4:30. Adm. 50¢. Tours: Guided only, limited to 10 persons; last ½ hr. Last tour begins 4. Food: No regular picnic area; bring box lunches. Rest rooms adjacent to parking lot. Handicapped: Get permission to drive to front door. Several steps in, but wheelchairs have made it.* (518) 828-0135.

Any castle worth its name should be loaded with just about everything that looks romantic, intriguing, rich and foreign. The home of Frederick E. Church, a foremost painter of the Hudson River School, contains treasures gathered on his trips around the world. He designed his castle in what he called Personal Persian, and his wife named it

Olana, Arabic for Our Place on High. Artists will be interested to discover many of Church's paintings throughout the house, as well as those of other "greats," including his teacher, Thomas Cole. Especially noteworthy are the windows. Each was specially designed in Persian or Moorish style to frame a scenic view. Photographers may snap pictures as they go. Frederick Church had a still more novel idea. As he looked southward over the mountainous landscape, there was the Hudson River on his right, but on the left was a dark mass of woodland. It didn't balance. So he built a lake; beautifully contoured, this gave light to his dark area. We get a good view of it as we drive back to the highway.

American Museum of Fire Fighting, Hudson, N.Y. 12534. *Open Apr. to Dec., daily 9-5, free. Rest rooms. Handicapped: ramps.* (518) 828-7695.

Here is one of the few places where buffs can see everything pertaining to fire fighting, well displayed in a fine, modern museum. Reputedly the oldest such collection in the country and possibly the largest, it contains thousands of items, from old-time fire engines to speaking trumpets. Old Timers will find the displays, dating from 1731 to 1926, bring back memories. Youngsters will probably learn things they didn't know about safety measures at this museum, which the New York Firemen's Association maintains here at the Firemen's Home.

House of History and Van Alen House, Kinderhook, N.Y. 12106. *Open end of May until Labor Day Tues. thru Sat. 10:30-4:30, Sun. 1:30-4:30. Open weekends, rest of Sept. Closed Mon. Adm. Adults $1.25. Sr. Cit. $1. 12-18 75¢, combination rate for both houses; student rates. Under 12, free. Tours: Guided (optional); last about half hour at each house.* (518) 758-9265.

You may be referring to this remote, picturesque, historical village every day of your life. Whenever you use the expression "Okay" you are quoting the rallying cry of the Van Buren faction in the presidential campaign of 1836, for their candidate, Martin Van Buren, was born in Old Kinderhook, or O.K.

Our tour starts at the House of History, which has a fine collection of Duncan Phyfe and Chippendale furniture and documents once owned by Martin Van Buren, eighth President of the U.S.

The second building on the Tour is the Van Alen House, built 1737; recently restored and now a National Historic Landmark because of its distinctive architectural features. Washington Irving frequented the house. The whole area is filled with things both historical and romantic. Visitors can browse through Kinderhook, looking up the house where Benedict Arnold stayed when still loyal, the one in which President Van Buren was born, the place where Irving's Ichabod Crane taught school.

Ask the guides at the House of History for a list, also for names of good dining places.

FOR THE DRIVER: From Hawthorne Circle take the Taconic State Pkwy. north toward Albany and drive to the exit to NY 199 to Red Hook. Turn left (west) toward Red Hook and proceed past US 9 to jct. with NY 9G. Turn right (north) on this toward Germantown. A short distance ahead, across from a gas station, follow sign on your left to Clermont State Park.

Return to NY 9G and turn left (north). Soon you'll see the Rip Van Winkle Bridge to Catskill; about the same time on your right you approach a road up the hill, right; take this, to Olana Castle.

Back to NY 9G and turn right. Just ahead is jct. with NY 23. Take this following signs to Hudson; bear left and continue north on 9G and 23B. Soon you pick up signs to Firemen's Home. Follow these, continuing one block beyond the point where Rtes. 9G and 23B turn right. The next corner is State St. Turn right, past the library, then bear left on Carroll to the next corner, Short St. Turn left (this is now Harry Howard Ave.) and proceed to top of hill where Firemen's Home is on your left. Drive to parking lot, at right of buildings. In the last building on left is the American Museum of Fire Fighting.

If continuing to Kinderhook: Turn left and proceed a short distance soon following Joslen Blvd. which goes to US 9. Turn left (north) on this and drive for about 15 minutes to Kinderhook. In town, about a block before a traffic light is the House of History, left. Van Alen House is part of the same tour.

Return Trip: Just above the Museum is jct. with NY 203. Turn right on this and drive to the Taconic State Pkwy. south—this takes you back to Hawthorne Circle.

If skipping Kinderhook: From the Fire Museum turn right and go back the way you came, turning on Carroll past the library on State St. Take any road left here and drive one block to Columbia St., (Rtes. 9G and 23B.) Turn left and proceed, following NY 23B East. This joins NY 23, which goes to the Taconic State Pkwy. Take this South to Hawthorne Circle, as you started.

Relics of the Shakers in the Berkshires

TRIP D-19 EXTENSION. *We'll Visit:*

SHAKER MUSEUM, Old Chatham, N.Y. (May thru Oct.)

DARROW SCHOOL, New Lebanon, N.Y.

HANCOCK SHAKER VILLAGE, Hancock, Mass. (June to mid-Oct.)

DISTANCE AND TOLLS: To Hancock Shaker Village, from NYC Exits, under 150 *m.*, mostly fast speeds. Direct to 3 Shaker sites and return 10 hrs. inclusive of stay. Via G.W. Bridge, 85¢; via Major Deegan & Thruway, also Hutchinson River Pkwy., 25¢. Plus return.

Shaker Museum, Old Chatham, N.Y. 12136. *Open May thru Oct. daily, 10-5:30. Adm. $2.50, 15-21 yrs. & Sr. Cit. $1.50, 6-14 yrs., 75¢. Group rates available. Combination ticket to include Hancock Shaker Village.*

Food: Picnic area, light snacks, Annual Shaker Festival, 1st Sat. in Aug., adm. fee.

Here is a unique opportunity to inspect the remains of what was once a thriving Shaker community, established late in the 18th century by a handful of dissidents from the English Society of Friends, known as Quakers. Because shaking their bodies to simulate ecstasy was part of their religious ritual they became known as the shaking Quakers, hence Shakers.

At the mother house of the order we will visit an excellent museum with more than 30 display galleries that show the beautiful, utilitarian, simply-designed products of the Shakers. A herb garden grows at the back. The library contains manuscripts and historic material. In the gift shop are books about Shakers and recordings of their music.

Darrow School, New Lebanon, N.Y. 12125. Phone (518) 794-7700. *Tours of grounds of former Shaker settlement, by appointment.*

The Darrow School is located on the grounds of the first Shaker settlement in the United States. The original village was settled about 1780. As celibacy was one of their customs, the Shakers did not multiply except by adoption or conversion. Thus after 150 years, decreasing numbers forced them to leave the village. More recently, a Shaker Work-group used part of the grounds in summer, teaching youths to reproduce Shaker crafts. This group eventually became inactive and its living quarters were acquired by followers of the Sufi faith.

Meanwhile, the Darrow School will gladly arrange a tour of the campus, which is so rich in history of the Shaker movement. Write or phone them.

Hancock Shaker Village, Pittsfield, Mass. 01201. *Open June thru mid-Oct., daily 9:30-5. Adults $3., 6-12 yrs., $1. Under 6, free. Combination ticket to include Shaker Museum. Tours at 10:30 and 3, or self-guiding all day. Food: Lunch shop daily from mid-June thru Sept. Picnic area.*

An original Shaker settlement dating back to 1790 has become an "outdoor museum" with 18 authentic buildings surrounded by fields and gardens. Ten of the buildings with about 70 rooms have been restored and are open to visitors. They include shops of the Brethren, with their chair-taping, broom-making, carpentry and tools; that of the Sisters displaying textiles, herbs and weaving. The Brick Dwelling contains a large communal kitchen and near it, the "Good Room" where the choicest foods were stored for special occasions. Landmark highlight of the village is the eye-catching Round Stone Barn, an enormous structure built in 1826. During the height of the season, late

June to mid-Sept., local women's groups prepare homemade baked goods and preserves to sell to visitors. Future plans call for selling craft work similar to that done by the Shakers.

Annual Shaker Kitchen Festival. *6 days in early August, daily 9:30-5. Check newspapers. Lunch shop daily 10-4. No extra charge for Festival.*

This is a demonstration of authentic Shaker cooking with "tastings" throughout the day. We'll sample delicacies like Shaker loaves and jams, Indian donuts, jumbles, cobblers, pink rice, butternut pudding. Every day a complete World's Peoples dinner is served, by reservation, at 6 p.m. On Sunday at noon.

FOR THE DRIVER: Exit Point for all: Hawthorne Circle. Take Taconic State Pkwy. North for over 100 miles until exit to NY 295. Continue North on 295 to a road, left, that runs along the Berkshire Spur of the NY Thruway and follow signs to Shaker Museum just ahead off County Road 13.

From Museum return to County Rd. 13 and turn left following signs to Brainard. At the end of Rte. 13 turn right into US 20 east. Continue on this toward Pittsfield. In New Lebanon next to church on left is a replica of the Shrine of Lourdes. Stay on US 20 passing jct. with NY 22 and after 22 turns left look for a small road, right, and sign Darrow School.

Near the School, on US 20, is Pittsfield State Forest. If it's azalea time, usually late May to mid-June, this has miles of roads banked with them. It will be crowded on weekends.

We continue on US 20 for a few miles to the Hancock Shaker Village.

Return Trip: Take Mass 41 just beyond the Shaker Village and drive south, to your right, to the Berkshire Spur of the NY Thruway, I-90. Take this west (toll) to Taconic State Pkwy. and go south to Hawthorne Circle.

Into Middle and Upper Connecticut

● *Our next trips take us across the New York line into Connecticut, mainly the middle and upper regions of the western part of the state.*

Most of these trips will be full-day EXTENSIONS as they cover territory beyond an average short drive from New York City. However, fast roads allow us to reach a wide variety of attractions easily.

Our first trip is on the New York side of the line; those to follow move into Connecticut. For hundreds of unspoiled Colonial towns filled with pre-Revolutionary homes, for entire areas that have been designated Historic Districts, for the quietly beautiful New England countryside, these drives are unexcelled.

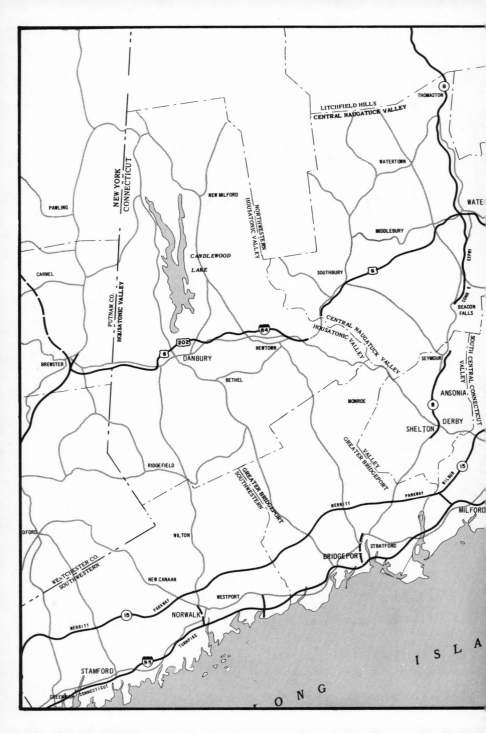

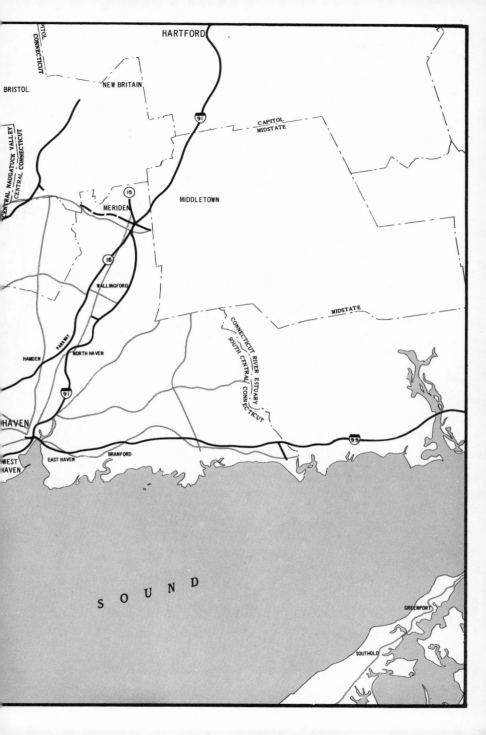

To reach Area E from New York City and environs, use these Exit Points: Hutchinson River Parkway and Hawthorne Circle. Main roads: Merritt Parkway, I-684 to Brewster.

From all sections, to reach Merritt Parkway, take Hutchinson River Parkway north. This becomes the Merritt in Connecticut (toll).

To reach I-684, from NY Thruway, take I-287 (Cross Westchester Expressway) toward White Plains and exit at I-684. From Hutchinson River Parkway, drive north to jct. with I-684.

From Prehistoric Dinosaurs to Living Beasts

TRIP E-1. *We'll Visit:*

DINOSAUR LAND PARK, Brewster, N.Y. (Late June to Labor Day. Closed Wed.)

SQUANTZ POND STATE PARK, New Fairfield, Conn.

DISTANCE AND TOLLS: From NYC Exits, 70-80 *m*, to Squantz Pond. Mainly fast speeds. Via G.W. Bridge, 85¢; Via Major Deegan & Thruway, also Hutchinson River Pkwy., 25¢. Plus return.

FOOD: On Rte. 7, and on way to the Park.

Dinosaur Land Park & Mineral Museum, Old Rte. 6, Brewster, N.Y. 10509. *Park open late May to mid-June, weekends 10-5; late June thru Labor Day, daily 10-5. Last tours starts at 4. Adm $1.25, 5-11 yrs 75¢. Special children's tour $.1. 5-11 yrs. 50¢. (914) 279-8557. Children under 5 not admitted. Gift Shop open year around; in summer, 10-5; winter, weekdays exc. Wed. 1-5, weekends 10-5. Closed during Danbury Fair. Tours hourly, last 1 hr., weather permitting; by appointment off season. Handicapped: Some walking in park. Museum is downstairs.*

This is an educational exhibit primarily for everyone interested in mineralogy. In the Dinosaur Park our guide shows us a large collection of Connecticut Valley dinosaur tracks; there is also a replica of an old mine and methods of panning gold. The guide and museum curator, Ronald Januzzi, can teach the beginner personal safety and how to avoid damaging valuable specimens in the field. Books and maps of mineral localities of this region are available in the gift shop, where protective glasses, geological hammers and chisels, and ultra-violet products may be purchased. There is also a good selection of hobby kits and articles made from natural stones.

Squantz Pond State Park, New Fairfield, Conn. *Open year around. Fees, in season, $1. per car (subject to change). Snacks in season. Picnics. Swimming, boating; boat or canoe for rent, or bring your own, under 7½ horsepower. No water skiing or surfing.*

A beautiful spot with a clear mountain lake for swimming or boating makes a fine place to top off a day spent with the dinosaurs. The drive to it, partially along Candlewood Lake, is likewise a scenic treat.

FOR THE DRIVER: Take I-684 to Brewster. Go past exit to I-84 to Danbury, and take first exit to US 6 & 202 east, toward Danbury. Continue on these a short distance, to Dinosaur Museum and Park (large pink dinosaur in front).

Continue on US 6 several miles to Danbury, where Rte 37 goes north to New Fairfield. Take this to junction with Rte 39 in New Fairfield, then turn right on Rte 39, passing Candlewood Lake, for about 4 *m.* to the park. There are snack places and a few restaurants nearby. Many more, if returning on Rte 7.

Return Trip: Back on Rte 39 to jct. with 37, then 37 south to I-84. Take this west, toward New York, then I-684 toward White Plains. OR: Continue north on Rte 39 nearly 10 *m* to Rte 7. South on this, past many eating places, to I-84. West on this, follow signs to New York, then White Plains.

Covered Bridges, Cascades, Blueberries, Americana

TRIP E-2. This trip will be good in laurel time, June, blueberry season, mid-July, or for fall foliage. In early October the famous Salisbury Antiques Fair is nearby; we'll tell you how to make connections. As it is primarily for the enjoyment of the drive it will be written out **For the Driver**.

We'll Visit:

NATURAL HISTORY MUSEUM, AKIN HALL LIBRARY, Pawling (May-Nov. Tues., Thurs. afts. Sat. all day)

BLUEBERRY PARK, Wingdale, N.Y. (Mid-July into Aug.)

HUNT COUNTRY FURNITURE, Wingdale

WEBATUCK CRAFT VILLAGE, Wingdale (Wed.-Sun.)

BULLS BRIDGE (COVERED) Conn.

MACEDONIA BROOK STATE PARK, Conn.

SLOANE-STANLEY MUSEUM OF EARLY AMERICAN TOOLS, Kent, Conn. (Memorial Day thru Oct. Closed Mon. and Tues.)

KENT FALLS STATE PARK, Kent, Conn.

SHARON AUDUBON CENTER, Sharon, Conn. (Closed Mon., Hol.)

HOUSATONIC MEADOWS STATE PARK

WEST CORNWALL COVERED BRIDGE

LAKE WARAMAUG STATE PARK

DISTANCE AND TOLLS: To Sharon (farthest point) from NYC Exits, about 100-110 *m.,* mainly fast or average speeds. From G.W. Bridge, 85¢; via Major Deegan & Thruway, 25¢; via Hutchinson River Pkwy., 25¢. Plus return tolls.

FOOD: In Patterson, L'Auberge Bretonne, closed Wed. and last 3 wks. in Jan. Birch Hill Inn & Cafe, closed Mon. & Tues. Lake Waramaug area, Hopkins Inn, June-mid-Oct. Boulders Inn, mid-June-Labor Day. Diners on US 7 on return.

FOR THE DRIVER: From Connecticut: If closer to US 7 to Danbury, take this north to jct. with I-84 and drive west on Rte. 84 toward Brewster. At jct. with NY 22, take this north toward Pawling.

Everyone else: Take I-684 north to Brewster then continue north on NY 22 toward Pawling.

Pass L'Auberge Bretonne and Birch Hill Inn and Cafe in Patterson. Soon NY 55 joins Rte. 22. Just above this jct. follow signs, right, on Quaker Hill Road for: Natural History Museum, Akin Hall Library, Pawling, N.Y. *Open May-Nov. Tues, and Thurs. 2-4:30; Sat. 10-4:30. Adm. fee.* Exhibits relate to political and natural history of the area.

Back to Rte. 22, turn right and continue north. At Wingdale, just beyond Harlem Valley State Hospital, NY 55 goes ahead and NY 22 forks left. Here we have a choice. If blueberries are in season, those who wish to pick berries follow Rte. 22 to the blinking light then turn left at sign to Wingdale and drive about 4 m. up winding road to Blueberry Park. *Season: Mid-July into Aug., depending on weather. Fee for use of picnic tables and for quantity picked. Bring your own containers; also, wear proper shoes — loafers or tennis shoes best.* A small, privately owned park, well-groomed and attractive. Less crowded during the week. Then back to Rte. 22 and jct. with NY 55. Take NY 55 ahead into Connecticut. Bear right, following signs to next attraction.

Hunt Country Furniture. Wingdale, N.Y. 12594. *Open year around daily and Sun. 9-5. Free. Handicapped have 2 steps into bldg., good railings to upper floors. Rest rooms.*

Early American furniture made on the premises is displayed appropriately in a picturesque 1747 homestead with its original flooring and beams. WEBATUCK CRAFT VILLAGE (adjacent): *Shops open Wed.-Sun. (914) 832-6522.* Craftsmen recently moved in and today their shops and barns surround the Hunt showrooms. We can watch artists at work on pottery, silver, leather, and stained glass. An art gallery and antique shop are in the group.

Go back to NY 55 and turn left, the direction you'd been going. Shortly ahead is the jct. with US 7. Turn left (north), passing immediately a tempting basket shop. This route is known as the Antique Trail. Proceed to Bulls Bridge and a traffic signal. For Covered Bridge, turn left on Bulls Bridge Road. You can drive across. Bulls Bridge, named after a prominent local family, was built over 200 years ago.

Back to US 7 and turn left. Shortly you are in Kent, a picturesque New England town with an atmosphere of well-groomed antiquity. In town, Conn 341 goes left to Macedonia Brook State Park. *Open year around, 8 a.m. to sunset. No fees for day use. Short term campsites available. Picnics, cooking, fishing. No concessions or boating.* A pleasant area includes deep woods, fields, streams, and hiking trails.

Return to US 7 and turn left. About a mile ahead is:

Sloane-Stanley Museum, Kent, Conn., 06757 (203) 566-3005. *Open mid-May through Oct. 10-4:30. Closed Mon., Tues. Adults 50¢, children 25¢.* This specialized collection of early American farm implements and tools is housed in a building typifying a New England barn. It was brought together by Eric Sloane, author and artist, and land and building were donated to the state by the Stanley tool manufacturing company of New Britain. Legends accompany the tools and tell how important trees were to the settlers.

Near the Museum is the old Kent Furnace, built in 1826; we can go down and look inside. Across the road from the museum is a bit of real nostalgia—the Fitzgeralds' Company Store.

Continuing north on US 7 we soon come to:

Kent Falls State Park. *Open year around, 8 a.m. to sunset. Free for day use. Short term campsites available. Fishing and hiking; no swimming or concessions.* Steep waterfall cascades down several levels to a brook. All around are pine forests with inviting trails for hiking including some scenic paths alongside the falls. Continue on Rte. 7 north to jct. with Conn 4. Turn left (west) and proceed several miles to:

Sharon Audubon Center, Sharon, Conn. 06069. *Open year around, Wed. thru Sat. 9-5, Sun. 1-5, closed Mon. and holidays. Fees: Adults $1, children 50¢. Rest rooms, no picnics.* (203) 364-5826.

Here are *580 acres* of meadows, forests, lakes and brooks. We take a self-guiding Tour, watch for birds from an observation blind, and view nature exhibits. In spring there are songbirds and the spring migrations. In the fall, migrating waterfowl—sometimes as many as 400 geese are on Ford Pond.

At this point, if you're going on to the annual Salisbury Antiques Fair, continue on Rte. 4 to Conn 41. Turn right to Lakeville, on US 44. Turn right (east) on 44, to Salisbury. To return from here to New York City; Go back on Rte. 44 (west) to Millerton and jct. with NY 22. Take this south, the way you started.

To continue the drive: After leaving Sharon, take Conn 4, right (east) back to jct. with US 7. Turn left (north); just above jct. is Housatonic Meadows State Park. *Open year around, 8 a.m. to sunset. Picnics, camping, fishing, hiking. No fee for day use.* A beautiful park on the Housatonic River includes both woodlands and waterfront.

Proceed 4 miles on US 7 to West Cornwall and jct. with Conn 128. Turn right and cross the Cornwall Covered Bridge. There is also a town called Cornwall Bridge nearby, but the bridge is in West Cornwall. This structure was built to replace a bridge flooded out in 1936. Art galleries, antique and gift shops are clustered together by the riverside in another attractive New England town.

Go back to Rte. 7, turn left and return as far as jct. with Conn 45 to Warren. Turn left and proceed several miles. You pass Hopkins Inn at Lake Waramaug just off Rte. 45 and Boulders Inn on Rte. 45 near the lake. Shortly is Lake Waramaug State Park. *Open year around, 8 a.m. to sunset. Parking fee in season. Picnics, cooking, snacks; swimming, fishing.*

Return Trip: Continue on Conn 45 to jct. with US 202. Turn right toward New Milford and proceed to jct. with US 7. Go south (left) on Rte. 7 toward Danbury. Pass a number of restaurants and diners here. Follow Rte. 7 when it merges with I-84 and take this for several exits.

Those who started via US 7: Continue on this, the way you came.

Everyone else, remain on I-84 after Rte. 7 branches, and follow signs to White Plains and N.Y. State. You pass the Danbury Fair Grounds, left. Then take I-684 south, toward White Plains and return the way you started.

On the Trail of General Putnam in Connecticut

TRIP E-3. *We'll Visit:*

PUTNAM MEMORIAL STATE PARK, near Redding, Conn.

SCOTT-FANTON MUSEUM, Danbury (Wed. thru Sun.)

HUNTINGTON HALL, Danbury (same as Museum)

DISTANCE AND TOLLS: To Danbury from NYC exits, 60-75 *m.*, fast and average speeds. Via G.W. Bridge, $1.05; via Major Deegan & Thruway, 20¢; via Hutchinson River Pkwy. 45¢. Plus return.

FOOD: Above Merritt Pkwy. Cobb's Mill Inn. On return, on US 7 below Danbury, Fox Hill Inn and Stonehenge Inn, both closed Mon. Diners in Danbury and on Rte. 7.

Putnam Memorial State Park, Redding, Conn. *Picnic area open most of year, 8 a.m. to sunset. Rest of park open in season. Museum open afternoons, weekends in June, weekdays in July & Aug. Free. Handicapped: Climbing in park, but not in picnic area.*

British forays into the Danbury area kept the Continentals busy in 1777. During the winter General Israel Putnam had an encampment here; the troops built shelters and maintained a commissary. Foundations of chimneys and ovens are visible. Part of the park is set aside as a memorial, and here the Museum shows relics of the war. An oak tree that sprouted from an acorn of the famous Charter Oak of Hartford is in a healthy state. A scenic picnic and play area is located around a small lake.

Scott-Fanton Museum & Historical Society, 43 Main St., Danbury, Conn. 06810. *Open year around, Wed. - Sun., 2-5, closed holidays. Donations: Guided Tours. Handicapped: Several steps into building. Good railings to 2nd floor.* (203) 743-5200.

In the early 1970's, history sleuths were amazed to find documented evidence that the Scott-Fanton House, presumed saved from British arsonists during the Revolution because of Tory ownership, actually was a house built in 1785 by John Rider, an ardent patriot. This dwelling was erected on the site of one which had been owned by another patriot and so, summarily, was burned along with the rest of Danbury town. The Rider House, still known as the Scott-Fanton Museum today holds an excellent collection of 18th-century furnishings gathered by the local historical society with their usual care for authenticity. An outstanding feature is the Charles Ives Parlor. The famed composer (1874-1954) was born in Danbury; his first piano is in the museum, as well as many other mementoes of his work.

Behind the house is the small Dodd Shop, reminding that Danbury hats have been famous since the days when hatting was the only industry in town. Tools used by the hatters are displayed, also models and records.

Huntington Hall, located behind the Scott-Fanton Museum. *Same hours. Exhibits on one level. Rest rooms. Donations.*

This modern structure contains the Museum offices and rooms for lectures and films. There are changing exhibits of industries and crafts, and arts and sciences.

FOR THE DRIVER: Take Hutchinson River Parkway north to Exit 42 to Rte. 57; follow 57 toward Weston to jct. with Rte. 53 north. At this jct. is Cobb's Mill Inn. Continue north on Conn 53 passing Saugatuck Reservoir, to Rte. 107. Turn right and go to its merger with Rte. 58. Here is Putnam Memorial Park—Museum at left, lake and picnic area at right.

Continue north on Rte. 58 to jct. with Rte 302. Take it left through Bethel into Danbury (South St.) When Main St. comes from the right, turn right to the Scott-Fanton Museum, next to Grand Union. Park in rear. Huntington Hall is behind the Museum. he Museum.

Return Trip: Continue on Main St., following signs to I-84 west. Take this toward New York. Rte 7 merges briefly with I-84. Choice: Follow Rte 7 south when it leaves I-84, and pass Fox Hill and Stonehenge Inns. Continue to jct. with Merritt Pkwy. and return to New York City. OR: Stay on I-84 to exit to White Plains via I-684. Take this south; eventually it merges with Hutchinson River Pkwy. to New York City.

A Day at the Great Danbury State Fair

TRIP E-4. *We'll Visit:*

THE DANBURY STATE FAIR

DISTANCE AND TOLLS: Via G.W. Bridge about 60 *m.*, 85¢ tolls; via Major Deegan & Thruway, 60 *m.*, 25¢; via Hutchinson River Pkwy., 40 *m.*, 45¢. Plus return.

The Great Danbury State Fair. *Open last weekend in September or in early October for 9 days, 9:30-7. Fees: Moderate, for admission and parking, exhibits free. Food: Restaurants, snacks, picnic areas. Handicapped: Walks are paved, useful for wheelchairs; Big Top can be entered from rear but is not suitable for chairs. Take lower walk to Dutch Village.*

This is one of the few surviving agricultural-industrial fairs in the East, recently past the century mark. There are ribbons and awards for the best displays and livestock gets inspected and admired; also the latest innovations in farming are shown. There are the parades, arena thrills and Cinderella's castle, games for the children and cotton candy.

We find three distinct sections, the New England Village, Gold

Town, and the Dutch Village, each with its own decor and specialties. The parade takes place every afternoon, while daily events include races, contests, judging of products. In the Big Top are grange exhibits; square dancing and country music at regular intervals add flavor. Weekdays are best for visits; it is crowded on weekends and school holidays.

FOR THE DRIVER: Take I-684 to Brewster, then I-84 east to Danbury. A few miles ahead are the Fair Grounds. Follow signs from highway. Via Hutchinson River Parkway: Go north into the Merritt Pkwy. and proceed to Exit 40 to US 7 north to Danbury (2nd exit). Drive almost to Fair Grounds, where signs direct you down side road, left.

Return Trip: Back on I-84 west toward New York, then south on I-684. For Hutchinson River Pkwy., take US 7 back to the Merritt toward New York.

A Trip to the Holy Land in Miniature

TRIP E-5 EXTENSION. *We'll Visit:*

HOLY LAND, U.S.A., Waterbury, Conn. (Catacomb Tours: afts., April — Oct. except Tues.)

MATTATUCK MUSEUM, Waterbury. (Afternoons. Closed Monday)

DISTANCE AND TOLLS: To Holy Land from NYC exits—70-80 *m.* via G.W. Bridge, $1.05; Via Major Deegan and Thruway, 45¢; via Hutchinson River Pkwy., 45¢.
FOOD: Near Holy Land, Holiday Inn.

Holy Land, U.S.A., Waterbury, Conn. 06720. *Open year around. Conducted Catacomb Tours: Apr.-Nov. (depending on weather), weekdays exc. Tues., and Fri. 1:30-4:30; weekends, 11-5. Tours hourly, last nearly an hour. Donations. Food; picnics. Restrooms. Catacombs have railings, but walks are on slope, unpaved. Canteen, weekends only. Bus reservations required for guided tours.* (203) 755-2456.

Here is a complete Holy Land in miniature located on a rugged hillside, composed of small replicas of places relating to the life of Christ. It includes a caravan climbing toward the Grotto of the Nativity; the temple with its section for the money changers; Solomon's Pool; the Court of Pilate and Jerusalem with twelve gates. Many inscriptions are lettered on stones, archways and walls. Above it stands a lofty cross; at night this glows with colored lights changing symbolically with the season.

In the catacombs we pass models of saints and martyrs depicting some of the suffering endured by the people forced to worship underground. We end in a grotto modeled after the one where Bernadette saw the vision.

The Village is a simple, hand-made project put together with reverence in the hope that those who see it may feel goodwill toward others of every creed. It is sponsored by the Catholic Campaigners for Christ, although many denominations have contributed to the display and the emphasis is non-sectarian.

Mattatuck Museum, 119 West Main St., Waterbury, Conn. 06720. *Open year around, Tues, thru Sat. 12-5. Sun. from 2; closed Hol., also Sun. in July, Aug. Free.* (203) 754-5500.

This interesting complex includes a Junior Museum with Indian and Colonial exhibits and demonstrations; an Industrial Museum with a replica of a 19th-century Yankee Pedlar's Wagon containing many locally-made items; the Main Museum with several period rooms as well as a gallery of fine arts.

FOR THE DRIVER: Take Hutchinson River Pkwy. into the Merritt Pkwy. in Connecticut. Proceed to Exit 52 to Conn 8 to Shelton, about 40 *m*. above NYC line. Drive north on Rte. 8 about 25 *m*. to jct. with I-84 at large cloverleaf. Follow signs 84 East to Hartford. On I-84 keep in middle lane briefly; take second exit, at Mill St. You'll see the Cross and the Village on hill to your right. Leaving the ramp, bear left. Do not go under highway; follow small signs To Holy Land, up the hill. Near top is entrance to Holy Land, U.S.A.

Go back down hill. If continuing to Mattatuck Museum go underneath Pkwy. at foot of hill. Follow main road, right, into town. You're on East Main St. At the town green you cross South Main St.; your road becomes West Main St. Just beyond, left, is the Mattatuck Museum, 119 W. Main. No parking here, but municipal parking lots are nearby. The annual Arts Festival is held on the green near the museum.

Return trip from Museum: In town, follow signs to I-84 West and take it briefly to jct. with Conn 8 south and return to Merritt Pkwy., becoming the Hutchinson River Pkwy.

Return trip from Holy Land: Back to bottom of hill and go under parkway, right. Immediately turn left up hill past hospital, to traffic light. Here is a Holiday Inn. At light, turn left for pkwy. and immediately turn left again following signs to I-84 West to Danbury. Proceed to jct. with Conn 8 South and return to Merritt Pkwy. the way you came.

Religious and Historical Sites in Connecticut

TRIP E-6 EXTENSION. *We'll Visit:*

GLEBE HOUSE, Woodbury, Conn. (Mon.-Wed., weekends)

REGINA LAUDIS NEAPOLITAN CRECHE, Bethlehem (Apr. thru Dec.)

GUNN MEMORIAL LIBRARY HISTORICAL MUSEUM, Washington (Tues., Thurs. & Sat. afts.)

MT. TOM STATE PARK

DISTANCE AND TOLLS: To Mt. Tom (farthest point) From New York Exits–90-105 *m.*, via G.W. Bridge $1.05. Via Major Deegan and Thruway, 45¢. Via Hutchinson River Pkwy., 45¢. Plus return. Mostly fast and average speeds. **FOOD:** In Woodbury near Glebe House, Curtis House Inn. Above Danbury on Rte. 7, on way home: The Hearth, Country Squire, White Turkey Inn; Howard Johnson's–below jct. with I-84. On US 7 below Danbury, Fox Hill Inn, closed Mon., Stonehenge Inn, closed Mon.

Glebe House, Hollow Road, Woodbury, Conn. 06798. *Open Apr.-Sept., Mon.-Wed. & Sat., Sun. 1-5. Rest of year Mon.-Wed. 1-4. Cl. Hol. Donations.*

This picturesque building, some of it dating back to 1690, was part of the glebe (property to be used by a minister) of a priest of the Church of England in 1771. Later, ten priests of the same church elected Samuel Seabury Bishop of Connecticut, the first bishop of any church to have a See in this country. The house has been restored and furnished with Americana from the 1700's.

Regina Laudis Neapolitan Creche, Bethlehem, Conn. 06751. *Open Apr. thru Dec. 10:30-4:30. Donations. Handicapped: Difficult for wheelchairs.*

A Neapolitan Creche appropriately housed in an antique barn may be found at a Benedictine Abbey in Bethlehem, Conn. It is a permanent exhibit, considered to be an authentic 18th-century work by artists of Naples. We can learn something of the art of making a creche—what part the master artist had to do himself and how his assistants helped with costumes and other appurtenances. Down the road at the Abbey there is an ART SHOP with articles for sale. The Abbey Chapel is open to visitors who come to attend Mass and Vespers. Abbey Fair 1st. Fri. & Sat. Aug. at noon. Barbeque.

Gunn Memorial Library Historical Museum, Washington, Conn. 06793. *Open year around, Tues. & Thurs., 2-5, Sat. 1-4. Donations. Some steps for handicapped.*

Here's an interesting place, crammed full of artifacts of the area. These include old-time toys, a big doll house, dressed figures, paintings, tools. An exceptional Indian collection was donated early in the century by the head of the U.S. Dept. of Indian Affairs. This consists of mementoes given him by the Oglala-Sioux Indians of South Dakota. Two local scientists have added their own collections, which date back to the Lamoka period, 3500 B.C.

Mt. Tom State Park, Conn. Rte. 25. *Open year around. Fees: $1 in season. Snacks, in season. Picnics with cooking. Fishing and swimming in the lake.*

From a lookout tower on top of the mountain we get splendid VISTAS of the Berkshire foothills.

FOR THE DRIVER: I-684 to I-84, east toward Danbury, to Exit 15. Via Rte 7, north into Merritt Pkwy., to Rte 7 north to Danbury (2nd exit). Take Rte 7 to I-84, which it joins in Danbury.

All: I-84 East to Exit 15. Follow US 6 at foot of ramp toward Woodbury, left. After several miles you pass the Curtis House in Woodbury. Just beyond is State Heritage sign on Hollow Road, left. Take this road down to Glebe House.

m384,   Back to US 6. Turn left and continue to jct. with Conn 61. Go left on this to town of Bethlehem. At sign, Entering Bethlehem, Flanders Road comes in from sharp left, just before a Texaco gas station. Turn left onto this and drive for about 10 minutes. At the top of a hill is a sign to Creche. Walk in from the parking area to Neapolitan Creche. Then turn left from the lot and continue a short way to Regina Laudis Abbey. There's a parking area above Art Shop.

Go back to jct. with Rte. 61. Turn left, the way you'd been going, and proceed to jct. with Conn 109. Turn left, toward Washington. At jct. with Conn 47 turn left and follow this, again to your left, after 109 branches right. In next town at the Village Green, 47 turns sharp right. Before this turn, straight ahead is the Gunn Historical Museum.

Go back the way you came, on Rte. 47, joining 109 briefly, but remain on 47 north. This arrives soon at US 202. Turn right and a few miles farther you'll pass Mt. Tom State Park, right. Drive up unpaved mountain road. Tower Trail is to your right; the beach to your left.

Return Trip: Take US 202 left to New Milford, then follow signs to US 7 to Danbury. Take US 7 south, passing restaurants and diners. (including The Hearth, Country Squire, White Turkey Inn, and just below jct. with I-84, a Howard Johnson's.) Stay on US 7 when it merges with I-84, then follow 7 when it goes south, leaving highway. You'll pass Fox Hill and Stonehenge Inns. Also some roadside stands. Take Merritt toward New York; this becomes Hutchinson River Pkwy. OR: At I-84 continue west into N.Y. and jct. with I-684. Take this toward White Plains.

To Litchfield and Its Historical Attractions

TRIP E-7 EXTENSION. *We'll Visit:*

SHRINE OF LOURDES, Litchfield.

LITCHFIELD HISTORICAL MUSEUM (Tues. thru Sat.)

TAPPING REEVE HOUSE and LAW SCHOOL (Tues. thru Sat. mid-May-mid-Oct.)

WOLCOTT LIBRARY (Tues. thru Sat.)

COBBLE COURT (shops)

WHITE MEMORIAL FOUNDATION NATURE CENTER

DISTANCE AND TOLLS: To Litchfield from NYC Exits, 95-105 *m.*, fast and average speeds. Via G.W. Bridge $1.05; via Major Deegan & Thruway, 45¢; via Hutchinson River Pkwy., 45¢. Plus return.

FOOD: In Litchfield, Mitchell's, Westleigh Inn.

Shrine of Lourdes. *Open daily year around. Masses and vesper services. Picnic area. Handicapped: Grotto is near parking lot.*

An outdoor chapel faces a replica of the Shrine of Lourdes; here the services are held. To one side, the Way of the Cross starts up a wooded trail which winds to the top of the hill, ending with a flight of steps leading to Calvary. Below is the gift shop and across the way, a picnic ground.

Litchfield Historical Society Museum, Noyes Memorial Bldg., Litchfield, Conn. 06759. *Open April to Dec. Tues.-Sat. 11-5. Closed Sun., Mon., hol., & Dec. 1-March.* (203) 567-5862. *Free. Handicapped: 4 steps into bldg. and some climbing inside. Rest rooms. Parking in streets.* Unlike many museums whose rooms are crammed full of Americana, this one is spacious and uncluttered so that every article on display stands out. The exhibits include figures in period clothing, locally produced silverware and clocks, some fine paintings, a section on country arts, tools, local history told by areas. You'll want time to browse here.

Tapping Reeve House & Law School, South St., Litchfield, Conn. 06759. *Open mid-May – mid-Oct. Tues.-Sat., 11-5. Closed July 4, Labor Day weekend.* (203) 567-5862. *Groups by appointment. Fees: Adults $1.50, under 16, 50¢. Handicapped: a few steps in, but crutches can manage.* Of particular interest to those studying the legal profession and its history is this famous house, the first law school in the country. It was a graduate course attended by students from universities such as Harvard, Yale. The imposing list of its more than 1,000 graduates includes Horace Mann, Vice Presidents Aaron Burr and John C. Calhoun, members of Congress, judges of higher courts, state governors. We'll see fine antiques of the Reeve family and mementoes of historical value. In the original school building adjacent to the house, a vault contains priceless documents and original law books.

Wolcott Memorial Library, South St., Litchfield, Conn. 06759. *Open year around, Tues. thru Sat. Hours: Tues. & Thurs. 10 a.m.-8 p.m. Wed., Fri., Sat., 10-5. Music Room Tues. & Thurs. 2-5. Rest rooms. Park in street or in parking area behind bldg.* The main library is new (1966) but it's attached to a house built in 1799 by Oliver Wolcott, Jr., whose father was a signer of the Declaration of Independence. The son served as Secretary of the Treasury and Governor of Connecticut. There are free exhibits of art, sculpture and photography including the works of Calder, Youngerman and Steinberg.

White Memorial Foundation: Litchfield Nature Center and Museum, Litchfield, Conn. 06759. *Open daily year around, weather permitting.*

MUSEUM: Daily in summer 9-5; Sun. from 2., closed Mon. Donation. At nearby Bantam Lake, small parking fee; also fees for swimming, boating and riding. Self-guiding tours through nature trails. Food: Picnics, Handicapped: Ramps to Museum. Could birdwatch from wheelchair. There are some 4,000 acres to this wildlife sanctuary and 25 miles of trails to be explored on foot, horseback or bicycle — but not by car. However, we may drive to Bantam Lake for a dip and perhaps a boat ride. At the Museum we'll see nature exhibits including habitat groups of life in the sanctuary. Field trips and nature study classes are available for all ages.

Birdwatchers will consider this visit something special. Beginners can get good help starting the hobby; a booklet, *Guide to Birding* gives tips on equipment and skills needed. It tells how to identify birds, and how to approach them. Two observation towers near the lake allow birdwatchers excellent views.

FOR THE DRIVER: Take Hutchinson River Pkwy. north into the Merritt and continue about 40 *m.* to Exit 52 to Conn 8 to Shelton. Take Rte. 8 north about 40 *m.* above Pkwy. exit to jct. with Conn 118. Take this toward Litchfield. Just before town a sign, right, directs to Shrine of Lourdes.

Back on Conn 118, turn right into Litchfield. The Village Green is just ahead and jct. with US 202 and 63. You are going to turn left on Rte. 63 but first may like a brief historical drive.

Before jct. with Rte. 63 you pass the beautiful Congregational Church, built in 1829 and restored just 100 years later. At the corner where 63 goes right toward Goshen, facing the Green is a handsome red brick building with white trim, the Litchfield Jail, built in 1812 and formerly used as both jail and inn. Today it houses the Connecticut Department of Corrections. Adjoining it is a curious companion, the First National Bank of Litchfield, founded in 1814.

By driving to the right on Rte. 63 past the bank you pass several notable houses including the Benjamin Talmadge House, which was visited by General Lafayette in 1775; Sheldon Tavern, where Washington stayed on his way to the historic meeting at the Webb House in Wethersfield; the site of Pierce Academy, founded by Sarah Pierce in 1792, the first girls academy in the country, and finally a house built in 1685 which today occupies the homesite of Lyman Beecher, who preached at the Congregational Church. The original house was the birthplace of Henry Ward Beecher and Harriet Beecher Stowe. None of the buildings on this street is open to the public however.

Now back across the Green on Conn 63; this becomes South St. Park wherever you can, and walk. All the places we'll visit are close together; we'll have an opportunity to see more of this historic Colonial town.

At the corner of the Green, left, is the Litchfield Historical Society Museum. On the right, look for a narrow road leading to a small area behind a number of quaint shops, Cobble Court. Continuing down South St., on the right are the Tapping Reeve House and Law School and the Wolcott Memorial Library. On Main St. is Mitchell's Restaurant; other dining places are in town. Drive back to the Green and cross it to jct. with US 202. Turn left following signs to New Milford. Within a few blocks on the right is the Westleigh Inn. A short distance beyond on your left watch for entrance to the Litchfield Nature Museum and White Memorial Foundation.

Return Trip: Go back on Rte. 202, turning right into Litchfield again. At the Green take Conn 118 which goes to Conn 8. Take Rte. 8 south to Merritt Pkwy.

Laurel Time in Northwest Connecticut

TRIP E-8 EXTENSION. The next trip is primarily a scenic drive, and its special appeal depends on the time of year. Early in June there are lavish displays of mountain laurel, which disclose why Connecticut is known as the Laurel State. As this is for the enjoyment of the drive it will be written out FOR THE DRIVER.

We'll Visit:

SOLOMON ROCKWELL HOUSE, Winsted (Mid-June thru Sept.)
BARKHAMSTED COMPENSATING RESERVOIR
HITCHCOCK CHAIR COMPANY, Riverton (Closed Sunday and Monday.) MUSEUM (same)
INDIAN LOOKOUT, Torrington (2 or 3 weeks in June)

DISTANCE AND TOLLS: From NYC Exits, round trip will be about 240 *m.* Fast and average speeds mainly. Via G.W. Bridge, $1.05; via Major Deegan & Thruway, 45¢, also via Hutchinson Pkwy. Plus return.

FOOD: On way up, near Patterson, N.Y., L'Auberge Bretonne, closed Wed. and in Jan.; Birch Hill Inn, closed Mon. and Tues. In Salisbury, White Hart Inn; Ragamont Inn, closed in winter. In Norfolk, Blackberry River Inn, closed Tues. In Riverton, Old Riverton Inn, closed Mon. & Tues. In Torrington, Yankee Pedlar Inn.

FOR THE DRIVER: Take I-684 through Brewster and continue north on NY 22. In Patterson, pass Birch Hill Inn and L'Auberge Bretonne. Some miles ahead is jct. with US 44. When Rte. 44 branches right, take this toward Lakeville. Go through Salisbury, where the annual Antiques Fair is held in early Oct. In town, pass White Hart and Ragamont Inns on Rte. 44. In Norfolk is the Norfolk Music Shed. Also, Blackberry River Inn.

Continue to Winsted, the Laurel City and hub of the season's festivities. There is a parade on the final day; that night a queen is crowned during the ball.

As you approach Winsted on Rte. 44 there is a traffic light at jct. where Conn 263 goes right toward Winchester Center. Take this to first corner, to the:

Solomon Rockwell House, 225 Prospect St. *Open mid-June thru Sept. daily exc. Wed. & Sun., 2-5; Adults 50¢, Children under 12, 25¢.* An 1813 home and one of the best examples of Federal period architecture, this is often referred to as Solomon's Temple. It contains period furnishings and some fine portraits.

By following Rte. 263 into Winchester Center you would be at the scene of the annual Blueberry Festival in early August.

Back to US 44, turn right and drive a few miles to New Hartford and jct. with Conn 219. Turn left on this and drive to the BARKHAMSTED COMPENSATING RESERVOIR. Bathing and boating available.

Continue to jct. with Conn 318 and take it to the left, crossing Saville Dam. VISTA parking on far side. Continue to jct. where Rte. 181 turns left at a small bridge. Just before this bridge, turn right through People's State Forest. This takes you to Riverton; you pass the Old Riverton Inn at jct. with Conn 20. Across the river from the Inn is:

Hitchcock Chair Company, Riverton, Conn. 06065. *Open year around, Tues. thru Sat., 10-5. Dec. to May, Sat. only. Free. Rest rooms.* (203) 379-1003.

Riverton was formerly named Hitchcocks-Ville. Here in 1826 Lambert Hitchcock, founder of the village, built a factory for the production of a special kind of chair decorated with fine stenciling that included his name and that of the town. The chairs became famous for quality and style, and today are considered valuable antiques. After the founder's death the works gradually became inactive. In 1946 a new company was formed to reproduce Hitchcock chairs and cabinet furniture. Today we will visit the gift shop, Connecticut House, where we can look through picture windows into the adjoining factory where the furniture is being machined. MUSEUM is in nearby church.

Take Conn 20 through town toward Winsted. Shortly you reach Conn 8. Take this south through Winsted to Torrington. Exit at Rte. 4 and take it west through town. At jct. with Rte. 8 is Yankee Pedlar Inn. On Conn 4 shortly after the business section, watch for a sign to the Mountain Laurel Display on Mountain Road. Turn right and drive to:

Indian Lookout. *Open during laurel season, usually near end of first or second week in June for early blossoms, then lasting 2-3 weeks following. Weekdays, 1-8:30 p.m. Sat. & Sun. 9 a.m.-8:30 p.m. Those unable to walk may drive up to the Lookout between 5 & 6:30 p.m. on weekdays only. Sundays especially crowded. No charge, but donations accepted. Groups arrange for special tours, also for fall foliage tours.*

In 1947 Paul Freedman began to clear his 6 acres of mountainside to allow the laurel on it to survive and spread. With his wife he landscaped the area mingling other plants and trees to provide the most natural balanced setting possible. The 6 acres grew to 100 and by 1958 the public was first invited to this fairyland of pink that hung like clouds over the whole mountain.

Return trip: Go back on Conn 4 through Torrington to Conn 8. Take this south to the Merritt Parkway to New York.

For a direct route to Indian Lookout, skipping rest of drive: Hutchinson Pkwy. and Merritt to Exit to Conn 8. North on this for over 40 *m.* to Torrington. Exit at Conn 4, drive west through town to Mountain Road and Indian Lookout.

Clocks and Locks of Old Connecticut

TRIP E-9 EXTENSION. *We'll Visit:*

AMERICAN CLOCK AND WATCH MUSEUM, Bristol (Apr. thru Oct., afts.)

LOCK MUSEUM OF AMERICA, INC. Terryville. (May-Oct.)

FARMINGTON MUSEUM, STANLEY-WHITMAN HOUSE

HILL-STEAD MUSEUM (Afts. Wed., Thurs., Sat. & Sun.)

DISTANCE AND TOLLS: To Farmington via Bristol, from NYC Exits about 100-110 *m.* Mainly fast speeds exc. in towns. Via G.W. Bridge, $1.05; via Major Deegan & Thruway, also Hutchinson River Pkwy., 45¢. Plus return.
FOOD: Near Bristol, Howard Johnson's, diners. In Farmington, Corner House.

American Clock and Watch Museum, 100 Maple St., Bristol, Conn. 06010. *Open April thru Oct. daily 1-5. Adm. fee — adults $2. 8-16, $1, under 8, free. Family $4.* (203) 583-6070. *Rest rooms. Ample parking. Some steps for handicapped.*

Connecticut was once the watch-making center of the country. Housed in a fine old building constructed in 1801 is a priceless display of clocks of every type. Horologists are aware of its value but this exhibit appeals to amateurs as well. The timepieces date from about 1820, when factories first started turning them out, up to the present. Tools of the trade are also on display.

Lock Museum of America, Inc. 114 Main St., Terryville, Conn. 06786. *Open May-Oct. daily exc. Mon. 1:30-4:30. Free. If closed, phone numbers on door.* (203) 589-9797.

Thousands of locks and keys, many made in Connecticut ("cradle of the lock industry") are of great interest to collectors and researchers. There are rare 19th century locks, and a variety used for handcuffs, leg irons, cabinets, trunks, safes, some ornate, others utilitarian. Worth a visit.

Farmington Museum—Stanley-Whitman House, National Historic Landmark, High St., Farmington, Conn. 06032. (203) 677-9222. *Open year around. Apr.-Nov. daily exc. Mon., 2-5. Wed., Sat. also 10-noon. Dec.-March, Fri., Sat., Sun. 2-5. Sat. also 10-12. Closed major hol. Fees: Adults $1., children 50¢. Parking area. Handicapped, a few steps. Special rest room facilities.*

Built about 1660, this is a good example of the "framed overhang" style, popular in England and brought here by the settlers. Local craftsmen made many of the furnishings and the exhibits include some rare antiques. Architects are especially interested in the construction.

Hill-Stead Museum, Mountain Road, Farmington, Conn. 06032. *Open year around, Wed., Thurs., Sat. & Sun. 2-5. Fees: adults $1.; children, 50¢. Tour lasts about an hour; last tour starts at 4. Handicapped: A few steps.* (203) 677-9064.

Now we turn to the ornate. This beautiful mansion, built in 1901, reminds us of Mount Vernon on the Potomac and is done throughout in the grand style. Among the valuable period furnishings and art objects from around the world is a collection of Impressionist paintings by such artists as Monet, Degas, Manet and Whistler. The grounds and the VISTAS from them are superb.

FOR THE DRIVER: Take Hutchinson River Parkway, then the Merritt to Exit 52 to Conn 8. Go north on Rte. 8 about 25 *m.* to jct. with I-84. Follow signs to I-84 east to Hartford. Proceed 12 *m.* to exit to West St., at Conn 229. Turn left from ramp toward Bristol and take Rte. 229 about 6 *m.* to the end, at jct. with US 6 – turn left and proceed 2 *m.* to jct. with Conn 69. At this point, where it turns right, you turn left, crossing railroad tracks. This is on Maple St. The following light is at the corner where the American Clock and Watch Museum is on your left. Back on US 6, left to Lock Museum, 114 Main St. in Terryville. Then back on Rte. 6, passing Howard Johnson's and many snack places. Continue to jct. with Conn 10, turn left toward Farmington. Watch for traffic light at Mountain Rd. Turn right for both museums. First comes High St., where the Farmington Museum is to your left. Just above is the entrance to Hill-Stead Museum, down a private lane. The streets to both museums are parallel. Continue ahead on either to the jct. with Conn 4. Turn left to center of town. At jct. with Conn 10 is Corner House restaurant (in motor inn), and other eating places.

Return trip: Back on Conn 10, follow signs in town to I-84 west toward Waterbury. Return the way you came, via Conn 8 south to the Merritt Pkwy.

Unusual Houses and Footprints in Connecticut

TRIP E-10 EXTENSION. *We'll Visit:*

WEBB HOUSE, Wethersfield (Closed Mon.)

ISAAC STEVENS HOUSE (Same)

SILAS DEANE HOUSE (Same)

THE OLD ACADEMY (Tues., Thurs., Sat. afts. mid-May to mid-Oct.)

BUTTOLPH-WILLIAMS HOUSE (Mid-May to mid-Oct.)

DINOSAUR STATE PARK, Rocky Hill (Apr.–Nov.)

DISTANCE AND TOLLS: To Wethersfield from NYC exits, about 100 *m.*, fast speeds. Via G.W. Bridge, $1.50; via Major Deegan & Thruway, 90¢; via

Hutchinson River Pkwy. 90¢. On return via Wilbur Cross & Merritt Pkwys., add 35¢. If via Connecticut Turnpike, $1.50.
FOOD; On Turnpike, Holiday House Service Area. Near Wethersfield, Clam Box, Howard Johnson's.

Webb House, 211 Main St., Wethersfield, Conn. 06109. *Open year around, Tues. thru Sat. 10-4. From mid-May to mid-Oct. also Sun. 1-4. Adults $1.50, special rates for children and groups. Special comb. ticket available for the 3 adjoining houses, listed below $4. Group rates. Guided tours last about an hour here; allow about 2 hr. 45 min. for all three. Parking in streets.* (203) 529-0612.

A house of distinction and a showcase of 18th century life in its finest sense, this historic dwelling was known as Hospitality Hall because of the number of important visitors in its day. We can visit the council room where Washington and Rochambeau planned what eventually led to the Battle of Yorktown and American independence. The Washington chamber contains the wallpaper that was hung in his honor when the Commander-in-Chief slept there. We also find priceless antiques, furniture, porcelain, tapestries, silver. This home is filled with real treasures, worth making the trip to see.

Isaac Stevens House, 215 Main St., Wethersfield, Conn. 06109. *Open same hours as Webb House. Small fee. Comb. ticket for the 3 houses available. Guided tour of this alone lasts about an hour.*

Less formal than the Webb House, this one shows the same excellent taste in furnishings and an unusual use of color in the paints used. There are fine antiques, and one whole bedroom has been converted into a children's museum.

Silas Deane House, 203 Main St., Wethersfield, Conn. 06109. *Open same hours as Webb House. Small fee. Comb. ticket to the 3 houses. Guided tour of this lasts about 45 minutes.*

Recently under restoration, this house of 1766 was built for the purpose of entertaining on a grand scale. Thus it has a spaciousness and elegance not found in other homes in the area. As with the other two, every item inside is either authentic or an accurate reproduction.

The Old Academy (Wethersfield Historical Society), 150 Main St., Wethersfield, Conn. 06109. *Open mid-May thru mid-Oct. Tues., Thurs. & Sat. 1-4. Small fee. Limited rest room facilities. Handicapped: Some climbing.* (203) 529-7656.

Built in 1801 by the First School Society, this later became the Town Hall and today is a museum of unusual value. Everything on display came from the archives of local families and includes Colonial artifacts and tools as well as Indian relics, records and documents. For those interested in the area's history, particularly that of Wethersfield, this is the place to come for information.

Buttolph-Williams House, Broad St., Wethersfield, Conn. 06109. *Open mid-May to mid-Oct. daily 1-5. Fees: 75¢ adults, children and groups, 25¢. Handicapped by arrangement.*

From 1692, when this house was built, to 1752, the date on the Webb House, some radical changes in living evidently occurred. The Buttolph-Williams House is a typical mansion house of an earlier and more rugged era and we have an unusual chance to observe the contrast as we visit both. Built in the Jacobean style, this has been faithfully restored to its original period. Of special interest: Ye Greate Kitchin, filled with many utensils of the times.

Dinosaur State Park, Rocky Hill, Conn. 06067. *Open daily exc. Christmas, 9-4. Free. Guided tours. Groups reserve in advance. Food: Snacks in season, picnics. Handicapped: Paths fairly level and paved. Wheelchairs accommodated through doors; rest rooms have grab rails.* (203) 566-2304, for tours.

The operator of a bulldozer turned up the first of the odd appearing markings. His find alerted scientists, who identified the marks as footprints belonging to dinosaurs of 185 million years ago. With the help of Governor Dempsey, the State Geological Survey, Yale's Peabody Museum and assorted paleontologists the fossilized footprints are being preserved. Some have been electrically heated and sanded, then covered with vinyl sheeting. The rest are being cared for inside a large plastic dome which is kept inflated by air pressure from within.

Geologists and paleontologists consider this discovery of 1,000 prints the rarest good fortune for it's one of the largest ever found of dinosaurs that lived during approximately the same period. Visitors may make their own plaster casts of one of the prints. This requires 10 lb. plaster of Paris and ¼ cup cooking oil (and rags). Each cast takes over ½ hr. to complete. Limited number of molds available. Dinosaur State Park has been designated a National Natural Landmark.

FOR THE DRIVER: Take Hutchinson River Pkwy. north into Merritt Pkwy. in Connecticut. Continue across Milford toll bridge, follow signs to Connecticut Turnpike. Take second entrance marked east to New London. Pass Holiday House Service Area. Continue about 15 min. to Exit 48 and take I-91 north. Drive about 35 m. to exit to Marsh St., Old Wethersfield. Turn off and follow signs into town and to Buttolph-Williams House. However, pass this house for the present and continue to Main St. At this jct. is the First Church of Christ, originally the Meeting House, with its landmark steeple.

Diagonally across from this are three historic houses. Turn left on Main St. for the Isaac Stevens house, the Joseph Webb House and the Silas Deane House. The Tour starts in the center one, Webb House.

Continue the same direction on Main St. Just beyond, across the street is The Old Academy.

To visit the Cove: Turn back on Main, passing the Meeting House (Church) and continue several blocks. It's best to park along the street and walk to the

Cove, just ahead off Main St. Near the Cove is the ancient Cove Warehouse, built before 1692 when Wethersfield was the northernmost point ships could reach on the Connecticut River and goods therefore had to be stored for distribution. This building eventually will be turned into a maritime museum. Check at The Old Academy for details.

Then go back on Main St. to jct. with Marsh, by the church. Turn left to Broad St. On the right is the Buttolph-Williams House.

Take Broad St., passing Village Green, and proceed to Maple St., Conn 3. Turn right on this to jct. with Conn 99, at light. Go left on 99 and proceed 2 or 3 *m.* Pass the Clam Box, and at jct. with I-91, a Howard Johnson's. Other eating places on this route. Continue to 3rd light after I-91 jct. Pick up signs to State Veteran's Hospital, bearing right. Turn as directed; across the road from the hospital is Dinosaur State Park.

Return Trip: Continue the same direction, passing the dome. A short way ahead is another entrance to I-91. Take this south, toward New Haven and NYC. Shortly you may prefer to take Exit 17 to Rte. 15 and return on the Wilbur Cross Pkwy. This becomes the Merritt, then the Hutchinson River Pkwy. Or stay on I-91 to the Connecticut Turnpike in New Haven and follow that back to the city.

A Memorable Day in Hartford

TRIP E-11 EXTENSION. For those who would like to savor that special atmosphere of a State Capital, Connecticut provides a treat. In Hartford are found not only the gold-domed Capitol building, the offices of State, both historic and modern, but also houses with wonderful memorabilia of people like Mark Twain and Harriet Beecher Stowe, a famous tower we may climb for VISTAS, two of our finer museums, and a park with a fabulous display garden. One of our few trips within a sizeable city, this will be made less confusing because we'll enter it "through the back door", thus avoiding freeway traffic and unfamiliar exits and streets. To start things off we'll look in on an excellent children's museum.

We'll Visit:

> CHILDREN'S MUSEUM OF HARTFORD, West Hartford
> ELIZABETH PARK
> CONNECTICUT HISTORICAL SOCIETY (Closed Sun. & Hol.)
> MARK TWAIN'S HOUSE (Closed Mon.)
> HARRIET BEECHER STOWE'S HOUSE (Same)
> CONNECTICUT STATE CAPITOL (Weekdays)
> CONNECTICUT STATE LIBRARY (Weekdays & Sat.)
> WADSWORTH ATHENEUM (Closed Mon.)
> CONSTITUTION PLAZA

TRAVELER'S INSURANCE BLDG. OBSERVATION TOWER (Mid-May–Oct.)

OLD STATE HOUSE (MUSEUM) (Tues. thru Sat. afternoons)

BUTLER-MC COOK HOMESTEAD

DISTANCE AND TOLLS: Round trip from NYC exits about 240 m. Mainly fast speeds; slower in city. Via G.W. Bridge, $1. plus bridge; via Major Deegan & Thruway, 25¢.; via Hutchinson River Pkwy., 25¢. Return trip, if taking Wilbur Cross Pkwy and Merritt, or Connecticut Turnpike, add tolls.

FOOD: Chain snack places and restaurants just off highways and also approaching the city. Snacks in season, also picnics in Elizabeth Park.

Children's Museum of Hartford, 950 Trout Brook Drive, West Hartford, Conn. 06119. *Open year around daily, 2:30-5 weekdays, Sat. from 10, Sun. from 1. July & Aug., Mon.-Sat. from 10, Sun. from 1. Closed major holidays. Free, Planetarium shows and Aquarium, adm. fees. Check schedules. Handicapped: Entrances to both buildings on ground level. One step to auditorium.* (203) 236-2961.

A handsome modern structure houses the fifth oldest museum in America. Two buildings feature Colonial displays, American Indian artifacts, an atmospheric Oriental room and garden, natural and scientific exhibits. Adults and children alike are attracted; this might be a good place to foster the natural curiosity of the very young child. The Planetarium provides popular and timely shows with its Space Transit Projector under a 40-foot dome.

Elizabeth Park, Asylum St. & Prospect Ave. *Open year around daily. Greenhouses, same. Free. Food: Snacks in season; picnics. Rest rooms near greenhouses. Parking areas.*

This is one of the finest parks in the region; its ROSE DISPLAY GARDENS are widely advertised. It is a beautiful spot for walking or driving through. Bring camera.

Connecticut Historical Society Museum and Library, 1 Elizabeth St., Hartford, Conn. 06105. *Museum open June thru Labor Day, weekdays 1-5, rest of year, Mon.-Sat. 1-5. Library open year around; Mon.-Fri. 9:30-5:30, Sat. 9-5. In summer, closes Sat. noon, also closed major holidays. Free. Parking area. Rest rooms. Handicapped: elevator; wheelchair.* (203) 236-5621.

The Museum displays important historical items, some of which once belonged to Israel Putnam, Nathan Hale and Mark Twain. Regional furniture as developed over the years, and portraits of many important Connecticut people also are shown. The Library contains a large collection of genealogies, early Connecticut papers and maps, manuscripts, Bible records and local history.

Mark Twain's House, 351 Farmington Ave., Hartford, Conn. 06105, (203) 525-9317. *Open year around, June 15-Labor Day, daily 10-4:30; rest of year, Tues.-Sat. 9:30-4: Sun. from 1. Closed major hol. Adm. fee for single house, adults $1.75; under 16 yrs., $1. Comb. tour to include Stowe House, adults $3., under 16, $1.75. (Subject to change.) Guided tours only, starting continuously, lasting about 45 min.; combined tour lasts about 1¼ hrs. and may be taken on different days. Handicapped: Many steps, inside and out.*

This is a colorful old house, perhaps best appreciated by those who have read the author's works and know his humor. We'll tour the south facade, modeled after a Mississippi River steamboat, the pilot-house styled dressing room, the fireplace with a window above it to allow Mark Twain to watch both the flames and the weather at one time. He lived here for nearly twenty years. His followers find Nook Farm a delight.

Harriet Beecher Stowe's House, 77 Forest St. *Open same hours as Mark Twain's House; fees, same. Guided tours only, lasting about ½ hour alone, or 1¼ hours with Mark Twain's. Groups by appointment only.*

Also living on Nook Farm was the author of *Uncle Tom's Cabin*, Harriet Beecher Stowe. Her personal touch, less flamboyant than that of her neighbor, is seen throughout this Gothic cottage style home. We'll see many fine antiques, the table on which she wrote part of her most famous book, her ten-sided bedroom and some of her own paintings. As at the Mark Twain house, a Victorian atmosphere prevails.

Connecticut State Capitol, Capitol Ave., (203) 566-3662. *Guided tours Jan.-mid-Nov. weekdays, 9:15, 10:30, 11:45 a.m., 1, 2:15 p.m. Free. Handicapped facilities.*

Built in 1878, this since has been the seat of the State government. It contains material tracing the development of Connecticut during its early years and also in the nation's wars. Statues and art exhibits are seen throughout.

Connecticut State Library, 231 Capitol Ave. *Open weekdays 9-5, Sat. 9-1. Closed Sun. and major holidays. Free.* (203) 566-3056.

Here are displays pointing up the importance of Connecticut's past. There are Indian relics, historical paintings, the Mitchelson Coin Collection, another of Colt Firearms, the original 1662 Royal Charter and even a piece of the famed Charter Oak.

Wadsworth Atheneum, 25 Atheneum Square North, Hartford, Conn. 06103. *Open year around Tues.–Fri. 11-3, Sat., Sun. 11-5. Closed major holidays. Adm. donation, adults $1., others 50¢. Under 12 free. Tours by appointment. Handicapped: Elevators. If advance notice is given, a* *side door will be opened to avoid stairs to main entrance. Food: Restaurant and snack bar.* (203) 278-2670.

One of the country's oldest and more important museums of art, the Atheneum contains 65 galleries of permanent displays. These include such rare art treasures as Renoir's *Monet Painting in the Garden at Argenteuil* and Rembrandt's *Portrait of Saskia.* Priceless 18th-century porcelains include the J. Pierpont Morgan collection. A greek pyxis (bowl) could be 3,000 years old. A recent account listed 39,350 works of art on view; that should provide something for nearly every taste.

Constitution Plaza. These elegant twelve acres of high-rise buildings and landscaped plazas show what can be done with urban renewal, and $40 million. Closed to traffic, it is the setting for many popular happenings, just one of which is the Mark Twain Frog Jumping Contest. Concerts, outdoor fashion shows, art exhibits are scheduled, along with the Christmas Festival of Light and an Easter Sunrise Service.

Travelers Insurance Tower Tours, One Tower Square, Hartford, Conn. 06115. (203) 277-2431. *Free group tours mid-May thru May 31, and Sept. 1 thru Oct. by reservation only. From June thru Aug. tours available to all, 8:30-3:30 Mon.-Fri. exc. major hol. No reservations needed. NOTE: 70 steps from where elevator stops to observation deck. No views en route.*

When this famous tower was built in 1919, only six buildings in America were taller. Its tip is 527 feet above sidewalk-level; 27 stories up is the observation area, where we can look over a stone balustrade. Still higher is the beacon with 24 3000-watt mercury vapor lamps, or 30 million candle power. From the Tower we get splended panoramic VISTAS of city and environs - a good place to start the movie story of your trip. Bring binoculars.

Old State House, 800 Main St., Hartford, Conn. 06103. *Open year around, Tues.-Sat. 12-4. Closed major holidays. Fees: Adults 50¢, children 10¢. Group rates. Group tours by appointment; religious, patriotic, educational groups free. Public rest rooms adjacent to bldg., parking in Plaza Parking Garages east of bldg. Handicapped: Can manage first floor, but there are stairs to a second, and no elevators. (may be closed for renovation.)*

A fine example of Federal architecture, this historic building was designed by Charles Bulfinch and completed in 1796 at the cost of $52,480. It contains original furnishings including some in use while it was the State's second capitol. We'll see excellent exhibits of Early American art; highlights are some beautifully executed public rooms such as the Council Chamber.

Butler-McCook Homestead, 396 Main St. *Open mid-May to mid-Oct. daily 12-4. Rest of year, Tues., Thurs., Sat., Sun. noon-4 p.m. Adm. fee. Adults $1. children 25¢.* (203) 522-1806.

One of the dwindling number of historic houses that did not get swallowed up by urban renewal changes, this is a well preserved home built 1782, filled with furnishings of the 18th and 19th centuries. There are collections of household items, toys, and objets d'art. Behind the building a Carriage House contains a museum.

FOR THE DRIVER: Take I-684 to Brewster, then I-84 east toward Danbury and Hartford. Continue to Exit 43 marked Park Road, West Hartford Center. After ramp turn right on Park Rd. At next corner turn left at light, on Trout Brook Drive, toward West Hartford Center. Shortly on right is sign to Children's Museum of Hartford Planetarium and Aquarium.

From Museum, turn right and continue on Trout Brook Dr. for 3 lights, to Asylum Ave., across from St. Joseph's College. Turn right on Asylum; a short distance ahead, right, is a park. We may enter it at corner on Steele Rd., or continue to entrance just beyond, at sign Elizabeth Park. This road leads to picnic areas and greenhouses where we can park then walk to Rose Gardens. To drive past the gardens, continue to next corner, Prospect Ave., and turn right, following signs.

For the Connecticut Historical Society, return to Asylum Ave. and turn right. Proceed for 2 more lights after Prospect Ave. to Elizabeth St. At this junction is the Connecticut Historical Museum and Library, with a large Hartford Fire Alarm Bell in front. Parking lot entered from Asylum Ave.

Go back up Asylum to Prospect Ave. and turn left. A couple of lights beyond is Farmington Ave. (Conn. 4). Turn left on this and proceed several blocks, passing shopping center. Just beyond, on right, is entrance to Mark Twain House. Keep in right lane for visitor parking lot on corner; this also serves the Stowe House. *Caution:* In Hartford streets are especially crowded from about 3:45 to 4:30 when the insurance companies let out.

Take Rte 4 to right and continue into town. We pass an enormous Colonial style structure, the Aetna Life Building (tours available). Just beyond is entrance to an Interstate Highway. *Before* this comes Broad St. Turn right on Broad and proceed to traffic light at Capitol Ave. Turn left; just ahead is the State Capitol. Some parking nearby, but best to look up a municipal parking lot, then walk. The next attractions are within a few blocks of one another.

Behind the Capitol is Bushnell Park. Across the street from the Capitol is the Connecticut State Library. Continue, walking or driving, on Capitol Ave. as far as it goes, to Main St. Turn left, passing the U.S. Court House. Just beyond, on the right, is the Wadsworth Atheneum. A little farther is the Travelers Insurance Co. Tower. A few blocks beyond is the Old State House, 800 Main St. Close by is Constitution Plaza.

Turn back on Main St. to No. 396 and the Butler-McCook Homestead.

Return Trip: To return the way you came, go back through town and follow signs to I-84 West. For a different route home: Follow signs to I-91 South, toward New Haven. On the way you have an opportunity to switch to the Wilbur Cross Parkway leading to the Merritt, then the Hutchinson River Pkwys. Use Exit 17 for this, at signs to Route 15. Or remain on I-91 to junction with the Connecticut Turnpike in New Haven and follow signs to NYC.

A Complete Restoration: Old Sturbridge

TRIP E-12 EXTENSION. *We'll Visit:*

OLD STURBRIDGE VILLAGE

DISTANCE AND TOLLS: From NYC exit, about 150 *m.* Fast speeds. Via G.W. Bridge, $1.75; via Major Deegan & Thruway, $1.15; via Hutchinson River Pkwy., $1.15. Plus return.
FOOD: On Conn. Turnpike, Holiday House Service Area; Howard Johnson's at Pkwy. exits.

Old Sturbridge Village, Sturbridge, Mass. 01566. (617) 347-3362. *Open Apr.-Oct. daily, 9:30-5:30. March & Nov. until 4:30. Dec.-Feb. daily exc. Mon., 10-4. (Open Mon. if hol. or school vacation.) Closed Christmas and Jan. 1. Fees: Adults $5.50, (less out of season, inquire) 6-14 yrs. $2. Under 6 free (subject to change). Covers all exhibits and demonstrations, carry-all rides, parking, picnic areas. Special group rates; dining reservations for groups on request. Food: Village Tavern serves buffet from 11:30 to 2:30 daily, late May to early November. Cafeteria from 11-3:30; Bar, 11:30-2:30 daily, Sun. 1-2:30 from late May to Dec. 1. Picnic areas. Handicapped: Much walking, paths not paved. Steps into houses, doors narrow; however, there are benches and shade. Seeing Eye dogs permitted in buildings. Pets: leashed, not in buildings. Hand camera only.*

A wonderful life-sized village showing New England as it was in 1790 and the years that immediately followed serves as a living history museum of how things were. It's a reconstructed town with nearly forty genuinely antique structures gathered from many sections of New England, including all buildings needed in a functioning town of the times. Here are the craft shops, village meeting house, grist mill, lawyer's office, tavern, schoolhouse, even the pillory and stocks.

In the bake house we buy our cookies hot out of the oven—raisin hobnails, grist mill grahams, walnut patties. A horse-drawn carry-all takes visitors on a free ride through the woods to the mills (carding, grist and saw), past Farmer's Nooning, a mid-day snack bar near the pond, and across the covered bridge, brought from Dummerston, Vermont. As we go, we hear a lively history of what we're passing and how it fitted into village life during America's early years of independence.

FOR THE DRIVER: Take Hutchinson River Pkwy. north into the Merritt Pkwy. and cross toll bridge at Milford. Here, follow signs to Connecticut Turnpike and take 2nd entrance marked East to New London. Continue about 15 min. to New

Haven, passing Holiday House Service Area. Take Exit 48 to I-91 north and drive to Hartford area where you pick up Rtes. 6 & 15 east to Providence and Boston. Get in left lane. Cross Charter Oak Bridge and proceed on Rte. 15 and I-86. About 45 *m* above Hartford take exit and follow signs to Old Sturbridge Village.

Return trip: Go back on Rte. 15 to Hartford joining I-91 south to New Haven and NYC. To avoid truck route take Exit 17 from I-91, following signs to Rte. 15 south via Wilbur Cross Pkwy. This becomes the Merritt, then Hutchinson River Pkwy.

From New York City Eastward Along Connecticut's Shore

• *We start at the eastern limit of the metropolis at City Island, then move through parts of Westchester County into southern Connecticut, and follow the shoreline of Long Island Sound almost to where Rhode Island begins. Some of these will be EXTENSION Trips, consuming a whole day. To reach Area F from New York City and environs, use Exit Points: George Washington Bridge toward New York City, Hutchinson River Parkway, Tappan Zee Bridge toward New York City and Throgs Neck Bridge from Long Island.*

Main roads: Hutchinson River Parkway, becoming the Merritt Parkway in Connecticut.

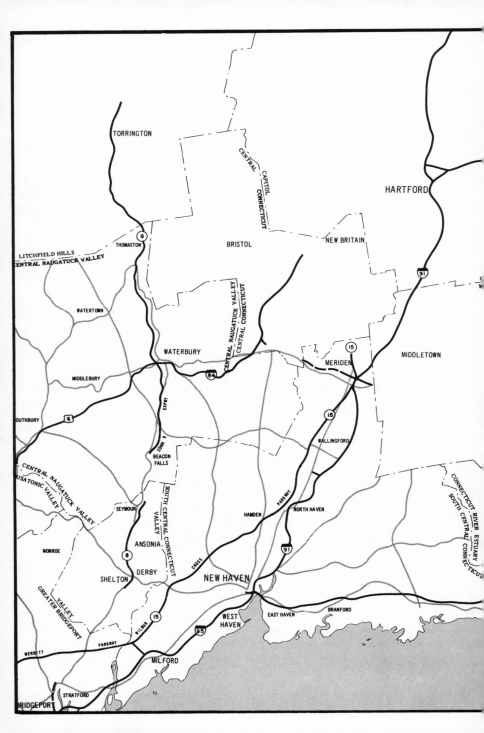

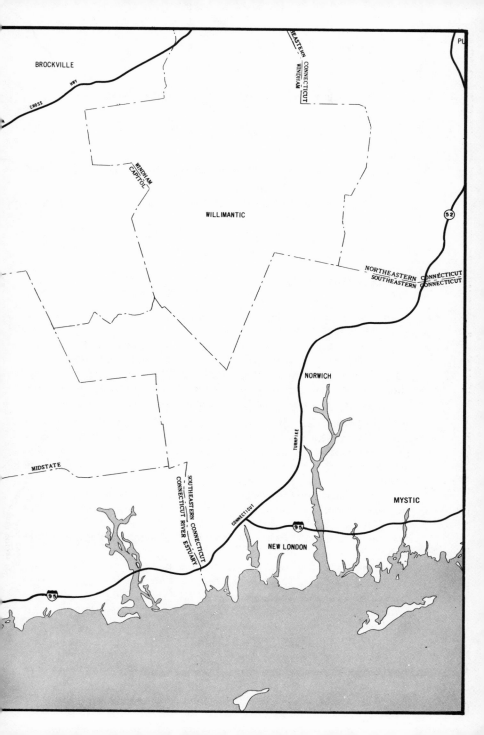

City Island and the Shore Road

TRIP F-1. *We'll Visit:*

CITY ISLAND, Bronx, N.Y.

RATSEY MUSEUM, City Island (Closed Sun.)

BARTOW-PELL MANSION, Bronx (Tues., Fri. & Sun. afts.)

ST. PAUL'S CHURCH, Mt. Vernon

THOMAS PAINE MEMORIALS, New Rochelle (Wed. thru Sun. afts.)

SQUARE HOUSE, Rye (Daily exc. Sat. & Mon.)

DISTANCE AND TOLLS: Mostly bordering on New York City; about 10-12 miles to Rye. Average or slow speeds. If taking Hutchinson River Pkwy. south, 25¢. Plus return toll.
FOOD: On City Island, Lobster Box, closed Mon. Thwaite's Inn. Plus snacks on island and in towns along the way.

City Island. Some of the finest yachts that ever sailed the Sound were built here at Kretzer's, Minneford's and other shops, and the sails from Ratsey's loft are famous. The place has Victorian landmarks. Many come here to sail and to enjoy seafood dinners. There are boat rental and fishing opportunities. Parking space is at a premium in season.

Ratsey Museum, E. Schofield St., City Island, N.Y. 10464. *Open year around, Mon.-Fri. 8-4:30, Sat. 8-12 noon. Free. Park in street. Stairs.* A small museum features ship models, instruments, documents and articles pertaining to sailmaking. Visitors may look into adjoining sail loft and watch craftsmen at work.

The approach to City Island is via Pell's Point, scene of a skirmish between Glover's Marblehead regiment and British after the battle of Long Island. There is a marker on the huge Glover's Rock. On the shore east of the highway is Orchard Beach, open Memorial Day until after Labor Day.

Bartow-Pell Mansion, Shore Road, Pelham Bay Park, Bronx, New York 10464. *House open year around Tues., Fri. & Sun. 1-5, gardens daily exc. Mon. Closed 2 weeks in summer. Fees: house 50¢; under 12, free with adult. Gardens free. Handicapped: Some climbing in house, but those on crutches could manage a good deal, also can walk to top of Sunken Gardens for fine views.* (212) 885-1461.

Built for descendents of the Pell and Bartow families, prominent in local history, this fine mansion is considered an outstanding example of domestic Greek Revival architecture. The rooms show a spacious simplicity and contain priceless furnishings, some of them loaned by the Metropolitan Museum of Art, the Museum of the City of New York and the Brooklyn Museum of Art. Still more came from members of the Internationl Garden Club, which restored the building and now holds its meetings here. Maintained by a garden club, the formal gardens are, naturally, superlative.

St. Paul's Church, 897 South Columbus Ave., Mount Vernon, N.Y. *Grounds open daily, year around. Guided tours by appointment. Self-guiding tours available. No charge.* This church has been designated the National Shrine of the Bill of Rights, commemorating the election of 1733 that led to the trial of John Peter Zenger, New York printer, and acquittal on the charge of seditious libel. The decision is a milestone in establishing freedom of the press. When the election was held on the Green, Quakers were denied the right to vote because they would not take an oath on the Bible. Zenger fought their case in his *Weekly Journal.* A small church on the Green was replaced later by the nucleus of the present structure, restored to its 1793 appearance. The graveyard contains graves of three centuries. In 1978 the church was made a National Park.

Thomas Paine Memorial Museum and Cottage, North & Paine Aves., New Rochelle, N.Y. *Open year around, Wed. thru Sun. 2-5. Verify before making special trip. Donations. Handicapped will find steps with good railings; doors of house narrow for wheelchairs. Guided Tours. Parking on Museum lot only.*

The great pamphleteer who wrote *Common Sense* and did so much in the cause of American freedom lived here only briefly. His neighbors, who were Huguenots, did not welcome him because of his radical views. Yet today it is the Huguenot Society that is preserving this memorial to Thomas Paine. His small cottage is furnished in the period when he was alive (1737-1809) but there are also some fine Victorian pieces.

In the Museum are cases of documents, including many of Paine's original manuscripts. This is not a large attraction, but pertinent because of Paine's influence on Revolutionary opinion.

Square House, Rte. 1 & Purchase St., Rye, N.Y. 10580. *Open year around, daily exc. Sat. & Mon., 2:30-4:30. Donations.*

The Rye Historical Society has headquarters in this fine old house where George Washington twice stopped in 1789, and which was visited by such notables as John Adams and Lafayette. There are seven rooms with period furnishings, also rotating displays of a historical nature.

FOR THE DRIVER: Exit Point for all: Hutchinson River Pkwy. Via G.W. Bridge from New Jersey take Cross Bronx Expressway east to Hutchinson River Pkwy. north. From areas above New York City line take Hutchinson River Pkwy. south, passing 1 toll booth.

All: From Hutchinson River Pkwy. take Exit 5 to Orchard Beach and City Island. At rotary follow signs to City Island. Proceed past Lobster Box, Thwaite's Inn and others to E. Schofield St., dead end, and turn left to the end, to Ratsey Museum, right. Park in street.

Return to the main avenue; turn left to drive to end of island (no parking) then back the way you came, passing Minneford's, Kretzer's and others. Cross bridge, go back to light and follow signs, right, to Shore Road north, thence to Bartow-Pell Mansion entrance gates on right.

From Mansion, return to Shore Road, go right, continue to light at Pelhamdale Ave. just beyond entrance to NY Athletic Club. Left on Pelhamdale to US 1, Boston Post Road. Take this left; continue underneath Hutchinson Pkwy. overpass. Just beyond at a light, turn right to Mt. Vernon, passing on left the Korvette Shopping Center. Cross bridge. At next light, Rte 22, Columbus Ave., turn left. St. Paul's Church is just ahead, left. Then back on Rte 22, this time staying to traffic light at Sanford Blvd., by Carvel's. Turn right and proceed going under Pkwy.; turn left to entrance to Hutchinson River Pkwy. north. Take this briefly to exit to New Rochelle Road. After ramp, turn right to light at corner, then left on Eastchester Road. Take this as far as it goes, to North Ave., then turn left passing high school and lake. At far end of both, beyond statue is a sign Thomas Paine Cottage; just ahead is the Museum.

Continue on North Ave. to 2nd light. Turn left on street after light, to Webster Ave. Turn right on Webster and go to end where it merges with the Pkwy. Follow right lane to Hutchinson Pkwy. north.

Continue to jct. with I-287, Cross Westchester Expressway, and take first entrance, east to Rye. Just ahead, join I-287 toward the Connecticut Turnpike and New England Thruway. Take Exit 11 south to Rye; you get off on Boston Post Rd. (US 1). Take this to right several blocks to jct. with NY 120. Here, US 1 bears left, but a side street takes you, right, to the Square House at this jct.

Return trip: Back on US 1 to entrance to Thruway, I-287 west to White Plains. Proceed to Hutchinson River Pkwy. exit 9 S (south) and 9 N (north). For NYC, follow signs to Hutchinson River Pkwy. and Whitestone Bridge (south) to where you started.

For G.W. Bridge area and Major Deegan and Thruway: Stay on I-287 almost to Tappan Zee Bridge. Follow lanes to left marked south to NY. For Thruway: continue on this, it becomes the Major Deegan Expressway in NYC. For G.W. Bridge via Saw Mill River Pkwy. leave at Exit 7 just after merger with Thruway to Saw Mill River Pkwy. southbound. This becomes the Henry Hudson Pkwy. in NYC and goes to G.W. Bridge.

For Play and Recreation at Playland

TRIP F-2. *We'll Visit:*

PLAYLAND, Rye, N.Y.

DISTANCE AND TOLLS: Via G.W. Bridge, under 30 *m.*, via Major Deegan & Thruway, about 20; via Hutchinson River Pkwy. about 15. Mostly fast speeds. New England Thruway (I-95) 25¢; Hutchinson River Pkwy., 25¢. Plus return. **FOOD:** Restaurants, snack bars at park.

Playland, Rye, N.Y. 10580. *Open year around on boardwalk and in nature areas. Amusement Park activities mid-May to Labor Day, daily. Thru June, Mon.-Thurs. 10-5:30. Fri., Sat. 1-midnight. Sun. 1-10. From July, Mon. thru Thurs. 1-11. Fri., Sat. until midnight. Sun. until 10. Fireworks Fri. 9. Swimming pool, from Memorial Day. Pier fishing, March to mid-May and early Sept. to Dec. Ice skating Oct. to March. Boats rented year around for fishing. Fees: Admission free. Parking Mon.-Fri. (to 6 P.M.) $1.25. Fri. (after 6) & Sat. & Sun.—$2. Hol. $3. (Subject to change.) Charges for rides, pool, pier fishing, ice skating, boats, concessions. Food: Restaurants, snack bars, free picnic areas. Handicapped: Benches along boardwalk, no steps. Fireworks 9 P.M. Wed. nights, July 4 thru Labor Day. Check papers for hours park is open.*

This is the only park of its kind in a wide suburban area. It has a 1,200-ft. beach, a boardwalk, a freshwater pool, and a marshland bird sanctuary beside Lake Playland.

And of course the rides—all the latest devices for producing feelings of exhilaration and excitement. The Playland Streamliner for the youngsters; the Dragon roller-coaster for the teen-agers, and many others. Golf for the more leisurely, competitive games for the skillful.

FOR THE DRIVER: Via G.W. Bridge, take Cross Bronx Expressway (I-95) and continue north on it when it becomes the New England Thruway, to Exit 11. Via Throgs Neck Bridge, follow signs I-95 north; it becomes New Eng. Thruway. Go to Exit 11. Via Hutchinson River Parkway below city line: Follow signs to New Eng. Thruway, go to Exit 11. Upper Westchester and Tappan Zee Bridge: Take I-287 (Cross Westchester Expressway) east to Rye. Exit at I-95 (New Eng. Thruway) and take this south to Exit 11 to Playland.

Return Trip: Go back the way you came.

Where General Isaac Putnam Won Fame

TRIP F-3. *We'll Visit:*

BRUCE MUSEUM, Greenwich, Conn. (Closed Sat.)

PUTNAM COTTAGE (May close Sun.)

BUSH-HOLLEY HOUSE (Closed Mon.)

MONTGOMERY PINETUM

DISTANCE to Pinetum via the others: From G.W. Bridge about 40 *m.* From other NYC exits, about 30. Fast or average speeds. **TOLLS:** Via G.W. Bridge,

$1.05; via Maj. Deegan & NY Thruway, 50¢, via Hutchinson River Pkwy. 50¢. Plus return.
FOOD: Near Bruce Museum, Showboat Inn; Manero's. Near Putnam Cottage, Near Pinetum, Clam Box.

Bruce Museum, Bruce Park, Steamboat Rd., Greenwich, Conn. 06830. *Open year around: Mon.-Fri. 10-5, Sun. 2-5, closed Sat. & Holidays. Free. Handicapped: No wheelchairs. 1 step up graded walk to door. Can see many displays on 1st level. Rest rooms on 1st floor.* (203) 869-0376.

We might call this the "everything museum." The viewing areas are quite small but an amazing use is made of space; there is no monotony. Displays include live animals, geological specimens, butterflies, tools of our forefathers, Indian relics. We are reminded that as recently as 350 years ago this area was in the Stone Age, the people living here knowing only stone or bone implements. The museum has a permanent fine art collection.

Museum of Cartoon Art, 384 Field Point Rd., Greenwich, Conn. 06830. *Open Tues.-Fri., 10-4; Sun. 1-5. Donations: Adults $1., under 12 & Sr. Citizens, 50¢.*

Thousands of original cartoons, some dating from the past century, are displayed, from the "Yellow Kid" era to Disney and Peanuts. Sun. aft., vintage animated cartoons shown; 1st Sun. of each month, cartoonists demonstrate.

Putnam Cottage, 243 E. Putnam Ave. (US 1) Greenwich, Conn. 06830. *Open year around. Mon.- Sat. 10-5. May be open Sun. from 2. Adults $1. Children free. Handicapped: Some steps. Parking area in rear. Check first; museum may be closed.* (203) 869-9697.

Originally the Knapp Tavern, a stagecoach stop along the Boston Post Road, this small house, built about the end of the 17th century, is a museum dedicated to General Israel Putnam. "Old Put" was a guest here in 1799 when he discovered a large number of British troops coming up the Post Road. Hurrying from the house, he urged his horse down the side of the cliff, making his escape. The local D.A.R. Chapter has its headquarters here and is responsible for the fine period furnishings.

Bush-Holley House, 39 Strickland Rd., Cos Cob, Conn. 06807. *Open year around, daily exc. Mon. 10-12, 2-5. Sun. 2-4. Nov.-March 2-4. Fees: Adults $1. Children 25¢. Guided tours. Handicapped: Steps into house and more inside. Easy access from parking lot, at rear. Paths to several buildings on the grounds. Rest rooms, equipped for handicapped.* (203) 622-9686.

If you have time for only a limited number of historic houses, perhaps this should be one. Built in 1685, a somewhat enlarged version of a saltbox, this beautiful old home has some interesting features, including the room once used as a counting house and office, with ancient wallpaper made before 1760 picturing a tax stamp of King George II of England. Across from an enormous fireplace in the kitchen, a picture window looks out upon the herb gardens. Many writers and artists gathered here in the past and an art colony met here for a time. An avant garde group went to Europe and returned with French Impressionist paintings.

Behind the house a small building has been made into a museum to contain examples of Rogers groups of statuary. John Rogers of Salem, Mass., for over 30 years made sculptures of homely people and situations which became extremely popular. Nearby is the Art Barn where the Greenwich Historical Society meets. Here we'll find paintings by Elmer Livingston McRae, who had his workshop here. A gift shop upstairs sells an unusual assortment of wares that includes antiques.

Montgomery Pinetum, Bible St., Cos Cob, Conn. 06807. *Open year around, daily 8-4:30; closed weekends and holidays from mid-Nov. to mid-March. Free. Garden Center: Daily Mon. thru Fri. 9-4, from Sept. thru June. In July, daily 9-1; closed Aug. Flower Container Shop: Open weekdays 9-4. Food: Picnic area with grills. Rest rooms in Garden Center (upstairs). No pets. Handicapped: Mostly climbing. On a Sat. in May (watch for notice) is held the annual May Market of garden supplies.*

We're in a Pinetum—a 61-acre arboretum with about 100 different species of coniferous trees, many quite rare. Miles of nature trails through this unusual forest are made easier to hike because of lack of the underbrush normally found in such areas. Wildflowers, flowering bulbs and shrubs appear in season. Picnickers sit among hemlocks overlooking a brook. This should especially appeal to everyone interested in nature or conservation.

FOR THE DRIVER: Take Hutchinson River Parkway to I-287 (Cross Westchester Expressway); take this East toward Rye, to jct. with I-95. Follow signs marked north on Conn. Tpke. to Bridgeport, from left lanes. Proceed on Tpke. into Conn., to Exit 3. At end of ramp bear right to Steamboat Rd. Cross this and continue up hill in Bruce Park following signs to Bruce Museum.

Then back down to Steamboat Rd. (To your left on this are Showboat and Manero's.) Turn right, go under Turnpike then R.R. tracks to where road becomes one way. Turn right one block, at an island, then left. This is Milbank Ave. Continue several traffic lights to a traffic circle. Stay in same direction on Milbank, to jct. with US 1. Turn right a short way to red bldg. on left, Putnam Cottage. Parking in rear.

Back onto US 1 and turn left. Watch for sign for Cos Cob. Shortly after the sign is a major intersection and traffic light at Strickland Ave. Here a small sign directs you to the right; follow it to River Road. On your right, just before the Conn. Tpke. overpass, is the Bush-Holley House. Parking lot just before you reach house.

Return the way you came, to US 1. Turn right, passing a school, left; at the far end is Orchard St., at another light. Turn left on Orchard and follow signs to Montgomery Pinetum on Bible St. In this section is the Clam Box, 453 Post Rd.

Return Trip: Back to US 1 and turn right, passing Putnam Cottage again. Three blocks beyond it is Maple St., with a sharp angle turn to right. Take this and bear right onto North St. Follow this to fhe Merritt Pkwy., this becomes the Hutchinson River Pkwy. in N.Y.

Maggie and Jiggs, A Castle and Pigs

TRIP F-4. *We'll Visit:*

MUSEUM OF CARTOON ART (Closed Mon., Sat.)

STAMFORD MUSEUM AND NATURE CENTER, Stamford, Conn.

BARTLETT ARBORETUM, Stamford (Weekdays)

Museum of Cartoon Art, Comly Ave., Port Chester, N.Y. 10573. (914) 939-0234. *Open Tues.-Fri. 10-4. Sun. 1-4. Cl. Mon., Sat., hol. Adults $1. Sr. Cit. & under 12 yrs. 50¢. Gift Shop. Rest rooms.*

Over 40,000 original cartoons by nearly 1,000 cartoonists are here, along with displays showing how cartoons are made. Movies lasting 20-30 min. are shown on request during the week and continuously on Sundays exc. the first Sun. of the month when famous cartoonists demonstrate their art.

Stamford Museum & Nature Center: 39 Scofieldtown Rd., Stamford, Conn. 06903. (203) 322-1646. *Open year around daily, 9-5; Sun., hol. 1-5. From Nov. to March Mon. hrs. 1-5. Closed Christmas, New Year's, Thanksgiving, and afternoons before each holiday. Fees: Parking, Conn. cars $1. Out of state cars $2., collected all year. Small fees for Planetarium Shows, weekends: Sat. 11 & 3:15, Sun. at 3. Observatory Fri. 8 p.m. Food: Picnics, light snacks. No fires. Handicapped: Can see the farm; you may also drive up to main building. One of the Nature Trails is being prepared to allow wheelchairs to travel through the woods. Numerous benches and shade. Rest rooms.*

The fabulous estate that once belonged to Henri Bendel today looks down upon a picture-book farm, a small gem of a lake dotted with waterfowl, a pool of seals, a handsome nature center and miles of trails. The Farm was established through the Heckscher Foundation for Children and 10-14-year-old junior curators are volunteer farm hands. The Zoo houses animals native to the region plus a few outsiders like seals and woolly monkeys. The main display in the mansion has natural history exhibits, art galleries, the Edgerton Memorial Planetarium, a black-light display on space, a functioning weather station. The gift shop carries an enormous selection of related subjects at prices agreeable to children. Special event: Shearing of the sheep, one Sun. in early May.

Bartlett Arboretum, University of Connecticut, 151 Brookdale Rd., Stamford, Conn. 06903. (203) 322-6971. *Open year around, 8:30 to sunset. Free. Tour arrangements in advance. No picnics. No dogs. No rest rooms.*

This is a fairly new arboretum that is becoming increasingly popular with naturalists, conservationists, tree specialists and youth groups. Eventually it will include a greenhouse, a library, and educational displays. At present we may visit at least ten acres of lush shrubbery and beautiful tree specimens. Over 2,000 varieties of plants are here and the demonstration gardens will provide suggestions for home land-scaping. The Arboretum is operated by the University of Connecticut College of Agriculture. Ask them about lecture series and courses.

FOR THE DRIVER: Take Hutchinson River Pkwy. to exit to King St. Turn right from ramp toward Port Chester. Drive under 1 mile to Comly Ave. on left (red brick church on corner). Left on Comly to entrance on left to Ward Castle & Museum. Then back to Hutchinson R. Pkwy. into Conn. Take this, now Merritt Pkwy., (1 toll). Proceed to Exit 35. At foot of ramp turn left and drive 3/4 mile to where a road branches left. At this jct., turn left into entrance to Stamford Museum and Nature Center. You can leave it from two exits: If taking the upper road past the Observatory, turn left and shortly you'll be back at the jct. where you started, where you next turn left. Or return through the gate where you entered and turn left.

ALL: On the main road, Conn 137, continue past the reservoir; just beyond, on left, is sign to Bartlett Arboretum on Brookdale Road. The last stretch is un-paved.

Back to Conn 137, turn right, again passing Stamford Museum, and continue to Merritt Parkway. Go back the way you came via Merritt Parkway.

Special Interest Tour

TRIP F-5. For this trip, you may have to arrange the best sequence: One gallery is open afternoons all year, another, weekends only, while the third is open in summer and fall. You may prefer to start with the Gardens and work your way back.

We'll Visit:

SILVERMINE GUILD OF ARTISTS, New Canaan, Conn. (Afternoons)

ALDRICH MUSEUM OF CONTEMPORARY ART, Ridgefield, Conn.

HAMMOND MUSEUM, North Salem, N.Y. (Late May thru Dec.)
ORIENTAL STROLL GARDENS, North Salem (Late May to late Oct., Wed.-Sun.)

DISTANCE AND TOLLS: To Hammond Museum via the other two from NYC Exits: About 55-65 *m.* fast and average speeds. Via G.W. Bridge $1.05; via Major Deegan and Thruway, also Hutchinson River Pkwy., 45¢. Plus return tolls.
FOOD: Near Silvermine Guild, Silvermine Tavern, closed Tues. Dec. thru Easter. Near Aldrich Museum in Ridgefield, The Inn at Ridgefield; The Elms Inn.

Silvermine Guild of Artists, Silvermine Rd., New Canaan, Conn. 06840. (203) 966-5617. *Hays Hall and Vassos Gallery open daily year around 12:30-5., exc. Mon. and some holidays. Free Food: Picnic area. Handicapped: A doorstep into Vassos Gallery; one step into Hays Hall. Exhibits on one floor, also rest rooms.*

This famous year-round art center has exhibits in all fields. Three galleries are open to the public, with displays changed every three weeks or so. In mid-June, the New England Exhibition of Painting and Sculpture opens lasting one month. Some time after Thanksgiving comes the Christmas Art Festival, held daily, where various art works in all price brackets are sold. The Children's International Festival is held in spring, while the summers are noted for Chamber Music Concerts.

The Aldrich Museum of Contemporary Art, 258 Main St., Ridgefield Conn. 06877. (203) 438-4519. *Sculpture Garden open year around. Galleries Wed., Sat., Sun. 1-5. Closed 2 wks. mid-Apr. & mid-Sept. Also end of Dec. Groups by appointment. Gallery tours Wed. & Sat. 2:30, last about 1 hr. Fees: Adults $1. Children, Sr. Cit. 50¢. Handicapped: 2 sets low steps to entrance; most displays are upstairs; stairs have good railings. You can visit the (free) sculpture garden outside, adjoining the parking area. Rest rooms upstairs.*

Anyone who understands contemporary art, or who would like to try, should stop in here. An increasing number of visitors are discovering *avant garde* works of merit in this unlikely setting of a small New England town.

Hammond Museum and Oriental Stroll Gardens. (See Trip D-11)

FOR THE DRIVER: Take Hutchinson River Pkwy. north into Merritt Pkwy. Proceed to Exit 37 to Conn 124 and follow signs to New Canaan (less complicated route). In New Canaan Conn 106 merges, from left. Shortly, turn right on Rte. 106 and proceed to where your road turns left. This is Silvermine Road; turn right on this ¿nd drive several blocks to parking area, right, for Silvermine Artists' Guild. At next corner, turn left for the Silvermine Country Store and across from it, the Silvermine Tavern. Then return past the Artists' Guild.

Back the way you came to jct. with Conn 106, from your left. This time, continue straight ahead on it and follow signs to its jct. with Conn 33. Make sharp left turn onto Rte. 33 and proceed several miles into Ridgefield. In town watch for Conn 35 coming in from your left. Just beyond this jct. on your right is the Aldrich Museum. Parking in rear, beside Sculpture Garden.

To locate The Inn at Ridgefield: Go back to corner where Conn 35 turned into Main St. and follow it briefly to The Inn. Then return to Aldrich Museum. From here, continue through town on Main St. Pass the Elms Inn on right. Proceed to where the road branches at blinking light and go straight ahead on Conn 116 about 8 *m.* At jct. with NY 124 in Salem Center, turn right briefly on 124 past June Farm Nursery, to Deveau Road. Follow sign, right, to the Hammond Museum and Oriental Stroll Gardens.

Return Trip: Back to 124, left to jct. with 116 and go back to Ridgefield. Here, take Conn 35 through town then follow Conn 33 back to jct. with Conn 106; turn right passing turn-off to Silvermine, thence back to Conn 124; left on this to Merritt Pkwy. to New York.

For a different route back; take NY 124 to left, after Museum road, to jct. with NY 116 at next corner. Turn right on 116 past Titicus Reservoir to I-684. Go south on this to jct. with Saw Mill River Pkwy. south to Hawthorne Circle, or branch left on I-684 to Hutchinson River Pkwy.

Old MacDonald's Farm
Lures Young and Old

TRIP F-6. *We'll Visit:*

NATURE CENTER FOR ENVIRONMENTAL ACTIVITIES, Westport, Conn.

OLD MAC DONALD'S FARM, South Norwalk. (In season.)

SHERWOOD ISLAND STATE PARK, Westport

DISTANCE AND TOLLS: To Sherwood Park, via the others, from NYC Exits 40-50*m.* Mainly fast speeds, some average. Via G.W. Bridge, $1.55; via Major Deegan & Thruway, 95¢; via Hutchinson River Pkwy. 95¢. Plus return.
FOOD: At Pkwy. exit to Westport, The Three Bears; The Red Barn. Restaurant at Old MacDonald's, Red Coach Grill, Cook's, Pancake House, etc. Near Sherwood Island Pk., Clam Box.

Nature Center for Environmental Activities, 10 Woodside Lane, Westport, Conn. 06881. *Open year around, Mon. thru Sat. 9-5, Sun. 1-4. Closed some Hol. Free. Handicapped: 1 curb; doors okay for wheelchairs. Rest rooms on main floor.* (203) 227-7253.

This is a small, imaginatively designed showcase for natural history featuring live animals of the area as well as fossils, shells, and some good dioramas. A small garden grows in the center courtyard and several miles of marked nature trails lead from the building. A gift shop sells books on natural history and related subjects.

Old MacDonald's Farm, Post Road, South Norwalk, Conn. *Open daily mid-May to mid-Sept. 11 a.m. to 6 p.m.; weekends from mid-Apr. and to mid-Nov. Adm. $3.25 (includes all rides); under 2 yrs., free.* (203) 866-5955. *Food: snacks; restaurant and grill. Handicapped: Paths good, some hilly areas. Plenty of benches and shade. Ample free parking.*

Here at the very farm which we've been singing about all our lives, or a reasonable facsimile, a brightly painted, picturebook quality sets an exciting mood for our trip. After crossing the covered bridge we'll find a variety of popular exhibits that includes an area where children can mingle with friendly animals, a maternity ward where they can not, and enclosures with monkeys, seals, bears, llamas. Through it all will be a constantly moving pattern of rides on frontier trains, antique cars, ponies, carousel and, of course, the slow, bumpy hayride. A well stocked Country Store adds appeal for chaperones as well as youngsters. Birthday parties that include food and favors may be arranged with the management.

Sherwood Island State Park: Westport, Conn. *Open year around. Fees: $1 parking, May thru Sept., daily in summer, weekends in Sept. Food: Picnics, cooking; snacks.*

This popular park includes a long beach, some typical shore areas, rocks and hills and many picnic groves with fine VISTAS of the Sound as well as of neighboring coves and peninsulas. Swimming, hiking, ball playing in season; a good place for the youngsters to romp any time.

FOR THE DRIVER: Take Hutchinson Pkwy. north into Merritt Pkwy. in Conn. Proceed to Exit 41, Conn 33 at Westport. At this jct. the Red Barn restaurant is on 33 just south of the exit while the Three Bears is to the north. Take Conn 33 south toward Westport and continue to first traffic light, at Kings Highway. Turn right on this and proceed a short distance to Woodside Ave. where you pick up signs, right to Nature Center for Environmental Activities.

Back the way you came to jct. with Conn 33, at light. Turn right and proceed briefly to jct. with US 1. Continue across US 1, following Conn. 33 to the Conn. Turnpike. Watch for signs marked jct. Rte. 95 to New York, to your right at a light and follow this. Westbound on Turnpike (1 toll) drive to Exit 13. Turn right from exit, and proceed to US 1. Turn right again, passing Red Coach Grill, Cook's, other snack places. Just across the road is Old MacDonald's Farm. Parking in rear, at far end.

Back to Conn. Turnpike (I-95) this time to the east. Proceed to Exit 18 and follow signs to Sherwood Island State Park. Nearby, at jct. with Rte. 1, is the Clam Box.

Return Trip: Take Conn Turnpike back to Exit 17 (west) to Conn 33 toward Westport & Rte. 1. Continue on Rte. 33, returning to the Merritt Pkwy. to New York.

Something New in Bird Sanctuaries

TRIP F-7. *We'll Visit:*

OLD POST HOUSE, Southport, Conn. (Closed Sun.)

SOUTHPORT HARBOR

FAIRFIELD HISTORICAL SOCIETY, Fairfield (Week days)

BIRDCRAFT MUSEUM (weekend afts.)

LARSEN SANCTUARY

DISTANCE AND TOLLS: To Larsen Sanctuary via the others: From NYC exits 50-60 *m.*, fast and average speeds. About 10 miles less on return trip. Via G.W. Bridge $1.05; via Major Deegan & Thruway 45¢; via Hutchinson River Pkwy. 45¢. Plus return tolls.

FOOD: On US 1 below Southport, Clam Box. In Fairfield, Howard Johnson's. Plus diners along Rte. 1.

Old Post House, 3519 Post Rd., Southport, Conn. 06490. *Open year around, daily 10-6. Fri. Eves. Closed Sun.*

A small frame house with several eye-catching antiques outside is also a gift shop plus an outlet for Hebert Candies (white chocolates) and gourmet foods. Fresh-baked pies from the Oronoque Orchards are brought in daily; perhaps its greatest distinction however is peanut butter ground to order without preservatives. A pleasant place to stop and browse.

Fairfield Historical Society Museum, 636 Old Post Rd., Fairfield, Conn. 06430. *Open year around Mon.-Fri. 9:30-4:30. No weekends or holidays. Donations. Handicapped: Several steps in; no ramps. You can see much on 1st level. Rest rooms. Parking adjacent.* (203) 259-1598.

This handsome building has fine exhibits, attractively shown. Permanent displays include Staffordshire china, paintings, clocks, toys, antique furniture. Special exhibits cover many related subjects. A research library is open daily.

Birdcraft Museum, 314 Unquowa Road, Fairfield, Conn. 06430. *Open year around. Sat. 10-5; Sun. 12-5. Closed hol. Donations. Handicapped: Steps into bldg., but exhibits are on 1 level. Rest rooms. Park in street or nearby lot.* (203) 259-6305.

A museum that started as a display center for a few native animal specimens has become a showcase for all wildlife of the area and even some from other parts of the world. A number of the birds and animals, which died from natural causes, were mounted early in the century by the curator. However, there is none of the mustiness or dullness of feather and fur sometimes found in such specimens. These are all beautifully prepared, excellent subjects for study. One prominent exhibit is a set of Charles "Shang" Wheeler decoys. Wheeler, considered tops in his field, decided instead of killing animals he would create lifelike models of them. The Connecticut Audubon Society operates both Birdcraft Museum and the Larsen Sanctuary.

Larsen Sanctuary, 2325 Burr St. *Open year around daily, sunrise to sunset weather permitting. Museum open Tues.-Sat. 9-5; Sun. 12-5. Closed holidays. Donations Adults $1. Children 50¢. Under 12, free. Best seasons: Spring and fall. Self-guiding tours; a booklet available here or at Birdcraft Museum lists walks from one to three hours long. Handicapped: A Braille Trail enables the blind to walk some distance and smell and touch many natural specimens along the way. Handicapped on crutches may also manage the trail. Headquarters of Connecticut Audubon Society.* (203) 259-6305.

6½ miles of nature hikes may be taken through habitats including wooded areas, open fields and marshes. About 100 different kinds of birds & animals are found as well as wildflowers, ferns and many fine tree specimens. A special delight is the "Singing and fragrance walk for the blind", co-sponsored by the Bridgeport Garden Club and the Connecticut Audubon Society. Soft paths with smooth wood handrails wind through a good-sized area not far from the entrance. The walk crosses murmuring streams; evergreens and shrubs along the pathside may be felt and sniffed. Songs of birds are everywhere. A handsome Nature Center building is headquarters for nature lectures, classes, information.

FOR THE DRIVER: Take Hutchinson River Pkwy. north into Merritt Pkwy. in Conn. and proceed to Exit 42, Conn 57. Follow signs at ramp (left) to Westport, and almost at once take Conn 136 and 57 south (to right). At jct. with US 1, turn left toward Southport. Shortly you pass the Clam Box, across from entrance to Sherwood Island State Park. Proceed on Rte. 1 and watch on right for the Pequot Motor Inn. Just before this is the Old Post House.

The corner just beyond the Inn is Center St. Take this to your right and stay on it as far as it goes, to Southport Harbor, a quaint, picturesque spot. Drive right for VISTA, then return. However, this time continue along the water on Harbor Road, finally crossing bridge at far end. This road leads up to Sasco Hill Road. Turn right, briefly, to Old Field Road which begins on your left; drive left on this into town, where your road becomes Old Post Road. Continue to the Green. On your left is the Fairfield Historical Society Museum. Parking in rear.

Then continue on Old Post Rd. to next corner, Beach Road. Turn left and go 1 block to US 1. For Howard Johnson's, turn right briefly on Rte. 1, then return to this jct. Turn left from Beach Rd. and proceed on US 1 a short distance to a jct. where there is a Community movie theater across the street. This is Unquowa Road (*not Unquowa Place*) and it crosses the tracks to your right. Take this across tracks, soon passing a school; just beyond on your right is the entrance to Audubon Society Birdcraft Museum. Parking in street.

To continue to the Sanctuary, stay on Unquowa Rd. and proceed to the first full stop sign, at Mill Plain Road. Turn right on this and drive north about 4½ miles. Eventually this becomes Burr St. Proceed past the Merritt Pkwy. underpass; shortly beyond on your left is the Larsen Sanctuary.

Return Trip: Go back to the street just the other side of the Pkwy.—Congress St. Turn left and drive to entrance to Merritt Pkwy. to New York.

To the Dogwood Festival

TRIP F-8. *We'll Visit:*

DOGWOOD FESTIVAL AT GREENFIELD HILL

DISTANCE AND TOLLS: From NYC exits, 45-55 *m*. Fast speeds. Via G.W. Bridge, $1.05; via Major Deegan & Thruway, 45¢; via Hutchinson River Pkwy., 45¢. Plus return.

FOOD: On longer drive home, Spinning Wheel, Cobb's Mill Inn, and Three Bears.

Dogwood Festival at Greenfield Hill. *Usually 2 weeks in mid-May. Free. During weekdays lunch is served in the Congregational Church; for reservation write Women's Guild of Church, 1045 Old Academy Rd., Fairfield, Conn. On weekends, snacks are sold by the Youth Fellowship of the Church. Handicapped: Some walking on the Green. You might add a trip to Larsen Sanctuary and the Braille Trail, only a few blocks away.* (203) 255-0421.

When a whole area turns into a fairyland of blossoms against a setting that includes a New England Village Church on the Green, a gift tent on the lawn, art exhibits and home-baked foods, then it usually becomes an annual tour for everyone who visits it once. We park on nearby streets then walk among the blossoms, perhaps dropping in at the art gallery or auction as we nibble home-made cookies. The Festival happens regardless of how far out the buds may be. They usually bloom in the city area a few days earlier than here. Fortunately there are both early and late varieties, which insures blooms for at least two weeks. Dogwood also provides a colorful foliage in the fall. If coming then, you might add a drive to nearby Southport Harbor and include some of the Fairfield attractions. (F-7)

FOR THE DRIVER: Take Hutchinson River Pkwy. north into Merritt Pkwy. and proceed to Exit 44 at Black Rock Turnpike, under an hour from the city. After ramp, do not go to the Turnpike but turn right on Congress St. Here signs, right, direct you to Dogwood, leading to the Dogwood Festival at Greenfield Hill Congregational Church.

Return Trip: Follow signs from the Church back to Merritt Pkwy. to New York.

For an alternate route home, longer, but very scenic: Go back to Merritt Pkwy., and jct. with Conn 58, Black Rock Turnpike. Turn left on 58 and proceed north, passing several reservoirs. Near Redding you'll pass the Spinning Wheel restaurant. Continue to jct. with Conn 107; at this jct. is Putnam Memorial State Park (E-3). Turn left on 107 and proceed to jct. with Conn 53. Turn left again and stay on 53 to jct. with Conn 57. At this point is Cobb's Mill Inn. Take 57 to Merritt Pkwy. and follow sign to New York. You pass Three Bears Restaurant.

Note: For a nearby nature sanctuary and Braille Trail: Start back toward the Merritt Pkwy., eventually turning right on Congress St. Shortly is jct. with Burr St. Turn left here, and proceed a short distance to Larsen Sanctuary. (F-7.)

In the Footsteps of P. T. Barnum

TRIP F-9. *We'll Visit:*

MUSEUM OF ART, SCIENCE & INDUSTRY, Bridgeport, Conn.

(Tues. thru Sun. afts.)

BEARDSLEY ZOOLOGICAL GARDENS

DISTANCE AND TOLLS: From NYC Exits, 50-60 *m.*, mostly fast speeds. Via G.W. Bridge $1.05; via Major Deegan & Thruway 45¢; Via Hutchinson River Pkwy. 45¢. Plus return.

Museum of Art, Science & Industry, Ninety Acres Park, Bridgeport, Conn. *Open year around, Tues. thru Sun. 2-5. Closed Holidays. Fees: Adults 50¢, students under 18, 25¢. Planetarium Tues., Thurs., Sat., Sun. Adm. to both museum and planetarium, adults $1.50, students 75¢. Under 6 not admitted to planetarium. Food: Picnic area in adjacent park. Handicapped: Drive to back door, one short step into bldg., elevators to all floors. Rest rooms on every floor. Ample free parking.* (203) 372-3521.

Whether our taste leans toward Indians, fine antiques, circus memorabilia, helicopters or space travel, we'll doubtless find something especially for us here. The Sikorsky mock-up of a helicopter cockpit and rotor is a popular attraction. The Planetarium provides excellent programs suited to all ages from the second grade up while the adjacent Du Pont Wheeler Gallery of the Skies has a model of Tel-Star. The circus gallery is fascinating, Bridgeport being Barnum-land. In the museum are parts of his study and dining room. Also clothing and mementoes that once belonged to Jenny Lind and General Tom Thumb, the 28-inch Bridgeport citizen of international fame. Rounding it out are a full-size ticket wagon in gala paint, and some superb miniatures of circus wagons.

Beardsley Zoological Gardens, Noble Ave. & E. Main St., Bridgeport, Conn. 06610. (203) 576-8082. *Open year around exc. Thanks., Christmas, New Years. Adm. 50¢ (Bridgeport residents); all others $1. All children, 25¢ Children's Zoo: Adults 35¢, children, 25¢ Special group rates. Ages 5 & under free.*

Quite an assortment of animals lives here, some outdoors, others—mainly monkeys and birds—housed in a large building. A seal pool is nearby and for the farm-minded, a barnyard enclosure filled with a variety of fowl. Close by is the popular Bunny Village. The setting is especially attractive during blooming seasons for a greenhouse and some well-tended gardens are also on the premises.

FOR THE DRIVER: Take Hutchinson River Pkwy. north into the Merritt, to Exit 17 at Park Ave., about an hour from NYC. From ramp drive toward Bridgeport and proceed to the Museum of Art, Science and Industry, left. Handicapped: Drive to next corner, turn left along unpaved road to rear of bldg.; no steps, use elevator.

Turn right on Park Ave., go back to Merritt Pkwy. Take it toward New Haven, to Exit 50 at Conn 127. Follow signs at ramp to Bridgeport. Shortly on right are several entrances to Beardsley Park and Zoo. Zoo is at far end; take any entrance.

Return Trip: Go back on Conn 127 to Merritt Pkwy., take it toward New York.

To Stratford and the Globe Theatre

TRIP F-10. *We'll Visit:*

BOOTHE MEMORIAL PARK, Stratford, Conn.

JUDSON HOUSE (Wed., Sat., Sun. Apr.-Oct.)

AMERICAN SHAKESPEARE THEATRE grounds, Stratford

ORONOQUE ORCHARDS

INDIAN WELL STATE PARK

DISTANCE AND TOLLS: To Stratford: From NYC exits 60-70 *m.* Mostly fast speeds, a few average. Add about 15 *m.* if including Indian Well State Park. Via G.W. Bridge $1.05; via Major Deegan & Thruway, 45¢. Via Hutchinson River Pkwy., 45¢. Plus return.

FOOD: Near Merritt Pkwy. at Stratford Motor Inn, Mermaid Tavern. Near Shakespeare Theatre, Fagan's, closed Mon. Also Howard Johnson's. Plus diners, in town.

Boothe Memorial Park, Main St., Stratford. *Open year around, daily. Bldgs., Mem. Day – Labor Day. Free. Handicapped: There are paths; you can see rose display gardens from parking area.*

No one passes for the first time this group of strangely constructed buildings without doing a double-take. Built at random by two eccentric brothers, it includes a windmill, a large structure full of baskets from all over the world, an enormous pipe organ in yet another building, a blacksmith shop, and more. The park is situated on a hill with some marvelous VISTAS of the whole area. A particular delight is the Jackson & Perkins Trial Rose Garden. Photographers will have to snap pictures just to prove it's real.

Judson House, 967 Academy Hill, Stratford, Conn. 06497. *Open April-Oct., Wed., Sat. & Sun. 11-5, and by appointment. Closed some hol. Fees: Adults $1.50, children 75¢. Handicapped: Some steps into house.* (203) 378-0630.

Built in 1723 on a foundation constructed nearly a hundred years earlier, this well-preserved house is filled with typical furnishings from the 18th century. Of special interest is the architecture which has been restored to its original state so the paneling and fireplace may be seen. We visit the parlor chamber, the spinning room, and dining room with a collection of over 200 pieces of China Export. The cellar holds something rare in the North—slave quarters, equipped with a huge fireplace and numerous farm implements of the times.

American Shakespeare Theatre, Stratford, Conn. 06497. (203) 375-5000 (or in New York City): (212) 966-3900. *Open for viewing, year around. Performances from mid-June thru Labor Day. Food: Picnic area on grounds. Marina available for those attending performances by boat. Parking charge in season. Handicapped: At Theatre, special provisions are made for wheelchair visitors.*

It could easily become a habit, visiting this attractive grey replica of the famous Globe Theatre in London, in its scenic riverside park, in order to watch some exceptional performances of Shakespeare. Visitors don't have to wait for the season to open, however; they may drive in anytime and view the buildings on the banks of the Housatonic River.

Oronoque Orchards: 6911 Main St., Stratford. *Open year around, daily, all day.*

We'll see posted at the driveway the name of today's special home-baked pie. By the time we arrive at the counter we've passed an enormous assortment of oven-fresh breads, muffins, cakes, turnovers. There are nearly 30 species of pie alone, with insulated containers for the frozen ones. Also, as if more were needed, candies, jams, gourmet foods, and a roomful of gifts for sale.

Indian Well State Park, Shelton, Conn. *Open year around. Activities in season. Fees: Parking: $1. in season. Food: Picnics, cooking, snacks. Rest rooms.*

The park is in a scenic location with the Housatonic running past, and boating and water skiing to watch or engage in. Playfields for the energetic, and plenty of hiking including to nearby waterfall, round things out nicely.

FOR THE DRIVER: Take Hutchinson River Pkwy. north into Merritt Pkwy. Proceed to Exit 53S, the first one, about 1 hr. 10 min. from city. Turn right, after ramp, on Conn 110, toward Stratford. Watch for first small road, right, Main St. & Putney,—with signs to Board of Education Offices. Take this road, then bear left. Just ahead, left, is Boothe Memorial Park.

Continue on Main St.; shortly it re-joins Conn 110. Proceed through town. Soon you merge with Conn 113. Take this, bearing right. You'll cross US 1 (Barnum Ave.), then railroad tracks. Finally, just beyond the Conn Turnpike, watch for Broad St. The smaller street just ahead is Academy Hill; turn left on this following sign to Judson House, 967 Academy Hill.

Proceed to next corner, Elm St., turn right and cross Stratford Ave., then follow signs to the American Shakespeare Theatre. In this area look for Fagan's (restaurant) on US 1 near the river. Also nearby at Exit 31 from Conn Turnpike is a Howard Johnson's.

Go back to Conn 113 and return through town, merging with Conn 110 and following signs to the Merritt Pkwy. Just beyond the pkwy. is the Stratford Motor Inn with its Mermaid Tavern. At the first corner beyond the entrance is a traffic light and sign to the Oronoque Orchards (store) to your left.

Back on Conn 110 and turn left. Soon after passing Conn 8, watch for a road, right, to Indian Well State Park.

Return Trip: Follow signs in town to Conn 108, right. This goes to Merritt Pkwy. to NYC. (slower, but less mileage.) Or return on Conn 110 to Pkwy.

One Day at Yale and New Haven

TRIP F-11 EXTENSION. *We'll Visit:*

YALE UNIVERSITY, New Haven, Conn.

UNIVERSITY ART GALLERY (Tues. thru Sun.)

NEW HAVEN COLONY HISTORICAL SOCIETY MUSEUM (Closed Mon.)

PEABODY MUSEUM OF NATURAL HISTORY

DISTANCE AND TOLLS: To New Haven from NYC Exits 65-75 *m.* Fast speeds. Via G.W. Bridge, $1.50; Via Major Deegan & Thruway, 90¢; Via Hutchinson River Pkwy, 90¢. Plus return.

Yale University Tours, New Haven, Conn. 06520. *Guided tours start at Phelps Gateway on College St. between Chapel and Elm. No advance*

*arrangements necessary. Schedule: Mon. thru Fri., 10 & 2. Sat. 11 & 2.
Sun. 1:30 & 3.* These cover the Old Campus, Residential Colleges,
Graduate & Professional Schools (Art, Drama, Law, Music), the Beinecke
Rare Book Library. Also, Mon. thru Fri. *at 11:30 is a tour of Science
facilities. Summer recess schedule: Mon.-Sat. 9:15, 1:30, 3. Sun. 1:30,
3. Science Tour Mon. 10:30. Guided Tours last about 1 hour; no charge.
Self-guiding Tours: Brochures available in English, French, Spanish,
German and Japanese, from University Information Office, Phelps
Gateway. Tour schedule subject to change.* (203) 467-6927.

The Tour Brochure describes the buildings within walking range.
These include: The Old Campus, Connecticut Hall, Harkness Tower.
Several of the Colleges, each with its own facilities, may be seen, as well
as the new Art and Architectural Building, Wrexham Tower, Mory's (at
whose tables sang the Whiffenpoofs), the Payne Whitney Gymnasium,
the Sterling Law Buildings. At the Hewitt Quadrangle is the Beinecke
Rare Book and Manuscript Library and outside, a sculpture garden in a
sunken courtyard.

Yale University Art Gallery, Chapel & High Sts. *Open year around,
Tues. thru Sat. 10-5; Thurs. also 6-9., Sun. 2-5. Closed Mon. & holidays.
Free. General tours on Tues. at 2:30, repeated Thurs. at 1:00 &
7:30 p.m. Continued all summer, exc. the 7:30; last about 1 hour.
Handicapped: Some steps with railings into bldg. Elevators. Rest rooms
on a lower level. Wheelchairs available for handicapped.*

Permanent collections include painting, sculpture and art. We'll find
Medieval and Baroque sculpture, Pre-Columbian art, American and
European paintings. Early American silverware includes some by Paul
Revere. There is a pleasant atmosphere, not the least effective part
being campus views from enormous picture windows.

New Haven Colony Historical Society Museum: 114 Whitney Ave., New
Haven, Conn. 06510. *Open year around Tues. to Fri. 10-5., Sat., Sun.,
Holidays 2-5. Closed Mon. Free. Handicapped: A few steps in;
elevators. Rest rooms near entrance.* (203) 562-4183.

Stop here for an unusually complete collection of early New Haven
memorabilia. Exhibits include explanations of such things as the
"touchmarks" on Connecticut pewterware, the names Saltbox and
Cape Cod for houses. There's information, too, about inventors who
came from New Haven; we can see the original model of Eli Whitney's
cotton gin and another of a wood-carving machine by Hezekiah Augur.
The Colony Shop sells quality china, brass, glass, as well as less
expensive items.

Peabody Museum of Natural History: 170 Whitney Ave., New Haven,
Conn. 06510. *Open year around, daily. From March thru Oct., 9-5.*

Rest of year, 9-4:30. Sun. & holidays 1-5. Closed major holidays. Fees: Tues., Thurs. & weekends: Adults 75¢, children 25¢. Rest of week free. Tours: Acoustiguides (with headsets) describe most main exhibits; adults 50¢. Under 12, 25¢. Handicapped: Several steps into bldg., no railings. Elevators. Rest rooms near entrance. (203) 436-0850.

This is one of our finer natural history museums. In it are minerals, fossils, mammals, relics found on Yale expeditions, and some excellent habitat groups. We can see exhibits of life through the ages from the earliest records, to man. Also shown, the world around us, North American environments from desert to seashore. A special hall features archaelogy, geology and ecology of New England.

FOR THE DRIVER: Take Hutchinson River Pkwy. north into the Merritt and drive over an hour, crossing the bridge (toll) at Milford. Here follow signs to the Conn. Turnpike and take this east toward New London.

About 15 minutes from here, watch for exit on left marked Down Town New Haven. Take this to ramp to Orange St. & Church St. You continue one block to Church St. then turn right, passing Macy's. To all drivers: Parking may be difficult. You may find it quickest to locate a central parking place and walk. Take the left lane on Church St. and turn left on the second street, Crown St., past Macy's. There's a large parking lot here. Others are around the block, to your left.

We'll assume you're walking, for the University Tour. Take any street parallel to Church St. and continue the direction you had been going. A block ahead is the Green. Phelps Gateway is on College St. between Chapel and Elm Sts. Get your Tour Folder here, or arrange for guided tour.

Back at the corner of College and Chapel Sts. (near Phelps) walk to the corner of High St., the next beyond College, to the University Art Gallery. A few blocks from this are the Historic Society Museum and Peabody Museum. You can drive to these, or walk. From the campus, (or from parking lot) go back to Church St., the one you entered on, and turn left. Shortly the road bends left and you're on Whitney Ave. Just above this, Temple St. comes in from your left. At this jct., also left, is the New Haven Colony Historical Society Museum. On the corner just above this, Sachem St., is the Peabody Museum of Natural History.

Return Trip: Bear right on Temple St., passing the Historical Museum, and proceed to Chapel St. Turn right, passing the Yale Campus, and continue on this—Conn 34 west. It eventually takes you past the Walter Camp Memorial and the Yale Bowl. Rte. 34 continues to jct. with Wilbur Cross Pkwy. Take this toward New York, into the Merritt Pkwy.

The Trolley Car is Now Historical Americana

TRIP F-12 EXTENSION. *We'll Visit:*

BRANFORD TROLLEY MUSEUM, East Haven, Conn. (Apr. thru Nov.)

DISTANCE AND TOLLS: From NYC Exits, 70-80 *m*. Fast speeds. Via G.W. Bridge, $1.50; via Major Deegan & Thruway, also Hutchinson River Pkwy., 90¢. Plus return.
FOOD: On Conn. Turnpike near New Haven, Holiday House Service Area. Plus diners in town and near turnpike exits.

Branford Trolley Museum, Branford Electric Railway Assoc., P.O. Box 457, Short Beach, Conn. 06405. (203) 467-6927. *Open Sundays Apr. thru Nov. Weekends & hol. from late May thru Oct. Daily June 25 thru Labor Day. Hours 11-5, (last full trip & tour). Fees: Adults $2. 5-11 yrs. $1. (Unlimited rides.) Charter for private trolley ride by advance arrangement. Food: Picnic area. Handicapped − steps into Museum; high step onto trolleys. Pets, leashed.*

Remember those weather-filled mornings standing on the corner waiting for the trolley? Griping at paying our nickel for the crowded, jouncy ride? Then one day the trolley never came again.

Today we're going to drive approximately 2 hours over nearly 80 miles of highways to visit one of these creatures from out of our past. We'll ride for the equivalent of from 20 to 40 of our old fares. And chances are we're going to love every minute.

We start at the Sprague Museum, named after Frank Julian Sprague, Father of Electric Traction, where are memorabilia including photographs of many familiar old cars. Our Trolley Ride may be on the open "breezer" that once ran to the Yale Bowl. On our return trip we disembark at the Car Barn and picnic grove where we can stroll past rows of these old acquaintances. Some can be boarded, others are antiques and we can only look.

A souvenir shop is well-stocked with hobby items. We may charter a private trolley for a special occasion by writing some time in advance to the address given above.

There is a cheerful spirit among the patrons. Children consider the exhibit about one half step this side of the Conestoga Wagon, while their elders wonder, "What happened? Where did they go?"

FOR THE DRIVER: Take Hutchinson River Parkway north into the Merritt and continue to toll bridge at Milford, a little over an hour from the city. After toll, follow signs to Conn. Turnpike and take it east toward New London. On Turnpike, pass Holiday House rest area. Proceed to Exit 51, Frontage Road. Drive past A & P to traffic light at Forbes Place where you pick up signs to the Trolley Museum.

Return Trip: Go back through town. You can turn right toward Foxon at sign. This goes to Conn. Turnpike, avoiding part of town. Take Turnpike west to New York, to exit to Milford and Merritt Parkway.

Wonderful New England Houses

TRIP F-13 EXTENSION. *We'll Visit:*

THOMAS GRISWOLD HOUSE, Guilford (Closed Mon., summer)

WHITFIELD HOUSE (Closed Mon. and Tues., also mid-Dec. to mid-Jan.)

HYLAND HOUSE (Summer)

HILLTOP ORCHARDS

DISTANCE AND TOLLS: To Guilford from NYC exits, 90-100 *m.* Via G.W. Bridge, $1.75; via Major Deegan & Thruway, also Hutchinson River Pkwy., $1.15. Fast speeds.

FOOD: On Conn. Turnpike, 2 service areas with Holiday House. In Guilford, Bernice's, closed Mon.; Captain's Table, closed Mon. and May; Little Stone House, open summer, closed Mon.

Thomas Griswold House, 171 Boston St., Guilford, Conn. 06437. *Open mid-June – Labor Day, daily 11-4 exc. Mon. Fee: $1. adults. Comb. ticket to all 3 houses available. Children free. Guided tours. Handicapped: Some steps. No rest rooms. Parking in adjacent lot.* (203) 453-3176.

An excellent example of a Colonial saltbox house, this was once pictured on a commemorative stamp, is both a museum and headquarters of the Guilford Keeping Society. It serves as repository for documents, records, pictures and artifacts dating back to 1735. We'll see the "borning room", the "keeping room", the buttery, as well as Guilford style furniture, and costumes from 1880 and later. A barn museum outside holds a collection of farm tools.

Henry Whitfield House, Whitfield St., Guilford, Conn. 06437. *Open April to October, Wed.-Sun. 10-5. Rest of year, to 4. Closed hol. and from mid-Dec. to mid-Jan. Fee: 50¢ adults, 25¢ age 6-17. Comb. ticket to 3 houses available. Handicapped: Some steps. Rest rooms.* (203) 453-2457.

This strikingly handsome stone house, the oldest in Guilford, belonged to the founder of the town, the Reverend Henry Whitfield, who led a group of parishioners to America from England to avoid religious persecution. Here they built a typical English manor house, unaware of the rugged American winters which had taught their predecessors to construct smaller, more easily heated rooms. The Great Hall, 33 feet long and 15 wide, required a fireplace at either end and a partition in the middle to allow it to become two rooms when needed. Walls were 22 to 24 inches thick. Here the minister and his family and servants lived, but the house was primarily a church meeting place.

Hyland House, 84 Boston St., Guilford, Conn. 06437. *Open mid-June thru September, daily except Mon. 10-4:30. $1. fee; combination ticket to 3 houses available; children free. No rest rooms. Handicapped: Some stairs.* (203) 453-9477.

Here is another fine example of a Colonial saltbox, built about 1660. The rooms are set up not so much like those in a museum as in a home. We'll see where the inevitable lean-to and wings were added. In fact, the "keeping room" was built onto the back of the house. Furnishings include locally made pieces. Upstairs we find sewing rooms, closets of period clothing, and wool and flax wheels.

Hilltop Orchards, US 1, Branford, Conn. *Open year around, daily, 7 days a week, 8-6.*

The emphasis here is on pies—home baked and fragrant, or unbaked and frozen. They'll box them for you to take home. In season, there's also a farm stand.

FOR THE DRIVER: Take Hutchinson River Parkway north into the Merritt. A little over an hour from the city, after toll bridge follow signs to Conn. Turnpike. Take 2nd entrance, east to New London. On Turnpike, pass 2 Holiday House Service Areas.

Proceed to Exit 58 at Guilford at Conn 77. Pick up signs here to the three houses and to Rte. 77. Continue to Village Green, make left turn to the end, then turn right to the other end, at Boston St. Turn left on Boston for two of the houses; temporarily skip Hyland House and continue to the Thomas Griswold House a little farther, right.

Get directions here for back roads to the Henry Whitfield House.

Continue from Whitfield House to Whitfield St. For restaurants, at the dock end on Whitfield St. are Little Stone House, also Captain's Table. Also on this street is Bernice's. Returning from the house, turn right on Whitfield and proceed to Boston St., Conn 146. Turn right, passing the Green. Just beyond is Hyland House.

While in town, park and browse through antique and craft shops. Then drive back past the Green to Rte. 77, the way you came, and return to the Conn. Turnpike. Take this west toward New Haven.

To stop at Hilltop Orchards, leave at Exit 56 and follow signs to orchards, turning right on US 1. Then return to Turnpike west. Proceed to exit to Milford and the Merritt Parkway.

A Ferry Ride to a Castle

TRIP F-14 EXTENSION. *We'll Visit:*

PRATT HOUSE, Essex (June-Oct., Tues., Thurs., Sat.)

VALLEY RAILROAD & RIVERBOAT, Essex
(Daily, summer. Weekends, Spring & Fall.)

CHESTER-HADLYME FERRY (Seasonal)

GILLETTE CASTLE STATE PARK (Castle: Memorial Day to Columbus Day)

FLORENCE GRISWOLD HOUSE

LYME ART ASSOCIATION SUMMER ART SHOW

NUT MUSEUM (May–Nov.)

DISTANCE AND TOLLS: To Gillette Castle: From NYC exits 120-130 *m.* Mostly fast speeds. Via G.W. Bridge, $2. Via Major Deegan & Thruway, also Hutchinson River Pkwy., $1.40. Plus return tolls. Add 25¢ for ferry for car and driver; passengers 5¢.

FOOD: On Turnpike, 2 service areas with Holiday House. At jct. with Rte. 9 on Turnpike, Howard Johnson's. On Rte. 9 at jct. with Rte. 154, Flagship Inn. In Essex, Griswold Inn. If via E. Haddam, Gelston House, closed Mon. in winter. In Old Lyme, Ferry Tavern.

Pratt House, 20 West Ave., Essex, Conn. 06426. *Open June to October, Tues., Thurs., Sat. 1-5 and by appointment. Adm. fee. Check first.* (203) 767-1737.

This small 17th-century house is filled with antiques including items from the Griswold collection. It has been restored to the 18th-century period by the Society for the Preservation of New England Antiquities.

Valley Railroad and Riverboat, Essex, Conn. 06426. *Early May-late Oct., weekends; daily in summer. Single train trips, or combination with boat available.* (203) 767-0103.

A full-sized vintage train whistles and chugs its way up the scenic Connecticut River to Chester. Here, passengers have option of transferring to a Riverboat for an additional one or two hour voyage farther up river, passing landmarks like Gillette Castle and Goodspeed Opera House. A train returns travelers to Essex from the boat dock.

Chester-Hadlyme Ferry. *Seasonal, depending on weather and river conditions or need for mechanical repairs. Runs: April to Oct. daily, 7 a.m.-8 p.m. Fees: 25¢ for car and driver; 5¢ each passenger.*

Gillette Castle State Park, Hadlyme, Conn. 06439. *Park open year around. Castle tours: Memorial Day to Columbus Day daily, 11-5. Fees: 50¢. Food: Picnics, snacks. Handicapped: Climbing in castle; grounds hilly.* (203) 526-2336.

High above the pastoral Connecticut River perches a dream castle built by the great turn-of-the-century actor and portrayer of Sherlock Holmes, William Gillette. A native of Hartford, Gillette chose this site because of the superb view. He decided not only would he have a castle here but he would plan-it-himself, the results taking workmen 5 years to carry out. We'll tour 24 rooms filled with fascinating devices and unconventional structural effects.

Florence Griswold House, Old Lyme, Conn. 06371. (203) 434-5542. *Open June-Aug. Tues.-Sat., 10-5; Sun. from 1. Rest of year, Wed.-Fri., & Sun. 1-5. Cl. hol. Free.*

A handsome Greek Revival house of 1817 contains rare antiques, marine exhibits and treasures from around the world. There are works by artist Henry W. Ranger, a boarder. Recently a superb doll collection was added.

Lyme Art Gallery Association, Old Lyme, Conn. 06371. *Exhibitions weekdays 10-5, Sun. 1-5. Adm. 50¢, age 12 & over. Closed between shows. Rest rms.*

At the turn of the century, artist Henry W. Ranger came to Old Lyme to paint the local land and seascapes. He helped form the Lyme Art Colony and nurtured American Impressionist painting. The Gallery has 3 shows each season.

The Nut Museum, Ferry Rd., Old Lyme, Conn. 06371. (203) 434-7636. *Open May-Nov. Wed., Sat., Sun. 2-5. Adm. 1 nut, plus $1. donation.*

In a large room of a Victorian mansion is a display of nuts and nut products from around the world, exotic nut novelties, nut jewelry, nut mini-furniture, paintings of nuts and, on request, songs about nuts.

FOR THE DRIVER: Take Hutchinson River Pkwy. north into Merritt Pkwy. and proceed a little over an hour to bridge at Milford. After toll, follow sign to Conn. Turnpike and take entrance East to New London. Pass two Holiday House rest areas. Proceed to Exit 69 to Conn 9 and take 9 north to Essex. At jct. with Turnpike is a Howard Johnson's. On Rte. 9 at jct. with Conn 154 is Flagship Inn. Continue to Exit 3 and follow signs to Historic Essex Village. Park here and walk through town. Pratt House is on West St., the one you come in on. Also in Essex, Griswold Inn. New: A Conn. Valley Steam R.R. runs in season.

Back to Rte. 9, take it north toward Middletown. Leave at Exit 6 to Conn 148, following signs to Chester & Hadlyme and Gillette Castle State Park. Turn right, toward the ferry. *If Ferry is running:* Take it across to a point below the castle and follow signs. *If not running:* Take Conn 148 toward the ferry to Rte. 9A; go north on this to Conn 82 and cross the river to East Haddam. The first building on the other side is the famous Goodspeed Opera House. Across from it is Gelston House restaurant. Continue on Rte. 82 several miles following signs to Gillette Castle State Park.

Back to Conn 82 and turn right; proceed to jct. with Conn 156, turn right toward Hamburg and the Connecticut Turnpike. Just before reaching Tpke. take Conn 51, left. A short distance beyond a shopping center, left, is the Lyme Art Gallery Association. Next door is the Florence Griswold House. Nearby on Ferry Rd. just off Rte 156, is the Nut Museum.

Return Trip. Back to jct. with the Conn. Tpke., take it west to exit at Milford to the Merritt Pkwy.

To A Seafaring Community of A Century Ago

TRIP F-15 EXTENSION. *We'll Visit:*

MYSTIC SEAPORT, Mystic, Conn.

MYSTIC MARINELIFE AQUARIUM

OLDE MISTICK VILLAGE (Shopping center)

STONINGTON LIGHTHOUSE, Stonington, Conn. (Summer)

DISTANCE AND TOLLS: To Stonington from NYC Exits, 130-140 *m.* Fast speeds. Via G.W. Bridge, $2.; via Major Deegan & Thruway, also Hutchinson River Pkwy., $1.40. Plus return.

FOOD: At jct. to Mystic Seaport from I-95, Howard Johnson's. In Seaport, Seaman's Inne, closed Mon. En route Stonington at Mystic Motor Inn, Flood Tide. On Conn. Turnpike, 2 Holiday House rest areas.

Mystic Seaport, Mystic, Conn. 06355. (203) 536-2631. *Open year around daily 9-5 exc. Thanksgiving & Christmas. In winter, 10-4. In summer, grounds open until 8 p.m. Also open evenings during Christmas season. Adm., summer, adults $5., Sr. Cit. & students, $4. 6-15 yrs., $2.50. Less in winter. All year, after 5 p.m., small fee. Small fee for Planetarium show. Food: picnics, snacks. cafeteria, also Seaman's Inne, closed Mon. exc. cafeteria which opens daily 11-3. Handicapped: Some streets cobblestone; a few steps into bldgs. but those on crutches can manage. Ramps; special rest rooms. Free parking. HARBOR CRUISES weekends May & Oct., daily June-Sept., additional charge.*

Thirty-seven acres of waterfront along a small river have become a major tourist attraction. Here is a maritime village, a unique living museum right out of the 19th century, where we may tread cobblestoned streets, watch craftsmen at work doing tasks pertaining directly to ships and the sea, ride a horse-drawn "barge" along unpaved country roads, and go shopping in quaint stores. The Pynchon Junior Museum contains touchable objects and a wonderful play section built like a ship's bridge, where youngsters can take their turn at the wheel, look through telescopes, climb the ship's rigging. The Planetarium presents several shows during the afternoon that include demonstrations of the science of celestial navigation. For many, the big thrill comes in boarding the seven historic ships along the waterfront. Perhaps the best known is the *Charles W. Morgan*, a 113-foot square-rigged wooden sailing ship, berthed along Seaport Street. Other smaller vessels include the *L.A. Dunton*, a Gloucester fishing schooner, and the famous Danish training ship, the *Joseph Conrad*. Over 100 smaller craft are likewise on view.

Mystic Aquarium. *Open year around. Adm. fee: $4. adults; children, $1.75 (less in winter). Under 4, free.* (203) 536-3323.

Dolphins, sharks, pilot whales are seen in action in this popular new enterprise dedicated to recreation and education.

Olde Mistick Village is a complete shopping center, almost a town, dressed up as an 18th-century village, with gristmill, meeting house, bricked walks. Opened in 1973, it is so well designed that visitors sometimes mistake it for the Seaport.

Stonington Lighthouse, Stonington, Conn. *Open July to Labor Day, daily exc. Mon. 11-4:30. Adm. 75¢. Under 12, 25¢.*

Built in 1841 and now run by the Stonington Historic Society, this contains a museum with exhibits of whaling implements and historical items of the area.

FOR THE DRIVER: Take Hutchinson Parkway north into the Merritt; cross toll bridge and follow signs to Conn. Turnpike east to New London. Proceed about 50 miles, passing 2 Holiday House rest areas, to Exit 76 to US 1 and I-95 to New London. Remain on I-95 after Rte. 1 branches off.

Soon you approach exit to Conn 27 and the Mystic Seaport. Do not get off at Mystic Street—wait for Seaport.

Just before your exit comes a Scenic Overlook where you can pull off the road for a fine VISTA of the Seaport. Photographers may capture good opening panoramic shots before reaching the village.

At the exit, take Rte. 27, right. At this jct. is a Howard Johnson's. Just ahead is Mystic Seaport. At same jct. are the Mystic Marinelife Aquarium and Olde Mistick Village.

You may decide to visit Stonington first, and end at the Seaport. In either case, you pass Mystic on the way to Stonington. For the latter, continue on Conn 27 to jct. with US 1. At this jct. is the Mystic Motor Inn with the Flood Tide restaurant. Turn left (east) on Rte. 1 to Stonington Village. You enter town near the Green. Park anywhere and walk, or drive to the end of town either on Main St. or one parallel. Eventually, arrive at the Stonington Lighthouse.

Return to the Green and go back to Rte. 1. Turn left, to Mystic. At jct. with Conn 27 turn right to the Seaport.

Return Trip: Take Conn 27 to I-95 west. Proceed to exit below New Haven to Milford and Merritt Parkway.

Touring in Long Island

• *Our next trips take us to that famous 125-mile long fish-shaped piece of glacial deposit called Long Island. This runs east and west, following the shoreline of Connecticut just across Long Island Sound.*

We'll be traveling a more or less straight line, first along the North Shore where historical, New England-type towns flourish, then the South Shore with miles of beaches that apparently come and go at the will of the Atlantic Ocean.

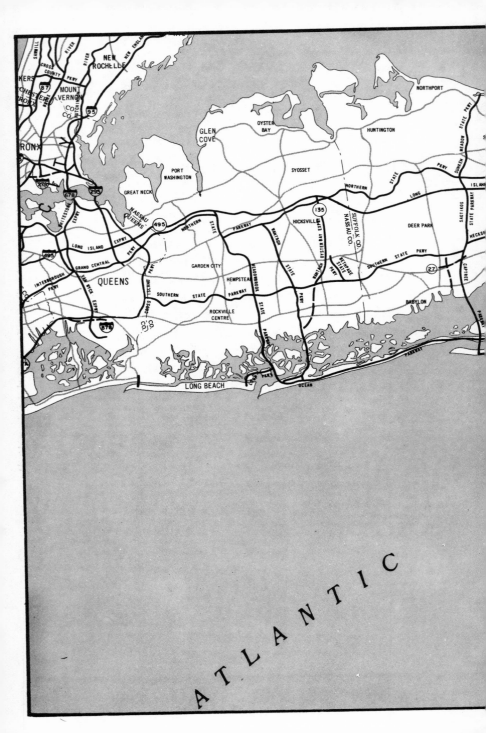

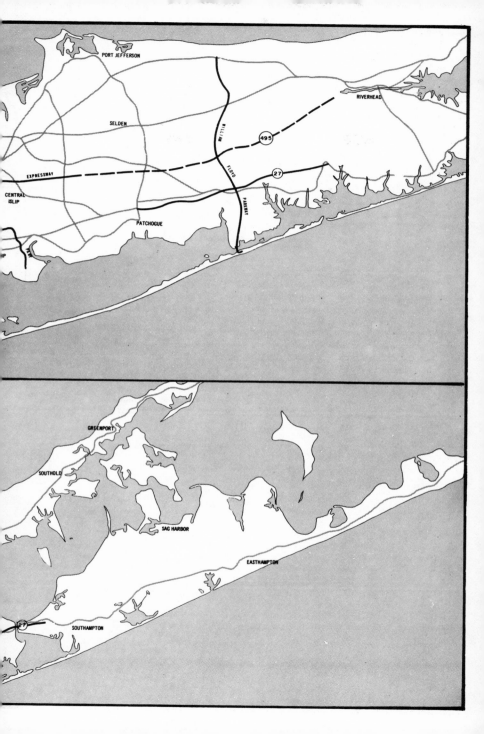

To reach Long Island from New York City and environs: Use Exit Points Throgs Neck Bridge or Verrazano Bridge.

Main roads: Northern Boulevard, NY 25A (not to be confused with Northern State Parkway); Long Island Expressway (I-495); Northern State Parkway (which begins in the city as Grand Central Parkway); Southern State Parkway.

To reach all roads from Verrazano Bridge: Follow signs after bridge to Long Island on the Belt Pkwy. System (Shore Pkwy.) Continue to Southern State, Northern State, Long Island Expressway or Northern Boulevard (in that order).

From all other sections: Take Throgs Neck Bridge. Continue straight ahead on I-78 to: Northern Blvd. (NY 25A), Long Island Expressway (I-495), Grand Central Pkwy. (becoming Northern State Pkwy.) For Southern State Pkwy., after bridge follow signs to Cross Island Parkway and Jones Beach. This goes to the Southern State Pkwy.

To a Marine Academy and a Tidal Mill

TRIP G-1. *We'll Visit:*

THE SADDLE ROCK GRIST MILL (Apr. thru Oct., Wed. thru Sun.)

U.S. MERCHANT MARINE ACADEMY (Weekend & Hol. afts.)

THE MANHASSET VALLEY SCHOOL (Apr. thru Oct., Wed. thru Sun.)

NASSAU COUNTY MUSEUM OF NATURAL HISTORY, GARVIE'S POINT DIVISION

DISTANCE AND TOLLS: To Garvie's Point after other stops; via Throgs Neck Bridge, about 35 *m.* bridge 25¢. Via Verrazano, about 60 *m.*, bridge 50¢. Plus return. Mainly fast and average speeds.

Saddle Rock Grist Mill, Saddle Rock, L.I. *Open Apr. thru Oct., Wed. thru Sun. 9:30-4:30. Free. Handicapped: Climbing, both to the mill and within.* (516) 420-5288.

A 1700 building still serves the purpose for which it was built. Now utilizing electric power instead of the tides, the grist mill continues to demonstrate how grain was ground before the big roller mills put stone mills out of business.

U. S. Merchant Marine Academy, Kings Point, Long Island, N.Y. 11024. *Regimental Reviews in May, June, Sept. & Oct., Sat. mornings at 10:30, weather permitting. Free. Tours: Groups arrange in advance. No picnics. Ample parking. Rest rooms. Handicapped: Can watch the Reviews, close to the entrance. Good paths.* (516) 482-8200.

This comparatively new Federal Academy already has a fine record of achievement with graduates having served in three wars. It is in an exceptionally attractive location, the main administrative center, Wiley Hall, having once been the country home of Walter P. Chrysler. We may visit some of the grounds, and watch the Regimental Reviews, which last about 45 minutes.

Manhasset Valley School, Manhasset Valley Park, Rte. 25A, Manhasset, L.I. *Open Apr. thru Oct., Wed. thru Sun. 1-5. Free. Rest rooms. Parking.*

Situated within a beautiful small park, this is an authentic restoration of a common school built in 1806 at the cost of approximately $400. We'll see the desks, the old-time textbooks, examples of penmanship.

Nassau County Museum of Natural History, Garvies Point Division, Barry Drive, Glen Cove, N.Y. 11542. *Open: Museum—Year around, 9-5. (closed some holidays). Fees: 25¢. Nature Preserve, year around, daily, 8 a.m. to dusk. Free. Food: Picnics. Rest rooms in Museum and Preserve. Handicapped: 1 curb to Museum; everything on 1 level inside. Some climbing in Preserve. No dogs allowed.*

The Museum is one of several county museums, each dedicated to a different aspect of its historical past. In this we'll trace the archeological and geological background of the region, with dioramas showing the coming of man to the area in 3,500 B.C., his cultural progress, and the decline of the Indian over the years. A large picture window looks into the adjacent Carlyle S. Smith Archeological Laboratories, where we can see the work in progress. There is a good reference library of scientific material. The Nature Preserve has 5 miles of trails winding through more than 72 acres of forests, meadows, high bluffs and a beach strewn with boulders from New England, brought here by an ancient glacier.

FOR THE DRIVER: Exit Point for all: Take Northern Boulevard, Rte. 25A, east. Watch for a fork in the road to your left, at a light. Sign here to Merchant Marine Academy—this is Great Neck Road. Turn left, continue straight ahead after road becomes Bayview Ave. to village of Saddle Rock. Turn left at sign to Saddle Rock Grist Mill.

Go back to road you came on and turn left, following signs to the Merchant Marine Academy.

You leave the Academy on Steamboat Rd. Stay on this and continue to Middle Neck Rd. (County Rte. 11). Turn right and proceed to NY 25A, Northern Blvd. Turn left here (east) toward Manhasset. You'll come to Manhasset Valley Park on your left, across the road from a pond. Drive to corner beyond light and turn in for parking area. Signs here for Manhasset Valley School.

Back on 25A, again turning left (east). Continue through Roslyn to where a sign directs you left to Glen Cove. Turn left and proceed about 4 miles to jct. with NY 107, coming in from your right. Continue on Rte. 107, passing turn-off to Glen Cove, for as far as the road goes. Fire House is just ahead. Pick up signs here to Garvies Point. Follow these to the Nassau County Museum of Natural History.

Return Trip: Go back the way you came, following signs Glen Cove Bypass. At foot of hill, the Fire House is on your right. Turn here to left, then proceed straight ahead—this becomes NY 107. Take it to jct. where it branches left; you bear right, remaining on Glen Cove Road back to Rte. 25A. Turn right, and return to city.

To the Splendid Gardens of Old Westbury

TRIP G-2. *We'll Visit:*

OLD WESTBURY GARDENS and WESTBURY HOUSE (Early May to late Oct., Wed. thru Sun. & Holidays)

DISTANCE AND TOLLS: From Throgs Neck Bridge, about 20 *m.*, bridge 25¢. From Verrazano, under 45 *m.*, bridge 50¢. Plus return. Fast speeds.

FOOD: Near gardens, on NY 25, Jericho Turnpike, Red Coach Grill; Carl Hoppl's Westbury Manor. Plus diners, snacks.

Old Westbury Gardens and Westbury House (Phipps Mansion). For information, P.O. Box 265, Old Westbury, L.I., N.Y. 11568. *Open early May to late Oct., Wed. thru Sun. and all holidays, 10-5. Fees; Garden: Adults, $2.50, children 50¢. Additional charge to Mansion: Adults, $1.50, children, $1. Under 6 free. Self-guiding tours.* (516) 333-0048.

Food: Picnic area. Handicapped: A good deal of walking; paths are gravel, on different levels. Stairs in house; no railings. Free parking. No pets.

Gardens: Eight different styles include a Boxwood Garden with a reflecting pool, a fragrant English Rose Garden, a walled Italian Garden which we enter through wrought iron gates, a lovely Cottage Garden, once the playground of the Phipps children, with a thatched cottage and picket fence. Superb specimens of shrubs bloom in season. Photographers will be delighted with the manner in which every garden is laid out to afford beautifully composed pictures, many with the mansion in the background.

The Mansion: The Georgian manor house of the late John S. Phipps is an example of the finest in luxurious living during the early years of the century. Many of the furnishings are museum pieces. Photographers may take pictures indoors, and are advised to use strong flash bulbs.

FOR THE DRIVER: Take Long Island Expressway, I-495 east about 7 miles beyond the jct. with Cross Island Pkwy., to Exit 39S at Guinea Woods Rd., South. Exit on ramp facing Guinea Woods Rd. Continue across this and proceed parallel to the Expressway, following signs to Old Westbury Gardens. For restaurants: Continue on Old Westbury Rd. to NY 25, Jericho Tpke.

Return Trip: Back the way you came, to Long Island Expressway.

Sagamore Hill,
the Home Theodore Roosevelt Loved

TRIP G-3. *We'll Visit:*

PLANTING FIELDS ARBORETUM, STATE UNIVERSITY, Oyster Bay (Apr.-Oct., daily. Rest of year, weekends.)

RAYNHAM HALL, Oyster Bay (Closed Tues.)

THEODORE ROOSEVELT MEMORIAL SANCTUARY and TRAILSIDE MUSEUM (May thru Nov.)

SAGAMORE HILL, ROOSEVELT'S HOME, Oyster Bay

DISTANCE AND TOLLS: To Sagamore Hill via Throgs Neck Bridge, 25 *m.*, bridge 25¢. Via Verrazano, 50 m., 50¢. Plus return. Mainly average speeds after Pkwys.

FOOD: On Rte. 25A near Oyster Bay, Rothmann's; Howard Johnson's.

Planting Fields Arboretum, State University of New York, Oyster Bay, L.I. N.Y. 11771. *Open year around. Weekends & hol. all year. Weekdays late Apr. to late Sept. Cl. Christmas. Adm. fee: adults, $1.50; under 12, free. Bus, $6. (Subject to change.) Greenhouses, Wed.-Fri. 10-4, weekends from 1. Closed hol. Handicapped: paths not too hilly, but there is some distance to cover.* (516) 922-9200.

Some of the finest collections of plantings in the East are to be found at this 409-acre Arboretum. There are superb specimens of trees, shrubs and flowers, and the displays are lavish. Winding paths take us past the 600 or more rhododendron and azalea plants that include many hybrids. Five acres of shrubs contain over 400 different plants that thrive in this area, arranged alphabetically for study purposes. This is called a Synoptic Shrub Collection, being a synopsis of the superior species and varieties best as ornamentals. The beautiful Elizabethan mansion, originally the estate of the late William Robertson Coe, is being used by the State University's Agricultural and Technical Institute at Farmingdale for the training of students in ornamental horticulture.

Raynham Hall, 20 W. Main St., Oyster Bay, L.I., N.Y. 11771. *Open year around, daily exc. Tues., 10-12, 1-5. Sun. 1-5. Closed major Hol. Fees: Adults 50¢, children with adult free. Tours: Guided. Handicapped: Some climbing inside. Parking on street.* (516) 922-6808.

This 18th-century clapboarded Colonial home was once owned by Samuel Townsend, the father of Robert Culper, Jr., New York City intelligence agent of General Washington. Here, after Long Island was taken by the British during the Revolution, the Queen's Rangers made their headquarters.

This historic house has been restored by the local chapter of the D.A.R., using mainly its original 18th-century and Victorian furnishings.

Theodore Roosevelt Memorial Sanctuary and Trailside Museum, Oyster Bay, L.I., N.Y. 11771. *Open May thru Nov. 2-5 exc. Tues. and Sun. Occasionally closed—check before making a special trip. Free. Tours: Self-guiding. Parking in adjacent area for both sanctuary and for Roosevelt's grave. (Grave, daily, sunrise to sunset.)*

A 12-acre wildlife sanctuary has been established in the woodland where Theodore Roosevelt, 26th President of the United States, once walked. The trail we take is also a model wild bird sanctuary. The National Audubon Society maintains this and recently has added a Trailside Museum where natural history items are for sale.

Sagamore Hill, Oyster Bay. For information: Supt. 26 Wall St., New York, N.Y. 10005. *Open year around daily 9:30-5, in summer until 6. Closed Thanksgiving, Christmas and New Year's. Orchard Museum, same hours. May be closed during winter months, inquire. Fees: House, ages 16 and over, 50¢. Museum free. Adm. free to holders of Golden Eagle and Golden Age passports (available here). Tours: Self-guiding, with brochure. Museum shows movies of Theodore Roosevelt's life. Snacks sold on premises, in season. No picnics. Handicapped: Walks somewhat hilly; stairs to and inside house. A National Historic Site.* (516) 922-4447.

This fine old Victorian home is furnished as it was when Theodore Roosevelt lived in it. Completed in 1885, it carries out many of his personal desires, including a large piazza with rocking chairs where the family could sit and watch the setting sun; a bay window with a southern view; enormous fireplaces. We'll see objects collected on his trips around the world, gifts from the famous, family heirlooms, trophies, and personal mementoes such as the "Clara-doll" in the playroom and the Teddy Bears, named after him. "Nothing," said Roosevelt, "can take the place of family life." A real family lived here and today visitors find themselves stopping for a second look at a way of life that may have provided only one bathtub for a large family, but produced healthy, happy, and loyal citizens.

Orchard Museum is in a nearby building, the home of one of Roosevelt's sons. Here are shown photographs, documents, color slides and a stirring movie of some of the highlights in the President's life.

FOR THE DRIVER: Take Northern Blvd. (NY 25A) east about 11 *m.* after jct. with Cross Island Pkwy. At foot of a hill at a light is Wolver Hollow Road where signs direct you left to State University Planting Fields. Turn right at next main jct., on Chicken Valley Road, to the Planting Fields.

Continue on same road briefly to its end then turn left to next road, Mill Hill Road. Turn right on this and proceed to West Shore Road, then turn right again. This becomes West Main St., just before center of town (Oyster Bay). Watch on left for a small Colonial house, Raynham Hall. Parking in street.

Continue to light at corner, South St., and jog left, then right again on East Main, following signs to Theodore Roosevelt's Grave and Bird Sanctuary. Just beyond, a road goes left along Oyster Bay Harbor. Take this to Sagamore Hill.

Return Trip: Back to jct. near Sanctuary. Turn right into town. Here, turn left on South St. (NY 106) and proceed south to jct. with NY 25A. Turn right, passing Howard Johnson's and Rothmann's, also other eating places. Return the way you started.

Whaling Gear and Walt Whitman

TRIP G-4. *We'll Visit:*

STATE FISH HATCHERY, Cold Spring Harbor

WHALING MUSEUM

HECKSCHER MUSEUM, Huntington (Closed Mon.)

POWELL-JARVIS HOUSE (Cl. Mon. & Sat.)

CONKLIN HOUSE, HUNTINGTON HISTORICAL SOCIETY (Closed Mon. & Sat.)

WALT WHITMAN HOUSE

STATE UNIVERSITY AGRICULTURAL and TECHNICAL COLLEGE, Farmingdale, L.I. (Farm, daily; grounds, May-Oct.; greenhouses, weekdays.)

DISTANCE AND TOLLS: To State University via the others: From Throgs Neck Bridge, 35 *m.*, 25¢. From Verrazano, 60 *m.*, 50¢, Pkwy. return add 10¢. Plus return. Mostly average speeds after Pkwys.

FOOD: Below Huntington, Mooring. Near Whitman House, Marcpiere.

State Fish Hatchery, Cold Spring Harbor, L.I. *Open year around daily, daylight hours. Office open 8-4:30. Free. Rest rooms in office bldg. Handicapped: Level ground; all displays outside.*

This small but always appealing exhibit includes several tanks of brook trout in various stages of growth. Vending machine dispenses fish food.

Whaling Museum, Cold Spring Harbor, L.I., N.Y. 11724. *Open Memorial Day thru Sept. daily, 11-5. Rest of year, weekends and hol. only. Closed major hol. Fees: Adults 75¢, 6-14, 25¢.*

The village of Cold Spring in the last century was home port to a fleet of whaling vessels; today a relatively new museum commemorates this with a varied collection of mementoes of that era. Biggest exhibit is a whaling boat completely outfitted with all the gear and tackle needed for operations before engines were introduced. Also: Try-pots, scrimshaw work, ship models, old prints and documents.

Heckscher Museum, Heckscher Park, Prime Ave. & Rte. 25A, Huntington, L.I., N.Y. 11743. *Open year around Tues.-Friday, 10-5, Sat.-Sun. 1-6. Some holidays 1-5. Free. Parking in street.* (516) 271-4440.

There's a true museum atmosphere here—it's quiet, cool, relaxing. It features a fine permanent collection of paintings by both American and European artists from the 15th century to today. Also are special exhibitions of sculpture, minerals, modern art.

Powell-Jarvis House, 434 Park Ave., Huntington, L.I., N.Y. 11743. *Open Tues.-Fri. and Sun., 1-4. Closed Hol. Fees: Adults 50¢, under 14, 25¢.*

Recently opened to the public by the Historical Society, this has a collection of memorabilia from the area including pottery made in Huntington, Indian artifacts, paintings, costumes and antiques.

Conklin House, Huntington Historical Society, New York Ave. and High St., Huntington, L.I., N.Y. 11743. *Open year around, Tues. thru Fri. and Sun. 1-4. Closed major holidays. Fees: Adults 50¢, under 14, 25¢. Guided tours. Handicapped: Some steps. Parking area behind house.*

This picturesque 18th-century farmhouse is a special delight to those who appreciate fine antiques as well as craft work of a past era. In the kitchen, besides the innumerable tools are examples of pottery made here in Huntington. Upstairs, bedrooms hold intriguing collections of children's toys and a four harness loom used in making rugs. Emphasis is on craft work and classes often visit to watch the steps in producing material such as wool. Craft classes are held at the Museum—anyone interested might inquire.

Walt Whitman House, off Rte 110, West Hills, L.I. (516) 427-5240. *Open year around; from Apr. thru Nov. 1-4 Wed. thru Sun. Rest of year weekends (weather permitting) upon request. Closed some hol. Free. Handicapped: some steps.*

In this small shingled farmhouse the poet Walt Whitman was born in 1819. The lower floor contains period furnishings; upstairs are documents, pictures, parts of many of his poems. As a young man, the poet came back to Huntington and established *The Long Islander*, the town's weekly newspaper. His birthplace is now a State Historic Site.

State University Agricultural and Technical College, Farmingdale, L.I., N.Y. 11735. *Open: Farm from 10 a.m., 7 days a week; milking time, 5 a.m., 3 p.m. Greenhouses, weekdays, exc. holidays. Grounds open May to Oct., dawn to dusk. Rose displays in June. Free. Group tours available by appointment.*

A 150-acre classroom for students of agriculture and horticulture is a popular oasis for visitors from many ways of life. Barnyard animals, pure-bred, fill pens, sties, coops, barns, fields. Cows get milked, sheep are shorn, eggs gathered. Gardens, conservatory and greenhouses hold lavish displays of thousands of herbaceous plants for study and for admiration, while the June rose garden is a highlight.

FOR THE DRIVER: Take Northern Blvd., Rte. 25A east and continue past Oyster Bay to Cold Spring Harbor on left. On your right is the State Fish Hatchery.

Continue on NY 25A; almost at once it turns into town. Many antique shops along this route. Watch on left for a small building, Whaling Museum.

Continue on Rte. 25A, passing restaurant Mooring in Cold Spring. In town of Huntington, just beyond jct. with NY 110 is Heckscher Park off Rte. 25A, left. In this is the Heckscher Museum. No driving permitted in park; visitors park on surrounding streets.

Continuing on Rte. 25A, just past the park is the Old First Church, a 1784 replacement for one built in 1715 which was used as a storehouse by the British in 1777.

Proceed on 25A to light at Park Ave. Turn right to N. Woodhull St. on left. At this corner is the Quaker Thomas Powell House.

Then return to Rte. 25A, turn left, to jct. with NY 110. Turn left toward Huntington Station. In a couple of blocks, almost directly in front of you is the Huntington Historical Society Museum, Conklin House. Park beyond the house.

For Walt Whitman House: Back on Rte. 110 and turn right. Continue to Jericho Turnpike, NY 25, at light. Cross this, but just beyond jct. watch for signs Whitman House. When a road branches right, take this to the Whitman House.

Take Rte. 110 the direction you had been going, turn right, and proceed about 5 m. On the right, at light at Melville Rd., is entrance to State University Agricultural and Technical College grounds.

Return Trip: For Throgs Neck Bridge: Back to Rte. 110, turn left and return about 3 m. to Northern State Pkwy. west. Take this to NYC.

For Verrazano Bridge: Back to Rte. 110, turn right and continue about 3 m. to Pkwy. west to NYC (it will be Southern State Pkwy). Follow signs to Verrazano Bridge.

The Baronial Opulence of a Vanderbilt

TRIP G-5. *We'll Visit:*

VANDERBILT MUSEUM, Centerport. (May thru Oct. Closed Mon.)
SUNKEN MEADOW STATE PARK

DISTANCE AND TOLLS: To Sunken Meadow Park: From Throgs Neck 55 *m.*,
25¢. From Verrazano, under 80 *m.*, 50¢. Plus return. Some fast, most
average speeds.
FOOD: Near Vanderbilt Museum, Al Dowd's Steak House; Geide's, closed Mon.
In Northport, Bali-Hai, closed Mon.

Vanderbilt Museum, Little Neck Rd., Centerport, L.I., N.Y. 11721.
Open May thru Oct., Tues. thru Sat. 10-4. Sun., Holidays 12-5. Fees:
Adults $1. Under 12, 50¢, exc. schools by appoint., also service men
and women in uniform of US or allies, and hospitalized veterans.
Guided tours. Handicapped: No wheeled vehicles indoors. Many paths
are cobblestone; also a good deal of climbing indoors and out. With
crutches, agile handicapped could manage most of it. (516) ANI-5656.
PLANETARIUM: *Shows Thurs.-Sun. eves., weekends & hol. also morn-*
ing and aft. Also weekdays July-Aug. Special program under 7 yrs., Sat.
11 a.m. Fees: Adults $1.75, Sr. Cit. & 6-12 yrs., $1. Under 6, to special
show, only, 75¢.

Eagle's Nest is one of four "baronial halls" built by grandsons of
Commodore Cornelius Vanderbilt. Our trips take in another at Hyde
Park, built by Frederick Vanderbilt (D-16 EXT). Today we'll visit one
that was transformed from a six-room country dwelling into an
impressive 24-room mansion by William K. Vanderbilt.

Exotic art treasures gathered by Vanderbilt in his world travels fill
dining room, bedrooms, library and sitting room. Special buildings
house enormous hobby collections. Natural history displays cover many
subjects including marine specimens said to be the only ones of their
kind in existence. Also here are mementoes of the auto racing for the
famous Vanderbilt Cup. Outside we'll see VISTAS through columns of
marble from the ruins of Carthage; Spanish-Moroccan buildings with
belltower and bells from 1715; courtyards and mosaic-bordered walks;
gardens overlooking picturesque Northport Harbor.

Sunken Meadow State Park. *Open year around. Bathing in Sound,*
Memorial Day thru Labor Day. Fees: Weekends from Mid-Apr., and
weekdays from late May, $1.50 per car. Mem. Day - Labor Day, daily,

$2. After Labor Day, weekends thru Columbus Day, and daily for 1 week only, $1.50. Swimming (L. I. Sound), weekends from Mem. Day, daily, mid-June thru Labor Day.

One of the larger state parks on Long Island, this is also one of the safest. It's located on the Sound, thus swimming is in calmer waters than on the South Shore. There are two 9-hole golf courses and driving ranges; also playgrounds, a good-sized boardwalk, and many picnic areas in wooded sections. Excellent bathing facilities.

FOR THE DRIVER: Take Northern State Pkwy. east for about 20 miles to NY 110 to Huntington. Proceed north on 110 into Huntington; you pass Walt Whitman's House, opp. the Whitman Shopping Center. Continue to jct. with NY 25A and turn right (east). Do not turn on Rte. 25–Jericho Tpke. Take 25A. Proceed about 5 miles to Centerport, near this is Al Dowd's Steak House. Also Geide's. Look for dolphin sign to Vanderbilt Museum to your left on Little Neck Road.

Back to Rte. 25A. Turn left and continue about 12 miles, passing Bali-Hai, to the parkway which goes to your left to Sunken Meadow State Park.

Return Trip: Take Sunken Meadow State Pkwy. to either Northern State Pkwy., the first one you reach, or the Long Island Expressway, NY 495, and return to New York City.

Modes of Living on Long Island

TRIP G-6. *We'll Visit:*

BULL STATUE, Smithtown

ORIGINAL ST. JAMES GENERAL STORE

MUSEUMS AT STONY BROOK: CARRIAGE MUSEUM (only) Closed Dec.-Apr.

THOMPSON HOUSE, Setauket (May-Oct., Fri.-Sun.)

SHERWOOD-JAYNE HOUSE, East Setauket (by appointment only)

DISTANCE AND TOLLS: To Sherwood-Jayne House, farthest: From Throgs Neck Bridge, over 70 *m.*, 25¢. From Verrazano, about 95 *m.*, 50¢. Plus return. Mainly fast speeds, slower in towns.
FOOD: In Smithtown, Mont D'Or, closed Mon. Frank Friede's Riverside, closed Tues. Howard Johnson's. In Stony Brook, Three Village Inn. In Port Jefferson, Elk Hotel. Diners in towns.

Bull Statue, Smithtown. How far could you ride in a day on bull-back? Richard Smith found out by trying, over 300 years ago. As their part of the bargain, the Indians granted him all the land he and his mount covered. If you don't believe it, here stands the bull in a small park in the center of town.

Original St. James General Store, Moriches and Harbor Hill Rds., St. James, L.I., N.Y. 11780. *Open year around, daily exc. Mon.* (516) 862-8333.

A descendant of the man who rode the bull built this store which, in 1977, celebrated its 120th birthday. Much of the original flavor still remains, with old fashioned foods, candies, spices as well as many accessories of that era. Connoisseurs will be surprised to discover a Tiffany glass workshop with tools of the trade. A music engravers' shop displays everything needed for printing sheet music, including the finished plates.

The Museums at Stony Brook, Stony Brook, N.Y. 11790. Phone (516) 751-0066. *Open year around, Wed.-Sun. and most Mon. Hol., 10-5, exc. Carriage Museum and adjoining period bldgs., which are closed Dec. thru Apr. Fees: Adm. to entire complex, Apr. thru Nov.: Adults, $2., students and Senior Citizens, $1.50, children 6-12, $1., under 6, free. From Dec. to Apr., adults, 75¢, students, Senior Citizens, 50¢, children, 25¢. Handicapped: Carriage Museum exhibit is on one floor, with ramps. Craft Center, some steps, but many exhibits on first floor. Steps to some period houses. Rest rooms in Carriage House, Art Museum and Craft Center. Gift Shop.*

In recent years, two popular attractions have expanded to include a group of period buildings and specialized exhibits.
Carriage Museum. Here 300 horse-drawn vehicles make an impressive display; included are fringed surreys, Wells Fargo coaches, a model of a Royal Stage Coach from England designed for George III, a Russian sleigh, a Conestoga wagon and some unusual utility coaches — remember the ones that dispensed popcorn and peanuts? Outside we visit a 1794 barn, a full-size harness and blacksmith shop, a schoolhouse of 1877, and a printing office. Nearby is an Art Museum, opened 1974, containing many displays formerly in the Suffolk Museum. Emphasis is on the works of the 19th-century American genre artist, William Sidney Mount, a Stony Brook resident. Changing exhibits are seen here; there is also a reference library, open by appointment.
The History Museum, opened 1977, is across the road; its collections include more from the former museum, costumes, household items, toys, and miniature rooms of historical significance.

Leaving this area, the drive into town goes past a 1751 grist mill, on left, between the mill pond and Stony Brook Harbor. **The Craft**

Center, originally the Suffolk Museum, has changing exhibits covering crafts of yesterday and today. Craft workshops are conducted here.

Thompson House, North Country Rd., Setauket, L.I., N.Y. 11785. *Open May-Oct., Fri.-Sun. 1-5. Adults $1. Under 14 yrs., and Sr. Cit. 50¢. Guided tours.* (516) 941-9444.

One of the houses maintained by the Society for the Preservation of Long Island Antiquities, this 1700 saltbox remained in the same family for nearly 180 years. Displays under unusually high ceilings include interesting paneling, Long Island chairs, linen bedding made from flax grown in this area, rare antiques.

Sherwood-Jayne House, Old Post Road, East Setauket, L.I., N.Y. 11733. *Hours same as Thompson House, but by appointment only.* (516) 941-9444.

The Jayne family built this saltbox house around 1730; as the need for larger quarters grew, so did the house and in 1790 an east end was erected. Unlike most historic homes, this has not been restored entirely to its earlier period; instead, it retains an interesting assortment of 18th-century furnishings plus a modern kitchen with built-in bar. Yet somehow the old blends with the new. Outside, sheep graze in the East Pasture, while ancient trees and beautiful gardens surround the picturesque house.

FOR THE DRIVER: Take Northern State Parkway east about 30 miles to the Sunken Meadow State Pkwy. at Exit 44N. Drive north briefly to Exit SM 3 east, to Jericho Tpke. (NY 25). After ramp, turn right at the light—you'll be on Rte. 25 east.

Soon NY 25A joins NY 25 in Smithtown. At this jct., to your left is a small park with the statue of the Smithtown Bull. Also at this jct. is Frank Friede's Riverside Inn. In center of town is a Howard Johnson's; on Rte. 25A is the Mont D'Or Restaurant.

Shortly Rtes. 25A and NY 111 turn left. Follow 25A north (left) for a couple of miles and watch for sign at traffic light just beyond town, to the St. James General Store, to your left.

Continue on NY 25A to Stony Brook. Here 25A turns right, while the road to Stony Brook goes ahead. A block before this is   the entrance to the Carriage Museum on right.

Then take road to Stony Brook; you'll shortly come upon the picturesque Village Green. Here is the Three Village Inn. In the next block, on Christian Ave. is the Craft Center on your left. Parking in street.

Continue on Christian Ave., bearing left. Watch for small sign to Setauket at Bailey Hollow Rd. Turn right at sign: All Points East. Proceed to stop sign at N. Country Road. Turn right to Thompson House, left.

Continue to next corner, NY 25A, and turn left (east). Just beyond town, before gas station is Old Coach Road and small signs to Sherwood-Jayne House. Turn right—soon Old Post Road merges with yours—and continue to the house.

Return Trip: Continue on Old Post Road to jct. with Main St., Rte. 25A, at stop sign. Turn right. For Elk Hotel and restaurant, turn left into town. For New York: Take Rte. 25A, right; soon comes NY 112. Continue ahead on Rte. 112 to jct. with NY 347 at light. Turn right, west, on 347 toward Smithtown. Continue after Rte. 347 ends—you're now on Veteran's Memorial Highway—and follow signs to Northern Pkwy. to New York. Keep left, toward city.

Natural History and Fire Engines

TRIP G-7. *We'll Visit:*

ROCK HALL, Lawrence (Apr. thru Nov., closed Tues.)

NASSAU COUNTY MUSEUM OF NATURAL HISTORY, Seaford
TACKAPAUSHA PRESERVE, Seaford

DISTANCE AND TOLLS: To Seaford via Whitestone Bridge, under 40 *m.*, 25¢. Via Verrazano, under 60 *m.*, 50¢; add 10¢ on return. Mostly average speeds, slower in towns.

Rock Hall, 199 Bway, Lawrence, L.I., N.Y. 11559. *Open Apr. thru Nov. daily exc. Tues., 10-5. Sun. 12-5. Free. Handicapped: Some exhibits are on upper floors and in basement, but you can see much on one level. 4 steps into the bldg., with railings. Limited rest room facilities. Parking area.*

This house was first noted in records dated 1767 when Josiah Martin, a planter from Antigua, West Indies, purchased 600 acres with buildings which may have included the present Rock Hall. Today it is administered by the Society for the Preservation of Long Island Antiquities. The rooms are unusually large and filled with fine antiques of the former period.

Nassau County Museum of Natural History, Seaford Div., Seaford, L.I., N. Y. 11783. *Open year around, Monday thru Saturday 10-5. Sunday 1-5 (closed some holidays). Fee 25¢. Food: Small picnic area. Handicapped may enter from ramp behind building. Rest rooms down one flight (railings).* 516) 292-4266.

This small modern museum provides background for the study of regional wild life. The displays combine specimens, scale models and pictures and cover subjects such as the eras of geological time, the story of the origin of Long Island, inhabitants of the Ice Age and th mineralized upper forearm of one of them. A weekend theater has free programs on various related topics. The Museum is connected with the one at Garvies Point (G-1).

Tackapausha Preserve. Adjacent to the Seaford Museum are 80 acres with over 5 miles of nature trails. A brochure is available for a Self-Guiding Tour through the glacial outwash plain where over 40 species of birds nest.

FOR THE DRIVER: Those coming from Long Island: Take Southern State Pkwy. to Exit 19 South, then Peninsula Blvd. toward Rockville Center. At Woodmere Blvd. at a light, turn left to Broadway. Turn right for a mile to Rock Hall, left.

Everyone else: From Verrazano, Whitestone or Throgs Neck Bridges, follow signs to Kennedy Airport, but do not turn in. Instead, take Rockaway Blvd. (exits from all parkways, marked) and drive past northern end of the airport. After truck route branches right, remain in left lane to continue on Rockaway Tpke., smaller road. Several blocks later cross railroad tracks; soon comes Broadway, at a light. Turn right several blocks to Rock Hall, left.

Back on Broadway, turn right and proceed a mile to Woodmere Blvd., just before shopping center. Turn left and drive to Peninsula Blvd., then turn right. About 3 *m.* ahead is jct. with NY 27, Sunrise Hwy. Take this east (right) to jct. with Merrick Road. Then continue on this.

In 10 *m* you'll pass jct. with NY 135, the Wantagh-Oyster Bay Expressway. A few blocks farther are signs to turn left to Nassau County Natural History Museum. Tackapausha Preserve is adjacent.

Return Trip: Go back the way you came, turning right on Merrick Road, and proceed to NY 135, the Wantagh-Oyster Bay Expressway. Take this north toward Oyster Bay, to jct. with Southern State Pkwy. For New York, take Pkwy. west and follow signs to your bridge. On Parkway, pass entrances to Hempstead Lake State Park and Valley Stream State Park.

Pre-Civil War Days Recreated

TRIP G-8. *We'll Visit:*
OLD BETHPAGE VILLAGE RESTORATION
BETHPAGE STATE PARK

DISTANCE AND TOLLS: To the Restoration: From Throgs Neck Bridge about 30 *m.*, from Verrazano, over 50 *m.* Add about 6 *m.* to Park. Fast speeds. Throgs Neck Bridge, 25¢, Verrazano, 50¢. If returning via Southern State Pkwy. add 10¢.

Old Bethpage Village Restoration, Round Swamp Road, Old Bethpage, L.I., N.Y. Phone (516) 420-5280. *Open year around, daily July & Aug., rest of year, closed Mon. Hours: 10-5, exc. from Dec.-Feb., 10-4. Closed most hol. Adm: Adults, $2.25; 5-17, $1.50. Food: Picnic areas, cafeteria. Handicapped: Ramps into Visitor's Reception Center. Grab bars in rest rooms. Roads unpaved but mainly level, except for hill to the church (optional). Steps into the houses, doors narrow. Little shade along roadways; few benches. Best time, weekday mornings, less crowded.*

This is the beginning of a big project. A typical Long Island farm community of a century ago is being recreated. Emphasis is on the period 1830 to 1850, when the agricultural age was becoming influenced by industry. Opened to the public in 1970, the restoration may take 10 years to complete, with buildings of architectural and historical significance being moved in from many parts of the island. While under way it should provide unusual opportunities to observe the meticulous reconstruction process.

Our visit begins with an excellent orientation movie, then we start down the dirt road past the cornfield into the village. Several houses and shops are open, and costumed guides are on hand to explain their period furnishings. Occasionally there may be a demonstration of farming, crafts or cooking. A wagon ride will transport us to various parts of town. The developing village can mean a refreshing day in another era, a fascinating look at a page of history.

Bethpage State Park, Farmingdale, L.I. *Open year around. Parking $1.50 on weekends, spring and fall, weekdays from Memorial Day into Sept. Nominal fees for golf, including lessons; horseback riding, skiing. No swimming. Food: Restaurant open all year; cafeteria, snacks, picnic areas. Polo Games: Late May – mid-Oct., Sun. at 3:00. Adm. $2., under 12, free.*

This beautifully groomed park includes features not found in most. There are five 18-hole golf courses, including one known as the Champion Tournament Course. Professional instruction is available. Riding stables and 8 miles of bridle paths are popular. So, also, are tennis courts, a regulation baseball field, areas for small games, and in winter, ski slopes and ski tows plus toboggan slopes. Hiking trails and picnic areas complete the picture.

FOR THE DRIVER: Take Northern State Pkwy. east about 17 *m*. Just beyond jct. with Rte. 135 (Seaford-Oyster Bay Expressway) the Long Island Expressway (Rte. 495) crosses yours, bearing right. You cut off a mile or so by switching to this, keeping in right lane. Exit at Round Swamp Road, and follow sign t

Farmingdale. Almost at once, at light, Round Swamp Road goes left; take it to entrance to Old Bethpage Village Restoration.

To return directly to the city, skipping the park: Turn right and follow signs to either Long Island Expressway west or to Northern State Pkwy. west.

For the park: Turn left from Village and follow signs to park, bearing right. Pass Bethpage Polo and Riding Stable, also golf courses. At traffic circle is a sign to Farmingdale. However, do not take this, but bear right, shortly passing entrance to golf courses and restaurant. Ahead, another sign to Bethpage, to right. Continue this direction to sign, right, to Bethpage State Pkwy., Golf courses, polo field and picnic area. Turn here for picnics, following signs. Near this jct. is sign to Rte. 135 to Northern State Pkwy.

Return Trip: Go back to jct. with NY 135. For Throgs Neck Bridge take Rte. 135 north to Northern State Pkwy. Take Pkwy. west (2nd entrance) and return. For Verrazano Bridge take Rte. 135 south to jct. with Southern State Pkwy. Take Pkwy. west, toward N.Y. City and follow signs to Verrazano Bridge.

To Jones Beach and Beyond

TRIP G-9. *We'll Visit:*

JONES BEACH STATE PARK
CAPTREE STATE PARK
ROBERT MOSES STATE PARK

DISTANCE AND TOLLS: To Robert Moses Park, farthest: From Throgs Neck Bridge, over 40 *m.*, 35¢; via Verrazano Bridge, 55 *m.*, 60¢. Fast speeds. Plus return. One road toll includes all three state parks.

Jones Beach State Park. *Open year around. Causeway Toll, mid-May – mid-Sept. $1. per car, round trip. Rest of year, 50¢. Plus parking fee, $2, same dates. Parking free rest of year. Swimming: Weekends from late May, daily, early June-Labor Day. (Beaches.) Pools, from late June daily. Food: Restaurant, all year; cafeteria, snack bars, picnic areas. Handicapped: Special facilities.*

Anyone who's been caught in the automotive holding pattern extending over Long Island on summer weekends must realize a blockbuster attraction is in the area. He's right. Eleven mammoth parking lots are waiting to accept some 20,000 cars bringing in five times that number of bathers to one of the largest state parks along the Atlantic Ocean.

Besides the 5 miles of sand and ocean we'll discover other bathing areas in Zach's Bay or in a salt water pool. There's fishing, 2 miles of boardwalks, free dancing, star gazing. In winter, fishing, deck games, roller skating, kite flying. In summer the Jones Beach Marine Theater puts on elaborate musicals.

Captree State Park. *Same as for Jones Beach State Park; same dates. Open year around. Parking fee & causeway toll. Picnic areas; snacks.*

Here is a seashore park ideally situated for those with fishing interests. Open fishing boats leave regularly; charter boats are available for parties, by reservation. There are piers for still more fishing.

Robert Moses State Park. *Open year around. Fees: parking fee and causeway toll same as for Jones Beach; same dates. Food: Picnic areas; snacks. Handicapped: Special facilities.*

The western end of the famous Fire Island, home of writers and artists over the years, has been opened to the motoring public, but the road goes no farther than the state park at its tip. A bridge opened in 1964 allows us to drive to this 1,000-acre seashore area, in bygone days the scene of many shipwrecks, now a fine backup for the overflow from Jones Beach. There's excellent surfbathing. Playgrounds and picnic tables are set among the rugged sand dunes.

FOR THE DRIVER: Take Southern State Pkwy. east about 9 miles to the Meadowbrook State Pkwy. then follow signs to Jones Beach, about 9 miles farther. If this road is too crowded you may continue on Southern State Pkwy. to the exit to Robert Moses Causeway and cross there for either Captree or Robert Moses State Parks, or to approach Jones Beach from the other end.

After Jones Beach, if taking an additional drive: Continue, following signs to Tobay Beach, a bird and game sanctuary, Gilgo State Park, undeveloped but available for outings, by permit, and finally, Captree State Park. From here, follow signs to Robert Moses State Park, across Fire Island Inlet.

Return Trip: Take Robert Moses Causeway back to Southern State Pkwy. westbound (toward NYC) and return the way you came.

Visit to a Great Arboretum

TRIP G-10. *We'll Visit:*

BAYARD CUTTING ARBORETUM (Closed Mon. & Tues., exc. hol.)
HECKSCHER STATE PARK

DISTANCE AND TOLLS: Via Throgs Neck Bridge, 40 *m.*, 35¢; via Verrazano Bridge, 55 *m.*, 60¢. Plus return. Fast speeds.

Bayard Cutting Arboretum, Great River, L.I. Address inquiries to Arboretum, Oakdale, N.Y. 11769. *Grounds open year around, Wed.-Sun., 10-4:30. Adm. fee: $1 per person late-April – late-Sept. Also* *weekends and hol. all year. Food: Snacks, same dates. No picnics. Self-guiding tours with maps. Handicapped: Paths level; few steps into snack bars. Benches. No pets.* (516) 581-1002.

Under development since 1887, this magnificent collection of fine trees includes many of the original plantings. Beneath are banked rhododendron and azaleas. The scenic Connetquot River flows by, attracting colonies of breeding birds. We may take specially planned walks through the Pinetum (25 min.), the Rhododendrons (1 hour— these peak in late May to mid-June), the Wildflower section (40 min.), the Swamp Cyprus (25 min.), and finally a popular hike for birdwatchers along the river to a bird sanctuary.

Heckscher State Park, East Islip, L.I. *Open year around. Fees: Weekends, from mid-Apr., and weekdays from late May, $1.50. Weekends in June, and daily, late June thru Labor Day, $2. After Labor Day, weekends thru early Oct., and daily into early Sept., $1.50. Swimming weekends from early June (beach only); daily late June thru Labor Day (beach and pool). Food: Snacks, when parking lot open; picnics, cooking.*

Facing Great South Bay, this scenic 1,600-acre park, a natural wildlife refuge, includes three different bathing areas on protected waters along three miles of waterfront. There are large picnic sections, playgrounds, game areas, softball diamonds and small boat launching ramps.

FOR THE DRIVER: Take Southern State Pkwy. east for about 32 *m.* to exit at Montauk Hwy. (NY 27A). Follow signs to Bayard Cutting Arboretum.

Return the way you came, to the parkway. Here, follow signs to Heckscher State Park.

Return Trip: Take Southern State Parkway west to New York City.

Adventures on Staten Island

• *You know that giant footstool, 14 miles long and 8 miles wide, over which you zip on super-highways between Brooklyn and New Jersey? You'll be interested to know it has a name, a history, and some most attractive rural neighborhoods and parks.*

STAATEN EYELANDT was its first name, given by Henry Hudson on his 1609 voyage, some 85 years after Giovanni da Verrazano apparently saw it in 1524. STATEN ISLAND is our goal for our visit today. Our drives take in several sections. They'll be divided into 2 trips.

To reach Staten Island: From Brooklyn, Manhattan, Connecticut, Long Island, use the Verrazano Bridge. From New Jersey, take Goethals Bridge.

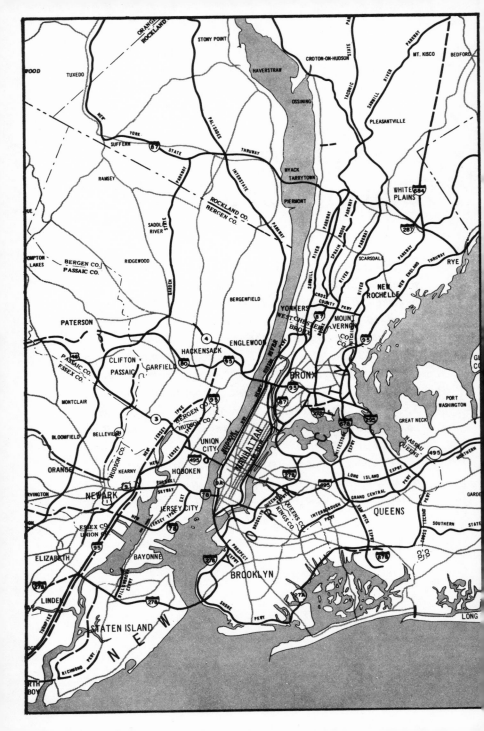

In the Footsteps of Garibaldi

TRIP H-1. *We'll Visit:*

FORT WADSWORTH MUSEUM (Closed Tues., Wed.)

VON BRIESEN PARK

GARIBALDI MEMORIAL (Closed Monday)

STATEN ISLAND INSTITUTE OF ARTS & SCIENCES (Closed Monday)

SAILORS' SNUG HARBOR

STATEN ISLAND ZOO

DISTANCE AND TOLLS: From any approach, all attractions are within a few miles. Bridges from N.J. $1.50 round trip. Verrazano Bridge 75¢, plus return.

Fort Wadsworth Museum: *Open year around, Mon., Thurs., Fri. 1-4. Sat. 10-5, Sun. 1-5. Closed hol. and for 10 days over Christmas & New Year's, or by appointment. Free. Parking area. Rest rooms. Handicapped: Exhibits on one level. (Check first: some Army units are being moved.)*

If your youngsters, especially the males, have been good sports about trailing you through museums of art and antiquities you might consider rewarding them with a trip to this one. Their seniors might be impressed, too. Located in the oldest continually manned military installation in the country, here is a museum devoted to the history of the U.S. Army and the Fort as well. In it is a collection of military crests and insignia; war mementoes from many conflicts, captured flags, uniforms, Red Cross supplies, full scale models of soldiers in a bunker, cannon to the right of us . . .

The museum is fairly small, but imaginatively constructed. Outside we can view a trapezoidal Battery Weed built in the mid-1800's, together with a number of artillery batteries from about the time of W W I.

Von Briesen Park, adjacent to Ft. Wadsworth. *Open year around for viewing.*

This unique VISTA overlooks the Narrows providing superb views of ocean-going traffic, the distant city and some of its mighty bridges.

Garibaldi Memorial, 420 Tompkins Ave., Rosebank, S.I., N.Y. 10305. *Open year around Tues.-Sat. 10-5, Sun., holidays, 1-5. Fees: Donations. Parking in street. Handicapped: Steps up to gardens, more into house. Main exhibits on first level.*

How much do you know about the man who was famous as the hero of two worlds, leader in wars to free South America, and who in 1860 led his Thousand to unite Italy? Giuseppe Garibaldi, fighter for democracy, lived a short time on Staten Island. The house he shared with an inventor, Antonio Meucci, has been designated a New York City Landmark, maintained by the Order of the Sons of Italy in America.

The eventful story of Garibaldi's life is seen in pictures, documents and letters in the Memorial Hall. The memorial is also dedicated to Antonio Meucci, whom many consider the inventor of the telephone. A model of a bipolar phone with a horse-shoe magnet which he designed in 1854 is on display.

Staten Island Institute of Arts & Sciences Museum, 75 Stuyvesant Place & Wall St., St. George, S.I., N.Y. 10314. *Open year around, daily exc. Mon. 10-5. Sun. 2-5 (Closed major holidays). Free. Handicapped: 3 low steps into bldg.; many exhibits on first level.*

A small but significant museum covers a variety of subjects relating to the history, archaeology and culture of Staten Island. Dioramas and habitat groups depict life in the nearby salt marshes and in New York Bay, conservation problems, Indian burials—their grounds are still being uncovered on Staten Island.

Sailors' Snug Harbor, Richmond Terrace, New Brighton. *Open by appointment.* (212) 448-2500.

This world-renowned home for retired sailors was founded in 1801 by Robert Randall. Its 100 acres face the waters of Kill Van Kull while about 50 buildings, including five of Greek Revival style, house the men. A Sung Harbor Cultural Center opened recently. See papers for events.

Staten Island Zoo, Barrett Park, West New Brighton. *Open year around daily 10-4:45. Closed 3 hol. Fees: 75¢ Adults, Children 50¢. Senior Citizens & under 6, free. Food: Light snacks in vending machines. Box lunches permitted, no picnic areas. Handicapped: One low step into bldg. Everything is on 1 level. Rest rooms. Parking in street. No dogs allowed.* (212) 442-3100.

They call it the Biggest Little Zoo on Earth, and as a place to enjoy a varied collection of animals, reptiles, fish and birds without spending the whole day, this is hard to beat. The Zoo takes pride in possessing the largest collection of rattlesnakes in the world. Outdoor cages allow for further viewing apes, lions, exotic birds and the less exotic.

A children's zoo in a miniature farm is a recent addition. Open daily May-Oct., 10-4:45.

FOR THE DRIVER: Via Verrazano Bridge: Immediately after toll watch for sign to Bay St. Exit here, turn right and proceed to traffic light at Bay St. Turn right, toward the bridge.

Via Goethals Bridge: Continue across Staten Island on I-278. Just before the toll booths for the Verrazano Bridge, exit at Bay St. Follow signs, crossing left under the bridge then turning right. At traffic light at Bay St. turn right, toward the bridge.

All, starting on Bay St.: About a block ahead is the entrace to Fort Wadsworth where an M.P. will direct you to the nearby Museum and also the adjoining Von Briesen Park.

Then go back the way you came to Bay St., this time proceed straight ahead on it. Soon at traffic light is Hylan Blvd., also signs to several piers. Turn left briefly, then at another light turn right on Tompkins Ave. A block or so ahead on your left is the Garibaldi Memorial Museum.

Continue on Tompkins Ave. the direction you were going, and take the next major street, Vanderbilt Ave., back to Bay St., right. Turn left on Bay, continuing along the waterfront. Presently you're in St. George, where the ferries leave for Manhattan. Your street turns to the right and goes to the ferry slips; however, keep in left lane for a left turn at the light, where again you'll be driving by the water, on Richmond Terrace.

Immediately watch for streets going up the hill to your left. The first are one-way coming toward you. Then you pass the Family Court Building, beyond which is a small street, Hamilton. You can take this a block up to Stuyvesant Place then turn left, to the Staten Island Institute of Arts and Sciences on your left. Metered parking here. If you miss Hamilton, continue a block or two to where a street forks back up the hill, and cross over to this, bearing left. This is Stuyvesant Place—continue on it to Museum.

After the Museum take first street to your left (Wall St.) back down hill to Richmond Terrace; turn left and proceed. A mile or so farther you pass the buildings of Sailors' Snug Harbor.

Continue on Richmond Terrace briefly to Bard Ave. Turn left and proceed to intersection where you would have to jog right to go ahead. This is Forest Ave. Turn right on Forest and proceed for several blocks until sign to S.I. Zoo, on Broadway. Turn left to the Zoo. Parking in street.

Continue on Broadway to corner and full stop sign. Here, merge with Clove Road, bearing left. Pass Clove Lake Stables and Clove Lake Park. Restaurant, picnic areas here.

Return Trip: Clove Road continues to jct. with I-278 to the bridges. Follow signs and return the way you started.

History in Staten Island

TRIP H-2. *We'll Visit:*

BILLIOU-STILLWELL-PERINE HOUSE (Summer, weekends.)
JACQUES MARCHAIS CENTER OF TIBETAN ART (Summer)

RICHMONDTOWN RESTORATION
CONFERENCE HOUSE (Closed Monday)

DISTANCE AND TOLLS: A few miles total from any approach. Bridge to Staten Island from N.J. $1.50 round trip. Verrazano Bridge 75¢, plus return.

Billiou-Stillwell-Perine House, 1476 Richmond Rd., Dongan Hills, Staten Island, N.Y. 10306. *Open Apr. thru Oct. weekends 2-5. Fee 25¢, children free.*

This is a picturesque house, or set of houses—one of them the oldest building on Staten Island and now maintained by the Staten Island Historical Society. The first section was built in 1662 by a French Walloon, Pierre Billiou, when the Dutch still ruled New Netherland. Later his son-in-law, Capt. Thomas Stillwell, added some typically English parts, and finally the Perine family in 1760 added more wings. We visit the 1830 wing, the kitchen, and the original section of the house.

Jacques Marchais Center of Tibetan Art, 340 Lighthouse Ave., Richmondtown, S.I., N.Y. 10306. *Open Apr. 1-Nov., weekends 1-5. Also June-Aug., Thurs., Fri. Adults $1. Children 50¢. Under 12, free.*

On just three acres of steep hills are found eastern style exotic gardens surrounding a temple built like a Tibetan lamasery. The late Mrs. Jacques Marchais owned an art gallery and although she had never been to Tibet, the subject fascinated her to the extent that she spent 25 years collecting the finest Oriental objects d'art. In the museum are exquisite gold filigreed work, richly colored robes and accessories, shrines and many forms of Buddha seated against different backgrounds. The emphasis is on the Tibetan type of Buddhism.

Richmondtown Restoration, Staten Island Historical Society and the Dept. of Parks, City of New York, Richmondtown, Staten Island, N.Y. 10306. Phone (212) 351-1611. *Several restoration buildings open, May-Oct. In July & Aug., Tues.-Fri. 10-5; Sat. from noon; Sun. from 2 p.m. May-June, and Sept., Oct., weekends only, 2-5. Adults $1.50. 6-18 yrs. 50¢. (Incl. Historic Museum). Groups by appointment.* (212) 351-9414. *Also includes Museum.*

In 1770 the settlement was called Cocclestown because of the presence of so many shellfish in the surrounding waters. By 1730 it had become a village with its name changed to Richmondtown. It withstood the Revolutionary War and the population continued to increase and prosper after its end. About 1880 its name had been shortened to Richmond, a thriving village now the county seat. However, in 1898

Staten Island became part of Greater New York and many county functions were moved elsewhere. By 1920 most of the former county buildings were out of use and the town's inhabitants had begun moving away.

A few years later in the 1930's the Staten Island Historical Society began to acquire the old buildings for its own use. In 1952 the Dept. of Parks of the City of New York joined in an ambitious plan to restore Richmondtown as a showcase of the development of a typical American village of the 17th, 18th and 19th centuries. That is the project under way at this time.

Presently we can visit the HISTORICAL SOCIETY MUSEUM. *Open the year around, Tues. thru Sat. 10-5, Sun. 2-5. Fee: 50¢ adults, 25¢ children. Rest rooms on 2nd floor. Store sells souvenirs, candy, material for buffs.*

The museum is filled with Americana and period rooms. This is also the focal point for information on the Restoration.

In addition, presently from Apr.-Oct. by appointment we can go through the VOORLEEZER'S HOUSE (1696), possibly the oldest elementary school still standing in the United States; the LAKE-TYSEN HOUSE (1740), STEPHENS HOUSE & STORE (1837), BENNETT HOUSE (1839) a CARPENTER SHOP (1870) and PRINT SHOP (1850). Eventually there will be 36 buildings located on streets closed to traffic.

This is the only project of this nature in the Metropolitan area. It probably will warrant frequent visits during the interesting process of reconstruction.

Conference House-Billopp Mansion, Conference House Park, Tottenville, Staten Island, N.Y. 10307. *Open year around, Wed.-Sun. Spring thru fall, 1-5 p.m. Winter, to 4. Fees; 50¢. Under 12, free with adult. Handicapped: Several steps into house and some climbing inside.*

A conference to end the American Revolution was held here in 1776 between the British naval commander, Lord Howe, and members of the Continental Congress, among them Benjamin Franklin and John Adams. Lord Howe offered amnesty to all if the country returned to British rule. The Continental delegates explained that a Declaration of Independence had been voted on July 4th and asked recognition. The meeting failed.

The house has been restored and is today a National Historic Landmark. In it two floors and a basement are open to visitors; in one of the bedrooms is a museum dedicated to Benjamin Franklin. Watch the newspapers in September for an announcement of the annual Conference House Day Celebration, held to commemorate the meeting that took place Sept. 11, 1776.

FOR THE DRIVER: Via Verrazano Bridge: After toll continue briefly to exit to Richmond Road and Clove Road. After ramp, stay to left on local road parallel to Expressway to 2nd light at Richmond Road. Turn left and proceed.

Via Goethals Bridge: Exit at Richmond Road and Hylan Blvd. sign (*not* Richmond Ave.) After ramp go to first light, at Richmond Rd. Branch right before light, to turn right, and proceed.

All: Continue on Richmond Road over a mile to the Billiou-Stillwell-Perine House, left.

Continue on Richmond Road, soon passing the New Dorp Moravian Church and Cemetery, right. Just beyond, follow signs to right, to Richmondtown. Continue to Lighthouse Ave., right. Turn here for the Tibet Museum. The road bears right, up the hill; just beyond, right, is the Jacques Marchais Center of Tibetan Art.

Go back to Richmond Road, turn right and shortly you are entering the Richmondtown Restoration.

For the next part of trip, new roads will bring newer routes. Check locally for best way to Hylan Blvd. to Tottenville. One way presently: Take Arthur Kill Rd., left, from Richmond Rd., and proceed to jct. with Richmond and Drumgoole. Follow signs to Outerbridge Crossing. Just before bridge, at rotary, take road going left, Page Ave. Proceed to Hylan Blvd. a short way ahead; turn right on Hylan and drive about a mile to its end and the Conference House.

Return Trip: For Outerbridge Crossing, Goethals Bridge or Verrazano Bridge, return to Page Ave., turn left and follow signs.

To go directly from the city to the Restoration: A new highway, Richmond Parkway, is under construction and will go to Richmondtown Restoration from I-278, from both bridges. Watch for opening.

Performing Arts

There are many opportunities to attend plays, concerts, operas and ballet performances in the New York periphery. They may be combined with trips, or objectives of your drive. Advance reservations are best. Wheelchair visitors often attend. Theaters are listed in the order in which they appear in this Guide. Dates are often announced in New York newspapers. Additional theaters are located in college towns, major resorts, and cities.

SURFLIGHT SUMMER THEATRE, Beach Haven, N.J. 08008. Phone (609) 492-2986. Late June to early Sept. Bway. musicals. All seats reserved. *(A-5 EXT)*

GARDEN STATE ARTS CENTER, Box 116, Holmdel, N.J. 07733. On Garden State Pkwy. Mid-June thru Aug., 9 p.m. No Sundays. See papers for listings: symphony, pop artists, ballet, opera. *(A-8)*

ST. JOHN TERRELL'S MUSIC CIRCUS, Lambertville, N.J. 08530. Phone (609) 397-1500. June to early Sept. Bway. shows, pop groups, well-known artists. *(A-14)*

BUCKS COUNTY PLAYHOUSE, New Hope, Pa. 18938. Phone (215) 862-2041. May to Oct. Bway. plays, revues, well-known casts. *(A-14)*

OPEN AIR THEATRE, Washington Crossing State Park, N.J. Theatre Committee, Washington Crossing Assn. of N.J., Box 1776, Titusville, N.J. 08560. Summer festival of performing arts: concerts, opera, plays, musicals. *(A-15)*

UPSALA COLLEGE, CARRIAGE HOUSE THEATRE, East Orange, N.J. Phone (201) 266-7144. Summer theatre, well-known plays. *(Nr. B-2, B-3)*

PAPER MILL PLAYHOUSE, Brookside Dr., Millburn, N.J. 07041. Phone (201) DR 6-4343. Year around exc. before Easter., Tues. thru Sun. Top Bway. productions, musicals. Children's Theatre. *(B-5)*

HUNTERDON REPERTORY CO., Clinton Music Hall, 23 W. Main St., Clinton, N.J. 08809. Phone (201) 782-8316. Repertory company presents 8 productions each yr. plus concerts nearly every weekend. *(B-10)*

WATERLOO VILLAGE RESTORATION MUSIC FESTIVAL, Stanhope, N.J. 07874. Phone (201) 347-5544, 45. 8:30 p.m. See papers for advt. for Metropolitan Opera soloists, orchestras, vocalists, etc., in 2,000-seat tent theatre. *(B-17)*

FOOTHILL PLAYHOUSE, Beechwood Ave., Middlesex, N.J. 08846. Phone (201) EL 6-0462. May thru Sept. Wed. thru Sat. Bway. hits in a barn theatre. Children's programs. *(Nr. B-13, B-10)*

GRISTMILL MUSICAL PLAYHOUSE, US 206, Andover, N.J. 07821. Phone (201) 786-5800. Mid or late June to Sept. Tues. thru Sun. Bway. musicals. *(Near B-16, B-17)*

PLAYHOUSE ON THE MALL, Bergen Mall, Paramus, N.J. 07652. Phone (201) 845-3040. At shopping center, Rte. 4. Year around. Bway shows, musicals. Dinner-theater parties. *(B-14)*

POCONO PLAYHOUSE, Mountainhome, Pa. 18342. Phone (717) 595-7456. Bway. hit plays and musicals with well-known casts. *(B-22 EXT)*

NEWFOUNDLAND ARTS CENTER, Newfoundland, Pa. 18445. Phone (717) 676-3384. Year around; musical productions, concerts, fashion, art shows, choral & dance festivals in theatre-in-the-round. *(B-22 EXT)*

TAPPAN ZEE PLAYHOUSE, Nyack, N.Y. 10960. Phone (914) EL 8-5800. In New York: (212) KI 9-7050. Late June thru Aug., Mon. thru Sat. New productions each week include top stars in Bway. shows. Marina nearby for those coming by boat. *(C-4)*

CORNWALL-ON-HUDSON PLAYHOUSE, Route 218. Summer theatre, well-known plays. *(Nr. C-11, C-12)*

WARWICK PLAYHOUSE, Warwick, N.Y. Phone (914) 986-3837. At 8:30, in summer. Bway. plays. *(C-10)*

MOUNTAIN DALE PLAYHOUSE, Box 132, Mountain Dale, N.Y. 12763. Phone (914) 434-9481. Early July thru Aug., Thurs. thru Sun. Top Bway. musicals, in former church bldg. *(C-16 EXT)*

SHAKESPEARE FESTIVAL, Fallsburgh, N.Y. 12779, at Olympic Hotel, about 4 wks., late Apr. into May. *(C-16 EXT)*

WOODSTOCK, N.Y. Opera, folk music, Sun. aft. concerts, Woodstock Playhouse, new Bway. comedies, serious plays & classics. *(C-24 EXT)*

KENSICO DAM PLAZA, July & Aug. "Music under the stars." Folk, country music; square dancing. Westchester Pops band & soloists. *(D-3)*

CARAMOOR FESTIVAL, Katonah, N.Y. 10536 Phone (914) 232-4206. Starts with June Festival, mid to late June to mid-July, then weekends for several more weeks. Seat of cultural & educational foundation for the arts of music, ballet, theater, architecture and painting. *Near D-10)*

CECILWOOD THEATRE, Fishkill, N.Y. 12524. Late June to mid-Sept. See papers. Straw Hat Circuit; Bway. plays & musicals. *(Near D-14, D-15)*

HYDE PARK PLAYHOUSE, Hyde Park, N.Y. 12538. Phone (914) 229-8047. Check papers. Plays all summer. *(D-17 EXT)*

BERKSHIRE FESTIVAL, TANGLEWOOD, Lenox, Mass. 01240. Early July thru Aug., Fri., Sat. & Sun., a nine-week schedule. Summer home of Boston Symphony Orchestra: 24 concerts in the 6000-seat Music Shed. Sat. morning rehearsals also open to public. Special performances almost daily. *(Near D-20 EXT) (D-20)*

JACOB'S PILLOW DANCE FESTIVAL, Box 287, Lee, Mass. 01238. Phone (413) 243-0745. Late June thru Aug. Tues. thru Sat. Special Dance Appreciation Evenings, usually on Sun. 8:30 p.m. Founded by Ted Shawn to train American males to become career dancers. Also a University of the Dance for resident students. Located in vicinity of Tanglewood. Mass. Tpke. to exit at Lee, then US 20 toward Springfield for 8 miles and follow signs. *(Near D-20 EXT)*

SHARON PLAYHOUSE, Sharon, Conn. 06069. Late June thru Aug., Bway plays by professional equity members. *(E-2 EXT)*

CANDLEWOOD THEATRE, New Fairfield, Conn. 06810. Phone (203) 746-2451. Late June to mid-Sept. Mon. thru Sat. From Brewster *(E-1)* I-84 east to exit to Rte. 37, then north.

LUMIA, THEATRE OF LIGHT, Box 224, Sandy Hook, Conn. 06482. Phone (203) 426-4579. *April till fall, Sat. night, 8:30, $3. adm. Connecticut's only avant garde theater, small and intimate. Whirling colors projected on screen. Groups by arrangement.*
From Brewster *(E-1)* east on I-84 to Rte. 34, Sandy Hook, ff. signs toward New Haven., about 5 miles.

SOUTHBURY PLAYHOUSE, Southbury, Conn. 06488. Phone (203) 264-8216. From late June, Mon. thru Sat. eve. Bway. plays. From Brewster *(E-1)* east on I-84 to Southbury exit; at jct. with Rtes. 6 & 67.

TRIANGLE PLAYHOUSE, Farmington, Conn. Summer shows. *(E-10 EXT)*

NORFOLK MUSIC SHED, Yale University Summer School of Music and Art, Norfolk, Conn. 06058. Phone (203) 542-5719. July 4 to late Aug., Fri. eves. 8:30. Orchestra, chamber music, choral, contemporary music by Yale Quartet, Yale Summer School Orchestra. Free art exhibit in Stoeckel Hall every week. *(E-9 EXT)*

WESTPORT COUNTRY PLAYHOUSE, Westport, Conn. 06880. Phone (203) 227-4177. Mid-June to early Sept., Mon thru Sat. Bway. & pre-Bway. productions. *(F-6, F-7)*

AMERICAN SHAKESPEARE FESTIVAL, Stratford, Conn. 06497. Phone (203) 378-7321 or 375-4457. In New York: (212) WO 6-3900. Mid-June thru Labor Day. Special student season, spring & fall. Superlative productions in atmospheric setting. Docking facilities for private boats near theatre. *(F-10)*

GOODSPEED OPERA HOUSE, East Haddam, Conn. 06423. Phone (203) 873-8668. Mid-June to early Sept. Mon. thru Sat. Worthwhile shows, some revivals, some world premieres, in 1876 landmark house, restored 1959. *(F-14 EXT)*

IVORYTON PLAYHOUSE, Ivoryton, Conn. 06442. Phone (203) 767-8258. Straw Hat Circuit summer theater; Bway. shows with top casts. Follow signs from Essex. *(F-14 EXT)*

OAKDALE MUSICAL THEATRE, Wallingford, Conn. 06492. Phone (203) 265-1551. Mid-June to late Sept. Mon. thru Sat. Bway. musicals, concerts by pop musical groups & soloists. Hutchinson-Merritt-Wilbur Cross Pkwys. to Exit 64 & follow signs.

ADELPHI UNIVERSITY LITTLE THEATRE, Garden City, L.I., N.Y. 11530. Phone (516) 747-2200. Thurs., Fri., Sat. Summer Theatre Workshop; also productions during academic year by Dept. of Speech & Dramatic Art. Grand Central Pkwy. (Northern State) to Exit 26 at New Hyde Pk. Rd., cont. to Stewart Ave., left to Nassau Blvd., right to South Ave., left to Univ.

WESTBURY MUSIC FAIR, P. O. Box 86, Westbury, L.I., N.Y. 11590. Phone (516) 333-0533. Late June thru Aug. Top musicals and dramas, name stars, concerts, children's shows. Grand Central Pkwy. (Northern State) to Exit 34. Turn right at Brush Hollow Rd., ff. signs. Near Old Westbury Gardens. *(G-2)*

STONY BROOK MUSIC FESTIVAL, Stony Brook, L.I., N.Y. 11790. In Dogwood Hollow Amphitheatre. July & Aug., Sat. at 8:30. Top pop music and stars. *(G-6)*

JONES BEACH MARINE THEATRE, P. O. Box 1300, Wantagh, L.I., N.Y. 11793. Phone (516) CA 1-1000. Late June thru Labor Day, 7 nights a week at 8:30 to 11:15. One production per summer, done on grand scale, followed by dancing to Guy Lombardo's Orchestra, free to theatre patrons. *(G-9)*

Index

ART MUSEUMS, GALLERIES, ART COLONIES

CRAFTS: SHOPS, SHOWROOMS, DEMONSTRATIONS

HISTORIC HOUSES, HISTORICAL MUSEUMS

RESTORED VILLAGES, HISTORICAL TRAILS AND TOURS

HOUSES OF FAMOUS PEOPLE

HOBBIES, SPECIAL INTERESTS, SCIENCE AND INDUSTRY

RELIGIONS AND ETHNICS

MILITARY ACADEMIES AND MUSEUMS

FOOD AND DRINK

SHOPPING CENTERS, MALLS

NATURE TRAILS

WATERFALLS

GARDENS, ARBORETUMS, PARK DISPLAYS

ANIMALS, ZOOS, GAME PARKS

AMUSEMENT PARKS

Asbury Park, N.J. A-2, 6, 7
Bertrand Island Park, Lake Hopat-
  cong, N.J. B-16, 64, 65
Great Adventure, Jackson, N.J.
  A-3(A) 8, 9

Playland, Rye, N.Y. F-2, 210, 211
Pocono's Magic Valley, Pa. B-23 Ext.,
  79, 81
Seaside Park, N.J. A-4, 10

GENERAL INDEX

Acorn Hall, N.J. 44, 45
Aldrich Museum, Conn. 215, 216
Allaire State Park, N.J. 7, 8
American Clock & Watch Museum,
  Conn. 193
American Museum Fire Fighting,
  N.Y. 170, 171
American Shakespeare Theatre, Conn.
  223, 224
Appalachian Trail Pure Maple Syrup
  Co., N.Y. 161, 162
ASBURY PARK, N.J. 6, 7
ATLANTIC CITY, N.J. 14
Audubon Center of Greenwich, Conn.
  143-4

Barnegat Lighthouse State Park, N.J.
  12
Bartlett Arboretum, Conn. 214-15
Bartow-Pell Mansion, N.Y. 208, 209
Basking Ridge Oak, N.J. 44, 45
Bass River State Forest, N.J. 12
Batsto Village, N.J. 13
Bayard Cutting Arboretum, L.I. 255-6
Bear Mountain State Park, N.Y. 98
Beardsley Park & Zoo, Conn. 222-3
Bedford Court House Museum, N.Y.
  145
Belleayre Ski, Summer Lift, N.Y.
  126-7
Bergen Mall, N.J. 60, 61
Bertrand Island Amusement Park,
  N.J. 64-5
Bethlehem Art Gallery, N.Y. 110, 112
Bethpage State Park, L.I. 252-3
Bible Gardens of Israel, N.J. 54
Big Pocono State Park, Pa. 75, 76

Billiou-Stillwell-Perine House, S.I.
  261-2
Black River & Western R.R., N.J. 22,
  23
Blue Mountain Reservation, N.Y.
  152-3
Boscobel, N.Y. 157, 159, 160
Bowcraft's Sport Shop, Playland, N.J.
  52-3
Branch Brook Park, N.J. 33
Branford Trolley Museum, Conn.
  227-8
Brigantine Wildlife Refuge, N.J. 13
Bronck House Museum, N.Y. 130,
  131
Brotherhood Winery, N.Y. 111, 112
Bruce Museum, Conn. 211, 212
Buck Hill Falls, Pa. 77, 78
Bush-Holley House, Conn. 211-213
Bushkill Falls, Pa. 79, 81
Butler-McCook Homestead, Conn. 198,
  201
Buttolph-Williams House, Conn. 194,
  196
Campgaw Mtn. County Reservation,
  N.J. 103
Captree State Park, LI. 254, 255
Carson City, N.Y. 116, 129, 130
Catskill Game Farm, N.Y. 129
Cedar Brook Park, N.J. 54, 55
Cheesequake State Park, N.J. 16
Children's Museum of Hartford,
  Conn. 197-8
Circus Museum, N.Y. 155, 156
Clermont State Park, N.Y. 170
Clinton Historical Museum, N.J. 49,
  50
Clinton House, N.Y. 162, 163